AF806130

Social Science Methodologies for Management Research

Social Science Methodologies for Management Research

Vissanu Zumitzavan

Social Science Methodologies for Management Research

From Philosophy to Practice in the AI Era

Springer

Vissanu Zumitzavan
College of Local Administration
Khon Kaen University
Khon Kaen, Thailand

ISBN 978-981-95-4317-5 ISBN 978-981-95-4318-2 (eBook)
https://doi.org/10.1007/978-981-95-4318-2

© The Editor(s) (if applicable) and The Author(s), under exclusive license to Springer Nature Singapore Pte Ltd. 2025

This work is subject to copyright. All rights are solely and exclusively licensed by the Publisher, whether the whole or part of the material is concerned, specifically the rights of translation, reprinting, reuse of illustrations, recitation, broadcasting, reproduction on microfilms or in any other physical way, and transmission or information storage and retrieval, electronic adaptation, computer software, or by similar or dissimilar methodology now known or hereafter developed.
The use of general descriptive names, registered names, trademarks, service marks, etc. in this publication does not imply, even in the absence of a specific statement, that such names are exempt from the relevant protective laws and regulations and therefore free for general use.
The publisher, the authors and the editors are safe to assume that the advice and information in this book are believed to be true and accurate at the date of publication. Neither the publisher nor the authors or the editors give a warranty, expressed or implied, with respect to the material contained herein or for any errors or omissions that may have been made. The publisher remains neutral with regard to jurisdictional claims in published maps and institutional affiliations.

This Springer imprint is published by the registered company Springer Nature Singapore Pte Ltd.
The registered company address is: 152 Beach Road, #21-01/04 Gateway East, Singapore 189721, Singapore

If disposing of this product, please recycle the paper.

I dedicate this textbook to my beloved parents, Mr. Sompoch Zumitzavan and Mrs. Duangyiva Zumitzavan. Although my father is no longer with us, I know he would take immense pride in my accomplishment of completing this work. Many of the examples presented here are drawn from the treasured conversations shared between my father, my mother, and me.

They selflessly set aside their own dreams to nurture my aspirations, allowing me to flourish. Their unwavering faith and steadfast support throughout every stage of my journey have been a profound source of strength. I could not have brought this textbook to fruition without their encouragement and love. They are the very essence of my being, and I am eternally grateful for their boundless wisdom and inspiration.

Preface

Research in the discipline of management is an art integrating philosophical inquiries with scientific rigour. *Social Science Methodologies for Management Research: From Philosophy to Practice in the AI Era* serves as a comprehensive guide through this complex terrain. It starts by exploring the philosophical foundations of research, specifically ontology and epistemology, developing a robust base for grasping how knowledge is constructed in management. The book then proceeds into practical methodologies, furnishing a clear roadmap through qualitative, quantitative, and mixed methods approaches, research design, and data analysis. It explores key concepts such as hypothesis development, validity, reliability, and ethical considerations, ensuring that researchers are provided with the methodologies to pursue meaningful and rigorous studies.

By harmonising theory and practice, this text strives to inspire a thoughtful, methodologically sound approach to management research, bolstering a deeper understanding of both its challenges and its impactful potential. To situate these methodologies in the present moment, it also probes the profound ways artificial intelligence is beginning to reshape the landscape of academic inquiry and augment the capabilities of the modern researcher. Whether for students, researchers, or established scholars, it serves as a valuable resource in mastering the art and science of research.

Vissanu Zumitzavan
College of Local Administration
Khon Kaen University
Khon Kaen, Thailand

Acknowledgements

I am deeply grateful to Professor Dr. Jonathan Michie and Associate Professor Dr. Titinun Auamnoy for their invaluable insights into research philosophy, methodologies, designs and techniques, and for their steadfast guidance throughout this journey. Their expertise has been an enduring source of encouragement.

My sincere thanks go to Professor Dr. Supachai Pathumnakul and Professor Dr. Woothisarn Tanchai for their thoughtful feedback, which has significantly enhanced the quality of this textbook.

I am especially indebted to the founder and current deans of the College of Local Administration at Khon Kaen University, Associate Professor Dr. Peerasit Kamnuansilpa and Assistant Professor Dr. Sirisak Laochankham, for their unwavering support, I am also deeply grateful to Khon Kaen University as an institution for providing the authorised license for IBM SPSS Statistics (Version 29), a resource that was essential for this work. My sincere thanks also go to my colleagues and administrative staff for their kindness and assistance.

Special thanks go to Assistant Professor Dr. John Draper, my expert proofreader, and to my dedicated Teaching Assistants, Athitiyaporn Sudee and Wannapappa Kanjanakod, for their attention to detail and commitment in refining this work. I am equally grateful to those friends whose guidance and encouragement brought clarity to the final version.

Finally, my deepest gratitude to my family, the foundation of my journey. To my parents, my siblings—Mr. Sompoch, Mrs. Daungyiva, Mr. Pasit Zumitzavan, Karuna Arromdee and Assistant Professor Somjintana Tungkawachara—and my cherished nieces and nephew, Jiratana Tungkawachara, Mameena Arromdee and Jaden Tungkawachara: your love, support and unwavering belief in me have guided every step of this journey. This achievement is a testament to your enduring inspiration

Contents

List of Figures

List of Tables

Chapter 1
Foundation of Research Philosophy

1.1 Introduction

This chapter elucidates the significance of ontology and epistemology in management research, both of which are pivotal in shaping our understanding and investigation of organisational realities and knowledge. Ontology examines whether organisational structures are objective entities or constructed through social interactions, whilst epistemology explores how knowledge is acquired and validated, ranging from empirical evidence to subjective interpretations. These philosophical foundations collectively steer research methodologies and theoretical frameworks, thus influencing our approach to studying organisational dynamics and advancing management practices.

1.2 Principle of Research Philosophy in Management Research

The principles of ontology and epistemology are fundamental in shaping how management scholars perceive and scrutinise organisational phenomena, leadership dynamics, decision-making processes, and human behaviour within organisational contexts (Mir & Greenwood, 2021). For instance, when investigating 'Organisational Culture', the ontological perspective influences how researchers conceptualise culture. An objective ontology known as a 'Realist Perspective' treats organisational culture as a tangible entity existing independently of individual perceptions, leading to the use of standardised surveys and metrics to measure it. In contrast, a subjective ontology referred to as a 'Constructivist Perspective' views organisational culture as a social construct that varies based on individual experiences, concentrating on how individuals interpret and give meaning to their environment.

Similarly, epistemology shapes how researchers gather and interpret knowledge. In research on leadership effectiveness, a positivist epistemology might lead

© The Author(s), under exclusive license to Springer Nature Singapore Pte Ltd. 2025

V. Zumitzavan, *Social Science Methodologies for Management Research*,
https://doi.org/10.1007/978-981-95-4318-2_1

researchers to use quantitative methods, such as surveys and statistical analyses, to identify universal traits associated with effective leadership. In contrast, a constructivist epistemology might drive researchers to use qualitative methods, such as interviews and case studies, to understand how leadership effectiveness is perceived in different contexts, recognising that knowledge is context-dependent and subjective. These philosophical underpinnings guide the development of research methodologies and theoretical frameworks, thereby advancing management theories and practices (Denzin et al., 2023).

1.3 Philosophical Foundations of Knowledge Acquisition in Management Research: Ontology and Epistemology

In the context of understanding organisational reality, ontology in management research addresses fundamental questions concerning the nature of organisational existence (Morgan, 1998). It explores the entities present within organisations, their interactions, and the underlying nature of organisational phenomena (Scotland, 2012).

For example, consider the concept of 'Organisational Members' Motivation' within an organisation. An ontological perspective might question whether organisational members' motivation is an objective entity that exists independently of individual experiences or if it is a subjective construct created by personal perceptions and organisational contexts. From an objective ontology recognised as a 'Realist Perspective', organisational members' motivation might be observed as a quantifiable phenomenon which could be measured through standardised instruments such as surveys and performance metrics. Researchers would focus on categorising concrete factors driving motivation, such as levels of compensations, values and belongings within the organisation, or work environment, assuming these factors exist independently of individuals' perceptions.

Conversely, from a subjective ontology ascribed as a 'Constructivist Perspective', organisational members' motivation is observed as a socially constructed phenomenon that varies based on individual experiences and organisational culture. Researchers would explore how different organisational members perceive and experience motivation differently, considering factors such as personal values, workplace relationships, and organisational climate. This perspective acknowledges that motivation is shaped by individual and collective interpretations within the organisational contexts. Thus, ontology helps in understanding whether organisational phenomena like organisational members' motivation are seen as objective realities or subjective constructs, which in turn influences how researchers investigate and interpret these phenomena.

Realism posits that organisations and their structures exist objectively, independent of human perception. Researchers adhering to a realist perspective employ quantitative methods to reveal the underlying structures, mechanisms, and causal relationships that govern organisational behaviour. Their goal is to identify universal principles that can be applied across a variety of organisational contexts (Smith, 2024).

For instance, in investigating the impact of leadership styles on organisational members' performance, a realist researcher might conduct a large-scale survey across cross-sectional organisations to quantitatively assess the relationship between different leadership styles and measurable performance outcomes. By utilising statistical scrutiny to identify patterns and correlations, the researcher aims to uncover objective, generalisable insights into how leadership influences performance, presuming that these relationships are consistent regardless of individual perceptions or specific organisational settings.

Furthermore, the researcher might explore bidirectional causal relationships. For example, they could investigate whether effective leadership styles not only improve employees' performance but also attract high-performing individuals to the organisation, creating a positive feedback loop. Conversely, the researcher could examine whether increased employees' performance might lead to the emergence or reinforcement of effective leadership styles within the organisation (Michie & Zumitzavan, 2016). By analysing such dynamics, the researcher seeks to understand not only how leadership styles impact performance but also how improved performance can influence leadership effectiveness, aiming to establish universal principles that apply broadly to organisational improvement and dynamics.

In contrast, constructivist ontologies assert that organisational reality is socially constructed through human interactions, interpretations, and shared meanings within organisational cultures (Bryman & Bell, 2022). Researchers adopting a constructivist perspective focus on the subjective meanings attributed by individuals and groups to organisational phenomena. They favour qualitative methods, such as interviews, case studies, or ethnography, to investigate how organisational members construct identities, negotiate meanings, and influence practices within specific contexts (Weiss, 2010).

For example, in studying how team members create a shared sense of identity within an organisation, a constructivist researcher might use interviews and observe daily activities to see how organisational members understand and perform their roles. By looking at how organisational members interact and form their identities, the researcher aims to understand how the organisation's culture is influenced by and influences these personal experiences. This approach focuses on how individuals' interactions and their views shape organisational practices and identities, offering insights into the social dynamics within the organisation.

Epistemology examines how knowledge is acquired, validated, and justified within organisational contexts, guiding researchers' beliefs about what constitutes valid knowledge and the selection of appropriate research methods (Easterby-Smith et al., 2018).

For example, in studying the effectiveness of different management training programmes, a researcher with a positivist epistemology might use structured surveys and statistical analyses to objectively measure the impact of the training on organisational members' performance. This approach assumes that valid knowledge can be obtained through quantifiable data and aims to generate generalisable results. Conversely, a researcher with a constructivist epistemology might conduct in-depth interviews and case studies to understand participants' personal experiences and perceptions of the training. This perspective values subjective insights and aims to deliver a richer, context-specific understanding of how the training is experienced and perceived by organisational members. Thus, epistemology helps determine the methods utilised to gather and interpret data, influencing how researchers approach the study of management practices.

As Creswell (2014) recommends, the use of empiricism within epistemology emphasises systematic observation, measurement, and empirical evidence to generate reliable knowledge about organisational behaviour. Empiricist researchers utilise methods such as surveys and experiments to uncover patterns and causal relationships within data. For instance, researchers might utilise surveys to gather data on employee performance before and after the implementation of a training programme. By analysing this data, they aim to identify any significant patterns or causal links between the training and changes in organisational members' performance. This approach relies on concrete, measurable evidence to test hypotheses and determine the impact of management practices, such as training programmes, on organisational outcomes. Thus, empiricism provides a rigorous framework for evaluating how such practices influence organisational members' performance through systematic data collection and analysis.

Conversely, interpretivist epistemologies challenge positivist objectivity by focusing on subjective perspectives and the meanings attributed to organisational phenomena. Interpretivist researchers value qualitative methods such as interviews, participant observation, and narrative analysis to explore organisational members' experiences, perceptions, and interpretations within their socio-cultural contexts (Creswell & Poth, 2024).

For instance, if a researcher proposes to understand how organisational members perceive and experience organisational changes driven by dynamic globalisation, they might conduct in-depth interviews and perceive daily interactions within the organisation. By analysing these personal accounts and observations, the researcher seeks to acquire insights into how globalisation influences organisational members' experiences of organisational change, including how such changes impact their work environment, job roles, and attitudes. This approach prioritises understanding the rich, contextual meanings that individuals attach to organisational phenomena, offering a nuanced view of how globalisation and other external factors shape organisational members' experiences and interpretations within specific socio-cultural settings.

Critical epistemologies critique dominant organisational knowledge structures and power dynamics. Critical theorists advocate for research that exposes and challenges inequalities, power relations, and ideological biases within organisations, promoting social justice and transformative change through rigorous research practices (Alvesson & Willmott, 2016).

For instance, a critical researcher might examine how organisational policies impact different organisational members' groups, such as investigating whether diversity and inclusion initiatives are genuinely effective or if they perpetuate existing power imbalances. By using methods like in-depth interviews and critical discourse analysis, the researcher aims to uncover how these policies might reinforce biases or marginalise certain groups. This approach seeks to highlight and address the underlying inequalities and power structures within the organisation, advocating for reforms that foster greater fairness and equity.

In management research, diverse philosophical approaches underpin various methods of knowledge acquisition. The deductive approach, aligned with quantitative methods, involves formulating hypotheses derived from literature reviews and subjecting them to statistical analysis, adhering to positivist or scientific principles (Abu-Bader, 2021).

For example, a researcher might hypothesise that implementing a performance-based incentive scheme improves organisational members' productivity. They would then gather data through structured-question surveys across cross-sectional departments and use statistical techniques to analyse whether the incentive scheme leads to measurable improvements in performance measures.

Conversely, the inductive approach aligns with qualitative methods, where researchers develop concepts and theories based on data findings, rooted in phenomenological philosophy (Saunders & Townsend, 2016). This approach entails an in-depth analysis of qualitative data to explore organisational phenomena. For instance, a researcher might conduct semi-structured interviews with organisational members to develop an understanding of how organisational culture influences their job satisfaction, identifying key themes from the interviews to form new theories about workplace culture.

Moreover, knowledge acquisition in research encompasses several established methodologies. Hart (2018) states that literature reviews involve systematic evaluations of existing research to identify knowledge gaps and refine research questions. For example, a researcher might review previous studies on levels of organisational members' engagement strategies to identify gaps in understanding the effectiveness of remote work initiatives, then refine their research question to explore how specific engagement practices impact remote organisational members' motivation and productivity.

Furthermore, Robson (2024) suggest that observations entail direct data collection through the monitoring of respondents, events, or processes to understand natural behaviours. For example, a researcher might observe team interactions during project meetings to study how team dynamics affect real-time decision-making and collaboration.

Fowler (2013) notes that surveys include gathering data from large respondent pools via questionnaires or interviews in order to quantify attitudes, behaviours, or traits. For instance, a researcher might distribute a survey to organisational members across several branches of an organisation to measure their satisfaction with recent management changes and identify common trends and issues.

However, experiments can manipulate variables to observe their effects and establish cause-and-effect relationships (Garson, 2013). For example, a researcher might conduct an experiment by introducing a new leadership training programme to one group of managers and comparing their team performance with a control group that did not receive the training in order to evaluate the programme's impact on managerial effectiveness and teams' productivity.

Yin (2012) emphasises that case studies provide in-depth analyses of individual cases, groups, or organisations in order to investigate complex behaviours, norms, or organisational dynamics. For instance, a researcher might conduct a case study of an organisation undergoing a major digital transformation to explore how the transition affects organisational members' roles, organisational structure, and overall organisational performance.

Hence, in management research, different philosophical approaches guide knowledge acquisition. The deductive approach uses quantitative methods to test hypotheses, whilst the inductive approach utilises qualitative methods to ground theories from data. Methods include literature reviews to pinpoint gaps, observations to capture natural behaviours, surveys to measure attitudes, experiments to determine cause-and-effect, and case studies to explore complex dynamics. Each method provides unique insights, tailored to address specific research questions.

1.4 The Emerging Role of Artificial Intelligence (AI) in Augmenting Research Practices

The contemporary research landscape is more and more formed by the integration of AI introducing both profound opportunities and critical challenges to the recognised philosophical foundations of management research. Rather than presenting a new philosophy, AI acts as a powerful tool that augments existing methodologies, inducing knowledge acquisition, validation, and interpretation across ontological and epistemological paradigms. From a practical standpoint, AI meaningfully improves the efficiency and scope of established research methods. To illustrate, in conducting literature reviews, AI-powered algorithms can systematically scrutinise thousands of academic papers to identify thematic trends, knowledge gaps, and nascent theoretical connections far more rapidly than manual processes; therefore, refining the formulation of research questions (Bolanos et al., 2024).

In addition, AI provides transformative capabilities in data analysis that align with both deductive and inductive approaches. For researchers adopting a realist ontology and positivist epistemology, AI can scrutinise vast quantitative datasets from surveys or experiments to uncover complex, non-linear patterns and predictive associations that might otherwise remain obscured (Kshetri et al., 2023). This improves the deductive process by allowing more sophisticated hypothesis testing. On the other hand, for those following a constructivist and inductive path, AI tools can assist in the thematic analysis of qualitative data from interviews or case studies, identifying sophisticated sentiments and emergent concepts from textual data, thus accelerating theory development (Christou, 2024).

Beyond augmentation, AI serves as a powerful catalyst for research creativity by permitting scholars to synthesise information and generate novel insights in unprecedented ways. By processing and juxtaposing findings from studies rooted in opposing philosophies—such as quantitative, realist data and qualitative, constructivist narratives—AI can reveal unexpected connections between objective phenomena and subjective interpretations. This capability for cross-paradigmatic synthesis inspires researchers to articulate more innovative and holistic theories bridging traditional divides (Lim, 2024).

Furthermore, generative AI can function as an ideation partner, suggesting unconventional hypotheses or novel research designs based on the patterns it identifies; thus, stimulating the creative process of knowledge generation. This moves the researcher's role beyond mere analysis and towards a more dynamic engagement with AI as a tool for intellectual exploration. However, the proliferation of AI requires a rigorous examination of its implications for research validity and reliability. Whilst AI models can provide high reliability through consistent data processing, their validity is contingent on the quality and representativeness of the training data. Biases inherent in the data can be amplified by AI systems, potentially perpetuating the very power imbalances that critical epistemologies pursue to challenge (Raza, 2024). Therefore, the researcher's role evolves from merely a data collector and analyst to a critical validator of AI-generated outputs. Ensuring the transparency, ethical application, and epistemological alignment of these advanced computational tools is paramount to harnessing their creative potential responsibly and advancing robust, credible knowledge in management research.

1.5 Chapter Summary

In summary, ontology and epistemology offer essential frameworks for understanding organisational realities and guiding research methodologies in management studies. The integration of Artificial Intelligence further improves these practices by augmenting data analysis and literature synthesis, providing unprecedented efficiency and depth to both quantitative and qualitative inquiries. Whilst AI can act as a powerful catalyst for research creativity, it also requires researchers to maintain critical oversight to address potential biases and ensure the ethical application of these advanced tools. By steering these philosophical perspectives and employing appropriate research methods, management researchers can contribute to evidence-based practices, organisational development strategies, and leadership interventions enhancing organisational effectiveness and societal impact.

1.6 Questions for Further Reflection

1. The chapter aligns realism with quantitative methods and constructivism with qualitative methods. Critically evaluate the assertion that a researcher's ontological and epistemological stance must dictate their choice of methodology. Could a researcher with a realist ontology legitimately employ qualitative methods like case studies? Justify your position with a hypothetical research example.
2. Critically assess how a researcher's personal ontology can compromise scholarly objectivity, even when operating within a defined philosophical tradition. What are the key implications of this inherent influence?
3. Empiricism is presented as a means to create reliable knowledge through systematic observation and measurement. What are the potential limitations or criticisms of relying merely on empirical evidence in the study of complex organisational phenomena, such as institutional trust or ethical decision-making?
4. The chapter contrasts objective and subjective ontologies. Consider the concept of 'organisational strategy'. Argue whether strategy is best conceptualised as an objective reality (a formal document and set of planned actions) or a subjective, socially constructed phenomenon (an emergent pattern of behaviour and shared understanding). Could it, perhaps, be both?
5. Realism is associated with uncovering 'causal relationships', often through experiments. How might a constructivist researcher approach the concept of causality? Can causality be established within a paradigm that posits reality as socially constructed and context-dependent? (e.g., For example, do highly skilled professionals tend to be drawn to financially prosperous organisations, or do such organisations attain high profitability as a result of employing a substantial proportion of highly skilled professionals?)
6. Imagine a research project designed to assess the 'effectiveness' of a corporate social responsibility (CSR) programme. How would a positivist, an interpretivist, and a critical theorist each frame the research question, choose their methods, and define what constitutes 'effectiveness'?
7. The chapter distinguishes between deductive (theory-testing) and inductive (theory-generating) approaches. Discuss the cyclical relationship between theory and data. At what point in an inductive study might deductive reasoning become necessary, and vice versa?
8. The text lists several data collection methods (surveys, experiments, case studies). Select two of these techniques and analyse the inherent, frequently unstated, ontological, and epistemological assumptions that underpin each one.
9. Critical epistemology advocates for research endorsing social justice. Is it the responsibility of all management researchers to implement a critical stance, or is there a legitimate place for research that is purely descriptive or explanatory without an explicit transformative agenda? Defend your viewpoint.

10. A manager commissions you to research high staff turnover in their organisation. Your initial literature review suggests that both low pay (a measurable, objective factor) and a 'toxic culture' (a subjective, experiential factor) are to blame. Outline a research design that acknowledges this complexity. Which philosophical stance (e.g., positivism, constructivism, pragmatism) would best justify your methodological choices, and why?

References

Abu-Bader, S. H. (2021). *Using statistical methods in social science research: With a complete SPSS guide*. Oxford University Press.

Alvesson, M., & Willmott, H. (2016). *Making sense of management: A critical introduction*. Sage Publications.

Bolanos, F., Salatino, A., Osborne, F., & Motta, E. (2024). Artificial intelligence for literature reviews: Opportunities and challenges. *Artificial Intelligence Review, 57*(10), 259.

Bryman, A., & Bell, E. (2022). *Business research methods* (6th ed.). Oxford University Press.

Christou, P. A. (2024). Thematic analysis through artificial intelligence (AI). *The Qualitative Report, 29*(2), 560–576.

Creswell, J. W. (2014). *Research design: Qualitative, quantitative, and mixed methods approaches* (4th ed.). Sage Publications.

Creswell, J. W., & Poth, C. N. (2024). *Qualitative inquiry and research design: Choosing among five approaches* (5th ed.). Sage Publications.

Denzin, N. K., Lincoln, Y. S., Giardina, M. D., & Cannella, G. S. (Eds.). (2023). *The Sage handbook of qualitative research*. Sage Publications.

Easterby-Smith, M., Thorpe, R., & Jackson, P. R. (2018). *Management and business research* (6th ed.). Sage Publications.

Fowler, F. J. (2013). *Survey research methods* (5th ed.). Sage Publications.

Garson, G. D. (2013). *Hierarchical linear modeling: Guide and applications*. Sage Publications.

Hart, C. (2018). *Doing a literature review: Releasing the research imagination* (2nd ed.). Sage Publications.

Kshetri, N., Hughes, L., Louise Slade, E., Jeyaraj, A., Kumar Kar, A., Koohang, A., et al. (2023). "So what if ChatGPT wrote it?" Multidisciplinary perspectives on opportunities, challenges and implications of generative conversational AI for research, practice and policy. *International Journal of Information Management, 71*, 102642.

Lim, W. M. (2024). What is qualitative research? An overview and guidelines. *Australasian Marketing Journal*. https://doi.org/10.1177/14413582241264619

Michie, J., & Zumitzavan, V. (2016). The impact of 'learning' and 'leadership' management styles on organizational outcomes: a study of tyre firms in Thailand. In *Leadership in the Asia Pacific* (pp. 165–188). Routledge.

Mir, R., & Greenwood, M. (2021). *Philosophy and management studies: A research overview*. Routledge.

Morgan, G. (1998). *Images of organization: The executive edition*. CA.

Raza, H. (2024). Ai-driven assessment: Reliability, bias, and ethical implications. *AI EDIFY Journal, 1*(2), 36–47.

Robson, C. (2024). *Real world research*. John Wiley & Sons.

Saunders, M. N., & Townsend, K. (2016). Reporting and justifying the number of interview participants in organization and workplace research. *British Journal of Management, 27*(4), 836–852. https://doi.org/10.1111/1467-8551.12182

Scotland, J. (2012). Exploring the philosophical underpinnings of research: Purposes, approaches and assumptions. *European Journal of Social Work, 15*(1), 9–16. https://doi.org/10.5539/elt.v5n9p9

Smith, J. A. (2024). *Qualitative psychology: A practical guide to research methods*. Sage Publications.

Weiss, R. E. (2010). Bayesian methods for data analysis. *American Journal of Ophthalmology, 149*(2), 187–188. https://doi.org/10.1016/j.ajo.2009.11.011

Yin, R. K. (2012). *Applications of case study research* (Vol. 34, 3rd ed.). Sage Publications.

Chapter 2
Research Framework: A Guide to Research Structure

2.1 Introduction

This chapter outlines the study design elements, including research questions, objectives, and framework, necessary to provide a comprehensive guide for management research.

2.2 Research Design and Framework: A Guide to Research Structure

In the dynamic and ever-evolving landscape of social science research, understanding contemporary phenomena necessitates a sophisticated approach grounded in epistemological principles. Social science aims to unravel the complexities of human behaviour, organisational dynamics, and management practices, all of which are influenced by swift fluctuations in the external environment. For example, the emergence of remote work has profoundly rehabilitated management practices by challenging traditional methods of supervision and team cohesion (Gajendran & Harrison, 2007; Mariani et al., 2023).

As organisations navigate this transformation, researchers must investigate how virtual teams can sustain productivity and engagement, requiring a detailed examination of remote work dynamics and their effects on management strategies (Golden, 2006; Allen et al., 2015). To remain relevant and insightful, research must continually adapt to these shifting influences.

Central to this exploration are concepts, constructs, and theories, which together construct the foundation of social science research. Concepts act as the building blocks of understanding, distilled from extensive academic and practice-based investigations. They represent predominant topics and trends within society, such as those impacting organisational performance and management practices. For example, the

© The Author(s), under exclusive license to Springer Nature Singapore Pte Ltd. 2025
V. Zumitzavan, *Social Science Methodologies for Management Research*,
https://doi.org/10.1007/978-981-95-4318-2_2

rise of remote work has fundamentally transformed how organisations operate and manage their organisation. This shift has sparked significant interest in understanding how organisations can maintain productivity and organisational members' engagement in a remote work environment (Sonidou, 2024; Delfino & Van Der Kolk, 2021).

Concepts related to remote work include organisational performance and organisational members' engagement, which are both critical to understanding the influence of this trend. Constructs, such as organisational productivity and organisational members' satisfaction, are more specific and measurable elements supporting to operationalise these concepts. For instance, constructs might include measures such as outputs per employee or levels of engagement as reported in surveys (Allen et al., 2015). Another example of a construct is the frequency of virtual meetings, which can be assessed to determine its effects on team cohesion and communication effectiveness within remote teams (Hoffmann et al., 2021). Such measures provide invaluable insights into how remote work arrangements influence organisational dynamics and organisational members' interactions (Sonidou, 2024; Delfino & Van Der Kolk, 2021).

Theories build on these concepts and constructs by providing a structured framework for illustrating and foreseeing phenomena. Theories are developed through rigorous research methodologies and are validated by probing how well they explain observed patterns and relationships (Steenhuis & Bruijn, 2006). In the case of remote work, theories might explore how different management practices influence productivity and engagement in virtual settings, drawing on established constructs such as communication effectiveness and work-life balance (Zeschke & Zacher, 2023).

Understanding these elements—concepts, constructs, and theories—enables researchers and practitioners to effectively address contemporary challenges and adapt to evolving organisational environments. By leveraging these frameworks, organisations can improved navigate the complexities introduced by remote work and develop informed strategies to enhance performance and organisational members' satisfaction in a remote context.

For instance, by applying theories of remote work, such as those addressing work-life balance and communication effectiveness, organisations can design tailor-made interventions to address common issues confronted by remote organisational members. Constructs like communication frequency and work autonomy can be measured and analysed to determine their impact on productivity and job satisfaction. Concepts such as organisational culture and remote team dynamics provide a broader understanding of how remote work influences and is influenced by a variety of factors within the organisation (i.e. Organisational Size, Availabilities and Accessibilities of Supported Facilities, and Leadership Styles) (see, for example, Hunton, & Norman, 2010; Kaluza &Van Dick, 2023).

By systematically investigating these areas through well-defined constructs and validated theories, organisations can implement evidence-based practices optimising remote work arrangements. This approach helps in creating supportive work environments, nurturing levels of organisational members' engagement, and ultimately achieving organisational goals despite the physical separation of team members

(Allen et al., 2015; Chatterjee et al., 2022). Therefore, the application of conceptual frameworks and theoretical insights permits organisations to address the complexities of remote work responsively and strategically. This results in more effective management practices, improved organisational members' experiences, and enhanced organisational performance in the face of ongoing and future challenges.

To effectively address these evolving challenges, it is indispensable to frame research questions and objectives within the context of established social science concepts. Concepts serve as the foundational elements of inquiry, encapsulating prevalent issues and inclinations ensuring thorough examination. However, to develop a complex understanding and derive robust solutions, it is imperative to advance beyond these fundamental concepts to more sophisticated theoretical frameworks.

Theories, more advanced and intricate than individual concepts, offer a structured approach to analysing and interpreting these concepts through rigorous research methodologies. The formulation of theories encompasses a systematic process of scrutinising and validating concepts, often utilising both deductive and inductive reasoning (Meredith, 1993; Guba & Lincoln, 1994). Deductive reasoning requires testing hypotheses stemming from existing theories to confirm or repudiate their validity, whereas inductive reasoning involves generating new theories from empirical observations and data (Adams & McGuire, 2022).

For example, in investigating the impact of remote work on organisational performance, researchers might start with broad concepts such as work-life balance and productivity. They would then define specific constructs, such as measures for organisational members' engagement and communication practices, and apply theories clarifying the relationships between these constructs. Theories such as Social Exchange Theory or Job Demands-Resources Theory can provide insights into how remote work affects organisational members' productivity and levels of organisational performance (Bakker & Demerouti, 2007; Cook & Hahn, 2021).

By situating research questions within well-established theories, researchers can design studies that not only address immediate concerns but also contribute to a deeper understanding of organisational behaviour and management practices. This approach ensures that the research is grounded in a robust theoretical framework, leading to more reliable and generalisable findings. Thus, integrating established social science concepts into research design and incorporating theories to illuminate these concepts provide a comprehensive framework for addressing contemporary organisational challenges. This methodical approach polishes the capacity to develop effective strategies and solutions in response to complex and evolving issues.

To understand the phenomena presented in contemporary circumstances, it is crucial to adopt appropriate methodologies informed by the philosophy of knowledge to formulate research questions and objectives (Gabrielian, 1999). In the rapidly changing landscape of environments, surroundings, and external factors, social science research is stirred by the need to comprehend evolving circumstances. These circumstances are inherently connected to the concepts and theories examined within various social science disciplines (Bell et al., 2022).

Concepts represent distinguished and scrutinised ideas, supported by extensive academic and practice-based research. They encapsulate current societal issues such as those related to beliefs, cultures, humanities, religions, societies, and politics (Corbin & Strauss, 2015). For instance, the COVID-19 outbreak exemplifies a global phenomenon—that of the pandemic—that has profoundly influenced nearly every region of the world Drayton, (2024). This widespread incident has generated significant interests in understanding how organisations can steer and continue in the reverberations of such a catastrophe (Sharma et al., 2024).

In this context, a relevant research question might be, "How can organisations sustain themselves and maintain operational effectiveness following the COVID-19 pandemic?" To address this question effectively, it is crucial to investigate specific cases, such as for-profit service organisations, and relate the inquiry to relevant social science concepts and theories (Swanson & Chermack, 2013). This involves aligning the research with established theoretical frameworks to provide a comprehensive understanding of how organisations can adapt and thrive in the face of such unprecedented challenges (Bakker & Demerouti, 2007). By grounding the research question in the relevant concepts of social science, researchers can develop well-informed objectives and methodologies enhancing the relevance and applicability of their findings (Allen et al., 2015).

Moreover, theories are significantly more developed than concepts. Theories are essentially concepts that have been rigorously scrutinised and examined through both deductive and inductive approaches. The validation and acceptance of theories are achieved through empirical research and methodological scrutiny (Easterby-Smith et al., 2021; Eisenhardt, 1989). Theories can be seen as grounded in concepts. For instance, concepts related to organisational success or performance need to be operationalised into constructs to be effectively investigated. Constructs are defined as specific, measurable elements extracted from broader concepts. In the context of a successful organisation, constructs might include the effective utilisation of both tangible and intangible resources (Kruesi & Bazelmans, 2023).

Tangible resources in this context can be quantified by measures such as organisational revenues, organisational assets, and organisational capital. Conversely, intangible resources might encompass elements such as organisational shared values, organisational culture, and organisational reputation (Barney, 1991; Grant, 1991). Each construct comprises variables that are components used to measure specific attributes from the data samples. These variables are assessed using statistical techniques to appraise hypotheses, thereby contributing to the development and modification of theories (Denis, 2021).

Therefore, once variables are collected and analysed through rigorous statistical methods, they provide insights into the constructs, which in turn support the theoretical framework. This process of measurement and hypothesis testing is crucial for the development and validation of theories, ensuring they are vigorous and applicable to real-world phenomena (Fig. 2.1).

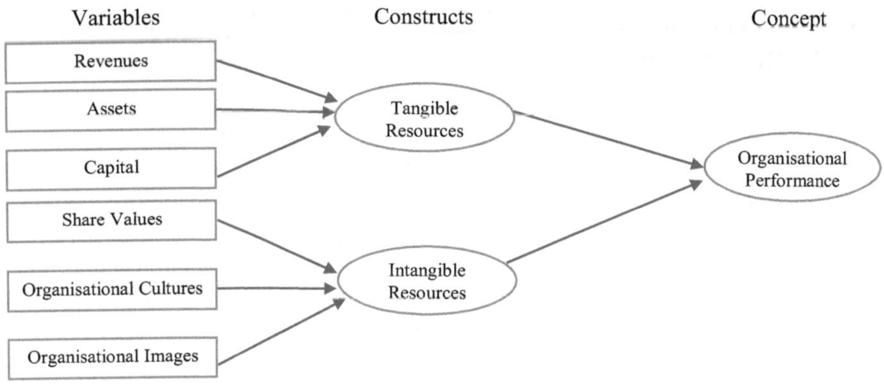

Fig. 2.1 Framework of the development of theories. (Source: Bryman & Bell, 2022; Hair et al., 2019)

As shown in Fig. 2.2, the research question could be 'How do Tangible and Intangible Organisational Resources impact the development of Organisational Performance?' Then, the research objectives could be 1. To categorise Tangible Organisational Resources (e.g., revenues, assets, and capitals) and Intangible Organisational Resources (e.g., share values, cultures, and images) within the organisational contexts; 2. To analyse how Tangible (e.g., revenues, assets, and capitals) and Intangible (e.g., share values, cultures, images) Organisational Resources are associated with Organisational Performance; and 3. To provide practical recommendations for optimising Tangible and Intangible Organisational Resources to improve Organisational Performance.

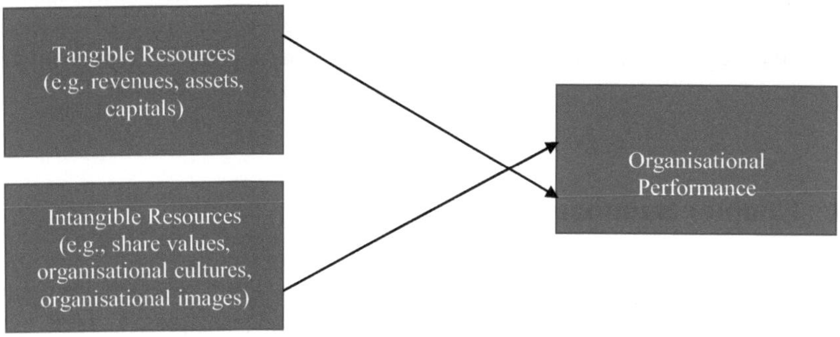

Fig. 2.2 Framework of organisational resources and organisational performance

2.3 The Art and Science of Framework Development in the AI Era

The construction of a research framework, whilst grounded in the rigorous science of theory and methodology, is also an act of intellectual art. The researcher, much like an artist, creatively selects and combines concepts and constructs to shape an exceptional theoretical structure capable of enlightening a specific phenomenon (Collins, 2025). This creative process comprises seeing novel associations between disparate ideas and envisioning how established theories might be utilised in new contexts. It is this synthesis of systematic rigour and creative insight allowing a framework to be not only robust but also truly innovative.

The advent of AI presents a powerful new dimension to this creative-scientific process, functioning as a collaborative partner in framework development. AI tools can systematically evaluate massive bodies of literature to identify underexplored associations between variables or recommend novel constructs; thus, sparking human creativity and accelerating scientific discovery (Sawyer & Henriksen, 2024). To illustrate, when developing a framework for remote work effectiveness, AI can process thousands of studies to propose a novel interaction between 'digital communication frequency' and 'employee psychological safety'—a connection a human researcher might overlook. This transforms AI from a mere analytical tool into a catalyst for theoretical innovation.

In addition, AI improves the 'science' of framework construction by aiding in the operationalisation of complex constructs. By identifying patterns in large datasets, AI can instruct precise, measurable variables effectively capturing the essence of an abstract concept, thus emphasising the framework's empirical validity and testability (Abisoye,2024). Therefore, the modern researcher's role is evolving; it now encompasses skilfully directing these computational tools to augment their own creative and critical faculties. This partnership between human intellect and artificial intelligence represents a significant advancement, promising more sophisticated and impactful theoretical frameworks in management research (Mirzani, 2024).

2.4 Chapter Summary

Understanding contemporary phenomena in social science research necessitates a sophisticated approach grounded in epistemological principles. Central to this endeavour are concepts, constructs, and theories, which collectively reinforce the research framework. Concepts, developed from extensive scholarly and practical investigation, encompass predominant societal issues such as organisational performance and the impact of remote work. Constructs operationalise these concepts into specific, measurable variables, such as productivity metrics or engagement levels. Theories, which emerge from rigorous methodological scrutiny and empirical validation, offer structured frameworks for explaining and predicting observed phenomena. The construction of this framework is an act of both creative art and rigorous science. Furthermore, AI can now function as a powerful partner in this process, augmenting human creativity and enhancing scientific validation. By incorporating established concepts into research design and implementing theories for interpretation, researchers can effectively address contemporary challenges, develop evidence-based strategies, and enhances organisational outcomes in a rapidly changing environment.

2.5 Questions for Further Reflection

1. The chapter identifies 'organisational culture' as an intangible resource. Propose a clear construct to represent one facet of this concept. Then, identify at least three distinct variables you would utilise to measure this construct, justifying why they are appropriate indicators.
2. The text presents a framework where concepts are broken down into constructs and then variables. Critically evaluate this linear model. To what extent does empirical research, particularly applying an inductive approach, follow this neat sequence?
3. The chapter mentions Social Exchange Theory and Job Demands-Resources Theory in the context of remote work. Select one of these theories and explain precisely how it could function as a framework to link the constructs of 'work-life balance', 'communication effectiveness', and 'organisational performance'.
4. Imagine you are tasked with researching the influence of a newly introduced four-day work week on organisational innovation—a phenomenon for which slight established theory exists. Would you utilise a primarily deductive or inductive approach? Justify your choice by outlining the initial steps of your research design.
5. Review the research objectives presented for the framework in Fig. 2.2. Critique their specificity and scope. What potential limitations or ambiguities exist within these objectives, and how might you refine one of them to make it more robust for a quantitative study?
6. Discuss the inherent difficulties and methodological compromises involved in quantifying an intangible construct like 'organisational reputation'. Your answer should consider how the choice between different levels of measurement (nominal, ordinal, interval, and ratio) reflects these compromises.
7. The chapter states that theories are "significantly more developed than concepts." At what point does a complex conceptual framework, which explains the relationships between multiple constructs, cease to be only a framework and initiate to serve as a theory? Discuss the defining characteristics that mark this transition.

8. How might a researcher's commitment to Resource-Based View (RBV) theory influence how they define and measure the concept of 'Organisational Performance', compared to a researcher guided by Stakeholder Theory (i.e., shareholder value vs. multi-stakeholder value)?
9. A study concludes that "managerial empathy positively influences organisational employees' retention in remote teams." Deconstruct this finding by identifying the core concept it addresses, the primary constructs it connects, and the probable variables measured.
10. Imagine your research on remote work reveals that the construct 'frequency of virtual meetings' has a positive statistical relationship with the construct 'team cohesion' but a negative relationship with 'individual productivity'. How would you interpret this apparent contradiction, and what further research might it recommend?

References

Abisoye, A. (2024). A conceptual framework for integrating artificial intelligence into STEM research methodologies for enhanced innovation. *International Journal of Research and Innovation in Social Science.*

Adams, K. A., & McGuire, E. K. (2022). *Research methods, statistics, and applications.* Sage Publications.

Allen, T. D., Golden, T. D., & Shockley, K. M. (2015). How effective is telecommuting? Assessing the status of our scientific findings. *Psychological Science in the Public Interest, 16*(2), 40–68. https://doi.org/10.1177/1529100615593273

Bakker, A. B., & Demerouti, E. (2007). The job demands-resources model: State of the art. *Journal of Managerial Psychology, 22*(3), 309–328. https://doi.org/10.1108/02683940710733115

Barney, J. (1991). Firm resources and sustained competitive advantage. *Journal of Management, 17*(1), 99–120. https://doi.org/10.1177/014920639101700108

Bell, E., Bryman, A., & Harley, B. (2022). *Business research methods.* Oxford University Press.

Bryman, A., & Bell, E. (2022). *Business research methods* (6th ed.). Oxford University Press.

Chatterjee, S., Chaudhuri, R., & Vrontis, D. (2022). Does remote work flexibility enhance organization performance? Moderating role of organization policy and top management support. *Journal of Business Research, 139*, 1501–1512. https://doi.org/10.1016/j.jbusres.2021.10.069

Collins, H. (2025). *Creative research: Research theory and practice for the creative industries.* Bloomsbury Publishing.

Cook, K. S., & Hahn, M. (2021). Social exchange theory: Current status and future directions. In S. Abrutyn & K. McCaffree (Eds.), *Theoretical sociology* (pp. 179–205). Routledge.

Corbin, J., & Strauss, A. (2015). *Basics of qualitative research* (Vol. 14). Sage Publications.

Delfino, G. F., & Van Der Kolk, B. (2021). Remote working, management control changes and employee responses during the COVID-19 crisis. *Accounting, Auditing & Accountability Journal, 34*(6), 1376–1387. https://doi.org/10.1108/AAAJ-06-2020-4657

Denis, D. J. (2021). *Applied univariate, bivariate, and multivariate statistics: Understanding statistics for social and natural scientists, with applications in SPSS and R.* John Wiley & Sons.

Drayton, M. (2024). *Leading hybrid organisations: How to build trust, collaboration and a high-performance culture.* Taylor & Francis.

Easterby-Smith, M., Jaspersen, L. J., Thorpe, R., & Valizade, D. (2021). *Management and business research.* Sage Publications.

Eisenhardt, K. M. (1989). Building theories from case study research. *Academy of Management Review, 14*(4), 532–550. https://doi.org/10.2307/258557

Gabrielian, V. (1999). Qualitative research methods: An overview. *Handbook of Research Methods in Public Administration, 2*, 167–206.

Gajendran, R. S., & Harrison, D. A. (2007). The good, the bad, and the unknown about telecommuting: meta-analysis of psychological mediators and individual consequences. *Journal of Applied Psychology, 92*(6), 1524. https://doi.org/10.1037/0021-9010.92.6.1524

Golden, T. D. (2006). The role of relationships in telecommuter satisfaction. *Journal of Managerial Issues, 18*(3), 294–311. https://doi.org/10.1002/job.369

Grant, R. M. (1991). The resource-based theory of competitive advantage: Implications for strategy formulation. *California Management Review, 33*(3), 114–135. https://doi.org/10.2307/41166664

Guba, E. G., & Lincoln, Y. S. (1994). Competing paradigms in qualitative research. In N. K. Denzin & Y. S. Lincoln (Eds.), *Handbook of qualitative research* (pp. 105–117). Sage Publications.

Hair, J. F., Black, W. C., Babin, B. J., Anderson, R. E., & Tatham, R. L. (2019). *Multivariate data analysis* (8th ed.). Pearson Education.

Hoffmann, C., Nißen, H., Scheel, L., & Willim, L. (2021). *Winners and losers of telework?: A meta-analysis of the predictive validity of teleworker's personality for performance.* Institute of Psychology.

Hunton, J. E., & Norman, C. S. (2010). The impact of alternative telework arrangements on organizational commitment: Insights from a longitudinal field experiment (retracted). *Journal of Information Systems, 24*(1), 67–90. https://doi.org/10.2308/jis.2010.24.1.67

Kaluza, A. J., & van Dick, R. (2023). Telework at times of a pandemic: The role of voluntariness in the perception of disadvantages of telework. *Current Psychology, 42*(22), 18578–18589. https://doi.org/10.1007/s12144-022-03047-5

Kruesi, M. A., & Bazelmans, L. (2023). Resources, capabilities and competencies: A review of empirical hospitality and tourism research founded on the resource-based view of the firm. *Journal of Hospitality and Tourism Insights, 6*(2), 549–574. https://doi.org/10.1108/JHTI-10-2021-0270

Mariani, M., Wamba, S. F., Castaldo, S., & Santoro, G. (2023). The rise and consolidation of digital platforms and technologies for remote working: Opportunities, challenges, drivers, processes, and consequences. *Journal of Business Research, 160*, Article 113617. https://doi.org/10.1016/j.jbusres.2022.113617

Meredith, J. (1993). Theory building through conceptual methods. *International Journal of Operations & Production Management, 13*(5), 3–11. https://doi.org/10.1108/01443579310028120

Mirzani, Y. (2024). Artificial intelligence and innovation management: Transformative forces shaping organizational creativity. *EPRA International Journal of Multidisciplinary Research (IJMR)*, 511–518.

Sawyer, R. K., & Henriksen, D. (2024). *Explaining creativity: The science of human innovation.* Oxford University Press.

Sharma, G. D., Kraus, S., Liguori, E., Bamel, U. K., & Chopra, R. (2024). Entrepreneurial challenges of COVID-19: Re-thinking entrepreneurship after the crisis. *Journal of Small Business Management, 62*(2), 824–846. https://doi.org/10.1080/00472778.2022.2089676

Sonidou, E. (2024). *The impact of flexible working arrangements on employer attractiveness: A Comparative study between startups and large companies* (Master's thesis).

Steenhuis, H. J., & de Bruijn, E. J. (2006). Building theories from case study research: The progressive case study. In *OM in the new world uncertainties: Proceedings (CD-ROM) of the 17th Annual Conference of POMS, 28 April – 1 May 2006, Boston, USA.* Production and Operations Management Society (POMS).

Swanson, R. A., & Chermack, T. J. (2013). *Theory building in applied disciplines*. Berrett-Koehler Publishers.

Zeschke, M., & Zacher, H. (2023). Is it bad because it is boring? Effects of idle time on employee outcomes. *European Journal of Work and Organizational Psychology, 32*(6), 886–901. https://doi.org/10.1080/1359432X.2023.2261661

Chapter 3
Research Methodologies and Designs

3.1 Introduction

This chapter explores core research methodologies positivism, interpretivism, inductivism, and deductivism and their influence on research design. It also outlines essential design elements and the use of primary and secondary data in both quantitative and qualitative approaches.

3.2 Understanding for the Inquiries of Research Methodologies

In a rapidly fluctuating organisational environment, existing challenges and issues are increasingly demanding modernisation and adaptation in light of shifting circumstances. Social science purposes to shape associations with the day-to-day responsibilities and events occurring within the organisation under investigation. In addition, it is essential to ensure that the findings of social scientific inquiries are made accessible to broader researchers and practitioners (Babbie, 2021; Giddens, 2009).

Scientific or objective knowledge is frequently regarded as a true representation of reality, and scientific explanations are expected to be universally applicable (Shearmur, 2005). This is particularly true when distinguishing facts from specific instances in a given situation; in this context, objective knowledge is reflected in the identification of causal processes (Babbie, 2021; Savin-Baden & Major, 2023). For example, in management research, objective knowledge is critical for understanding the ramifications of leadership styles on organisational members' performance. Studies such as those by Judge and Piccolo (2004) have implemented rigorous statistical analyses to identify how transformational leadership positively affects organisational members' motivation and performance, indicating a clear causal relationship.

© The Author(s), under exclusive license to Springer Nature Singapore Pte Ltd. 2025
V. Zumitzavan, *Social Science Methodologies for Management Research*,
https://doi.org/10.1007/978-981-95-4318-2_3

As recommended by scholars, objective knowledge is grounded in empirical evidence and stringent analysis, assuring that findings are based utterly on the facts being investigated (Bibi et al., 2022; Yin, 2014). For instance, Delery and Doty (1996) employed empirical data to explore the effects of human resource management practices on organisational performance. Their research findings offered evidence that high-performance work systems, characterised by comprehensive training and development, have a significant positive effect on organisational effectiveness. Such findings are the results of detailed empirical investigation and contribute to the broader understanding of effective management practices.

In another example, a study by Bamberger and Meshoulam (2000) analysed the association between strategic human resource management and organisational performance. By utilising a range of empirical methods, comprising surveys and case studies, they established how strategic alignment of HR practices with organisational goals can improve organisational performance. This research emphasises the importance of evidence-based approaches in management research, where research findings are acquired from systematic data collection and analysis.

In the realm of scientific research, the credibility of findings hinges on the robustness of the data and the accuracy of the interpretations sourced from it (Denzin & Lincoln, 2011). More importantly, it is essential that scientific inquiries are conducted with methodological rigour and that findings are disseminated with clarity, as this is vital to progressing knowledge and enlightening practice (Silverman, 2021).

In the social sciences, including management research, factual knowledge can be pursued through both deductive and inductive approaches, each functioning distinct purposes dependent upon the research contexts. Deductive reasoning, typically aligned with quantitative methods, begins with a general theory or hypothesis and endeavours to test its validity through empirical evidence. For example, a researcher might analyse the hypothesis sourced from transformational leadership theory that transformational leaders improve organisational members' performance more effectively than transactional leaders. Researchers then collect and analyse quantitative data to test whether the empirical evidence supports this theoretical expectation (Hargis et al., 2011).

In contrast, the inductive approach, often associated with qualitative methods, entails building theories or generalisations founded on specific observations and patterns. For instance, a researcher might conduct in-depth interviews to explore how a variety of aspects of organisational culture influence organisational members' satisfaction, developing a new theoretical framework based on the emergent themes from the qualitative data (Gioia et al., 2013). Whilst deduction is valuable for testing established theories, induction is vital for generating new insights grounded in empirical observations. The selection between these approaches depends on the nature of the research questions and objectives, highlighting their complementary roles in advancing knowledge within

It is crucial, however, to avoid cementing a false dichotomy that aligns the case study almost exclusively with a qualitative, interpretive paradigm. The case study is a methodologically flexible research design, not one intrinsically bound to a specific epistemological commitment. Its defining characteristic is the intense focus on a single, bounded unit; the framework itself remains fundamentally agnostic as to whether the evidence collected from that unit is qualitative or quantitative. A case study can be robustly positivist, for example, through a longitudinal statistical analysis of a single firm's performance or an econometric model of one nation's economy. Therefore, the essential distinction between a case study and a cross-case analysis is one of scope—a focus on one case versus many—not a predetermined commitment to a particular type of data (Gerring, 2006; Yin, 2014),the management discipline (Bell et al., 2022).

Although these designs vary, they share resemblances in their ability to deliver comprehensive insights. Cross-case studies are valuable for constructing an overarching understanding of a phenomenon by comparing and contrasting multiple cases. An example of this is a cross-case study on different organisational cultures across multiple organisations, which can reveal general patterns and implications of cultural practices on organisational members' performance (Morgeson et al., 2010; Wang et al., 2024b). In contrast, a case study provides a more in-depth analysis of a single instance, providing detailed insights into its unique aspects. For example, a case study of a particular organisation's implementation of a new technology can offer complex understandings of the challenges and successes encountered by that specific organisation, which might not be apparent in broader cross-case studies (Eisenhardt & Graebner, 2007; Siggelkow, 2007).

It is challenging to imagine a cross-case study that does not draw on case study research, or a case study that disregards the relevance of similar cases. Cross-case studies rely on the detailed knowledge attained from individual cases to provide the rich, more sophisticated data necessary for meaningful comparison and generalisation. Conversely, single-case studies benefit from comparisons with similar cases to contextualise their findings and identify broader tendencies. Thus, these designs, though distinct in scope, are synergistic tools in analysing the social world. They work together to offer a more comprehensive picture, with cross-case studies profiting from the depth of individual cases, and single cases gaining broader context through comparison (Voss et al., 2002; Yin, 2009a).

Qualitative research provides a diverse array of data collection methods designed to capture the richness of human experience. Key methods include interviews—conducted individually (in-depth interviews) or in groups (focus groups)—to capture personal narratives and collective attitudes; observation of behaviours, such as ethnography, for understanding phenomena in their natural context; and the analysis of documents and other artefacts to interpret existing texts and symbolic materials (Denzin & Lincoln, 2011). Whilst each method has unique strengths, this study focusses on interviewing techniques as they are particularly effective for obtaining comprehensive and sophisticated information directly from participants regarding their skills and perspectives (Creswell & Poth, 2024).

In-depth interviews, for example, entail conducting detailed, face-to-face conversations with participants to attain comprehensive insights into their experiences, perspectives, and motivations. This method is mainly effective for discovering complex phenomena where individual narratives provide valuable depth and context.

Unlike structured surveys, in-depth interviews are typically directed by a flexible interview guide or protocol, enabling an open-ended exploration of topics (Creswell & Poth, 2024). This approach enables a rich, detailed analysis and contributes to a more profound understanding of complex strategies, such as global management practices (Hayes et al., 2015).

Focus groups, also known as group interviews, include structured discussions with a small group of participants, typically ranging from six to twelve individuals. This method is prearranged to create a range of perspectives on a specific topic through interactive dialogue. The interactive nature of focus groups enables participants to construct upon each other's responses, potentially leading to the identification of common themes and divergent views that may not be apparent in individual interviews. This method offers valuable insights into the collective attitudes and experiences of organisational members (Krueger & Casey, 2014).

A core tenet of qualitative inquiry is its explicit valuation of subjectivity and the essential role of scholarly interpretation. In a departure from positivist paradigms seeking to minimise bias, the qualitative method posits that an individual's subjective standpoint—their unique experiences, values, and affective responses—is not a contaminant of the data, but rather constitutes its very substance. The objective is not to expunge the personal but to apprehend social phenomena through the lens of lived experience. Consequently, the researcher is not conceived as a neutral conduit for information but is an integral part of the analytical process, utilising a hermeneutic lens to synthesise disparate narratives and distinguish underlying thematic structures. It is this interpretive act that transforms raw testimony into theoretically-informed insight.

Methodologically, qualitative inquiry is essential for understanding the intricate dynamics of organisational life. Its varied methods move beyond surface metrics to explore the detailed realities of human experience. Their true value, however, lies not merely in the data gathered, but in their foundational embrace of participant subjectivity and the necessity of rigorous scholarly interpretation. The strength of these techniques is their capability to access subjective standpoints, whether through an individual's personal narrative, observed behaviours, or the social interaction of a group. This approach reveals the 'why' behind organisational behaviours, providing a textured understanding that quantitative data alone cannot provide.

This rich data calls for sophisticated interpretation to yield insight. The researcher is an active analyst, not a passive recorder utilising a hermeneutic lens to synthesise information and construct theoretical arguments. It is this deliberate engagement with subjectivity and interpretation that elevates qualitative inquiry, transforming detailed accounts of workplace life into a profound and actionable understanding of the modern organisation.

Generally speaking, whilst both deductive and inductive approaches offer significant insights and contribute to the richness of knowledge, neither essentially recommends that one paradigm is more crucial than the other. Each approach conveys its own set of strengths and limitations, particularly when addressing exploratory research questions. To illustrate, the inductive method, often used to derive data through observation, can provide valuable insights, much like the deductive method, which concentrates on hypothesis testing and empirical validation (Verma et al., 2024). Therefore, the distinction between quantitative and qualitative methods should not be viewed as an absolute contrast. Instead, Verma et al. (2024) argue for the fusion of both quantitative and qualitative approaches, enabling the complementary strengths of each to be leveraged, leading to a more holistic and refined understanding. By integrating these methodologies, researchers can maximise the potential of both approaches, enhancing the thoroughness and depth of their findings.

3.3 Research Methods and Designs

As articulated by Verma et al. (2024), adopting a multi-method approach facilitates a more comprehensive validation and verification of research findings. In addition, (Creswell & Poth, 2016) suggest that the integration of quantitative and qualitative techniques, along with the use of both primary and secondary data, is emphasised by many researchers. Primary data, collected through methods such as in-depth interviews, can be systematically categorised and analysed to illuminate the complex contexts in which participants have applied their experiences within their organisations. To illustrate, after collecting and analysing in-depth interview data, researchers can examine extreme outcomes to identify potential starting points for further quantitative analysis. If a majority of respondents identify four key factors as critical for improving organisational performance, the next step might involve utilising quantitative methods to test the relationships between these factors and performance levels. This approach permits researchers to determine whether these factors are statistically associated and so allows them to represent the strength of these correlations statistically (Jaga & Guetterman, 2021).

On the other hand, researchers might start with quantitative techniques to explore variable relationships and then utilise qualitative methods to validate and deepen their understanding of these associations. This sequential or concurrent application of methods ensures a robust and multifaceted examination of the research question (Johnson & Onwuegbuzie, 2004; Morse, 2016a, b; Rentschler & Liu, 2024).

Moreover, secondary data can be utilised to depict the overall picture of the unit of analysis. To assure the levels of reliability and validity of the data collection and analysis process, researchers can implement a multi-method approach (Bryman, 2023). For example, integrating financial performance measures with assessments of managers' learning styles, as defined by Honey and Mumford's typology, can deliver a more refined understanding of their impact on organisational success (Honey & Mumford, 2006; Zumitzavan, 2011).

In this way, Honey and Mumford (2006) classify managers into four distinct learning styles: Activists, Pragmatists, Reflectors, and Theorists. Activists thrive on engaging actively with new experiences, which may lead them to drive innovation within the firm. Pragmatists prefer applying ideas in practical contexts, potentially increasing levels of operational efficiency and contributing to improved profitability.

Reflectors, who learn by observing and contemplating, may excel in strategic planning and risk management, thereby bolstering stable financial outcomes. In the meantime, Theorists, who favour understanding theoretical underpinnings before application, might contribute to the development of strategic frameworks but could be slower to implement changes due to their need for thorough conceptual understanding.

To investigate the relationship between these learning styles and financial performance, researchers might analyse secondary data such as revenue growth, profitability, and cost management metrics. To illustrate, firms with a predominance of Pragmatist managers might demonstrate enhanced operational efficiency and superior financial results (Michie & Zumitzavan, 2012). Tashakkori, Johnson, and Teddlie (2020) suggest that complementing this quantitative analysis with qualitative data from in-depth interviews can further elucidate the relationship. Such interviews could reveal, for example, that Activists are instrumental in driving innovation yet encounter difficulties in executing practical solutions, whilst Theorists, although valuable in developing strategic frameworks and ensuring that strategies are theoretically sound, might experience delays in decision-making and implementation due to their thorough, conceptually driven approach. By triangulating quantitative financial data with qualitative insights, researchers can achieve a more comprehensive understanding of how managers' learning styles influence organisational performance, thereby offering more robust and actionable recommendations for enhancing management practices (Howell et al., 2023).

The selection and integration of these methodologies represent not only a scientific decision but also an act of research creativity. This creative process is now powerfully augmented by AI operating as a methodological partner rather than a mere tool. To illustrate, AI can analyse thousands of pages of qualitative interview data to identify novel, emergent themes that a human researcher might miss, which can then be utilised to creatively design a more sophisticated quantitative survey, thus bridging the inductive-deductive divide (Badawy et al., 2025). By revealing such unexpected patterns and connections within complex datasets, AI tools inspire new avenues of inquiry and empower researchers to construct more innovative and sophisticated multi-method designs (Chinnaraju, 2025). At last, this symbiotic association between human creativity and computational power is reshaping the landscape of research design, allowing a more profound synthesis of qualitative depth and quantitative scale (Quiñones-Gómez et al., 2025).

In social science research, the survey strategy is a crucial technique for deriving general conclusions, provided that samples are chosen appropriately. Survey research primarily underlines the opinions, attitudes, motives, values, and norms of the research subjects. Typically, the survey method is associated with the use of written questionnaires (De Vaus & de Vaus, 2013; Dillman et al., 2014).

In the context of this study, a survey technique is utilised as part of a deductive approach to gather empirical data from respondents (Bryman, 2023), whilst in-depth interviews are applied as a tool for collecting qualitative data from participants as part of an inductive approach (Creswell, 2014). For example, in a study examining organisational culture, researchers might use in-depth interviews to explore employees' perceptions and experiences in detail, thus uncovering themes and patterns that inform the development of new theories or models (Guest et al., 2012).

Lastly, it is therefore imperative that the unit of analysis is clearly defined and that both primary and secondary data are classified prior to data collection. This guarantees that information pertinent to the research topic is selected for analysis (Hall, 2020; Ishaq et al., 2025; Randolph & Myers, 2013; Tashakkori et al., 2020).

3.4 Unit of Analysis

In the discipline of management research, the selection of the unit of analysis is vital for ensuring that results are pertinent and generalisable. The unit of analysis defines the essential point of the research and varies dependent upon the research objectives. When the research objective is to understand phenomena at an individual level, such as personal traits, behaviours, or experiences, the individual serves as the unit of analysis. For example, a research project investigating the influence of different leadership styles on organisational members' performance might centre on individual managers as the unit of analysis.

In this scenario, researchers would conduct surveys or interviews with managers to evaluate their leadership styles and subsequently collect performance data from their subordinates. This approach facilitates a detailed exploration of how variations in individual managerial behaviours influence employee outcomes, offering insights into the personal attributes and actions of leaders (Legood et al., 2021; Park, 2019).

In contrast, when the research purpose is to investigate phenomena operating at a larger organisational level, such as organisational culture, structural changes, or strategic initiatives, the organisation itself becomes the unit of analysis. For instance, a study exploring the relationship between organisational culture and innovation would examine organisational-wide attributes. Researchers might survey multiple organisations to assess their cultural characteristics and innovation practices, thereby identifying patterns and relationships at the organisational level (Mhatre & Mehta, 2023; Martins & Terblanche, 2003). This approach provides insights into how collective cultural dimensions impact organisational innovation and overall organisational performance.

Moreover, there are instances where a multi-level approach is essential to acquire a comprehensive understanding of the interplay between individual and organisational factors. For example, a research project investigating how managerial behaviours influence organisational performance might integrate data from both individual managers and the organisation. This could involve analysing individual managerial practices and behaviours alongside organisational performance metrics and strategic initiatives. By combining these perspectives, researchers can explore how specific managerial actions affect broader organisational outcomes and how organisational factors, such as culture or strategy, shape individual behaviours (Ting et al., 2024; Afsar & Umrani, 2020). This integrated approach allows for a more sophisticated understanding of the complex interactions between individual and organisational dynamics, providing a richer and more comprehensive view of the unit of analysis.

3.5 Primary Data for Quantitative Techniques

The questionnaire is a widely utilised instrument for collecting survey data, involving the administration of a uniform set of questions to participants according to a standardised protocol. It offers numerous advantages for research, providing a straightforward and efficient method for examining attitudes, values, beliefs, and motivations (Bretschi et al., 2023; Saunders et al., 2019a). A primary benefit of using questionnaires is their ability to collect data from a large number of respondents rapidly and cost-effectively, making them ideal for studies requiring extensive reach and statistical analysis (Abowitz & Toole, 2009). Furthermore, they enable researchers to standardise responses, thereby enhancing the comparability and reliability of the data (Hair et al., 2015).

However, questionnaires also present notable limitations. A significant drawback is their reliance on respondents' willingness and ability to provide accurate and thoughtful answers, which can impact the quality of the data collected (Sternberg, 2000; Weiss, 2022). In addition, Bretschi et al. (2023) propose that the views individuals express might not always match their actual behaviours, and they may not fully reveal their genuine attitudes. This misalignment can result in incomplete or biased responses, potentially compromising the validity of the findings (Molina-Azorin, 2023).

For example, in management research assessing organisational members' satisfaction with a new performance appraisal system, respondents might exaggerate their satisfaction levels to avoid potential negative repercussions, thereby skewing the results (Alsafadi & Altahat, 2021). Similarly, if a questionnaire on organisational culture is poorly designed, for instance with leading questions, the data may not accurately reflect the true organisational climate, thereby affecting the research conclusions (Schneider & Barbera, 2014).

To address these issues, researchers should employ several strategies to improve data accuracy and reliability. Ensuring respondent anonymity, distributing pilot tests of the questionnaire, and providing clear instructions are crucial steps (Bretschi et al., 2023; Hair et al., 2015). Reliability refers to the consistency and stability of the measurement instrument over time and across different contexts, ensuring that results are repeatable and dependable (Forero, 2024). Researchers can ensure reliability by conducting pilot studies to refine the instrument, employing consistent administration procedures, and utilising established scales with demonstrated reliability (Shrivastava & Shukla, 2023).

In addition, ensuring the validity of respondents' responses involves verifying that the sample size is sufficiently large to draw reliable averages and maintain response validity (Zumitzavan, 2011; Zumitzavan et al., 2025). An adequate sample size is essential for achieving a representative and reliable set of responses, which is critical for the accuracy of research findings (Krejcie & Morgan, 1970).

To further ensure levels of validity and reliability, researchers may employ triangulation, which involves combining primary and secondary data sources and applying multiple methods to verify findings. For instance, researchers might assess participants' willingness to engage in the study and corroborate questionnaire data with secondary sources or qualitative data. Such an approach is particularly pertinent when analysing respondents in organisational contexts where managerial perspectives are crucial (Flick, 2023; Patton, 2014).

Additionally, the validity of the data can be tested using statistical methods to determine whether the data distribution is normal. In addition to the Shapiro-Wilk test (when sample size is approximately lower than 50), the Kolmogorov-Smirnov test (when sample size is approximately equivalent to or greater than 50) provides a robust method for assessing normality. This test compares the empirical distribution function of the sample with the cumulative distribution function of a normal distribution (Kolmogorov, 1933; Auamnoy, 2002). It is widely used for evaluating the goodness-of-fit and determining if a sample conforms to a normal distribution (Lilliefors, 1967).

3.6 Quantitative Approach

3.6.1 Attitude Scales

Attitude scales are a crucial attribute in questionnaire design, comprising a series of statements to which respondents specify their levels of agreement or disagreement with pre-coded options. This method allows for the assessment of a range of attitudes on a specific theme rather than being dependent upon a single question to gauge complex attitudes (Oppenheim, 2000). Among the most widely used scales is the Likert scale, which positions respondents' answers along an attitude continuum. As established by Likert (1932), this scale often employs multiple items (e.g., ranging from 1 to 6) to measure agreement or disagreement on various statements. However, biases may arise if respondents avoid extreme response categories or inaccurately assess their preferences. Balnaves and Caputi (2001) emphasise the importance of validating and ensuring the reliability of these scales. Cronbach's coefficient alpha is a prevalent method for assessing internal consistency, reflecting the inter-relationships among items used to measure respondents' attitudes (Auamnoy, 2002). This coefficient ranges from 0 to 1, with values closer to 1 indicating higher reliability; a minimum value of 0.7 is generally considered acceptable (Bell et al., 2022).

3.7 Primary Data for Qualitative Techniques

Qualitative research aims to uncover rich, refined insights and detailed descriptions in order to address complex research questions. This methodological approach concentrates on accumulating in-depth and contextually significant data to elucidate observed phenomena. Central to the success of qualitative research is the meticulous selection of participants, which profoundly influences the validity and reliability of the findings. For instance, in the realm of social sciences, including leaders or managers as main participants can provide critical insights into organisational dynamics. The selection of participants should be guided by several criteria in order to ensure their relevance and suitability.

Firstly, participants must possess direct experience or knowledge relevant to the research topic. For example, when studying the effects of different leadership styles on organisational members' performance, it is crucial to include both managers and employees who have interacted with various leadership approaches (Yukl, 2021). This ensures that the data collected are both relevant and informative. Secondly, participants should have appropriate expertise and experience related to the focus of research. Research on organisational change, for instance, should involve senior executives who have spearheaded change initiatives, as their perspectives offer valuable insights which are more reflective of high-level strategic decisions (Kotter & Cohen, 2014).

Additionally, researchers should consider the diversity of participants in order to enrich the data and provide a comprehensive understanding of the research subject. A study exploring corporate culture, for instance, would benefit from involving participants from various organisational levels and departments to capture a wide-ranging view of the organisational environment (Schein, 2016).

Furthermore, the accessibility and willingness of participants are crucial; ensuring that participants are both reachable and motivated to provide truthful and detailed responses is essential for obtaining high-quality data (Sharma et al.,2023). The ability of participants to communicate their experiences effectively and their openness to discussing sensitive topics are also important factors to consider (Charmaz, 2014).

In addition, the selection of participants for a study is contingent upon a range of criteria, including the research aims, the intricacy of the phenomenon under investigation, and the resources at one's disposal (Cohen et al., 2022). A larger number of participants can produce a more comprehensive and varied dataset, which is especially advantageous for probing multifaceted issues such as organisational culture or leadership paradigms (Bickman & Rog, 2009). This enhanced diversity in the sample can facilitate a more polished understanding of complex constructs and phenomena.

For example, a research project examining the effects of transformational leadership on organisational members' motivation might involve a large number of organisational members from various departments in order to capture a broad spectrum of experiences and perspectives (Black, 2023; Saunders & Lewis, 2017a). However, managing and analysing data from a larger number of participants can be demanding in terms of time, resources, and logistical coordination (Poth et al., 2023; Goodenough & Waite, 2012).

Conversely, a smaller sample of participants allows for a more concentrated and detailed exploration of specific cases or phenomena. This approach is often more manageable and cost-effective, simplifying a thorough and intensive analysis. For example, a case study probing the decision-making processes within a single organisation might involve in-depth interviews with a select group of senior managers. Such a method provides a comprehensive understanding of the complexities involved in decision-making within that particular context, e.g., decisions regarding the most effective methods for transferring knowledge, such as coaching, on-the-job versus off-the-job training, or lecturing. However, this may limit the generalisability of the findings to other settings (Trainor & Graue, 2013).

In contrast, a smaller sample of participants enables a more focused and detailed examination of specific phenomena. Such an approach is generally more manageable, entailing fewer logistical and financial limitations, and therefore enabling for a more intensive level of analysis.

A relevant illustration can be drawn from Indonesia, where a case study of a logistics firm employed in-depth interviews to identify the critical determinants of effective knowledge transfer among its staff (Sundiman et al., 2019). This method provides a sophisticated understanding of the complexities embedded within that particular organisational context. Nevertheless, this degree of specificity inevitably limits the extent to which the findings can be generalised to other settings—a well-recognised trade-off in case study research (Trainor & Graue, 2013). Similarly, a qualitative research project investigating the implementation of a new technological tool within a small start-up could involve all-inclusive observations and interviews with a select group of organisational members directly interacting with the technology. Whilst this enables an in-depth analysis of the tool's impact within that specific organisational settings, the findings may not be readily generalised to larger organisations or different sectors (Yin, 2013). These limitations highlight the importance of exercising caution when applying insights from case studies to wider contexts.

To ensure the appropriateness of the selected number of participants, researchers must carefully evaluate the following criteria: the relevance of participants' expertise to the research, their accessibility, and their willingness to deliver honest and detailed responses. Participants should be straightforwardly reachable and motivated to participate in the research process to ensure the reliability and validity of the data collected (Maxwell, 2013). Moreover, the criteria should comprise the participants' ability to provide rich, descriptive data that aligns with the research objectives, together with their suitability based on the specific focus of the research (Mason, 2010). By considering these factors, researchers can ensure that the numbers of participants and selection criteria effectively support the research aims and available resources.

3.8 Qualitative Approach

In qualitative research, an array of instruments is utilised to elicit rich, insightful data from participants, thereby enabling researchers to investigate complex phenomena in considerable depth. A primary method is interviews, which can be categorised into three distinct types: structured, semi-structured, and unstructured.

3.8.1 Methods of Interviews

Firstly, structured interviews are characterised by a fixed set of predetermined questions, assuring consistency across responses. This method is particularly advantageous for collecting specific information in a comparable manner, such as assessing the degree of organisational members' satisfaction across a variety of divisions (Davis, 2004). The rigidity of this format facilitates straightforward data analysis, yet may limit the depth of insight.

Secondly, semi-structured interviews strike a balance between directed questioning and the flexibility to explore participants' experiences more thoroughly. Researchers may initiate the discussion with core questions but hold the latitude to probe into unforeseen topics that emerge during the conversation. For example, when investigating perceptions of leadership, a researcher might inquire about specific experiences with different leaders whilst also investigating how these encounters shape broader views on leadership effectiveness (Bryman, 2011).

Thirdly, unstructured interviews, by contrast, offer participants the utmost freedom to express their views without predefined constraints. This approach is particularly valuable when exploring emergent or poorly understood areas, as it allows participants to share narratives and insights that researchers may not have anticipated. For instance, in studying organisational culture, an unstructured interview could discover valuable perspectives reflecting the composite social dynamics within the organisation (Chauhan, 2022). For example, in contexts where seniority plays a predominant role, most organisational members in many organisations are likely to respect, listen to, and defer to older individuals. However, in some, due to limitations in resources such as time and budget constraints, the levels of deference to seniority may vary (van de Mieroop, 2015). In such cases, employing unstructured interviews could prove particularly advantageous.

3.8.2 Focus Groups

In addition to interviews, focus groups represent another significant qualitative tool. These moderated discussions encourage interaction among participants, facilitating the exchange of diverse perspectives on a particular topic. This method can unearth collective attitudes and experiences that may remain hidden in individual interviews, enriching the data set (Akyıldız & Ahmed, 2021).

3.8.3 *Observational Research*

Next, observational research permits researchers to collect data through direct observation of participants in their natural environments. This method provides valuable context to behaviours and interactions, offering insights into the dynamics of teamwork, communication patterns, and organisational culture (Klonek et al., 2020).

3.8.4 *Diary Studies*

Diary studies invite participants to chronicle their thoughts and experiences over an extended period, permitting researchers to distinguish ongoing reflections and responses to specific events or changes within the workplace. This longitudinal approach can illuminate how attitudes and experiences evolve over time (Olorunfemi, 2024).

In conclusion, by utilising these varied qualitative instruments, researchers can amass comprehensive data capturing the complexity of human experiences whilst contributing a deeper understanding of the organisational context in which these experiences unfold. This rich qualitative data assists in complementing quantitative findings, ultimately offering a holistic perspective on the phenomena under investigation.

3.9 Secondary Data for Both Quantitative and Qualitative Approaches

Effective research often hinges on the strategic use of secondary data, which can significantly enrich the analysis and findings (Sekaran & Bougie, 2019). Mohajan (2017). categorises secondary data into three primary types: documentary data, survey-based data, and data compiled from multiple sources. Documentary data, in particular, plays a vital role in research. This category incorporates a diverse range of materials, including books, journal articles, newspaper articles, surveys, and publicly available government statistics, many of which are accessible online. The utilisation of a variety of forms of documentary data is instrumental in augmenting the examination of research questions and achieving research objectives, providing a robust foundation for analysis and interpretation.

The principal advantage of applying secondary data is significant savings in resources, such as time and financial costs. This method allows researchers to review, revise, and refine their analysis before presenting the findings. Secondary data is often readily accessible, relatively cost-effective, and swiftly obtainable (Ghauri et al., 2020). Saunders (2015) stresses that this approach facilitates more rapid access to data and may be the sole feasible option in certain contexts. These efficiencies enable researchers to allocate more resources towards conceptualising the research's theoretical frameworks and exploring its broader implications.

Nevertheless, several challenges are associated with the utilisation of secondary data. For instance, obtaining access to applicable data can sometimes be arduous or costly. Saunders and Lewis (2017b) note that whilst a broad array of online indexing systems delivers direct links to accessible data sources, these sources may not always be valid or reliable. Correspondingly, the use of secondary data from governmental reports or industry databases, whilst initially appealing due to their accessibility, may pose issues related to data accuracy and timeliness (Flick, 2023). It is thus crucial to verify the provenance and publication date of the data in order to ensure its credibility. In addressing these challenges, the inductive method, as outlined by Hakim (1987), offers an alternative approach by allowing researchers to explore deeper, refined insights through qualitative techniques such as in-depth interviews, which can complement and enhance the findings obtained from secondary data sources (Robson, 2024; Saunders et al., 2019a, b).

Furthermore, quantitative and qualitative techniques offer distinct advantages in research. Quantitative methods excel in making broad generalisations that extend beyond the research setting. Surveys, a key quantitative tool, provide a robust sampling framework and are often applied alongside qualitative methods in case studies to investigate specific situations, groups, or processes in greater details. In contrast, qualitative methods, such as in-depth interviews, distribute rich, detailed insights into individual cases, capturing the complexities of specific phenomena (Bryman & Harley, 2022).

In the social sciences, survey research is frequently a preliminary step rather than a conclusion, and it can also serve as a component within broader case studies (Mabry, 2008). Whilst quantitative methods are generally more time efficient, qualitative methods produce a deeper and more distinguished understanding. Therefore, integrating both approaches through triangulation can maximise their respective strengths and enhance overall research outcomes (Hirose & Creswell, 2023).

3.10 Chapter Summary

This chapter elucidated the core research methodologies and designs, detailing their respective advantages and disadvantages. It also scrutinised the utilisation of primary and secondary data in order to enhance research's credibility. The subsequent chapter presents the instruments for ensuring the validity and reliability of research within the management discipline.

3.11 Questions for Further Reflection

1. A company wishes to understand why its organisational members' turnover has recently increased. Propose a mixed-methods research design to investigate this issue. Justify your choice of a specific design (e.g., sequential exploratory) and explain precisely how the qualitative and quantitative findings would be integrated to offer a comprehensive answer.
2. The chapter asserts that a case study is a methodologically flexible design, not one intrinsically bound to qualitative data. Design a predominantly quantitative, single-case study to assess the effectiveness of a new strategic initiative implemented by one specific multinational corporation. What variables would you measure, and what sources of data would you use?
3. You are researching the factors leading to successful product innovation in technology firms. Discuss the advantages and disadvantages of selecting (a) the individual product development team or (b) the organisation as a whole as your primary unit of analysis. Which would you select, and what are the implications of this choice for your research design?
4. A researcher plans to utilise publicly available corporate annual reports (a form of secondary data) to analyse the relationship between a firm's stated commitment to sustainability and its financial performance. Critically evaluate the potential pitfalls and limitations of relying merely on this data source in terms of its validity, reliability, and objectivity.
5. The chapter notes that in qualitative inquiry, the researcher is an interpretive instrument. Discuss the concept of the 'interviewer effect' in the context of conducting semi-structured interviews with organisational members about their line managers. What practical steps could a researcher take to lessen this form of bias whilst still embracing their interpretive role?
6. Imagine you are planning to conduct in-depth interviews with junior organisational members to explore their perceptions of organisational power dynamics and career progression barriers. Identify the key ethical issues you would need to address before, during, and after the data collection process.
7. A researcher applies a single questionnaire item, "Please rate your overall job satisfaction on a scale of 1 to 5," to measure the construct of 'job satisfaction'. Drawing on the chapter's discussion of attitude scales and reliability, critique this approach. How would you design a more robust, multi-item Likert scale to measure this construct, and how would you assess its internal consistency?
8. Compare and contrast the sampling strategy you would adopt for a large-scale quantitative survey on managerial stress with the sampling strategy for a small-scale qualitative study on the same topic. Justify the differences in logic, referencing concepts such as probability sampling and purposive sampling techniques.
9. For a study exploring how a team of software developers collaborates on a complex project, which qualitative method—in-depth interviews, focus groups, or observation—would be most appropriate? Justify your choice by discussing

the unique insights each method could provide and the limitations each might present in this specific context.

10. The chapter distinguishes between deductive (theory-testing) and inductive (theory-building) approaches. If an inductive interview study revealed that organisational members in a creative industry consistently link their motivation to 'intellectual autonomy', what would be the next logical step in the research process to develop this emergent theme into a more formal, testable hypothesis?

References

Abowitz, D. A., & Toole, T. M. (2009). Mixed method research: Fundamental issues of design, validity, and reliability in construction research. *Journal of Construction Engineering and Management, 136*(1), 108–116. https://doi.org/10.1061/(ASCE)CO.1943-7862.0000026

Afsar, B., & Umrani, W. A. (2020). Transformational leadership and innovative work behavior: The role of motivation to learn, task complexity and innovation climate. *European Journal of Innovation Management, 23*(3), 402–428. https://doi.org/10.1108/EJIM-12-2018-0257

Akyıldız, S. T., & Ahmed, K. H. (2021). An overview of qualitative research and focus group discussion. *International Journal of Academic Research in Education, 7*(1), 1–15. https://doi.org/10.17985/ijare.866762

Alsafadi, Y., & Altahat, S. (2021). Human resource management practices and employee performance: The role of job satisfaction. *The Journal of Asian Finance, Economics and Business, 8*(1), 519–529. https://doi.org/10.13106/jafeb.2021.vol8.no1.519

Auamnoy, T. (2002). *Statistics and SPSS for 21st century research*. Chulalongkorn University.

Babbie, E. R. (2021). *The Practice of social research* (15th ed.). Cengage Learning.

Badawy, A. M., Elhamd, E. A., Shamma, H. M., & Kolaly, H. (2025). Artificial intelligence in marketing: implications and future research directions. *International Journal of Business & Economics (IJBE), 10*(1), 66–95.

Balnaves, M., & Caputi, P. (2001). *Introduction to quantitative research methods: An investigative approach*. Sage Publications.

Bamberger, P., & Meshoulam, I. (2000). *Human resource strategy: Formulation, implementation, and impact*. Sage Publications.

Bell, E., Bryman, A., & Harley, B. (2022). *Business research methods*. Oxford University Press.

Bibi, H., Khan, S., & Shabir, M. (2022). A critique of research paradigms and their implications for qualitative, quantitative and mixed research methods. *Webology, 19*(2), 7321–7335.

Bickman, L., & Rog, D. J. (Eds.). (2009). *The SAGE handbook of applied social research methods* (2nd ed.). Sage Publications.

Black, K. (2023). *Business statistics: For contemporary decision making*. John Wiley & Sons.

Bretschi, D., Schaurer, I., & Dillman, D. A. (2023). An experimental comparison of three strategies for converting mail respondents in a probability-based mixed-mode panel to internet respondents. *Journal of Survey Statistics and Methodology, 11*(1), 23–46. https://doi.org/10.1093/jssam/smab002

Bryman, A. (2011). Research methods in the study of leadership. In A. Bryman, D. Collinson, K. Grint, B. Jackson, & M. Uhi-Bien (Eds.), *The Sage handbook of leadership* (pp. 15–28). Sage.

Bryman, A. (2023). *Social research methods* (6th ed.). Oxford University Press.

Bryman, A., & Harley, B. (2022). *Social research methods*. Oxford University Press.

Charmaz, K. (2014). *Constructing grounded theory* (2nd ed.). Sage Publications.

Chauhan, R. S. (2022). Unstructured interviews: are they really all that bad? *Human Resource Development International, 25*(4), 474–487. https://doi.org/10.1080/13678868.2019.1603019

Chinnaraju, A. (2025). Partial Least Squares Structural Equation Modeling (PLS-SEM) In The AI Era: Innovative methodological guide and framework for business research. *Magna Scientia Advanced Research and Reviews, 13*(02), 062–108.

Cohen, L., Manion, L., & Morrison, K. (2022). *Research methods in education.* Routledge.

Creswell, J. W. (2014). *Research design: Qualitative, quantitative, and mixed methods approaches* (4th ed.). Sage Publications.

Creswell, J. W., & Poth, C. N. (2016). *Qualitative inquiry and research design: Choosing among five approaches.* Sage publications.

Creswell, J. W., & Poth, C. N. (2024). *Qualitative inquiry and research design: Choosing among five approaches* (5th ed.). Sage Publications.

Davis, G. (2004). Job satisfaction survey among employees in small businesses. *Journal of Small Business and Enterprise Development, 11*(4), 495–503. https://doi.org/10.1108/14626000410567143

De Vaus, D., & de Vaus, D. (2013). *Surveys in social research.* Routledge.

Delery, J. E., & Doty, D. H. (1996). Modes of theorizing in strategic human resource management: Tests of universalistic, contingency, and configurational performance Predictions. *Academy of Management Journal, 39*(4), 802–835.

Denzin, N. K., & Lincoln, Y. S. (Eds.). (2011). *The Sage handbook of qualitative research.* sage.

Dillman, D. A., Smyth, J. D., & Christian, L. M. (2014). *Internet, phone, mail, and mixed-mode surveys: The tailored design method* (4th ed.). Wiley.

Eisenhardt, K. M., & Graebner, M. E. (2007). Theory building from cases: Opportunities and challenges. *Academy of Management Journal, 50*(1), 25–32. https://doi.org/10.5465/AMJ.2007.24160888

Flick, U. (2023). *An introduction to qualitative research* (7th ed.). Sage Publications.

Forero, C. G. (2024). Cronbach's alpha. In A. C. Michalos (Ed.), *Encyclopedia of quality of life and well-being research* (pp. 1505–1507). Springer International Publishing.

Gerring, J. (2006). *Case study research: Principles and practices.* Cambridge university press.

Ghauri, P. N., Grønhaug, K., & Strange, R. (2020). *Research methods in business studies.* Cambridge University Press.

Giddens, A. (2009). *Sociology* (6th ed.). Polity Press.

Gioia, D. A., Corley, K. G., & Hamilton, A. L. (2013). Seeking qualitative rigor in inductive research: Notes on the Gioia methodology. *Organizational Research Methods, 16*(1), 15–31. https://doi.org/10.1177/1094428112452151

Goodenough, A., & Waite, S. (2012). Real world research: A resource for users of social research methods in applied settings (3rd ed.). *Journal of Education for Teaching, 38*(4), 513–515. https://doi.org/10.1080/02607476.2012.708121

Guest, G., MacQueen, K. M., & Namey, E. E. (2012). *Applied thematic analysis.* Sage Publications.

Hair, J. F., Wolfinbarger, M. F., Money, A. H., Samouel, P., & Page, M. (2015). *Essentials of business research methods* (3rd ed.). Routledge.

Hakim, C. (1987). *Research design: Strategies and choices.* Sage Publications.

Hall, R. P. (2020). *Mixing methods in social research: qualitative, quantitative and combined methods.* Sage Publications.

Hargis, M. B., Watt, J. D., & Piotrowski, C. (2011). Developing leaders: Examining the role of transactional and transformational leadership across business contexts. *Organization Development Journal, 29*(3), 51–66.

Hayes, R., Kyer, B., & Weber, E. (2015). *The case study cookbook.* Worcester Polytechnic Institute.

Hirose, M., & Creswell, J. W. (2023). Applying core quality criteria of mixed methods research to an empirical study. *Journal of Mixed Methods Research, 17*(1), 12–28. https://doi.org/10.1177/15586898221086346

Honey, P., & Mumford, A. (2006). *The manual of learning styles* (3rd ed.). Peter Honey Publications.

Howell, M. C., Babchuk, W. A., & Guetterman, T. C. (2023). Mixed methods-grounded theory: Best practices for design and implementation. In C. N. Poth (Ed.), *The Sage handbook of mixed methods research design* (pp. 291–292). Sage Publications.

Ishaq, M. I., Sarwar, H., Franzoni, S., & Palermo, O. (2025). The nexus of human resource management, corporate social responsibility, and sustainable performance in upscale hotels: A mixed-method study. *International Journal of Emerging Markets, 20*(13), 1–29. https://doi.org/10.1108/IJOEM-04-2022-0714

Jaga, A., & Guetterman, T. C. (2021). The value of mixed methods work-family research for human resource management: A review and agenda. *The International Journal of Human Resource Management, 34*(2), 286–312. https://doi.org/10.1080/09585192.2021.1964092

Johnson, R. B., & Onwuegbuzie, A. J. (2004). Mixed methods research: A research paradigm whose time has come. *Educational Researcher, 33*(7), 14–26. https://doi.org/10.3102/0013189X033007014

Judge, T. A., & Piccolo, R. F. (2004). Transformational and transactional leadership: A meta-analytic test of their relative validity. *Journal of Applied Psychology, 89*(5), 755–768. https://doi.org/10.1037/0021-9010.89.5.755

Klonek, F. E., Meinecke, A. L., Hay, G., & Parker, S. K. (2020). Capturing team dynamics in the wild: The communication analysis tool. *Small Group Research, 51*(3), 303–341. https://doi.org/10.1177/1046496420904126

Kolmogorov, A. N. (1933). Sulla determinazione empirica delle leggi di distribuzione. *Giornale Dell'Istituto Italiano degli Attuari, 4*, 83–91.

Kotter, J. P., & Cohen, D. (2014). *Change leadership: The kotter collection (5 Books)*. Harvard Business Review Press.

Krejcie, R. V., & Morgan, D. W. (1970). Determining sample size for research activities. *Educational and Psychological Measurement, 30*(3), 607–610. https://doi.org/10.1177/001316447003000308

Krueger, R. A., & Casey, M. A. (2014). *Focus groups: A practical guide for applied research* (5th ed.). Sage Publications.

Legood, A., van der Werff, L., Lee, A., & Den Hartog, D. (2021). A meta-analysis of the role of trust in the leadership-performance relationship. *European Journal of Work and Organizational Psychology, 30*(1), 1–22. https://doi.org/10.1080/1359432X.2020.1819241

Likert, R. (1932). A technique for the measurement of attitudes. *Archives of Psychology, 22*(140), 55.

Lilliefors, H. W. (1967). On the Kolmogorov-Smirnov test for the exponential distribution. *Journal of the American Statistical Association, 62*(318), 399–402. https://doi.org/10.2307/2283970

Mabry, L. (2008). Case Study in Social Research. In P. Alasuutari, L. Bickman, & J. Brannen (Eds.), *Case study in social research* (pp. 214–227). Sage Publications. https://doi.org/10.4135/9781446212165

Martins, E. C., & Terblanche, F. (2003). Building organisational culture that stimulates creativity and innovation. *European Journal of Innovation Management, 6*(1), 64–74. https://doi.org/10.1108/14601060310456337

Mason, M. (2010). Sample size and saturation in PhD studies using qualitative interviews. *Forum Qualitative Sozialforschung / Forum: Qualitative Social Research, 11*(3). https://doi.org/10.17169/fqs-11.3.1428

Maxwell, J. A. (2013). *Qualitative research design: An interactive approach* (3rd ed.). Sage Publications.

Mhatre, S. G., & Mehta, N. K. (2023). Review of phenomenological approaches and its scope in human resource management. *Journal of Organizational Effectiveness: People and Performance, 10*(1), 112–131. https://doi.org/10.1108/JOEPP-12-2021-0354

Michie, J., & Zumitzavan, V. (2012). The impact of 'learning' and 'leadership' management styles on organizational outcomes: A study of tyre firms in Thailand. *Asia Pacific Business Review, 18*(4), 607–630. https://doi.org/10.1080/13602381.2012.694724

Mohajan, H. K. (2017). Two criteria for good measurements in research: Validity and reliability. Annals of Spiru Haret University. *Economic Series, 17*(4), 59–82. https://doi.org/10.26458/1746

Molina-Azorin, J. F. (2023). Mixed methods prevalence studies, publishing strategies and reporting in business and management fields. In R. Cameron & X. Golenko (Eds.), *Handbook of mixed methods research in business and management* (pp. 110–122). Edward Elgar Publishing.

Morgeson, F. P., DeRue, D. S., & Karam, E. P. (2010). Leadership in teams: A functional approach to understanding leadership structures and processes. *Journal of Management, 36*(1), 5–39. https://doi.org/10.1177/0149206309347376

Morse, J. M. (2016a). *Mixed method design: Principles and procedures*. Routledge.

Morse, J. M. (2016b). *Qualitative health research: Creating a new discipline*. Routledge.

Olorunfemi, D. (2024). Diary studies in research: More than a research method. *International Journal of Market Research, 66*(4), 410–427. https://doi.org/10.1177/14707853231222139

Oppenheim, A. N. (2000). *Questionnaire design, interviewing and attitude measurement*. Bloomsbury Publishing.

Park, C. K. (2019). Transformational leadership and employee engagement from the HRD perspective. *Korean Review of Corporation Management, 10*(3), 19–36. https://doi.org/10.20434/KRICM.2019.10.10.3.19

Patton, M. Q. (2014). *Qualitative research & evaluation methods: Integrating theory and practice* (4th ed.). Sage Publications.

Poth, C. N., Bullock, E. P., & Eppel, E. (2023). Adaptive mixed methods research design practices to address complexity in business and management research. In R. Cameron & X. Golenko (Eds.), *Handbook of mixed methods research in business and management* (pp. 329–347). Edward Elgar Publishing.

Quiñones-Gómez, J. C., Mor, E., & Chacón, J. (2025). Data-driven design in the design process: A systematic literature review on challenges and opportunities. *International Journal of Human–Computer Interaction, 41*(4), 2227–2252.

Randolph, K. A., & Myers, L. L. (2013). *Basic statistics in multivariate analysis*. Oxford University Press.

Rentschler, R., & Liu, J. (2024). Methods and methodologies in arts and cultural management research. In J. Jung, Y. Vakharia, & M. Vecco (Eds.), *The Oxford handbook of arts and cultural management* (pp. C3S1–C3S11). Oxford University Press.

Robson, C. (2024). *Real world research*. John Wiley & Sons.

Saunders, M. N. (2015). *Research methods for business students*. Pearson.

Saunders, M., & Lewis, P. (2017a). *Doing research in business and management* (2nd ed.). Pearson.

Saunders, M., & Lewis, P. (2017b). *Research methods for business students*. Pearson.

Saunders, M. N. K., Bristow, A., Thornhill, A., & Lewis, P. (2019a). Understanding research philosophy and approaches to theory development. In M. N. K. Saunders, P. Lewis, & A. Thornhill (Eds.), *Research methods for business students* (8th ed., pp. 128–171). Pearson Education.

Saunders, M. N. K., Lewis, P., & Thornhill, A. (2019b). *Research methods for business students* (8th ed.). Pearson.

Savin-Baden, M., & Major, C. (2023). *Qualitative research: The essential guide to theory and practice*. Routledge.

Schein, E. H. (2016). *Organizational culture and leadership* (5th ed.). Jossey-Bass.

Schneider, B., & Barbera, K. (2014). *The oxford handbook of organizational climate and culture*. Oxford University Press.

Sekaran, U., & Bougie, R. (2019). *Research methods for business: A skill-building approach* (7th ed.). Wiley.

Sharma, L. R., Bidari, S., Bidari, D., Neupane, S., & Sapkota, R. (2023). Exploring the mixed methods research design: Types, purposes, strengths, challenges, and criticisms. *Global Academic Journal of Linguistics and Literature, 5*(1), 3–12. https://doi.org/10.36348/gajll.2023.v05i01.002

Shearmur, J. (2005). The logic of scientific discovery. In J. Shand (Ed.), *Central works of philosophy v4: Twentieth century: Moore to Popper* (4th ed., pp. 262–286). Routledge.

Shrivastava, N. K., & Shukla, A. V. (2023). Measuring an employer brand: A study towards valid scale development (as a second-order factor of a structural model). *International Journal of Organizational Analysis, 31*(2), 550–568.

Siggelkow, N. (2007). Persuasion with case studies. *Academy of Management Journal, 50*(1), 20–24. https://doi.org/10.5465/amj.2007.24160882

Silverman, D. (2021). *Doing qualitative research.* Sage Publications.

Sternberg, R. (2000). Innovation networks and regional development—evidence from the European Regional Innovation Survey (ERIS): Theoretical concepts, methodological approach, empirical basis and introduction to the theme issue. *European Planning Studies, 8*(4), 389–407.

Sundiman, D., Wu, C. H., Mursidi, A., Johan, S. B. P., & Indahingwati, A. (2019). Knowledge management key factors: An empirical research on small and medium-sized enterprises in Indonesia. *International Journal of Business and Systems Research, 13*(2), 139–161.

Tashakkori, A., Johnson, R. B., & Teddlie, C. (2020). *Foundations of mixed methods research: Integrating quantitative and qualitative approaches in the social and behavioral sciences.* Sage Publications.

Ting, C. W., Li, H. X., Chen, K. H., Lee, Y. S., & Yen, S. J. (2024). How can organizational leadership promote environmental behaviors through corporate social responsibility policy adoption? The moderating role of environmental awareness. *Sustainability, 16*(17), 7677.

Trainor, A., & Graue, E. (Eds.). (2013). *Reviewing qualitative research in the social sciences.* Routledge.

van de Mieroop, D. (2015). Social identity theory and the discursive analysis of collective identities in narratives. In A. De Fina & A. Georgakopoulou (Eds.), *The handbook of narrative analysis* (pp. 408–428). John Wiley & Sons.

Verma, R., Verma, S., & Abhishek, K. (2024). *Research methodology.* Publishing.

Voss, C. A., Tsikriktsis, N., & Frohlich, M. (2002). Case research in operations management. *International Journal of Operations & Production Management, 22*(2), 195–219. https://doi.org/10.1108/01443570210414329

Wang, W., Zhang, Y., & Chen, S. (2024b). The development of the sustainable innovation capabilities construct using grounded theory: Evidence from Chinese equipment manufacturers. *European Journal of Innovation Management, 27*(8), 2483–2521. https://doi.org/10.1108/EJIM-10-2022-0546

Weiss, D. (2022). Technological innovation systems: A critical review of quantitative methods. In *EU-SPRI 2022 conference.*

Yin, R. K. (2009a). *Case study research: Design and methods* (4th ed.). Sage Publications.

Yin, R. K. (2013). Validity and generalization in future case study evaluations. *Evaluation, 19*(3), 321–332. https://doi.org/10.1177/1356389013497081

Yin, R. K. (2014). *Case study research: Design and methods* (5th ed.). Sage Publications.

Yukl, G. (2021). *Leadership in Organizations* (9th ed.). Pearson.

Zumitzavan, V. (2011). *The impact of managers' learning styles and leadership styles on the effectiveness of their organisations: A case study from small retail tyre companies in Thailand* (Doctoral dissertation, University of Birmingham).

Zumitzavan, V., Prachumrasee, K., & Pathak, S. (2025). Transformational leadership cultivating innovation and transparency in local government organisations, Thailand. *Journal of Open Innovation: Technology, Market, and Complexity*, 100626.

Chapter 4
Levels of Validity and Reliability

4.1 Introduction

In management research, the credibility of findings is fundamentally dependent on the principles of reliability and validity, which vary in line with the methodological approach. Quantitative research ensures reliability—consistency in measurements—through test-retest, inter-rater agreement, and internal consistency assessments. Validity, in this context, pertains to the accuracy of the constructs measured, encompassing construct validity, content validity, and criterion validity. Conversely, qualitative research emphasises reliability through methodological consistency and validity (or trustworthiness) by adopting techniques such as member checking and prolonged engagement to ensure findings authentically represent participants' perspectives. Mastery of these concepts is essential for producing rigorous and insightful management research.

4.2 Pilot Study

A pilot study is a preliminary trial conducted on a limited scale prior to the full-scale research project. It is instrumental in appraising both reliability and validity. From the perspective of reliability, a pilot study scrutinises the consistency and dependability of research instruments and procedures, facilitating the identification and resolution of potential issues before the main study is launched. In terms of validity, it ensures that the research design and instruments accurately measure the intended constructs and address the research questions with precision. Consequently, a pilot study is essential for fine-tuning both the reliability and validity of the research methodology (Zumitzavan, 2011).

A pilot study or pilot test is an introductory investigation designed to evaluate the feasibility, time requirements, cost implications, and potential risks associated with

© The Author(s), under exclusive license to Springer Nature Singapore Pte Ltd. 2025

V. Zumitzavan, *Social Science Methodologies for Management Research*,
https://doi.org/10.1007/978-981-95-4318-2_4

a research methodology. It aims to refine and optimise the main research's design by testing the research instruments and procedures on a smaller scale before full-scale arrangement (Thabane et al., 2010; van Teijlingen & Hundley, 2001).

The purpose of the pilot study is to enhance the questionnaire in order to ensure that respondents encounter no difficulties in understanding and responding to the questions. It provides critical insights into the clarity of the question wording and the overall framework of the questionnaire (Baker & Edwards, 2012; Leon et al., 2011). Furthermore, it helps assess the validity and reliability of the data collected (Zumitzavan & Michie, 2015). Typically, a pilot test involves a sample size ranging from ten to thirty participants, which is generally deemed sufficient for larger surveys expecting to obtain 100 to 200 responses (Rahi, 2017; Kruger & Terblanche, 2024).

4.3 Conducting a Pilot Study in Academic Management Research

A pilot study is an essential preliminary stage in academic management research, serving to fine-tune research instruments and methodologies before embarking on a comprehensive research. The following steps describe a refined method to conducting a pilot study with rigour and precision.

4.3.1 Defining the Research Question

The initial step involves crafting a well-defined research question. This question should be precise and relevant to the management field, suggesting the research's objectives and focus (Ratten, 2023). A clearly articulated research question confirms that subsequent research activities are associated with the overall study goals.

4.3.2 Reviewing the Literature

An extensive review of existing literature is essential for understanding the up-to-date state of knowledge and identifying gaps. Researchers should critically analyse previous studies related to the research question to contextualise the research and pinpoint where new contributions can be made (Cohen et al., 2013). This review helps in refining the research question and developing a robust study framework.

4.3.3 Developing a Research Plan

Based on the research question and literature review, researchers must develop a meticulous research plan. This plan should outline the methodology and data collection techniques to be employed, ensuring that they are appropriate for addressing the research question (Halcomb & Hickman, 2015; Robinson, 2014). A well-structured plan is substantial for accomplishing valid and reliable results.

4.3.4 Selecting a Sample

Selecting a representative sample is indispensable for the pilot study's success. Researchers should select a sample that accurately reflects the population under investigation, utilising several sampling methods, such as Simple Random Sampling (Devlin, 2020). The sample's representativeness certifies that the findings from the pilot study are applicable to the larger population.

4.3.5 Collecting Data

The data collection phase encompasses implementing the selected methods, which may comprise surveys, interviews, or focus groups. This process should be conducted carefully to ensure that the data collected are relevant and reliable (Robson & McCartan, 2016). Appropriate data collection is crucial for the integrity of the pilot study.

4.3.6 Analysing Data

Once data have been gathered, they must be analysed by applying appropriate statistical or analytical techniques. This analysis helps identify patterns and insights crucial for understanding the research question (Haslam et al., 2024). The pilot study's findings provide valuable information for refining the research instruments and methodologies.

4.3.7 Interpreting Results

Interpreting the results requires analysing them within the contexts of the research question and existing literature. This interpretation helps draw meaningful conclusions and identify areas requiring further research (Merriam & Tisdell, 2015). A thorough interpretation ensures that the final research is well-informed and methodologically sound.

In conclusion, conducting a pilot study is a fundamental process in academic management research. It enables researchers to test and refine their methodologies, ensuring that the final research is robust and capable of generating valid and reliable results. By following these steps, researchers can enhance their research design and improve the overall quality of their research.

4.4 Levels of Validity

In management research, validity is fundamentally crucial as it ascertains whether a research instrument genuinely measures what it is intended to assess, thus ensuring that the findings are both credible and pertinent (Wallwey & Kajfez, 2023). Content validity specifically examines whether the instrument comprehensively encompasses the full spectrum of the construct it aims to measure. For instance, a survey questionnaire formulated to assess leadership styles must thoroughly address all relevant dimensions of leadership (Haynes et al., 1995). This type of validity is typically established through expert consultation and a thoroughly exhaustive literature review. To test the levels of validity of a pilot study, several methods can be applied.

Construct validity evaluates whether the measurement tool precisely replicates the theoretical construct that it is projected to measure. For example, a scale structured to measure 'organisational members' satisfaction' must genuinely capture the essence of satisfaction, rather than unrelated variables (Cronbach & Meehl, 1955). This validity is often assessed rigorously using factor analysis so as to confirm that the instrument aligns correctly with the theoretical construct.

Moreover, criterion validity effectively measures how well the tool predicts an outcome based on a validated benchmark. This includes both concurrent validity, which directly compares the tool with an existing measure at the same time, and predictive validity, which carefully assesses how well the tool predicts future outcomes (Cohen et al., 2022). Similarly, face validity pertains more superficially to the degree to which the tool appears to measure what it is supposed to measure. Although this is less rigorous, it remains crucial for ensuring that the instrument is perceived as relevant and appropriate by participants and stakeholders (Trochim, 2006).

Furthermore, internal validity primarily concerns the accuracy with which an experiment measures the relationship between variables, excluding the influence of confounding factors. This type of validity is vitally important for ensuring that observed effects are attributable to the experimental manipulation rather than other variables and are reliably supported by rigorous research design and control measures (Cook & Campbell, 2007). Finally, external validity broadly addresses the generalisability of the research findings beyond the specific sample and context of the study, evaluating whether results can be reasonably applied to other organisations or settings. This involves considering the representativeness of the sample and the applicability of study conditions to real-world scenarios (Wallwey & Kajfez, 2023).

Collectively, these various dimensions of validity ensure that research instruments in management research reliably provide accurate and applicable findings, thereby significantly enhancing the overall integrity and relevance of research outcomes. Hence, by applying one or more of these methods, researchers can evaluate the levels of validity of their pilot study and determine if any changes need to be made to improve the validity of their research.

4.4.1 Confirmatory Factor Analysis

Confirmatory factor analysis (CFA) is a statistical technique utilised to approve the factor structure of a set of observed variables. It is commonly applied in the fields of psychology, sociology, and management in order to validate theoretical constructs and measure latent variables. Within the discipline of management, CFA can be utilised to assess the validity of constructs, particularly in relation to the 'Umbrella of Management Disciplines' (Bollen, 1989; Black & Babin, 2019)

Specifically, within the context of factor analysis, the Kaiser-Meyer-Olkin (KMO) measure falls under the category of validity in management research. The KMO test assesses the adequacy of sampling for factor analysis by evaluating the degree to which variables are associated. A higher KMO value indicates that the data are appropriate for factor analysis, which supports the construct validity of the measurement instrument. Essentially, it helps determine whether the data can be effectively reduced to a smaller set of underlying factors, thereby validating the constructs being measured. In summary, KMO is a tool employed to establish the validity of the factor structure of a dataset rather than its reliability.

CFA, when conducted using SPSS (Statistical Package for the Social Sciences) or other similar statistical packages, offers a host of benefits to researchers in the social sciences, improving the efficiency, accuracy, and depth of their analytical endeavours.

One of the primary advantages of conducting CFA using SPSS is the platform's user-friendly interface, simplifying the analytical process. SPSS provides researchers with intuitive tools for data entry, manipulation, and analysis, enabling them to navigate complex datasets with ease. This accessibility lowers the barrier to entry for researchers, regardless of their levels of statistical expertise, allowing them to focus more on the interpretation of results rather than the technicalities of analysis.

Furthermore, SPSS facilitates efficient model specification for CFA. Researchers can utilise SPSS's graphical interfaces and syntax commands to define the relationships between observed variables and latent factors within their CFA models. This streamlined process of model specification minimises the likelihood of errors and allows researchers to articulate complex theoretical frameworks with clearness and precision, ensuring the accurate representation of underlying constructs.

Moreover, SPSS provides researchers with comprehensive output that facilitates the interpretation of CFA results. The software generates detailed reports containing fit indices, parameter estimates, and model fit statistics, allowing researchers to rigorously assess the goodness-of-fit of their CFA models. This rich output empowers researchers to evaluate the validity and reliability of their measurement instruments and make informed decisions about model refinement and further analyses.

Additionally, SPSS seamlessly integrates CFA analysis with other statistical procedures available within the software. Researchers can combine CFA with additional analyses such as descriptive statistics, correlation analysis, or regression analysis, within the same familiar environment. This integration enhances the coherence and depth of data analysis, enabling researchers to derive richer insights from their datasets and explore complex relationships between variables more comprehensively.

Furthermore, SPSS's widespread usage and familiarity among researchers contribute to its accessibility and utility. Many researchers are already well-acquainted with SPSS's interface and functionalities, reducing the learning curve associated with adopting new software packages. This familiarity facilitates resourceful data analysis and promotes collaboration and knowledge sharing within research communities, ultimately advancing scientific inquiry and understanding.

For example, in one management research project, there are 250 questionnaire respondents, the managers of small-to-medium enterprise firms. The questionnaires were distributed to explore the relationship between the different strategies that the managers apply to manage their firms with different levels of productivity. There are three different types of strategies in the questionnaire: (1) Cost Leadership, (2) Product/ Service Differentiation, and (3) Niche Market/ Focus Group Strategies. Each group of strategies comprises five different questions. To confirm whether those questions are classified into the appropriate component, CFA is applied.

As depicted in Fig. 4.1, firstly, select 'Analyse'. Secondly, select 'Dimension Reduction', and finally, select 'Factor'.

As shown in Fig. 4.2, firstly, select all variables into the 'Variables' box. Next, select 'Descriptives'. Then, on the Statistics, select 'Initial solution'. After that, on the Correlation Matrix, select 'Coefficients', 'Significant levels', and KMO and Bartlett's test of sphericity. Finally, select 'Continue'.

As illustrated in Fig. 4.3, firstly, select 'Extraction'. Next, on Method, by default, the principal components method has already been selected as it identifies linear combinations of the observed variables that capture the maximum amount of variance in the data. These combinations are called principal components. There are different methods available for selection. These are: (1) Common factor analysis, which extracts the common variance and puts them into factors; (2) Image factoring, which is based on a correlation matrix. The 'Ordinary Least Square Regression' method is used to predict the factor in image factoring; (3) Maximum likelihood method, which works on a correlation matrix basis but uses the maximum likelihood method to factor; (4) other method of factor analysis; Alfa factoring outweighs least

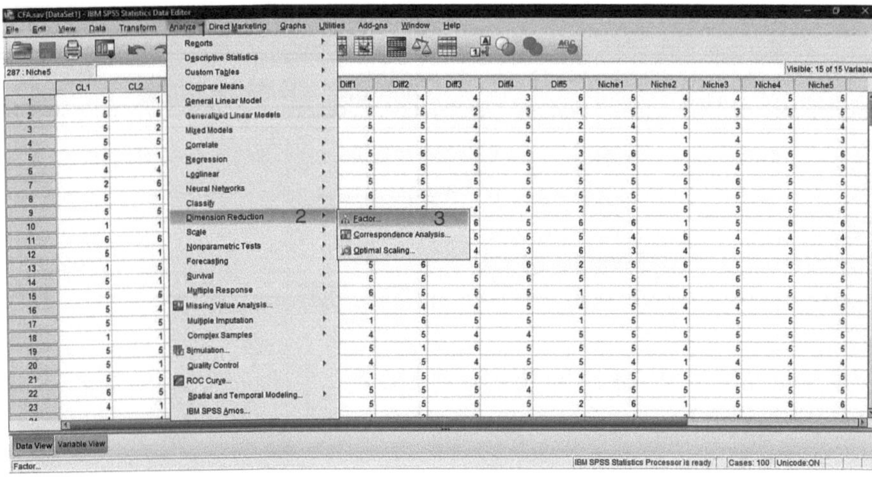

Fig. 4.1 Confirmatory Factor Analysis[1]

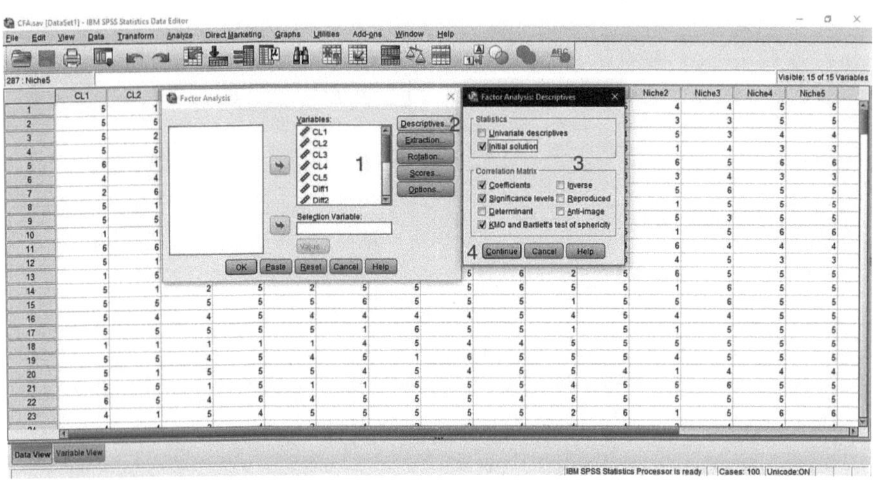

Fig. 4.2 Confirmatory Factor Analysis[2]

square. Weight square is another regression-based method which is used for factoring (Auamnoy, 2002).

In addition, on 'Analyse', it is possible to select 'Correlation matrix'. And on 'Display', select 'Unrotated factor solution, and Scree plot'. Next, on 'Extract', select 'Based on Eigenvalue, Eigenvalues greater than: 1'. Finally, continue 'Continue'.

As indicated in Fig. 4.4, firstly select 'Rotation'. Next, on 'Method', select 'Varimax'. Then, on 'Display', select 'Rotated solution'. Finally, select 'Continue'.

As shown in Fig. 4.5, firstly select 'Options'. Next, on 'Missing Values', select 'Exclude cases listwise'. Next, on Coefficient Display Format, select 'Sorted by

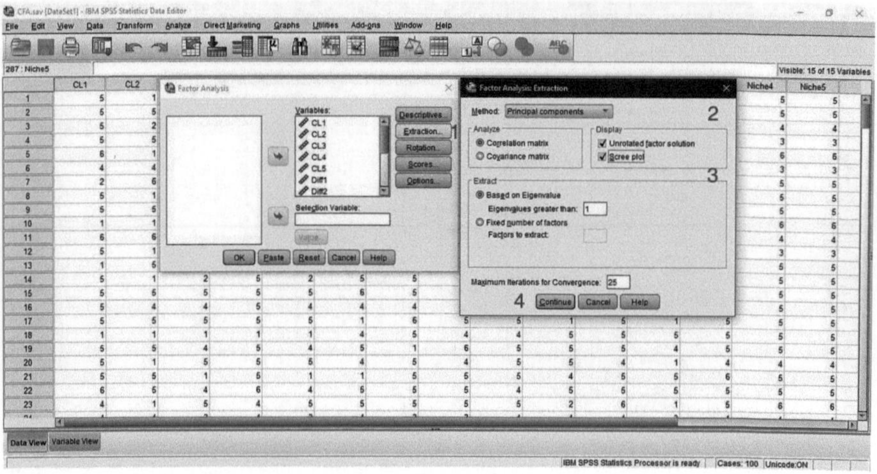

Fig. 4.3 Confirmatory Factor Analysis[3]

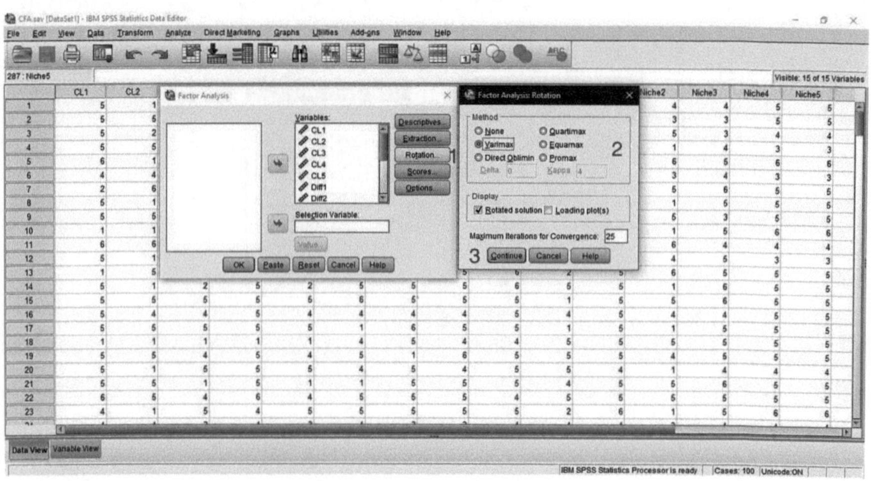

Fig. 4.4 Confirmatory Factor Analysis[4]

size, and 'Suppress small coefficients; Absolute value below 0.10'. Next, select 'Continue'. Finally, select "OK'.

As depicted in Fig. 4.6, in order to analyse data by using the CFA technique, the Pearson's Correlation Coefficients between the variables value should not be lower than 0.30 or 30 per cent. Here, the values of the Pearson's Correlation Coefficients between the variables in this dataset are not lower than 0.30; hence, the variables in this dataset are sufficient to proceed with the CFA technique.

As indicated in Table 4.1, the results of KMO value is 0.762, which is greater than 0.700, which is generally considered acceptable, suggesting that the variables

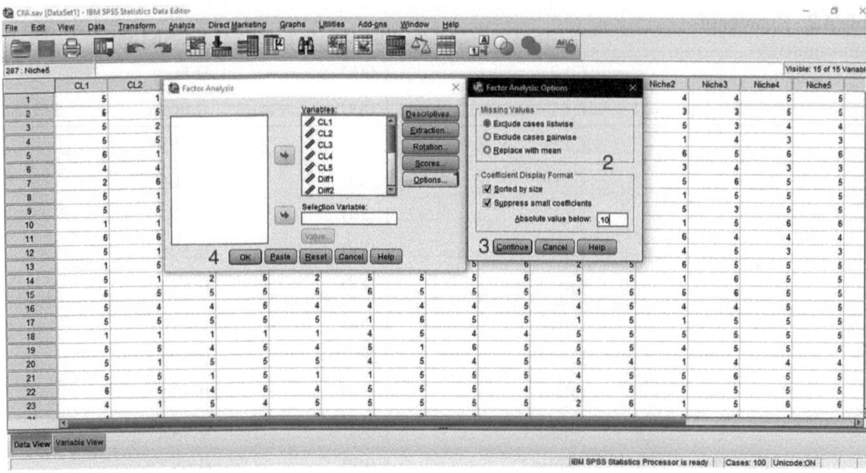

Fig. 4.5 Confirmatory Factor Analysis[5]

Variables		CL1	CL2	CL3	CL4	CL5	Diff1	Diff2	Diff3	Diff4	Diff5	Niche1	Niche2	Niche3	Niche4	Niche5
Correlation	CL1	1.000	0.693	0.673	0.840	0.802	0.481	0.424	0.399	0.314	.106	-.264	-.306	-.201	-.246	-.319
	CL2	0.693	1.000	0.623	0.648	0.700	0.434	0.424	0.435	0.223	.070	-.343	-.220	-.211	-.307	-.349
	CL3	0.673	0.623	1.000	0.801	0.856	0.500	0.439	0.496	0.297	.103	-.370	-.354	-.281	-.326	-.382
	CL4	0.840	0.648	0.801	1.000	0.684	0.496	0.443	0.525	0.342	.068	-.376	-.380	-.264	-.317	-.372
	CL5	0.802	0.700	0.856	0.684	1.000	0.491	0.408	0.402	0.269	.084	-.260	-.270	-.212	-.248	-.319
	Diff1	0.481	0.434	0.500	0.496	0.491	1.000	0.680	0.494	0.281	.206	-.355	-.423	-.363	-.400	-.452
	Diff2	0.424	0.424	0.439	0.443	0.408	0.680	1.000	0.458	0.282	.222	-.340	-.431	-.381	-.421	-.472
	Diff3	0.399	0.435	0.496	0.525	0.402	0.494	0.458	1.000	0.491	.172	-.359	-.345	-.203	-.266	-.271
	Diff4	0.314	0.223	0.297	0.342	0.269	0.281	0.282	0.491	1.000	.167	.025	-.017	-.034	.003	-.025
	Diff5	0.106	0.070	0.103	0.068	0.084	0.206	0.222	0.172	0.167	1.000	-.148	-.065	-.190	-.195	-.148
	Niche1	-0.264	-0.343	-0.370	-0.376	-0.260	-0.355	-0.340	-0.359	0.025	-.148	1.000	.734	.684	.766	.697
	Niche2	-0.306	-0.220	-0.354	-0.380	-0.270	-0.423	-0.431	-0.345	-0.017	-.065	.734	1.000	.581	.661	.749
	Niche3	-0.201	-0.211	-0.281	-0.264	-0.212	-0.363	-0.381	-0.203	-0.034	-.190	.684	.581	1.000	.880	.795
	Niche4	-0.246	-0.307	-0.326	-0.317	-0.248	-0.400	-0.421	-0.266	0.003	-.195	.766	.661	.880	1.000	.913
	Niche5	-0.319	-0.349	-0.382	-0.372	-0.319	-0.452	-0.472	-0.271	-0.025	-.148	.697	.749	.795	.913	1.000
Sig. (1-tailed)	CL1		0.000	0.000	0.000	0.000	0.000	0.000	.000	.000	.047	.000	.000	.001	.000	.000
	CL2	0.000		0.000	0.000	0.000	0.000	0.000	.000	.000	.136	.000	.000	.000	.000	.000
	CL3	0.000	0.000		0.000	0.000	0.000	0.000	.000	.000	.052	.000	.000	.000	.000	.000
	CL4	0.000	0.000	0.000		0.000	0.000	0.000	.000	.000	.142	.000	.000	.000	.000	.000
	CL5	0.000	0.000	0.000	0.000		0.000	0.000	.000	.000	.094	.000	.000	.000	.000	.000
	Diff1	0.000	0.000	0.000	0.000	0.000		0.000	.000	.000	.001	.000	.000	.000	.000	.000
	Diff2	0.000	0.000	0.000	0.000	0.000	0.000		.000	.000	.000	.000	.000	.000	.000	.000
	Diff3	0.000	0.000	0.000	0.000	0.000	0.000	0.000		.000	.003	.000	.000	.001	.000	.000
	Diff4	0.000	0.000	0.000	0.000	0.000	0.000	0.000	.000		.004	.347	.392	.296	.484	.344
	Diff5	0.047	0.136	0.052	0.142	0.094	0.001	0.000	.003	.004		.010	.155	.001	.001	.010
	Niche1	0.000	0.000	0.000	0.000	0.000	0.000	0.000	.000	.347	.010		.000	.000	.000	.000
	Niche2	0.000	0.000	0.000	0.000	0.000	0.000	0.000	.000	.392	.155	.000		.000	.000	.000
	Niche3	0.001	0.000	0.000	0.000	0.000	0.000	0.000	.001	.296	.001	.000	.000		.000	.000
	Niche4	0.000	0.000	0.000	0.000	0.000	0.000	0.000	.000	.484	.001	.000	.000	.000		.000
	Niche5	0.000	0.000	0.000	0.000	0.000	0.000	0.000	.000	.344	.010	.000	.000	.000	.000	

Fig. 4.6 Results of Correlation Matrix

are sufficiently related to each other to proceed with factor analysis (Kaiser, 1974; Lorenzo-Seva, 2003).

Table 4.1 Results of KMO and Bartlett's test

Kaiser-Meyer-Olkin Measure of Sampling Adequacy		0.762
Bartlett's Test of Sphericity	Approx. Chi-Square	3296.221
	df	105
	Sig.	0.000

Table 4.2 Results of communalities

	Initial	Extraction
CL1	1.000	0.804
CL2	1.000	0.669
CL3	1.000	0.789
CL4	1.000	0.805
CL5	1.000	0.823
Diff1	1.000	0.596
Diff2	1.000	0.584
Diff3	1.000	0.590
Diff4	1.000	0.599
Diff5	1.000	0.426
Niche1	1.000	0.742
Niche2	1.000	0.682
Niche3	1.000	0.785
Niche4	1.000	0.898
Niche5	1.000	0.869

Extraction Method: Principal Component Analysis

As shown in Table 4.2, as suggested by Tabachnick and Fidell (2019), the communalities in factor analysis represent the proportion of variance in each observed variable accounted for by the factors extracted in the analysis. Whilst there is not a strict rule regarding the minimum acceptable value for communalities, a common guideline is that communalities should ideally be greater than 0.5 or 0.6 to indicate that a substantial portion of the variance in each variable is explained by the factors. However, in some cases, communalities lower than 0.5 or 0.6 may still be acceptable, especially if the analysis is exploratory in nature or if the variables have low reliability. Here, no values of communalities of the variables are lower than 0.5; hence, the variables of this dataset can be analysed with CFA.

As indicated on the Table 4.3, the eigenvalues explain that each factor extracted from the observed variables has an associated eigenvalue. The eigenvalue epitomises the amount of variance explained by that factor. Higher eigenvalues indicate that the corresponding factor accounts for more variance in the observed variables. The eigenvalues of the three components are equivalent to 6.727, 2.665, and 1.268 suggesting that the first group has the greatest eigenvalues and followed by the second and third groups respectively.

As shown in Fig. 4.7, the scree plots show the position of each factor based on their eigenvalues of 6.727, 2.665, and 1.268.

As displayed in Tables 4.4 and 4.5, the values of the factor loading coefficients are represented both before and after rearranging in order. Table 4.4 shows that the factor loading coefficients of each variable are not reported in order. Therefore, some of the factor loading coefficients of the variables are categorised as crossing

Table 4.3 Results of total variance explained

Component	Initial eigenvalues			Extraction sums of squared loadings			Rotation sums of squared loadings		
	Total	% of Variance	Cumulative %	Total	% of Variance	Cumulative %	Total	% of Variance	Cumulative %
1	6.727	44.844	44.844	6.727	44.844	44.844	4.387	29.246	29.246
2	2.665	17.766	62.610	2.665	17.766	62.610	4.271	28.471	57.717
3	1.268	8.456	71.066	1.268	8.456	71.066	2.002	13.349	71.066
4	0.867	5.779	76.845						
5	0.745	4.967	81.812						
6	0.575	3.835	85.647						
7	0.475	3.169	88.816						
8	0.395	2.632	91.448						
9	0.318	2.118	93.566						
10	0.303	2.020	95.586						
11	0.255	1.700	97.286						
12	0.205	1.366	98.652						
13	0.128	0.855	99.507						
14	0.047	0.313	99.820						
15	0.027	0.180	100.000						

Extraction Method: Principal Component Analysis

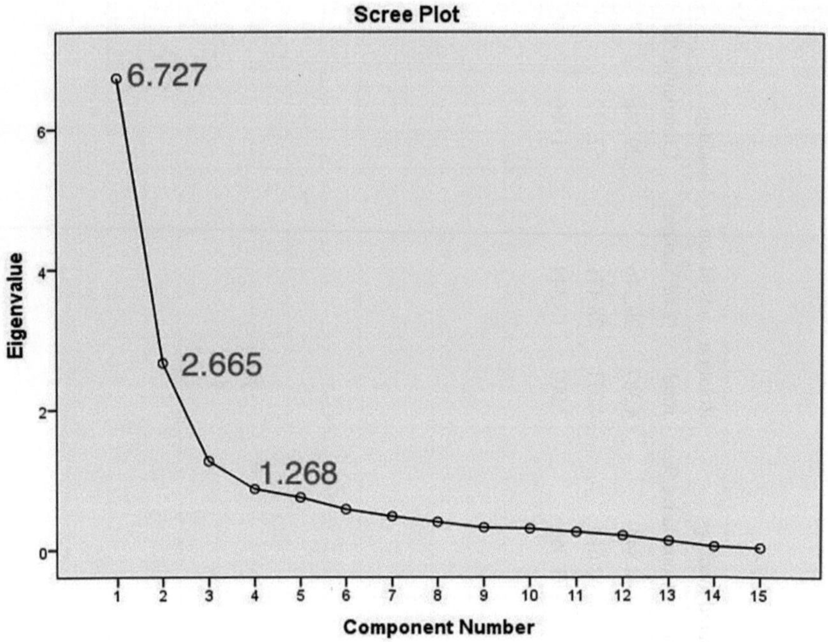

Fig. 4.7 Scree Plot

the components. As demonstrated in Table 4.6, in order to classify the factor loading coefficients of the variables into each component more properly, the suppress small coefficients; Absolute value below; 0.50 value needs to be adjusted.

As shown in Fig. 4.8, firstly, go back to the previous stage of CFA by choosing 'Options'. Next, on 'Coefficients Display Format' adjust number on the 'Absolute value below; 0.5'. Thus, the results display only those coefficients whose absolute values are less than 0.5. This ensures that coefficients with weak associations (absolute value less than 0.5) are be displayed in the output, making the output more concise and focused on stronger relationships. More elaborately, this setting can help researchers focus on the most important relationships in the model and ignore weaker ones, which may be less relevant or less reliable (Schumacker & Lomax, 2004). Moreover, the output is more user friendly and more straightforward to interpret.

As shown in Tables 4.6 and 4.7, the values of the factor loading coefficients have been sorted by size and suppress small coefficients by removing the values lower than 0.50. Hence, the variables are classified into each component.

In summary, CFA is a statistical technique widely employed in the social sciences, particularly in psychology, sociology, and management, to assess the validity and reliability of measurement instruments and to validate theoretical constructs. More importantly, conducting CFA using SPSS offers researchers a powerful toolkit for exploring and validating theoretical constructs. From user-friendly data handling and

Table 4.4 Component Matrix[a]

	Component		
	1	2	3
CL4	0.785	0.396	−0.179
CL3	0.779	0.379	−0.194
Niche5	−0.752	0.547	
CL1	0.733	0.467	−0.221
CL5	0.730	0.469	−0.265
Diff1	0.715		0.276
Niche4	−0.714	0.622	
CL2	0.694	0.367	−0.228
Niche1	−0.690	0.507	
Diff2	0.687		0.334
Niche2	−0.680	0.463	
Niche3	−0.641	0.611	
Diff3	0.621	0.248	0.377
Diff5	0.227		0.609
Diff4	0.323	0.432	0.554

Extraction Method: Principal Component Analysis
[a]3 components extracted

Table 4.5 Rotated Component Matrix[a]

	Component		
	1	2	3
CL5	0.893	−0.121	0.105
CL1	0.876	−0.120	0.145
CL4	0.853	−0.205	0.189
CL3	0.845	−0.215	0.170
CL2	0.792	−0.174	0.107
Niche4	−0.127	0.933	−0.109
Niche5	−0.214	0.902	−0.102
Niche3		0.874	−0.126
Niche1	−0.208	0.834	
Niche2	−0.215	0.792	
Diff4	0.268	. 0176	0.704
Diff5	−0.120	−0.139	0.626
Diff3	0.431	−0.169	0.612
Diff2	0.361	−0.383	0.554
Diff1	0.443	−0.355	0.524

Extraction Method: Principal Component Analysis
Rotation Method: Varimax with Kaiser Normalisation
[a]Rotation converged in 4 iterations

Table 4.6 Results of Component Matrix[a]

	Component		
	1	2	3
CL4	0.785		
CL3	0.779		
Niche5	0–0.752	0.547	
CL1	0.733		
CL5	0.730		
Diff1	0.715		
Niche4	0–0.714	0.622	
CL2	0.694		
Niche1	0–0.690	0.507	
Diff2	0.687		
Niche2	0–0.680		
Niche3	0–0.641	0.611	
Diff3	0.621		
Diff5			0.609
Diff4			0.554

Extraction Method: Principal Component Analysis
[a]3 components extracted

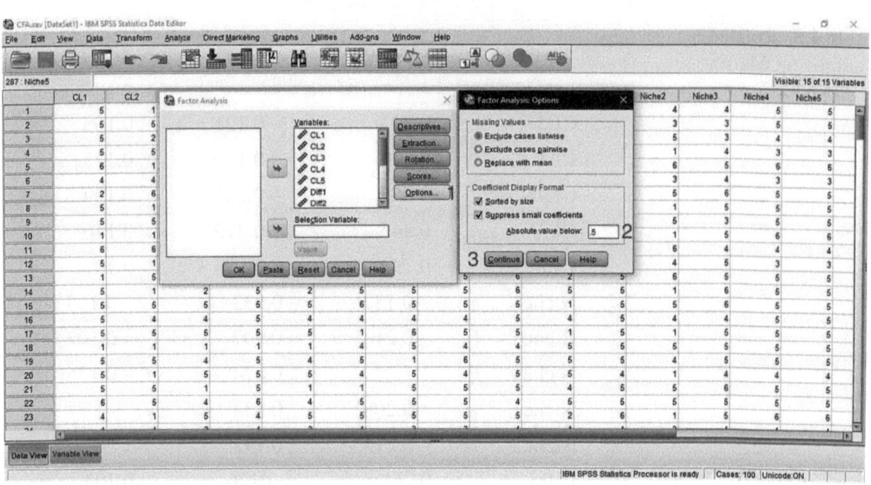

Fig. 4.8 Confirmatory Factor Analysis[6]

Table 4.7 Results of Rotated Component Matrix[a]

	Component		
	1	2	3
CL5	0.893		
CL1	0.876		
CL4	0.853		
CL3	0.845		
CL2	0.792		
Niche4		0.933	
Niche5		0.902	
Niche3		0.874	
Niche2		0.834	
Niche1		0.792	
Diff4			0.704
Diff5			0.626
Diff3			0.612
Diff2			0.554
Diff1			0.524

Extraction Method: Principal Component Analysis
Rotation Method: Varimax with Kaiser Normalisation
[a]Rotation converged in 4 iterations

efficient model specification to comprehensive output and seamless integration with other statistical procedures, SPSS enhances the rigour and validity of CFA analysis, enabling researchers to derive meaningful insights and advance knowledge in their respective fields.

4.5 Level of Reliability

To assess the reliability of a pilot study, several rigorous methods can be employed. Firstly, test-retest reliability involves administering the same pilot study to the same respondents on two distinct occasions and comparing the results. This method is measured using a correlation coefficient, which reflects the degree of consistency between the two sets of scores. If the results are statistically comparable across the two time points, it illustrates that the questionnaire demonstrates temporal stability and consistency, suggesting that the instrument is reliable over time (Kline, 2013).

Secondly, split-half reliability entails separating the pilot study into two halves and comparing the outcomes of each half. This approach is evaluated using a correlation coefficient. A coefficient of 0.7 or higher signifies that the two halves of the study are consistent with each other, suggesting that the items within the questionnaire are reliably measuring the same construct (Gulliksen, 1950). This method is instrumental in ensuring the internal consistency of the questionnaire.

Additionally, inter-rater reliability involves multiple raters independently assessing the same materials or data and comparing their evaluations. This reliability is also gauged using a correlation coefficient, which reflects the degree of agreement among the raters. A coefficient of 0.7 or greater indicates a high level of agreement among raters, suggesting that the questionnaire's items are interpreted consistently across different evaluators (Fleiss et al., 2013). This method is particularly valuable when expert judgement is involved, as it ensures consistent evaluation by different experts.

Moreover, intra-rater reliability requires a single rater to evaluate the same materials or data on two separate occasions. This is measured utilising a correlation coefficient, which demonstrates the consistency of ratings provided by the same individual over time. A coefficient of 0.7 or higher suggests that the rater's assessments are stable and consistent across different instances, supporting the reliability of the questionnaire (Gwet, 2014).

Finally, the application of one or more of these methods allows researchers to effectively measure the reliability of their pilot study. Whilst reliability is irrefutably vital, it is essential to recognise that it does not, in itself, assure validity. A research study can be reliable yet not valid; however, for research to be regarded as truly robust and credible, it must embody both reliability and validity (Cronbach, 1951).

4.5.1 *The Split-Half Alpha Coefficient*

The split-half alpha coefficient is a reliability measure used to assess the internal consistency of a test. It involves dividing a test into two halves, correlating the scores from each half, and then using the Spearman-Brown formula to estimate the reliability of the full test (Tashakkori et al., 2020). This method evaluates whether the two halves generate consistent results, thereby reflecting the test's reliability. Although straightforward and practical, it assumes that both halves are equally representative of the entire test, which may not always be the case. Consequently, it is often complemented by other reliability measures for a more comprehensive assessment. The below subsections discuss some of its advantages and disadvantages (George & Mallery, 2019):

4.5.1.1 Advantages of Using Split-Half Alpha Coefficient

The split-half alpha coefficient offers a straightforward and unpretentious method for assessing the internal consistency reliability of a scale. It requires fewer statistical assumptions compared to methods such as Cronbach's Alpha coefficient, making it more accessible to researchers with limited statistical expertise (Haws et al., 2023). Its simplicity in calculation and interpretation, along with its applicability to both binary and continuous data types, adds to its versatility in reliability assessment (Schmitt, 1996).

4.5.1.2 Disadvantages of Using Split-Half Alpha Coefficient

The split-half alpha coefficient is a practical approach for estimating the internal consistency reliability of a scale. However, it has several limitations. The reliability estimate can be influenced by chance fluctuations, mainly when the scale consists of a small number of items (Gliner et al., 2017). The accuracy of the split-half alpha coefficient also depends on the representativeness of the two halves; unequal splits can distort the reliability assessment (Graham, 2006). In addition, different approaches to splitting the scale can yield varying reliability estimates, and the method is limited to scales with an even number of items (Fay et al., 2010).

Ultimately, whilst the split-half alpha coefficient offers a useful and accessible measure of reliability, it should be utilised alongside other validity and reliability measures in order to ensure a comprehensive evaluation of a measurement instrument's properties.

4.5.1.3 Example of How to Calculate the Split-Half Alpha Coefficient

To calculate the split-half alpha coefficient by using statistical software such as SPSS or Excel, these are the steps:

1. Enter the responses for each respondent in a spreadsheet or data file. Each row is supposed to represent a respondent, and each column is supposed to signify an item on the questionnaire.
2. Split the items into two equal share-out by creating two new variables in the spreadsheet or data file. For example, if you have 30 items, you can split them into items 1–15 and items 16–30.
3. Calculate the total score for each respondent on each half of the questionnaire by summing the responses for the relevant items.
4. Use the statistical software (e.g., SPSS) to compute the correlation coefficient between the total scores on each half of the questionnaire.
5. Use the software to calculate the split-half alpha coefficient. In SPSS, use the Reliability Analysis function and select 'Split-Half' as the method. In Excel, use the 'ALPHA' function.

4.5.2 Cronbach's Alpha Coefficient

Cronbach's Alpha coefficient is a widely applied statistic for assessing the internal consistency or reliability of a measurement scale. It enumerates the degree to which a set of items or questions in a test measure the same underlying construct, ensuring that the scale yields consistent results across its items.

The coefficient is typically calculated using the formula:

$$\alpha = \frac{n.r^{-}}{1 + (N - 1).r^{-}}$$

where N represents the number of items and r^{-} is the average inter-item correlation.

Values of Cronbach's Alpha range from 0 to 1, with higher values indicating greater reliability. A value above 0.7 is generally considered acceptable, though this threshold may vary depending on the context and purpose of the research (Rosas & Camphausen, 2007). Cronbach's Alpha is valued for its simplicity and robustness, making it a cornerstone in psychometric evaluation and questionnaire design. However, it assumes unidimensionality, meaning that all items should reflect a single construct. If the scale is multidimensional, Cronbach's Alpha may not accurately signify the reliability of each dimension (DeVellis, 2016).

In summary, Cronbach's Alpha coefficient is a fundamental instrument for ensuring that a measurement scale is consistent and reliable, enhancing the validity of the research outcomes.

4.5.2.1 Advantages of Applying Cronbach's Alpha Coefficient

Cronbach's Alpha Coefficient contributes several notable advantages in the realm of research methodology. Primarily, it provides a robust measure of internal consistency reliability, determining whether or not a set of items within a scale cohesively measures the same underlying construct. This attribute is crucial for validating the coherence and reliability of measurement instruments (Wolf & Harbatkin, 2023).

One significant advantage of Cronbach's Alpha is its versatility across various types of data, including Likert-scale, binary, and continuous data. This adaptability enables researchers to apply the coefficient to a wide range of measurement tools and contexts, enhancing its usefulness in diverse research settings (DeVellis & Thorpe, 2021). Furthermore, Cronbach's Alpha is instrumental in categorising problematic items that may undermine the scale's reliability. By pinpointing items with low inter-item correlations, researchers can refine or eliminate such items, thereby improving the overall quality of the measurement instrument (Gliner et al., 2011).

Additionally, Cronbach's Alpha simplifies comparative analyses between different scales measuring the same construct. This comparative function allows researchers to select the most reliable instruments, thereby enhancing the precision and validity of their findings (Aljandali, 2016). The coefficient also aids in determining the appropriate sample size needed to achieve reliable results, providing indispensable insights for effective research design (Graham et al., 2011).

In conclusion, Cronbach's Alpha Coefficient is well regarded for its simplicity, versatility, and capacity to enhance the reliability and validity of research findings, making it a fundamental tool in the development and evaluation of measurement scales.

4.5.2.2 Disadvantages of Applying Cronbach's Alpha Coefficient

Despite its widespread utilisation in research and psychometrics to evaluate the internal consistency reliability of measurement instruments, Cronbach's Alpha coefficient has several notable limitations.

Firstly, the coefficient is contingent upon sample homogeneity. It presupposes that all items in the scale measure a uniform construct and exhibit equivalent relationships to this construct across the sample. Significant variability within the sample may compromise the accuracy of the reliability estimate (Dawson et al., 2024). Moreover, Cronbach's Alpha is not a measure of validity. It exclusively addresses internal consistency and does not incorporate other critical aspects of validity such as content, criterion, construct, or face validity (Debowska et al., 2024).

Another limitation is its sensitivity to scale length and homogeneity. Cronbach's Alpha is affected by the number of items and the degree of homogeneity among them. Shorter scales and those with heterogeneous items tend to generate lower Alpha values compared to longer and more homogeneous scales (Mumba & Alıcı, 2018). This sensitivity underscores the importance of scale length and item consistency in determining reliability.

In addition, Cronbach's Alpha assumes that the items or tests are parallel, meaning they measure the same construct with a consistent level of difficulty. This assumption may not hold true for non-parallel items, which can result in imprecise reliability estimates (Osburn, 2000; Schmitt, 1996). Furthermore, the coefficient is susceptible to item redundancy. Redundant items can artificially expand the Alpha value, potentially misleading researchers about the true reliability of the scale (Charry et al., 2016).

Finally, interpreting Cronbach's Alpha can be challenging. Misinterpretation of the coefficient may lead to inaccurate conclusions regarding the reliability and validity of the measurement instrument, thus affecting the overall research findings (De Schryver et al.,2018).

In summary, whilst Cronbach's Alpha is a valuable tool for assessing internal consistency, researchers must be cautious of its limitations and use it in conjunction with other validity and reliability measures to ensure a comprehensive evaluation of their measurement instruments.

In conclusion, Cronbach's Alpha is a valuable tool for assessing the internal consistency reliability of measurement instruments. It is straightforward to apply, adaptable to various data types, useful for identifying improvements, and helpful in comparing scales and informing research design. However, its limitations include its reliance on sample homogeneity, its focus solely on internal consistency without addressing other validity aspects, its sensitivity to scale length and item redundancy, and its assumptions about item parallelism. Therefore, whilst Cronbach's Alpha is effective, it should be complemented by additional validity and reliability measures for a comprehensive assessment.

4.5.2.3 Example of How to Calculate Cronbach's Alpha Coefficient

To calculate Cronbach's Alpha coefficient by using statistical software such as SPSS, R, or Excel, these are the steps:

After entering your data into a spreadsheet, each row of the data should represent a respondent, and each column should embody an item (a question) on the questionnaire.

Firstly, go to the 'Analyse' menu and select 'Scale' > 'Reliability Analysis'. Next, in the 'Reliability Analysis' dialogue box, select the items that you want to include in the analysis and move them into the 'Items' box. Then, under 'Statistics', select 'Descriptive' and 'Scale if Item Deleted'. Next, under 'Model', select 'Alpha' as the reliability coefficient. Lastly, click 'OK' to run the analysis.

SPSS will generate a table of results, including Cronbach's Alpha. It will also provide information about the mean and standard deviation for each item, as well as the Alpha coefficient if each item was deleted.

4.6 Augmenting Validity and Reliability with AI

The established principles of validity and reliability are increasingly augmented by the creative application of Artificial Intelligence (AI), providing a paradigm shift from static validation to dynamic, computational scrutiny. For example, researchers can now utilise AI-driven simulations to generate thousands of synthetic respondent datasets through the bootstrapping technique, enabling a more robust pre-emptive assessment of a questionnaire's reliability under diverse conditions, and moving beyond the limitations of a small-scale pilot study. In addition, AI can enhance construct validity by utilising Natural Language Processing (NLP) to evaluate enormous textual corpora, ensuring that the latent concepts within a survey accurately and creatively reflect their real-world usage in organisational discourse (Tummalapalli et al., 2025). This synergy between human research design and AI-powered validation does not replace foundational methods but creatively improves them, permitting the identification of latent inconsistencies and fostering the overall trustworthiness of management research findings (Ma et al., 2025).

4.7 Chapter Summary

This chapter highlights the significance of both validity and reliability in management research. By detailing the instruments used to ensure these aspects, valuable insights can be provided for conducting rigorous and credible research.

4.8 Questions for Further Reflection

1. The chapter labels its SPSS walkthrough as 'Confirmatory Factor Analysis'. Based on the described procedure (e.g., dimension reduction, varimax rotation), critically appraise this label. Describe the fundamental conceptual and procedural differences between Exploratory Factor Analysis (EFA) and Confirmatory Factor Analysis (CFA), and clarify which technique was actually demonstrated.
2. Imagine you have conducted a factor analysis and your output shows a KMO value of 0.55, and two of your questionnaire items have communality values of 0.35. What do these results indicate about your data and measurement instrument? What would be your subsequent course of action?
3. You have been tasked with developing a new questionnaire to measure the construct of 'Psychological Safety' within organisational teams. Explain the specific steps you would take to establish the content validity and construct validity of your new instrument before deploying it in a full-scale study.
4. A researcher is assessing the reliability of observers who are coding managerial behaviours during team meetings. Which specific type of reliability (e.g., test-retest, inter-rater, internal consistency) is most crucial in this scenario? Justify your answer and explain how this form of reliability would be calculated.
5. Propose a detailed plan for a pilot study for a new 20-item survey measuring 'Employee Resilience'. Your plan should specify the target sample size and, more importantly, state precisely what you would be evaluating in terms of both the questionnaire's design and the data's statistical properties (validity and reliability).
6. The chapter states that a study can be reliable but not valid. Provide a plausible management research example of a measurement demonstrating high reliability but poor validity. Explain your reasoning clearly.
7. The chapter notes that Cronbach's Alpha is sensitive to the number of items in a scale. Explain why a high Alpha value (e.g., >0.95) for a scale with many items might not necessarily be desirable and could, in fact, indicate a potential problem with the measurement instrument.
8. Compare and contrast the likely levels of internal and external validity in the following two studies: (a) a laboratory experiment testing the effect of time pressure on decision-making quality among business students, and (b) a large-scale survey of CEOs about their strategic decision-making processes. Which study's findings are more generalisable and which are more causally certain?

9. Whilst this chapter emphasises on quantitative metrics, how would a researcher conducting a qualitative study based on in-depth interviews establish the 'trustworthiness' or 'credibility' (the qualitative equivalent of validity) of their findings?
10. Upon reviewing the Rotated Component Matrix (Table 4.7), a researcher finds that one item from the 'Differentiation' scale has a high factor loading (e.g., 0.75) on the 'Cost Leadership' component instead of its own. What does this phenomenon, known as 'cross-loading', signify about the item, and what are the researcher's options for addressing it?

References

Aljandali, A. (2016). *Quantitative analysis and IBM® SPSS® statistics.* Springer International Publishing.

Auamnoy, T. (2002). *Statistics and SPSS for 21st century research.* Chulalongkorn University.

Baker, S. E., & Edwards, R. (2012). *How many qualitative interviews is enough*?. National Centre for Research Methods Review Paper.

Black, W., & Babin, B. J. (2019). Multivariate data analysis: Its approach, evolution, and impact. In B. J. Babin & M. Sarstedt (Eds.), *In The great facilitator: Reflections on the contributions of Joseph F. Hair, Jr. to marketing and business research* (pp. 121–130). Springer International Publishing.

Bollen, K. A. (1989). *Structural equations with latent variables.* John Wiley & Sons.

Charry, K., Coussement, K., Demoulin, N., & Heuvinck, N. (2016). *Marketing research with IBM® SPSS statistics: A practical guide.* Routledge.

Cohen, J., Cohen, P., West, S. G., & Aiken, L. S. (2013). *Applied multiple regression/correlation analysis for the behavioral sciences.* Routledge.

Cohen, L., Manion, L., & Morrison, K. (2022). *Research methods in education.* Routledge.

Cook, T. D., & Campbell, D. T. (2007). *Experimental and quasi-experimental designs for generalized causal inference.* Figures.

Cronbach, L. J. (1951). Coefficient alpha and the internal structure of tests. *Psychometrika, 16*(3), 297–334. https://doi.org/10.1007/BF02310555

Cronbach, L. J., & Meehl, P. E. (1955). Construct validity in psychological tests. *Psychological Bulletin, 52*(4), 281–302. https://doi.org/10.1037/h0040957

Dawson, P., Yan, Z., Lipnevich, A., Tai, J., Boud, D., & Mahoney, P. (2024). Measuring what learners do in feedback: The feedback literacy behaviour scale. *Assessment & Evaluation in Higher Education, 49*(3), 348–362. https://doi.org/10.1080/02602938.2023.2240983

De Schryver, M., Hughes, S., De Houwer, J., & Rosseel, Y. (2018). *On the reliability of implicit measures: Current practices and novel perspectives.* https://doi.org/10.31234/osf.io/w7j86

Debowska, A., Boduszek, D., Ochman, M., Hrapkowicz, T., Gaweda, M., Pondel, A., & Horeczy, B. (2024). Brain Fog Scale (BFS): Scale development and validation. *Personality and Individual Differences, 216*, 112427. https://doi.org/10.1016/j.paid.2023.112427

DeVellis, R. F. (2016). *Scale Development: Theory and Applications* (4th ed.). Sage Publications.

DeVellis, R. F., & Thorpe, C. T. (2021). *Scale development: Theory and applications.* Sage Publications.

Devlin, A. S. (2020). *The research experience: Planning, conducting, and reporting research.* Sage Publications.

Fay, K., Boyd, M. J., & Salkind, N. J. (2010). *Encyclopedia of research design.* Sage Publications.

Fleiss, J. L., Levin, B., & Paik, M. C. (2013). *Statistical methods for rates and proportions*. John Wiley & Sons.
George, D., & Mallery, P. (2019). *IBM SPSS statistics 26 step by step: A simple guide and reference*. Routledge.
Gliner, J. A., Morgan, G. A., & Leech, N. L. (2011). *Research methods in applied settings: An integrated approach to design and analysis*. Routledge.
Gliner, J. A., Morgan, G. A., & Leech, N. L. (2017). *Research methods in applied settings: An integrated approach to design and analysis* (3rd ed.). Routledge.
Graham, J. M. (2006). Congeneric and (essentially) tau-equivalent estimates of reliability: What they are and how to use them. *Educational and Psychological Measurement, 66*(6), 930–944. https://doi.org/10.1177/0013164406288165
Graham, J. M., Diebels, K. J., & Barnow, Z. B. (2011). The reliability of relationship satisfaction: A reliability generalization meta-analysis. *Journal of Family Psychology, 25*(1), 39–48. https://doi.org/10.1037/a0022441
Gulliksen, H. (1950). *Theory of mental tests*. John Wiley & Sons.
Gwet, K. L. (2014). *Handbook of inter-rater reliability: The definitive guide to measuring the extent of agreement among raters* (4th ed.). Advanced Analytics, LLC.
Halcomb, E., & Hickman, L. (2015). Mixed methods research. *Nursing Standard: Promoting excellence in nursing care, 29*(32), 41–47. https://doi.org/10.7748/ns.29.32.41.e8858
Haslam, S. A., McGarty, C., Cruwys, T., & Steffens, N. K. (2024). *Research methods and statistics in psychology*. Sage Publications.
Haws, K. L., Sample, K. L., & Hulland, J. (2023). Scale use and abuse: Towards best practices in the deployment of scales. *Journal of Consumer Psychology, 33*(1), 226–243. https://doi.org/10.1002/jcpy.1320
Haynes, S. N., Richard, D. C., & Kubany, E. S. (1995). Content validity in psychological assessment: A review of the literature and guidelines for test development. *Psychological Assessment, 7*(3), 238–247. https://doi.org/10.1037/1040-3590.7.3.238
Kaiser, H. F. (1974). An index of factorial simplicity. *Psychometrika, 39*(1), 31–36. https://doi.org/10.1007/BF02291575
Kline, P. (2013). *Handbook of psychological testing*. Routledge.
Kruger, F., & Terblanche, N. H. D. (2024). Working alliance theory in workplace coaching: A pilot study exploring the missing role of the organization. *The Journal of Applied Behavioural Science, 60*(2), 310–332. https://doi.org/10.1177/00218863221136125
Leon, A. C., Davis, L. L., & Kraemer, H. C. (2011). The role and interpretation of pilot studies in clinical research. *Journal of Psychiatric Research, 45*(5), 626–629. https://doi.org/10.1016/j.jpsychires.2010.10.008
Lorenzo-Seva, U. (2003). A factor simplicity index. *Psychometrika, 68*(1), 49–60. https://doi.org/10.1007/BF02296652
Ma, J., Wen, J., Qiu, Y., Wang, Y., Xiao, Q., Liu, T., et al. (2025). The role of artificial intelligence in shaping nursing education: A comprehensive systematic review. *Nurse Education in Practice, 104345*.
Merriam, S. B., & Tisdell, E. J. (2015). *Qualitative research: A guide to design and implementation*. John Wiley & Sons.
Mumba, B., & Alıcı, D. (2018). *Understanding quantitative versus qualitative dichotomies*. Available at SSRN.
Osburn, H. G. (2000). Coefficient alpha and related internal consistency reliability coefficients. *Psychological Methods, 5*(3), 343–355. https://doi.org/10.1037/1082-989X.5.3.343
Rahi, S. (2017). Research design and methods: A systematic review of research paradigms, sampling issues and instruments development. *International Journal of Economics & Management Sciences, 6*(2), 1–5.
Ratten, V. (2023). *Research methodologies for business management*. Routledge.

Robinson, O. C. (2014). Sampling in interview-based qualitative research: A sociological perspective. *Qualitative Research in Psychology, 11*(1), 25–41. https://doi.org/10.1080/14780887.2013.801543

Robson, C., & McCartan, K. (2016). *Real world research* (4th ed.). Wiley.

Rosas, S. R., & Camphausen, L. C. (2007). The use of concept mapping for scale development and validation in evaluation. *Evaluation and Programme Planning, 30*(2), 125–135. https://doi.org/10.1016/j.evalprogplan.2007.01.003

Schmitt, N. (1996). Uses and abuses of coefficient alpha. *Psychological Assessment, 8*(4), 350–353. https://doi.org/10.1037/1040-3590.8.4.350

Schumacker, R. E., & Lomax, R. G. (2004). *A beginner's guide to structural equation modeling* (2nd ed.). Lawrence Erlbaum Associates.

Tabachnick, B. G., & Fidell, L. S. (2019). *Using multivariate statistics* (7th ed.). Pearson.

Tashakkori, A., Johnson, R. B., & Teddlie, C. (2020). *Foundations of mixed methods research: Integrating quantitative and qualitative approaches in the social and behavioral sciences.* Sage Publications.

Thabane, L., Ma, J., Chu, R., Cheng, J., Ismaila, A., Rios, L. P., Robson, R., Thabane, M., Giangregorio, L., & Goldsmith, C. H. (2010). A tutorial on pilot studies: The what, why and how. *BMC Medical Research Methodology, 10*, 1–10. https://doi.org/10.1186/1471-2288-10-1

Trochim, W. M. (2006). *The research methods knowledge base* (2nd ed.). Atomic Dog Publishing.

Tummalapalli, H. K., Rao, A. N., Kamal, G., Kumari, N., & Kumar, J. R. S. (2025). Exploring AI-driven management: Impact on organizational performance, decision making, efficiency, and employee engagement. *Journal of Advanced Research in Applied Sciences and Engineering Technology, 52*(2), 148–163.

van Teijlingen, E., & Hundley, V. (2001). The importance of pilot studies. *Nursing Standard, 16*(40), 33–36. https://doi.org/10.7748/ns2002.06.16.40.33.c3214

Wallwey, C., & Kajfez, R. L. (2023). Quantitative research artifacts as qualitative data collection techniques in a mixed methods research study. *Methods in Psychology, 8*, Article 100115. https://doi.org/10.1016/j.metip.2023.100115

Wolf, B., & Harbatkin, E. (2023). Making sense of effect sizes: Systematic differences in intervention effect sizes by outcome measure type. *Journal of Research on Educational Effectiveness, 16*(1), 134–161. https://doi.org/10.1080/19345747.2022.2071364

Zumitzavan, V. (2011). *The impact of managers' learning styles and leadership styles on the effectiveness of their organisations: A case study from small retail tyre companies in Thailand* (Doctoral dissertation, University of Birmingham).

Zumitzavan, V., & Michie, J. (2015). *Personal knowledge management, leadership styles, and organisational performance: A case study of the healthcare industry in Thailand*. Springer.

Chapter 5
Ethics in Management Research

5.1 Introduction

Ethical considerations in management research are paramount for the continuation of scholarly integrity and the safeguarding of participants. It is essential that researchers secure informed consent, ensuring that participants are comprehensively briefed on the research's nature, objectives, and potential consequences prior to their involvement (Bryman & Bell, 2022). Confidentiality must be rigorously upheld to protect participants' personal data, and measures should be implemented to mitigate any risk of harm. Where deception is deemed necessary, it must be justified by compelling reasons, and participants should receive a thorough debriefing. The principles of integrity and honesty are fundamental, necessitating the accurate and transparent reporting of results, without any falsification. Researchers are required to disclose any conflicts of interest to avert bias and maintain objectivity. Respectful treatment of participants is imperative, and obtaining approval from ethics review committees is necessary to ensure compliance with established ethical norms. Moreover, researchers should evaluate the broader societal implications of their work and maintain transparency and responsibility through the entire research process.

5.2 Ethical Issues and Confidentiality of the Respondents and Participants

The data collection process is inherently associated with a spectrum of ethical considerations and the protection of respondents' and participants' confidentiality. It is imperative to guarantee that the process does not inflict any distress or encroach upon the privacy of those involved (Bryman & Harley, 2022). Participants, having complied to the research, retain the right to withdraw from the research at any point and to opt out of particular aspects of the research. Researchers must ensure that

© The Author(s), under exclusive license to Springer Nature Singapore Pte Ltd. 2025

V. Zumitzavan, *Social Science Methodologies for Management Research*,
https://doi.org/10.1007/978-981-95-4318-2_5

participants are not subjected to any activity that might cause distress or violate their privacy.

An additional core ethical principle involves upholding objectivity. During data collection, it is essential for researchers to assure that data are collected with accuracy and completeness, avoiding any form of bias or selective reporting. This principle is methodically interlinked with the research's validity and reliability.

Moreover, before initiating data collection, participants must be thoroughly informed about the research project, including the potential benefits and risks of their involvement. After providing a comprehensive explanation of the ethical issues and confidentiality measures, participants should be fully aware of their right to withdraw at any stage (Creswell & Poth, 2024). Consequently, it is advisable to present participants with a detailed consent form and to elucidate all pertinent matters clearly.

Example of Consent Form

College of Local Administration,
Khon Kaen University,
Thailand

CONSENT FORM

Title of research or thesis:
The Influence of Managers' Leadership Styles and the Effectiveness of their Organisations: A Case Study of X Industry in Thailand

Name and position of researcher:
Vissanu Zumitzavan, Researcher and Lecturer, Khon Kean University, Thailand

Please initial box

1. I confirm that I have read and comprehended the information sheet for the aforementioned study and been given the opportunity to ask any questions.
2. I acknowledge that my participation is entirely voluntary and that I retain the right to withdraw from the study at any stage of the data collection process.
3. I agree to play a part in the research.
4. I consent to the interview being recorded both audio-visually.
5. I give my permission for anonymised quotations to be used in publications.

Name of participants:	Date:	Signature:
Name of researcher:	Date:	Signature:

Remark: The data will be anonymised and used only for research-related activities. In particular, the data will be used entirely for academic purposes, and it will not be shared outside the academic context.

Developed from Saunders, Lewis, and Thornhill (2019b, p. 269).

5.3 Confidentiality and Privacy

Confidentiality and privacy are critical components of ethical research practice, demanding that researchers rigorously safeguard the personal information of participants. This entails implementing robust measures to ensure that the data collected during the research is securely kept and only accessible to authorised individuals. Protecting participants' privacy not only comprises securing personal identifiers but also encompasses maintaining the confidentiality of sensitive information that could potentially harm participants if disclosed. Upholding these standards is essential for preserving the trust between researchers and participants, as it reassures individuals that their involvement will not bring about unwanted exposure or misuse of their data (Creswell, 2014).

For example, if a researcher proposes to use collected data solely for academic purposes, they must clearly inform participants of this intent through a detailed consent form. This form should explicitly affirm that their data will be anonymised and utilised only for research-related activities, and that it will not be revealed outside academic contexts. Such transparency ensures that participants are fully conscious of how their data will be handled, reinforcing their trust in, and commitment to, the research (Easterby-Smith et al., 2021).

Furthermore, strict adherence to confidentiality fosters a more open and honest participation environment, thereby enhancing the overall reliability and validity of the research findings. By ensuring privacy, researchers establish respect for participants and their personal information, thereby reinforcing the ethical integrity of the research process.

5.4 Avoiding Harm

Avoiding harm is a fundamental ethical principle in research, necessitating that studies be meticulously designed and implemented to minimise any potential physical, emotional, or psychological harm to participants. Researchers must anticipate and mitigate risks associated with their research procedures to ensure that the study does not inadvertently cause distress or discomfort. This involves conducting a thorough risk assessment and implementing strategies to safeguard participants' well-being throughout the research procedure (Edmonds & Kennedy, 2016).

For example, in a study investigating the impact of leadership styles on organisational members' morale and productivity, researchers must be particularly careful to avoid causing psychological harm. This means being able to obtain feedback on potentially contentious leadership practices in a way that does not cause excessive stress or instil feelings of retaliation in organisational members (Zumitzavan, 2011; Zumitzavan et al., 2025). To mitigate these risks, researchers could anonymise responses to prevent the identification of participants and assure them that their feedback will not affect job security or performance evaluations. The research could also provide possibilities for participants to express concerns or discomfort about the research focus without pressure. Additionally, offering support mechanisms, such as access to human resources representatives or workplace mediators, can help address any issues arising during the study.

A concrete application of these ethical principles can be seen in research conducted in Singapore on workplace bullying—an inherently sensitive and potentially distressing topic. In a study exploring the social dynamics surrounding bullies, Hosier, Zhang, and Goh (2023) had to guarantee participants could speak freely about their traumatic experiences without distress of reprisal or further psychological harm. To accomplish this, the researcher implemented rigorous ethical safeguards, including obtaining explicit informed consent, guaranteeing strict confidentiality, and utilising pseudonyms to anonymise both the participants and their respective organisations. These measures were vital for constructing the trust required for candid disclosure, thereby protecting participants whilst allowing the collection of valid data on a damaging organisational phenomenon.

By incorporating these measures, researchers can shelter participants from potential negative impacts whilst still obtaining valuable insights into management practices and their effects on employee

5.5 Deception

Deception in research encompasses misleading participants vis-à-vis the study's true purpose or nature. It must be justified by arguing that it is essential for obtaining valid results and that no other methods are feasible. Once the study is completed, researchers must debrief participants promptly, exposing the true nature of the research and explaining why deception was necessary. This ensures that participants are not harmed by the misleading information and that ethical standards are maintained (Zumitzavan & Kantavong, 2018; Zumitzavan, 2022).

In a research project investigating the different levels of effectiveness of different management training programmes on organisational members' performance, researchers might use deception to ensure that participants' responses reflect genuine reactions rather than biases influenced by their knowledge of the study's true objectives. For example, participants could be told that the research is appraising their general work habits rather than specifically assessing the impact of the training programmes on their performance (Zumitzavan & Udchachone, 2014).

Whether or not this deceptive approach is used, it must be carefully justified by arguing that expressing the genuine purpose of the study would compromise the validity of the results or introduce bias. After the research is accomplished, researchers are required to conduct a thorough debriefing session with participants. During this session, researchers are must explain the real aim of the research—evaluating the effectiveness of various management training methods—and clarify why deception was necessary (Zumitzavan, 2020).

Additionally, the researchers should address any concerns that participants might have about being misled, and they must provide reassurance that their involvement will not negatively impact their professional evaluations or relationships within the organisation. Offering to answer any questions and providing support if the deception caused any distress are also important aspects of the debriefing process. This approach ensures that the use of deception is ethically justified and that participants are treated with respect and transparency, thus upholding the integrity of the research process.

5.6 Integrity and Honesty

Integrity and honesty in research require that researchers report their findings accurately and truthfully, without fabricating, falsifying, or manipulating data. This principle ensures that the research results are credible and reliable, permitting others to trust and build upon the findings. Upholding integrity and honesty maintain the overall quality and ethical standing of the research (Zou & Xu, 2023).

An example of integrity and honesty in management research can be demonstrated by a research project appraising the influence of a new management strategy on levels of organisational members' productivity. Suppose the researcher obtains data indicating only modest improvements but is minded to elaborate on the results in order to portray the strategy as more effective. Adhering to the principles of integrity and honesty demands reporting the actual findings accurately, even if they fall short of initial expectations (Zumitzavan, 2014).

For instance, if the data show a 10 per cent increase in productivity rather than the projected 20 per cent, the researcher should present these results straightforwardly, providing a comprehensive account of the research's methodology and of any limitations encountered. By maintaining such transparency, the researcher maintains the credibility of the research and ensures that subsequent decisions and further research are based on reliable and truthful information.

5.7 Conflicts of Interest

Conflicts of interest involve the obligation for researchers to disclose any financial, personal, or professional interests that could influence their research outcomes, potentially biasing their interpretations of data or reporting of results. For instance, in management research, a conflict might arise if a researcher is evaluating a performance management system established by their own organisation or a company and with which they have financial ties.

For example, if a researcher holding shares in a consultancy organisation is conducting a research project on the effectiveness of a new leadership training programme offered by that organisation, they must transparently disclose their financial stake. Such disclosure allows others to assess potential bias and scrutinise the findings appropriately (Michie & Zumitzavan, 2016). Another example could be a researcher who is also a board member of an organisation being researched for its innovative management practices; their personal stake in the organisation's success could influence their research outcomes. Transparent disclosure of these interests is crucial for maintaining the research's credibility and ensuring that conclusions are reliable and trustworthy (Zumitzavan & Michie, 2015). In addition, the necessity for such disclosures is particularly salient in research contexts where corporate, political, and personal interests are closely entwined. Research into corporate governance in Malaysia, for example, suggests a compelling illustration of this principle. A seminal study by Johnson and Mitton (2003) investigated whether politically connected firms received preferential treatment during the Asian financial crisis. Whilst the authors themselves maintained academic independence, their research scrutinised the very type of influential relationships—in this circumstance, political cronyism—that can create profound conflicts of interest. The study highlights a critical point: if external affiliations can fundamentally influence corporate outcomes, it is incumbent upon any researcher to declare similar personal or financial ties to the subject of their investigation. Such transparency is essential for permitting the academic community to rigorously assess the objectivity of the analysis and the credibility of its conclusions.

5.8 Respects for Participants

Respect for participants involves treating all individuals in research with dignity and consideration. This comprises recognising their autonomy, valuing their contributions, and ensuring their well-being throughout the study. In management research, for instance, when evaluating employees' satisfaction with a new organisational policy, researchers should begin by obtaining informed consent. This means clearly explaining the research's objectives, procedures, and how the data will be utilised, whilst reassuring participants that their feedback will be confidential and their participation voluntary, with the option to withdraw at any time without drawbacks (Zumitzavan, 2011).

Furthermore, researchers must handle sensitive feedback with care, ensuring comments are anonymised to avoid any potential retaliation or discomfort. If an employee raises concerns about the policy affecting their work environment, researchers should address these issues professionally and sensitively, providing support if needed. By upholding these practices, researchers demonstrate respect for participants and maintain ethical standards, fostering a trustworthy and respectful research environment (Saunders et al., 2009; Zumitzavan & Michie, 2015).

5.9 Ethical Review and Approval

Ethical review and approval encompass submitting research proposals to an ethics review board or institutional review board (IRB) before beginning a study involving human participants. This process certifies that the research meets established ethical standards and safeguards the rights and welfare of participants. The review board assesses various aspects of the study, including the research's design, methods, informed consent procedures, and potential risks to participants.

For example, in management research evaluating the impact of a new organisational members' performance evaluation system, researchers need to seek ethical approval before starting the study. The ethics review board reviews the proposal to ensure that the system's implementation does not negatively impact organisational members' job security or well-being. This review should include assessing how participants are informed about the research, ensuring that their consent is obtained, and evaluating measures to protect their privacy and address any potential psychological stress from participating in the study (Saunders et al., 2019a).

The importance of this review lies in its role as an additional layer of oversight. It helps to identify and address potential ethical issues before the research commences, ensuring that the study adheres to principles such as respect for participants, minimisation of harm, and integrity. By obtaining ethical approval, researchers demonstrate their commitment to conducting research responsibly and ethically, thus enhancing the credibility and trustworthiness of their findings.

5.10 Social Responsibility

Social Responsibility in research involves considering the broader societal impacts of the research and ensuring that the research contributes positively to society. Researchers must appraise how their findings might affect various stakeholders and strive to produce results that advance public well-being and contribute to social decent. This includes assessing potential negative consequences and actively working to mitigate them (Saunders & Townsend, 2016).

For instance, in management research evaluating the implementation of a new organisational diversity initiative, researchers should deliberate how their findings might influence broader industry practices and public perceptions of diversity and inclusion. They must ensure that their research does not inadvertently reinforce stereotypes or fail to address underlying issues of inequality. For example, if a study suggests that one gender performs better than another in managerial roles, it could perpetuate gender biases and ignore the complexities of individual performance and organisational context. Researchers should avoid such generalisations and instead focus on understanding and addressing the systemic factors that impact performance across different groups.

Researchers must also critically assess whether their methodology or findings could unintentionally marginalise certain groups or obscure significant challenges. By prioritising social responsibility, researchers contribute to meaningful improvements in workplace practices and support positive societal change, such as fostering a more inclusive work environment. This approach not only aligns with ethical standards but also maximises the potential benefits of the research for society at large, ensuring that initiatives designed to promote diversity and inclusion are genuinely effective and equitable.

5.11 Accountability and Transparency

Accountability and transparency in research involve being responsible for individual's research practices and openly sharing details about the methods and findings (Zumitzavan et al., 2025). Researchers must ensure that their research processes, data collection, and analysis are conducted with integrity and rigour. This includes providing clear and detailed descriptions of how the study was designed, the procedures followed, and how data were analysed (Saunders, 2015).

For example, in management research evaluating the effectiveness of a new leadership training programme, transparency requires that researchers disclose their methodology, including participant selection criteria, training delivery methods, and metrics used to assess outcomes. If the study finds that the programme significantly improves leadership skills, researchers should report both the successes and any limitations or challenges encountered. Additionally, any potential conflicts of interest, such as bonds to the training provider, should be divulged (Saunders, 2020).

By willingly sharing these matters, researchers allow others to scrutinise and replicate their work, which enhances the credibility and reproducibility of the research. This openness helps to build trust within the scientific community and with the public, ensuring that findings are reliable and can be verified or challenged as necessary.

5.12 Navigating the Ethical Frontier of Artificial Intelligence in Research

The integration of AI into management research presents a new frontier of ethical considerations, demanding a creative and proactive approach to upholding scholarly integrity. Whilst AI can improve data analysis, it also raises critical issues of accountability and data privacy. To illustrate, if an AI model is applied to analyse qualitative interview data, researchers must be transparent about the algorithms utilised and remain accountable for any biases the model might present or perpetuate, as AI systems can inadvertently amplify societal prejudices present in their training data (Mensah, 2023). In addition, the principle of confidentiality is amplified; researchers must ensure that vast datasets utilised to train AI do not contain personally identifiable information that could be reverse-engineered, generating a new layer of privacy risk (Hamilton et al., 2023). Therefore, ethical best practice now necessitates not only ensuring human participants but also conducting a rigorous "ethical audit" of the AI tools themselves, guaranteeing they align with principles of fairness, transparency, and social responsibility before they are organised in the research process (Hasija & Esper, 2022).

5.13 Best Practices for Addressing Ethical Issues in Management Research

Best practices for addressing ethical issues in management research involve several key strategies. First, developing a clear research plan is essential; this plan should explicitly project how each ethical concern will be addressed within the research design. For example, if researching organisational members' satisfaction with a new performance management system, the plan should detail how informed consent will be obtained, how confidentiality will be maintained, and how potential biases will be managed (Zumitzavan & Mumi, 2014).

Next, engaging with ethics committees delivers valuable guidance on navigating complex ethical dilemmas. For instance, before conducting a research on the effectiveness of a new organisational restructuring initiative, researchers might consult an ethics committee to ensure that their methods for evaluating organisational members' reactions do not inadvertently lead to undue stress or job insecurity. Similarly, when studying the implementation of a new incentive programme, ethics committees can help guarantee that the methods for collecting feedback from employees are designed to prevent any undue pressure or coercion (Robson & McCartan, 2016).

In addition, researchers should prioritise education by remaining informed about current ethical standards and providing regular training for their research teams. For example, if researchers are investigating diversity and inclusion in an organisation, they should ensure that their team is trained in recognising and avoiding unconscious biases and understands how to handle sensitive data respectfully. Additionally, if researchers are examining organisational members' feedback on sensitive issues such as discrimination or harassment, they should provide training on how to conduct interviews and surveys in a way that respects participants' privacy and psychological safety.

Finally, regularly reviewing and utilising up-to-date ethical practices ensures ongoing compliance with evolving standards. For instance, if a management research project initially approved involves new data collection methods, such as online surveys or remote interviews, researchers should reassess their ethical practices to ensure that these methods continue to protect participant confidentiality and comply with data protection regulations (Robson, 2024).

Correspondingly, if the research expands to include new participant groups or additional research sites, an updated review of ethical considerations is necessary to address any new potential risks. To sum up, by integrating these best practices into management research, researchers maintain the integrity of their studies and uphold the well-being of participants.

5.14 Chapter Summary

In summary, ethical considerations in management research are fundamental for ensuring scholarly integrity and protecting participants. Researchers must secure informed consent, fully briefing participants on the study's aims, potential risks, and their right to withdraw. Maintaining confidentiality is crucial, with rigorous measures to safeguard personal data and mitigate harm. If deception is necessary to ensure valid results, it must be carefully justified, with careful design and thorough debriefing provided afterwards. Integrity and honesty are essential, demanding the accurate and transparent reporting of findings, whilst any conflicts of interest must be revealed to avoid prejudice.

In addition, researchers must treat participants with respect, handling sensitive feedback with care, and acquire ethical approval from review boards to adhere to established standards. Evaluating the broader societal impact of research and ensuring transparency and accountability throughout the process reinforces ethical practice. Best practices consist of developing a detailed ethical plan, consulting ethics committees, providing regular training, and updating practices to align with evolving standards. These measures collectively uphold the research's integrity, ensuring that it contributes positively to societal knowledge whilst respecting and protecting all participants.

5.15 Questions for Future Reflection

1. A researcher plans to analyse thousands of public posts on LinkedIn and Glassdoor (a company review website) to study organisational members' sentiment towards a recent, controversial merger. As the data is publicly accessible, the researcher argues that informed consent is not required. From the perspective of an ethics review committee, critically evaluate this position. What ethical principles from the chapter might be compromised?
2. A study purposes to investigate whether managers display bias in promotion recommendations. To avoid socially desirable answers, the researchers want to tell participating managers they are participating in a study about general decision-making styles, not bias. Is this use of deception justifiable? Formulate the stringent conditions and debriefing procedures that would need to be in place for an ethics committee to approve such a study.

3. A doctoral student is conducting case study research on the effective implementation of a four-day work week. Their chosen research site is their own place of employment. Critically assess the potential conflicts of interest and power dynamics at play. What specific measures must the student apply to ensure objectivity and protect both themselves and their colleagues?
4. During an interview about organisational change, a participant becomes visibly distressed when recounting their experience of being made redundant. Along with the principles in the chapter, what are the researcher's immediate ethical obligations in this situation? What long-term responsibilities, if any, do they have towards this participant?
5. Review the sample consent form provided in the chapter. Whilst it is a strong example, identify two areas where it could be enhanced to provide participants even greater protection or clarity. For example, consider details about data storage, the duration for which data will be held, or who to contact with a complaint. Justify your suggestions.
6. A researcher wants to study workplace stress and is granted access to a company by a senior manager. The manager, wanting to present the organisation in a positive light, provides access only to employees from departments known for high morale. Identify the ethical and methodological problems this raises and propose how the researcher should address this situation with the manager.
7. In a qualitative study of a specialist senior management team in a niche industry, a researcher guarantees participants anonymity. However, given the small pool of individuals in such roles, direct quotes—even when anonymised—could make the participants easily identifiable to their peers. How should the researcher balance the duty of confidentiality with the need to present rich, authentic data in their publications?
8. A research study finds that a new AI-driven performance monitoring system significantly boosts productivity but also triples the level of reported employee anxiety and burnout. How should the researcher ethically approach the reporting and dissemination of these findings, considering their social responsibility to the wider business community and society?
9. A participant completes a lengthy interview but, a week later, contacts the researcher to withdraw their consent and requests that all their data be destroyed. The researcher has already transcribed and started analysing the data. What are the researcher's ethical obligations in this instance? Does the stage of the research process affect this obligation?
10. A study on corporate ethics is published and receives significant media attention. Another academic group challenges the research's findings, requesting access to the original (anonymised) data to verify the analysis. What do the principles of accountability and transparency require of the original researcher in this situation?

References

Bryman, A., & Bell, E. (2022). *Business research methods* (6th ed.). Oxford University Press.

Bryman, A., & Harley, B. (2022). *Social research methods*. Oxford University Press.

Creswell, J. W. (2014). *Research design: Qualitative, quantitative, and mixed methods approaches* (4th ed.). Sage Publications.

Creswell, J. W., & Poth, C. N. (2024). *Qualitative inquiry and research design: Choosing among five approaches* (5th ed.). Sage Publications.

Easterby-Smith, M., Jaspersen, L. J., Thorpe, R., & Valizade, D. (2021). *Management and business research*. Sage Publications.

Edmonds, W. A., & Kennedy, T. D. (2016). *An applied guide to research designs: Quantitative, qualitative, and mixed methods*. Sage Publications.

Hamilton, L., Elliott, D., Quick, A., Smith, S., & Choplin, V. (2023). Exploring the use of AI in qualitative analysis: A comparative study of guaranteed income data. *International journal of qualitative methods, 22*, 16094069231201504.

Hasija, A., & Esper, T. L. (2022). In artificial intelligence (AI) we trust: A qualitative investigation of AI technology acceptance. *Journal of Business Logistics, 43*(3), 388–412.

Hosier, S., Zhang, H., & Goh, H. S. (2023). Workplace bullying among nurses in Singapore: A quantitative survey. *The Malaysian Journal of Nursing (MJN), 14*(3), 55–66.

Johnson, S., & Mitton, T. (2003). Cronyism and capital controls: Evidence from Malaysia. *Journal of Financial Economics, 67*(2), 351–382.

Mensah, G. B. (2023). Artificial intelligence and ethics: a comprehensive review of bias mitigation, transparency, and accountability in AI Systems. *Preprint, November, 10*(1), 1.

Michie, J., & Zumitzavan, V. (2016). The impact of 'learning' and 'leadership' management styles on organizational outcomes: A study of tyre firms in Thailand. In *Leadership in the Asia Pacific* (pp. 165–188). Routledge.

Robson, C. (2024). *Real world research*. John Wiley & Sons.

Robson, C., & McCartan, K. (2016). *Real world research* (4th ed.). Wiley.

Saunders, M. N. (2015). *Research methods for business students*. Pearson.

Saunders, C. (2020). *Leadership*. Oxford University Press.

Saunders, M., Lewis, P., & Thornhill, A. (2009). *Research methods for business students*. Pearson education.

Saunders, M. N., & Townsend, K. (2016). Reporting and justifying the number of interview participants in organization and workplace research. *British Journal of Management, 27*(4), 836–852. https://doi.org/10.1111/1467-8551.12182

Saunders, M. N. K., Bristow, A., Thornhill, A., & Lewis, P. (2019a). Understanding research philosophy and approaches to theory development. In M. N. K. Saunders, P. Lewis, & A. Thornhill (Eds.), *Research methods for business students* (8th ed., pp. 128–171). Pearson Education.

Saunders, M. N. K., Lewis, P., & Thornhill, A. (2019b). *Research methods for business students* (8th ed.). Pearson.

Zou, P. X., & Xu, X. (2023). *Research methodology and strategy: Theory and practice*. John Wiley & Sons.

Zumitzavan, V. (2011). *The impact of managers' learning styles and leadership styles on the effectiveness of their organisations: A case study from small retail tyre companies in Thailand* (Doctoral dissertation, University of Birmingham).

Zumitzavan, V. (2014). The impact of different styles of 'Personal Knowledge Management' and 'Leadership' on 'Organisational Performance': A case of healthcare industry in Thailand. *WSEAS Transactions on Business and Economics, 11*(1), 430–441.

Zumitzavan, V. (2020). Learning preferences and brand management in the Thai housing estate industry. *International Journal of Management and Enterprise Development, 19*(1), 42–57.

Zumitzavan, V. (2022). Practical strategy for maintaining organisational performance in the hospitality industry of Thailand. *International Journal of Management Practice, 15*(1), 108–130. https://doi.org/10.1504/IJMP.2022.119923

Zumitzavan, V., & Kantavong, P. (2018). Increasing organisational success through management styles of managers in housing development industry. *Panyapiwat Journal, 10*, 110–123.

Zumitzavan, V., & Michie, J. (2015). *Personal knowledge management, leadership styles, and organisational performance: A case study of the healthcare industry in Thailand*. Springer.

Zumitzavan, V., & Mumi, A. (2014). An evaluation of 'subjective measures': Organisational performance influenced by personal knowledge management and leadership styles: An investigation into the healthcare industry in Thailand. *Recent Advances in Economics, Management and Development, 146*.

Zumitzavan, V., & Udchachone, S. (2014). The impact of different styles of leadership and levels of organisational innovation on organisational performance: A case of hospitality industry in Thailand. *WSEAS Transactions on Business and Economics, 11*(1), 272–282.

Zumitzavan, V., Prachumrasee, K., & Pathak, S. (2025). Transformational leadership cultivating innovation and transparency in local government organisations, Thailand. *Journal of Open Innovation: Technology, Market, and Complexity*, 100626.

Chapter 6
Sample Selection Methods

6.1 Introduction

This chapter describes approaches to sample selection, encompassing the delineation of the target population, the determination of sample size, and the application of various sampling techniques.

6.2 Population

The term 'population' refers to the entire set of individuals or units that are the focus of a research investigation. This can include all members of a particular group or the entire collection of entities relevant to the study (Silverman, 2024; Yousefi Nooraie et al., 2020). In this context, '*N*' denotes the total population.

For instance, if a research project aims to examine the attributes of the 'Marketing Mix' (4Ps: Product, Price, Place, and Promotion) and how these elements contribute to customer satisfaction for the 'X' beverage product, then the population comprises all customers of the 'X' beverage (Kotler & Keller, 2016; Zumitzavan, 2020). These customers are considered the population because they can provide insights into which aspects of the 4Ps are most effective at enhancing their satisfaction levels (Zou & Xu, 2023).

© The Author(s), under exclusive license to Springer Nature Singapore Pte Ltd. 2025
V. Zumitzavan, *Social Science Methodologies for Management Research*,
https://doi.org/10.1007/978-981-95-4318-2_6

6.3 Sample Size

A sample is a subset or component of the entire population that is randomly drawn and collected to represent the broader population (Fricker, 2008; Mulisa, 2022). In statistical terms, '*n*' denotes the sample size, which refers to the number of observations or data points encompassed in the sample. The goal of sampling is to ensure that the sample accurately reflects the characteristics of the entire population, thereby enabling the generalisation of findings from the sample to the population (Kumar, 2018; Zou & Xu, 2023).

For instance, in a management context, suppose a hi-tech enterprise is interested in assessing employees' job satisfaction. The unit of analysis in this case is the individual employee. To obtain meaningful results, the company might randomly select a sample of 300 employees from a total workforce of 5000. This sample of 300 employees is intended to be representative of the entire workforce. If the sample accurately reflects the characteristics and opinions of the entire employee base, the company can generalise the findings from this sample to the entire organisation, thus gaining insights into overall employee job satisfaction

6.4 Different Methods in Determining Sample Size

In addition, there are various methods for determining sample size, each of which is designed to ensure that the sample accurately represents the population and provides reliable and valid results.

6.4.1 *First Technique*

(This formula is used to calculate the size of samples when there is an infinite or a vast population; Cochran, 1997, p. 76.)

$$n = \frac{Z^2\sigma^2}{e^2}$$

Where:

N = Population
n = Sample Size
e = Error (The range of the error that we can accept that the sample size could represent the entire population; formula $e = x - \mu$; where x = sample means, and μ is population means.)

σ^2 = the variance of variables of the research

Z = Z-Score; $\alpha = 0.1$, or Confidence Interval = 90%; Z = 1.65
$\alpha = 0.5$, or Confidence Interval = 95% Z = 1.96
$\alpha = 0.01$, or Confidence Interval = 99% Z = 2.58

6.4.2 Second Technique

(This formula is used to calculate for the size of samples whilst there is the finite population; Babbie, 2021.)

$$n = \frac{NZ^2\sigma^2}{Ne^2 + Z^2\sigma^2}$$

Where:

N = Population
n = Sample Size
e = Error (The range of the error that we can accept that the sample size could represent the entire population; formula $e = x - \mu$; where x = sample means, and μ is population means.)

σ^2 = the variance of variables of the research

Z = Z-Score; $\alpha = 0.1$, or Confidence Interval = 90%; Z = 1.65
$\alpha = 0.5$, or Confidence Interval = 95% Z = 1.96
$\alpha = 0.01$, or Confidence Interval = 99% Z = 2.58

Note: In general, the variance of the variables of the research can be obtained from previous research.

There exists another formula which can help us to calculate for sample size (Yamane Taro, 1973; Field, 2024).

6.4.3 Third Technique

(This formula is used to calculate the size of samples when there is a finite population; Yamane, 1973, p. 1088.)

$$n = \frac{N}{1 + N(e)^2}$$

Where;

N = Population
n = sample size
e = Error (The range of the error that we can accept that the sample size could represent the entire population; formula $e = x - \mu$; where x = sample means, and μ is population means.)

6.4.4 Fourth Technique

Hair, Black, Babin, Anderson, and Tatham (2019) recommended that a ratio of 5:1 is the standard to achieve to ensure that the data collected is adequate to reflect the phenomenon being studied. More specifically, taking into account all the independent variables, a sample that is at least one-fifth of the target population size is required. Thus, the high response rate could further contribute to the representativeness of the data collected.

For instance, consider the case where the research is analysing 12 independent variables, i.e. Gender, Age, Experience, Education, Number of Employees, Activist, Pragmatist, Reflector, Theorist, Transformational Leadership, Transactional Leadership and Laissez-faire Leadership. Therefore, the minimum sample size required is estimated to be at least 60 (12 * independent variables * 5 = 60 participants in the sample).

6.5 Different Methods of Sample Selection

6.5.1 Sample

A sample, symbolised as '*n*', thus represents a selected subset of the population that is intended to accurately reflect the entire population. Employing appropriate sampling techniques enhances the validity and reliability of research findings whilst managing time and budget constraints effectively (Bartlett, 2005). Appropriate sample selection minimises researchers' bias and ensures that the sample accurately represents the population under investigation (Chartered Institute of Personnel and Development [CIPD], 2021).

Sampling methods are generally categorised into two main types: probability sampling and non-probability sampling techniques. Probability sampling methods involve random selection, ensuring that each member of the population has a known and equal chance of being included in the sample, thereby enhancing the representativeness and generalisability of the results (Field, 2024). Non-probability sampling methods, on the other hand, do not provide each member of the population with a known chance of selection, which can affect representativeness and potentially introduce selection bias (Abbott & McKinney, 2012).

6.5.1.1 Non-Probability Sampling

Non-probability samples are typically regarded as less desirable than probability samples due to their reduced representativeness. Unlike probability sampling, non-probability sampling does not guarantee that every member of the population has an equal chance of selection (Bellamy, 2011). Despite this, probability sampling may sometimes be impractical or excessively costly (Guetterman et al., 2023).

In such scenarios, researchers may not prioritise generalising findings to the broader population (Babbie, 2021). The validity of non-probability samples can be enhanced by approximating random selection and mitigating sources of bias as effectively as possible. Techniques to improve validity include several strategies, discussed below.

Quota Sampling

A quota sample is distinguished by the researcher's deliberate setting of proportions for different strata or levels within the sample. This method is employed to ensure that specific segments of the population are included. To maintain representativeness, the proportions assigned in the sample should closely mirror those in the population. Importantly, the establishment of quotas is conducted independently of the underlying characteristics of the population (Edmonds & Kennedy, 2016; Malhotra, 2019).

For example, suppose a researcher is examining the attitudes of individuals from various nationalities towards the taste of Thai food. In Thailand, a random sample might under represent Europeans, given their relatively small proportion compared to Thais. To ensure the adequate representation of Europeans, the researcher might set a quota of 3 per cent of Europeans within the sample. Although this approach ensures that European perspectives are included, it results in a sample that may not accurately reflect the true proportions of the population. As a result, the generalisability of the findings to the broader national population may be constrained. Nonetheless, the quota method guarantees that the views of Europeans are represented in the survey (Bennett et al., 2022; Robson & McCartan, 2016).

Purposive Sampling

A purposive sample is a non-representative subset of a larger population, selected to address a specific research need or objective. Researchers using purposive sampling may focus on particular groups, such as senior business executives, based on their relevance to the study. Defining the entire population can be challenging, as some members might be unrecognised or difficult to access (Loseke, 2012; Palinkas et al., 2015).

For example, a researcher investigating leadership styles in multinational corporations might choose a purposive sampling approach to focus specifically on senior business executives. These executives are chosen for the reason that their perspectives are particularly applicable to the research's purposes. Defining the entire population of senior executives can be challenging, as some individuals might be unrecognised or difficult to access. Consequently, the researcher might select a sample of 20 high-ranking executives from various industries to acquire insights into leadership practices that are directly applicable to the research objectives (Campbell et al., 2020).

Additionally, a subset of purposive sampling is the snowball sample, named for its method of accumulation—similar to a snowball gathering snow as it rolls. This technique involves starting with an initial participant who then refers the researcher to others suitable for the study. Snowball sampling is particularly useful for reaching hard-to-access populations, such as enthusiasts of niche sports teams or individuals with specific behaviours (Atkinson & Flint, 2001; Goodson & Phillimore, 2012).

Principally, in the management discipline, snowball sampling can be effective for investigating niche market segments, such as enthusiasts of supercars. For example, a researcher aiming to explore the purchasing behaviours and brand preferences of supercar buyers might start with an initial participant, an owner of a high-end supercar. This participant could then refer the researcher to other supercar holders within their network. As the researcher gathers more referrals, they build a sample of individuals deeply engaged in the supercar market. This approach is invaluable for reaching a highly specific and fairly exclusive group, permitting in-depth insights into the motivations and preferences of supercar enthusiasts, which might be difficult to access through other sampling methods (Robson, 2024).

Convenience Sampling

A convenience sample is characterised by selecting participants who are readily accessible, rather than through a structured or random process. This type of sampling, often referred to as an accidental sample, does not ensure that every member of the population has an equal chance of being included. Consequently, it does not meet the criteria for true random sampling, where every individual in the population should have an equal opportunity for selection (Ekanem, 2007; Mukherjee, 2019).

For instance, in a qualitative study investigating the effectiveness of a new management training programme within an organisation, a researcher might choose to interview only those managers who are available during specific times at the company's headquarters. Whilst this method allows for practical and timely data collection, it does not ensure that the sample is representative of all managers who participated in the training programme. The insights obtained may be skewed towards the views of those who are more accessible or available at the time, and may not reflect the broader perspectives of all programme participants (Poth, 2023; Dunwoodie et al., 2023).

In summary, non-probability samples, such as convenience samples, have limitations regarding generalisability. As they do not accurately represent the entire population, making valid inferences about the larger group from which they are drawn can be challenging. Nevertheless, convenience sampling can be advantageous in management research for obtaining rich, detailed data whilst operating within practical constraints, despite its limitations in terms of generalisability (Fraenkel et al., 2018; Khalid et al., 2012).

6.5.1.2 Probability Sampling

Probability sampling refers to a method of selecting a sample from a population where each member has a known, non-zero chance of being included. This technique ensures that the sample is representative of the population, allowing researchers to generalise findings accurately. The main types of probability sampling include simple random sampling, stratified sampling, and cluster sampling. Simple random sampling ensures every individual has an equal chance of selection, stratified sampling involves dividing the population into distinct subgroups and sampling from each, and cluster sampling selects entire clusters randomly, rather than individuals (Grønmo, 2023; Teddlie & Yu, 2007).

These methods are vital for reducing sampling bias and enhancing the reliability of statistical inferences. By employing probability sampling techniques, researchers can ensure that their samples more accurately reflect the broader population, which supports valid and generalisable results (Auamnoy 2002; Tashakkori et al., 2020). There exist various types of probability sampling techniques;

Simple Random Sampling

Simple random sampling is a probability sampling technique where each member of a population has an equal chance of being selected. This method ensures that every individual in the population has an equal probability of inclusion, which helps in obtaining a representative sample. Simple random sampling can be conducted with or without replacement, each having different implications for the sample and its analysis (Dattalo, 2009; Kremelberg, 2010).

Firstly, in sampling without replacement, once an individual is selected, they are not returned to the population pool. As a result, each individual can only be selected once. This method reduces the sample size gradually and is typically used when the goal is to ensure each member of the sample is unique. Sampling without replacement is preferred when the population size is finite and manageable, as it avoids duplication and provides a more accurate reflection of the population (Rosenthal & Rosnow, 2008).

Secondly, in sampling with replacement, once an individual is selected for the sample, they are placed back into the population pool and may be selected again. This approach maintains the original population size throughout the sampling process, allowing for the possibility of selecting the same individual multiple times. Sampling with replacement is particularly useful when the population is large or when the sampling is done repeatedly (Hedrih & Hedrih, 2022).

Finally, both methods aim to minimise selection bias and enhance the reliability of statistical inferences. The choice between sampling with or without replacement depends on the research objectives, population size, and practical considerations (Kremelberg, 2010; Hedrih & Hedrih 2022).

- Without replacement: Simple random sampling is similar to putting the names of all the students in a population in a hat, and then drawing 200 names without replacement. In this case, the chance of selection of each sample will be less and less since there is no replacement. Hence, this may affect the chance of errors in the process of sample selection because the smaller the number of the samples remaining in the hat, the greater chance of each sample being selected.
- With replacement: Simple random sampling is similar to putting the names of all the students in a population in a hat, and then drawing 200 names with replacement. In this case, all students have the equal chance of being selected at all times. However, this technique is not well-known since it consumes more time, energy, and budget.

A practical approach to implementing simple random sampling involves constructing a sampling frame or list. For example, one might create a list of all the students studying at the College of Local Administration (COLA) at Khon Kaen University, in Thailand, and then randomly select 200 names from this frame. On a smaller scale, random number generators or software tools can be employed to choose individuals from the frame. This method is beneficial due to its ideal statistical properties, ensuring that each individual within the frame has an equal probability of being selected. However, obtaining a comprehensive and accessible frame for the target population can be challenging (Salkind, 2019).

For instance, it might be difficult to access complete lists for populations such as Thai residents, customers of Big-C Superstores in Thailand, or potential credit card applicants. In such cases, more accessible but less precise frames, such as telephone directories and mailing lists, may be utilised. Whilst these approximations are practical, they may introduce some inaccuracies. For example, some Thai residents listed in telephone directories may no longer be at the provided address, possibly due to relocation for reasons such as military service, employment in remote areas, or other commitments. As a result, there may be discrepancies between the frame and the actual target population at the time of the survey (Slattery et al., 2011).

Systematic Sampling

A *k*-in-*1* systematic sample selects every *k*th subject on a list or a sequence. For example, every 10th customer entering the store may be approached for a survey, or every 25th number in the phone book may be called. Another example would be, in a retail management research project, a researcher might apply systematic sampling to evaluate customers' satisfaction. By selecting every 20th customer who makes a purchase in a month, the researcher ensures a regular and unbiased sample of shoppers (Haq, 2015). This methodical approach helps maintain a balanced representation of customers' opinions without the need for complex randomisation techniques.

In a case where there are 300 households in a particular area, and the required sample size is 5 households, the value of *k* can be established as follows; $k = \frac{N}{n}$; $\frac{300}{5} = 60$ (Cleff, 2019).

In this case, if we start from the first household **1**st; then the second one would be $= 1 + 60 =$ **61**st, the third, $61 + 60 =$ **121**st, the fourth, $121 + 60 =$ **181**st, and the fifth, $181 + 60 =$ **241st.**

Therefore, in this case, the samples are 1st, 61st, 121st, 181st, and 241st households.

Stratified Random Sampling

A stratified random sample partitions the population into subsets, called strata, and selects a simple random sample from each stratum. In the survey of the students of the College of Local Administration (COLA), Khon Kaen University, Thailand undergraduates, we may choose to draw 50 students from each of the freshman, sophomore, junior, and senior strata, instead of 200 students from the combined student population. In addition, in this case, the stratified technique is more likely to work well with the homogeneous backgrounds or attributes (Wilson, 2016). Thus, each group of students, whether freshman, sophomore, junior, or senior stratum, is homogeneous or similar in general, as within each stratum the sample is homogeneous in backgrounds or attributes. For example, the age of the students in the freshman stratum is almost certainly not older than 18 years old, the students will likely have similar lifestyles and preferences, and the students will possess the same or a very similar level of academic knowledge.

Cluster Sampling

Cluster sampling involves selecting entire groups or clusters at random when individual participants cannot be assigned to specific groups. This method first randomly chooses a subset of clusters from the available groups, and then includes all the members of these selected clusters in the sample.

For instance, consider a scenario where we have 5 classes, each comprising 40 students. In this case, each class is regarded as a cluster. Cluster sampling is particularly effective when these clusters are diverse and representative of the overall population, such as including a mix of freshmen, sophomores, juniors, and seniors, as well as male and female students. To enhance representativeness, it is advantageous to focus on general education classes rather than those specific to particular majors, which may be less heterogeneous (Lohr, 2021).

Another example can be found in studying resident preferences in the Northeast region of Thailand. The region comprises 17 provinces. To conduct the study, we might randomly select 5 provinces, with a sample of 100 residents from each. Here, each province functions as a cluster. This approach is likely to yield a sample that accurately reflects the diversity of the entire population, given the varied age, gender, and educational backgrounds within each province (Rassel et al., 2020).

Multi Stages Sampling

Multi-stage sampling is a sophisticated technique combining both probability and non-probability sampling methods to achieve a more practical and efficient sampling process. It typically involves several stages of selection, starting with a broad probability sampling method and narrowing down through subsequent non-probability sampling steps (Lohr, 2021).

For example, in the first stage, a researcher might use random sampling to select geographic regions or clusters. In the subsequent stages, within these selected regions, a non-random method such as convenience or purposive sampling might be used to select specific individuals or subgroups. This approach helps in managing large populations and reduces costs whilst aiming to maintain representativeness at different levels of the sampling process.

For instance, a researcher might first employ random sampling to select xxx subgroups from a larger set of yyy groups. Following this, individual members are randomly chosen from within each selected sub-group. This process often involves multiple stages of selection, with various sampling methods potentially applied at each stage or throughout the entire sampling process. This layered approach enhances both the precision and efficiency of the sampling strategy (Thompson, 2012).

For example, rather than selecting 2000 individuals directly from a population of 2,000,000 spread across 26 districts in Khon Kaen, Thailand, a multi-stage sampling approach might be employed. First, 7 districts are randomly chosen from the 26 districts, which represents the cluster sampling stage. Subsequently, within each of these 7 selected districts, 30 individuals are randomly sampled, which represents the individual sampling stage. This method streamlines the sampling process and ensures that the sample is both manageable and representative (Groves et al., 2011).

Exercise

In this case, we are interested in studying the different levels of satisfaction of the guardians of students who are studying at a school under the supervision of Khon

Kaen Municipality. There are 11 schools within the area of Khon Kaen Municipality comprising approximately 10,363 students in total. How can we apply different techniques of sample selection to attain the most accurate sample to generalise to the entire population?

1st formula: (This formula is used to calculate the size of samples when there is an infinite or a vast population; Thompson, 2012).

$$n = \frac{Z^2\sigma^2}{e^2}$$

When the population (N) is massive, or when the exact size of N is unknown but its variance is known.

Example 1 The National Statistical Office has announced that the standard deviation of the monthly income of a middle-class family is equivalent to 1200 baht. In this case, we would like to estimate the expenditure of the middle-class family whilst allowing for an error that is not greater than 50 baht at the 95% confidence interval. What should be the appropriate number of the sample?

(σ) Standard Deviation = 1200 baht
(e) Error = 50 baht
(Z) 95% Confidence Interval = 1.96

$$n = \frac{1.96^2 1,200^2}{50^2} = 2,212.76$$

Therefore, the sample should consist of approximately 2213 families.

Remarks: Generally, we do not know the variance of the population, but we can attain it from previous studies in related disciplines.**[(σ) = Standard Deviation; (σ^2) = Variance]**

$$s = \sqrt{\frac{\sum_{i=1}^{n}(x_i - \overline{x})^2}{n-1}}$$ **Standard Deviation of Sample**

$$\sigma = \sqrt{\frac{\sum_{i=1}^{n}(x_i - \overline{x})^2}{N}}$$ **Standard Deviation of Population**

2nd formula: (This formula is used to calculate the size of a sample when there is a finite population; Cochran, 1997, p. 76).

$$n = \frac{NZ^2\sigma^2}{Ne^2 + Z^2\sigma^2}$$

In case we know the finite population and the variance of the population.

Example 2 A village comprises 720 households. The variance of the monthly income is equivalent to 820 baht. If we would like to calculate the mean of the monthly income per household in a way in which the error should not be greater than 5 baht at the 95% and 99% confidence interval, what would be the appropriate number of the sample?

(N) Population = 720 households
(σ^2) variance of the monthly income = 820 baht
(e) Error = 5 baht

95% Confidence Interval; Z = 1.96
Therefore:

$$n = \frac{720x(1.96^2)x\,820}{720x(5^2) + (1.96^2)x(820)}$$

$$= 107.237 = 108 \text{ people}$$

99% Confidence Interval; Z = 2.58
Therefore:

$$n = \frac{720x(2.58^2)x\,820}{720x(5^2) + (2.58^2)x(820)}$$

$$= 167.529 = 168 \text{ people}$$

3rd formula: (This formula is used to calculate the size of a sample when there is a finite population; Yamane, 1973, p. 1088).

$$n = \frac{N}{1 + N(e)^2}$$

Example 3 In this case, the researchers aim to study a village in the countryside comprising 1500 people for the population. When the error is 5%, what should the appropriate number of the samples be?

(N) Population = 1500 people
(e) = error at 5% = 0.05
Therefore:

$$n = \frac{1500}{1 + (1500(0.05))^2}$$

$$= 315.789 = 316 \text{ people}$$

As the confidence interval level increases, the required sample size also increases to maintain statistical reliability. Conversely, a larger margin of error allows for a smaller sample size, though this may compromise the precision of the estimates.

6.6 Creative Sampling in the Digital Age: The Role of Artificial Intelligence

The contemporary paradigm of sample selection is being greatly redesigned by the creative application of AI, which augments the traditional statistical techniques discussed heretofore. AI allows researchers to move beyond static sampling frames, utilising machine learning algorithms to recognise and characterise nascent or hard-to-reach populations from vast, unstructured digital sources such as online forums or social media discourse; therefore, improving the precision of purposive sampling on an unprecedented scale (AdeyinkaOjo, 2025). Additionally, a particularly innovative development involves using generative AI to produce synthetic populations. This permits researchers to simulate a variety of sampling strategies, pre-emptively testing for potential biases and optimising sample designs before promising substantial resources to fieldwork (Aher et al., 2023). Nevertheless, it is compulsory upon the researcher to approach these methods with critical scrutiny, as algorithmic biases inherent in AI models can risk generating new forms of sampling error, potentially marginalising the very voices the research aims to include (Yang et al., 2020). Therefore, the future of rigorous sample selection lies in the judicious synthesis of time-honoured statistical principles with these powerful, AI-driven creative methodologies.

6.7 Chapter Summary

This chapter provided a comprehensive overview of sample selection techniques, including the definition of the target population, methods for determining sample size, and the application of various sampling strategies. The subsequent chapter will address the development of hypotheses.

6.8 Questions for Future Reflection

1. A researcher calculates a precise sample size of 316 using Yamane's formula but then gathers the data utilising convenience sampling technique from a single location. Critically evaluate this approach. Does the mathematical rigour of the

sample size calculation lend any credibility to the sample's representativeness, or is the effort nullified by the non-probability selection method?

2. You are commissioned to conduct a study on organisational members' morale but are given a very tight budget and deadline. Your manager argues for a non-probability method such as quota sampling for its speed and low cost. Argue against this choice, explaining the specific risks to the validity and generalisability of the findings. Conversely, how could you defend the use of quota sampling as a 'good enough' approach in this practical business context?
3. The chapter acknowledges that obtaining a perfect sampling frame is often difficult (e.g., using a telephone directory). At what point does the imperfection of a sampling frame undermine the statistical superiority of a probability sampling method such as simple random sampling technique? Could a meticulously planned quota sample potentially yield a more representative sample than a simple random sample technique drawn from a severely flawed frame? Justify your position.
4. The chapter presents Hair et al.'s (2019) 5:1 ratio for determining sample size based on the number of variables. Critique this approach. In what specific research scenarios could this rule of thumb be dangerously misleading, contributing to a sample that is either grossly insufficient or unnecessarily large?
5. Imagine a research project aiming to study job satisfaction at a multinational corporation with three distinct departments (Sales, Engineering, HR) and offices in five different countries. Which probability sampling method—stratified random sampling or cluster sampling techniques—would be more appropriate? Justify your choice by detailing the practical and statistical advantages for this specific scenario.
6. Snowball sampling technique is presented as an effective technique for reaching hard-to-access populations, such as supercar enthusiasts. Critically evaluate the primary sources of bias inherent in this method. What specific steps could a researcher take to mitigate the risk of ending up with a homogenous sample that simply replicates a single, interconnected social circle?
7. For the study on the 'X' beverage, the population is defined as 'all customers'. Critically analyse this definition. Who is potentially excluded (e.g., potential customers, former customers, or individuals who purchase the drink for others)? How would redefining the population to be more specific (e.g., 'frequent purchasers aged 18–35') alter the entire sampling strategy?
8. Systematic sampling technique (e.g., selecting every 10th customer) is presented as a probability technique. However, how could a hidden pattern (or 'periodicity') in the population list compromise the randomness of this method? Provide a hypothetical management research example where systematic sampling could lead to a biased sample.
9. The sample size formulas require the researcher to pre-determine an acceptable margin of error (e). Discuss the ethical and practical trade-offs a researcher makes when selecting this value. What are the implications of choosing a larger margin of error (e.g., 10% instead of 5%) to lessen the required sample size and, therefore, the cost of the study?

10. For the chapter's exercise (studying guardian satisfaction across 11 schools with 10,363 students), a simple random sample technique would be logistically difficult. Design a two-stage sampling plan to address this problem. Clearly define what would happen at each stage and justify why this multi-stage approach is superior to both simple random sampling and convenience sampling techniques in this context.

References

Abbott, M. L., & McKinney, J. (2012). *Understanding and applying research design*. John Wiley & Sons.

AdeyinkaOjo, S. (2025). *Digital and strategic qualitative research methodology*. Notion Press.

Aher, G. V., Arriaga, R. I., & Kalai, A. T. (2023). Using large language models to simulate multiple humans and replicate human subject studies. In *International conference on machine learning* (pp. 337–371). PMLR.

Atkinson, R., & Flint, J. (2001). Accessing hidden and hard-to-reach populations: Snowball research strategies. *Social Research Update, 33*. https://sru.soc.surrey.ac.uk/SRU33.html

Auamnoy, T. (2002). *Statistics and SPSS for 21st century research*. Chulalongkorn University.

Babbie, E. R. (2021). *The Practice of social research* (15th ed.). Cengage Learning.

Bartlett, K. R. (2005). Survey research in organisations. In R. A. Swanson & E. F. Holton III (Eds.), *Research in organisations foundations and methods of inquiry* (pp. 97–113). Berrett-Koehler Publishers, Inc.

Bellamy, C. (2011). *Principles of methodology: Research design in social science*. Sage Publications.

Bennett, K., Heritage, B., & Allen, P. (2022). *SPSS Statistics: A practical guide 5e*. Cengage AU.

Campbell, S., Greenwood, M., Prior, S., Shearer, T., Walkem, K., Young, S., et al. (2020). Purposive sampling: complex or simple? Research case examples. *Journal of Research in Nursing, 25*(8), 652–661. https://doi.org/10.1177/1744987120927206

Chartered Institute of Personnel and Development (CIPD). (2021). *Research methods and methodology*. CIPD.

Cleff, T. (2019). *Applied statistics and multivariate data analysis for business and economics: A modern approach using SPSS, Stata, and Excel*. Springer.

Cochran, W. G. (1997). *Sampling techniques* (3rd ed.). John Wiley.

Dattalo, P. (2009). *Strategies to approximate random sampling and assignment*. Oxford University Press.

Dunwoodie, K., Macaulay, L., & Newman, A. (2023). Qualitative interviewing in the field of work and organisational psychology: Benefits, challenges and guidelines for researchers and reviewers. *Applied Psychology, 72*(2), 863–889. https://doi.org/10.1111/apps.12414

Edmonds, W. A., & Kennedy, T. D. (2016). *An applied guide to research designs: Quantitative, qualitative, and mixed methods*. Sage Publications.

Ekanem, I. (2007). "Insider accounts": a qualitative research method for small firms. *Journal of Small Business and Enterprise Development, 14*(1), 105–117. https://doi.org/10.1108/14626000710727926

Field, A. (2024). *Discovering statistics using IBM SPSS statistics* (6th ed.). Sage Publications.

Fraenkel, J., Wallen, N., & Hyun, H. (2018). *How to design and evaluate research in education* (10th ed.). McGraw-Hill Education.

Fricker, R. D. (2008). Sampling methods for web and e-mail surveys. In N. Fielding, R. M. Lee, & G. Blank (Eds.), *The SAGE handbook of online research methods* (pp. 195–216). SAGE Publications.

Goodson, L., & Phillimore, J. (2012). Community research: Opportunities and challenges. *Community Research for Participation*, 3–20. https://doi.org/10.2307/j.ctt1r33pzb.6

Grønmo, S. (2023). *Social research methods: Qualitative, quantitative and mixed methods approaches* (2nd ed.). Sage Publications.

Groves, R. M., Fowler, F. J., Jr., Couper, M. P., Lepkowski, J. M., Singer, E., & Tourangeau, R. (2011). *Survey Methodology*. John Wiley & Sons.

Guetterman, T. C., Molina-Azorin, J. F., & Fàbregues, S. (2023). The need to rigorously develop common quality guidelines for reporting mixed methods research. *Journal of Mixed Methods Research, 17*(1), 6–11. https://doi.org/10.1177/15586898221143561

Hair, J. F., Black, W. C., Babin, B. J., Anderson, R. E., & Tatham, R. L. (2019). *Multivariate data analysis* (8th ed.). Pearson Education.

Haq, M. (2015). A comparative analysis of qualitative and quantitative research methods and a justification for the use of mixed methods in social research. *Annual PhD Conference, University of Bradford School of Management*, June 2014. http://hdl.handle.net/10454/7389

Hedrih, V., & Hedrih, A. (2022). *Interpreting statistics for beginners: A guide for behavioural and social scientists*. Routledge.

Khalid, K., Abdullah, H. H., Kumar, M., & D. (2012). Get along with quantitative research process. *International Journal of Research in Management, 2*(2), 15–29.

Kotler, P., & Keller, K. L. (2016). *Marketing management* (15th ed.). Pearson Education.

Kremelberg, D. (2010). *Practical statistics: A quick and easy guide to IBM® SPSS® statistics, stata, and other statistical software*. Sage Publications.

Kumar, R. (2018). *Research methodology: A step-by-step guide for beginners*. Sage Publications.

Lohr, S. L. (2021). *Sampling: Design and analysis*. Chapman and Hall/CRC.

Loseke, D. R. (2012). *Methodological thinking: Basic principles of social research design*. Sage Publications.

Malhotra, N. K. (2019). *Marketing research: An applied approach* (7th ed.). Pearson Education.

Mukherjee, S. P. (2019). *A guide to research methodology: An overview of research problems, tasks and methods*. CRC Press.

Mulisa, F. (2022). When does a researcher choose a quantitative, qualitative, or mixed research approach? *Interchange, 53*(1), 113–131. https://doi.org/10.1007/s10780-021-09447-z

Palinkas, L. A., Horwitz, S. M., Green, C. A., Wisdom, J. P., Duan, N., & Hoagwood, K. (2015). Purposeful sampling for qualitative data collection and analysis in mixed method implementation research. *Administration and Policy in Mental Health and Mental Health Services Research, 42*(5), 533–544. https://doi.org/10.1007/s10488-013-0528-y

Poth, C. N. (Ed.). (2023). *The sage handbook of mixed methods research design*. Sage Publications.

Rassel, G., Leland, S., Mohr, Z., & O'Sullivan, E. (2020). *Research methods for public administrators*. Routledge.

Robson, C. (2024). *Real world research*. John Wiley & Sons.

Robson, C., & McCartan, K. (2016). *Real world research* (4th ed.). Wiley.

Rosenthal, R., & Rosnow, R. L. (2008). *Essentials of behavioural research: Methods and Data Analysis* (3rd ed.). McGraw-Hill Education.

Salkind, N. J. (2019). *Statistics for people who (think they) hate statistics* (7th ed.). Sage Publications.

Silverman, D. (2024). *Interpreting qualitative data*. Sage Publications.

Slattery, E. L., Voelker, C. C., Nussenbaum, B., Rich, J. T., Paniello, R. C., & Neely, J. G. (2011). A practical guide to surveys and questionnaires. *Otolaryngology – Head and Neck Surgery, 144*(6), 831–837. https://doi.org/10.1177/0194599811399724

Tashakkori, A., Johnson, R. B., & Teddlie, C. (2020). *Foundations of mixed methods research: Integrating quantitative and qualitative approaches in the social and behavioral sciences*. Sage Publications.

Teddlie, C., & Yu, F. (2007). Mixed methods sampling: A typology with examples. *Journal of Mixed Methods Research, 1*(1), 77–100. https://doi.org/10.1177/2345678906292430

Thompson, S. K. (2012). *Sampling* (3rd ed.). John Wiley & Sons.

Wilson, V. (2016). Research methods: Content analysis. *Evidence-Based Library and Information Practice, 11*(1(S)), 41–43. https://doi.org/10.18438/B8CG9D

Yamane, T. (1973). *Statistics: An introductory analysis* (3rd ed.). Harper and Row.

Yang, Y., Youyou, W., & Uzzi, B. (2020). Estimating the deep replicability of scientific findings using human and artificial intelligence. *Proceedings of the National Academy of Sciences, 117*(20), 10762–10768.

Yousefi Nooraie, R., Sale, J. E., Marin, A., & Ross, L. E. (2020). Social network analysis: An example of fusion between quantitative and qualitative methods. *Journal of Mixed Methods Research, 14*(1), 110–124. https://doi.org/10.1177/1558689818804060

Zou, P. X., & Xu, X. (2023). *Research methodology and strategy: Theory and practice*. John Wiley & Sons.

Zumitzavan, V. (2020). Learning preferences and brand management in the Thai housing estate industry. *International Journal of Management and Enterprise Development, 19*(1), 42–57.

Chapter 7
Hypotheses Development

7.1 Introduction

This chapter discusses the formulation of hypotheses, demonstrating key concepts with relevant examples from the discipline of management to enhance the readers' comprehension. It also addresses different methodologies for hypothesis testing, including by explaining Type I and Type II errors, and provides relevant examples to elucidate these notions.

7.2 The Relationship Between the Quantitative Approach and Hypothesis Development

The quantitative approach is deeply rooted in the philosophy of positivism, speculating that knowledge is best accomplished through empirical observation and the application of scientific methods. This philosophical stance maintains that reality is objective and can be systematically measured and analysed using quantitative techniques such as statistical methods. Positivism highlights the belief that phenomena can be observed, quantified, and subject to rigorous testing to derive objective conclusions (Ghauri et al., 2020).

In the realm of management disciplines, the quantitative approach is instrumental for testing hypotheses and making predictions about a population based on sample data. This methodology involves the collection of numerical data through a variety of techniques such as surveys, experiments, and other structured data collection methods. Once collected, statistical techniques are employed to test hypotheses, interpret the data, and draw meaningful inferences.

For instance, consider a research project examining organisational members' satisfaction within an organisation. A researcher might use a structured survey with

© The Author(s), under exclusive license to Springer Nature Singapore Pte Ltd. 2025
V. Zumitzavan, *Social Science Methodologies for Management Research*,
https://doi.org/10.1007/978-981-95-4318-2_7

Likert scale questions to quantify the organisational members' levels of satisfaction with different aspects of their organisational environment. The collected data is then subjected to statistical analyses such as regression analysis or factor analysis to test hypotheses related to job satisfaction and organisational performance. This quantitative method enables accurate measurement of levels of satisfaction and facilitates predictions about how changes in specific variables, e.g., Work Conditions and Managerial Support, might affect overall levels of organisational members' satisfaction (Kline, 2023).

Another example may be found in the field of marketing management. Researchers might use experimental designs to assess the impact of different promotional strategies on consumers' purchasing behaviour. For example, an experiment could be designed to measure how variations in advertising messages influence consumers' likelihood of purchasing a product. By applying statistical techniques such as analysis of variance (ANOVA) or chi-square tests, researchers can determine whether the observed effects are statistically significant and make data-driven recommendations for improved marketing strategies (Kinnear & Gray, 2019). A study of Vietnamese SMEs provides a salient example of using Pearson's Correlation in business. Researchers found that organisational employee loyalty was far more strongly correlated with the quality of management and engaging work than it was with pay. This recommends that for enhancing staff retention, emphasising on leadership and job design is more impactful than simply improving salaries (Dai Quang & Vo-Thanh, 2025). The quantitative approach, whilst powerful, also necessitates a rigorous technique for data collection and analysis to avoid potential drawbacks such as sampling errors or biases. It is essential for researchers to reassure that their data collection methods are valid and reliable, and that their statistical analyses are appropriately conducted in order to avoid what are called Type I and Type II errors. Type I errors occur when a hypothesis is incorrectly rejected when it is actually true, whilst Type II errors occur when a hypothesis is inaccurately accepted when it is actually false (Aldrich, 2018).

In summary, the quantitative approach in management research provides a robust framework for hypothesis testing and predictive analysis through the utilisation of numerical data and statistical methods. By adhering to the principles of positivism and employing rigorous data collection and analysis techniques, researchers can derive objective insights and make informed decisions that drive effective management practices.

7.3 The Key Characteristics of the Quantitative Approach

The principal characteristic is objectivity. The quantitative approach strives for objectivity by using standardised methods for data collection and statistical analysis, thereby minimising the influence of the researcher's subjective interpretations. By adhering to consistent procedures and utilising rigorous statistical techniques, this approach proposes to ensure that any findings are based on empirical evidence rather than personal biases or subjective viewpoints. This emphasis on objectivity is crucial for producing results that are replicable and generalisable, thereby improving the reliability and validity of the research findings.

For example, an effective illustration of this objective is found in the evaluation of organisational members' performance using standardised assessments. For instance, researchers might investigate the influence of different performance appraisal methods on different levels of organisational members' productivity. To maintain objectivity, they would design a survey featuring a standardised questionnaire capturing numerical data on various performance measures, such as rates of task completion, quality of work, and adherence to deadlines.

By applying statistical techniques such as factor analysis to the collected data, researchers can objectively evaluate which appraisal methods most effectively increase levels of productivity. For example, they might compare the outcomes of traditional annual performance reviews with those of continuous feedback systems. Statistical tests such as t-tests or ANOVA are then applied to evaluate whether or not any observed differences in productivity are statistically associated (Goel, 2023).

This rigorous approach assures that the research findings are grounded in empirical evidence and not influenced by subjective biases. Consequently, it supports data-driven decision-making in performance management, leading to more effective appraisal practices and improved organisational performance.

7.4 Generalisability

The quantitative approach aims to make generalisations about a population based on samples collected. To accomplish this, it is essential to use a sufficiently large and representative sample to ensure that the findings are applicable to the complete population. The ability to generalise the results depends significantly on the approach of sample selection, which must be rigorous and systematic to accurately reflect the characteristics of the greater number of the population.

For example, a relevant example of generalisability in the management discipline is a research project examining levels of organisational members' satisfaction across different sectors of an industry. Suppose researchers are eager to generalise their research findings regarding the levels of job satisfaction to all organisational members within a specific industry. To ensure the results are broadly applicable, they would need to collect data from a sufficiently large and representative sample of organisational members across various sectors and job roles within that industry.

For instance, if a research project is conducted to assess overall levels of job satisfaction and its influence on levels of productivity, researchers might survey organisational members from multiple organisations within the industry, certifying that the sample comprises various demographic groups, job functions, and organisational sizes. By applying stratified random sampling or similar techniques, researchers can improve the representativeness of the sample. Statistical analyses can then be applied to determine if the findings are generalisable to the entire industry (Judge et al., 2001).

If the sample is adequately representative and the results are statistically significant, the researchers can confidently generalise their conclusions to the greater number of the population of organisational members within the industry. This technique highlights the importance of rigorous sampling methods to ensure that research findings are relevant and applicable on a larger scale.

7.5 Reductionism

The quantitative approach utilises reductionism by breaking down intricate phenomena into smaller, measurable components. This process enables researchers to isolate and scrutinise individual variables and their effects on specific outcomes of interest. By segmenting complex phenomena into manageable elements, researchers can systematically analyse how each component influences the overall results, leading to more precise and targeted insights.

For example, an illustrative example of reductionism in the management discipline is a research project investigating the impact of various leadership styles on organisational members' performance. To understand this complex relationship, researchers might decompose the broader concept of leadership into specific styles, such as transformational, transactional, and laissez-faire leadership. Each leadership style can be further broken down into distinct attributes or behaviours, such as motivational techniques, reward systems, and decision-making approaches.

Researchers can then design surveys or experiments to measure these attributes and their effects on employees' performance measures, such as different levels of productivity, job satisfaction, and organisational commitment. By separating and testing the impact of each leadership style and its attributes, researchers can determine which specific elements are most strongly associated with positive employee outcomes (Decuypere & Schaufeli, 2021). Thus, this reductionist approach enables a detailed examination of how individual variables, such as different leadership behaviours, affect performance outcomes. The insights gained can help managers refine their leadership strategies and implement practices that are empirically supported in order to enhance organisational members' performance and satisfaction.

7.6 Causality

The quantitative method seeks to establish cause-and-effect relationships between variables through experimental or quasi-experimental designs. In the social sciences, Structural Equation Modelling (SEM) is particularly useful for elucidating these causal relationships. SEM allows researchers to test the direction and strength of relationships between variables, providing insights into the extent of their associations.

For example, consider a well-known organisation, Organisation A, which is renowned globally for its innovative products and achieves significant revenue figures. This organisation attracts numerous highly skilled organisational members. In this context, researchers might explore the causal relationship between the organisation's reputation and the number of skilled organisational members it attracts. By applying SEM, researchers can assess whether Organisation A's high productivity and strong reputation are the result of its ability to attract skilled organisational members or whether its reputation itself draws skilled workers to the organisation.

Another pertinent example, a leading Philippine BPO company, to illustrate, could apply Structural Equation Modelling (SEM) to comprehend how to retain skilled talent. SEM would go beyond simply correlating factors such as service innovation and corporate reputation with organisational employee loyalty. Instead, it could determine the precise causal pathway: does innovation build reputation, which in turn boosts retention (a mediating effect), or do these factors act independently? This insight provides a clear strategic advantage by guiding investment in either branding or process improvements, a vital consideration in the competitive Philippine market (Bernardo et al., 2023).

Through SEM, the researchers can determine whether the organisation's reputation leads to a higher influx of skilled organisational members or if the presence of skilled organisational members increases the organisation's reputation and productivity. This analysis helps clarify the causal mechanisms at play and provide valuable insights into how various factors influence one another in organisational surroundings.

Whilst the quantitative method offers several advantages, such as its capability to generate accurate and objective data, it also has limitations. For instance, this approach may not fully capture the complexity of a phenomenon or provide a comprehensive exploration of subjective experiences (Cartwright & Igudia, 2023). Moreover, biases or errors may arise if the sample is not representative or if inappropriate statistical techniques are employed (Cronk, 2016).

Generally, the philosophy underpinning the quantitative method is rooted in the belief that knowledge can be accumulated through objective and empirical observation. This belief holds that such knowledge can then be used to make predictions and test hypotheses on a global scale (Rose et al., 2023).

7.7 Examples of Management Research Studies Applying the Quantitative Approach

In the realm of quantitative research, numerous practical applications illustrate the method's effectiveness in analysing numerical data and deriving insights. For instance, a company seeking to understand the factors influencing organisational members' satisfaction distributes a survey to its employees. This survey measures levels of satisfaction and gathers information on job responsibilities, compensation, benefits, and work environment. Statistical techniques are then employed to identify the factors most strongly associated with employee satisfaction. Similarly, researchers aiming to measure the effectiveness of a new marketing campaign design an experiment in which participants are randomly assigned to either a control group or a group exposed to the marketing intervention. By measuring changes in brand awareness and purchase intentions, and by applying various statistical tests, they assess whether or not the marketing campaign had significant effects.

In another example, researchers examine the relationship between the academic performance of students attending onsite classes versus those enrolled in online formats. They collect data on grades and attendance records, utilising independent sample t-tests to compare the academic outcomes between the two groups. Or, a restaurant chain endeavours to identify the factors influencing customer satisfaction by surveying its patrons about their dining experiences. The survey collects feedback on aspects such as food quality, service, atmosphere, and pricing. The chain then uses statistical techniques to discern which factors are most strongly associated with customers' satisfaction.

These examples illustrate how the quantitative method is applied to obtain numerical data, analyse it with statistical techniques, and test hypotheses to make predictions about a population based on a sample (Argyrous, 2011; Keith, 2019; Rose et al., 2023; Sekaran & Bougie, 2019).

7.8 In Relation to Hypotheses Testing

Hypothesis testing is a crucial statistical technique in academic management research utilised to assess the validity of hypotheses or predictions concerning the relationships between variables. Firstly, researchers formulate the null hypothesis (H_0), which asserts that there is no significant relationship between the variables under investigation. This null hypothesis is then contrasted with the alternative hypothesis (H_a), which suggests that a significant relationship does exist.

Secondly, researchers determine the levels of significance, which is typically set at 5% (corresponding to a 95% confidence interval) or 1% (corresponding to a 99% confidence interval). In social sciences, a 95% confidence interval is commonly used due to the less critical nature of the research outcomes. Conversely, in fields such as medical research, where outcomes can have more significant implications on critical matters such as health, a 99% confidence interval is often applied (Creamer, 2023).

Thirdly, data collection is conducted according to the research design. This stage involves selecting appropriate methods and channels for obtaining data, including online surveys distributed via email, blogs, or websites, as well as offline methods such as postal mail or in-person distribution. Effective planning is essential to address any potential issues arising during the data collection process.

Fourthly, the collected data is analysed using various statistical techniques. For instance, a t-test may be used to explore the relationship between two variables, whilst an F-test is appropriate for evaluating associations including more than two groups, such as comparing returns across organisations of different sizes (Field, 2024).

Finally, the results of the statistical analysis are interpreted by comparing the p-value obtained with the predetermined levels of significance. If the p-value is less than or equivalent to the levels of significance, the null hypothesis is rejected. If the p-value exceeds the significance level, the null hypothesis is not rejected (Kline, 2023). This systematic approach ensures a rigorous evaluation of hypotheses, enabling researchers to draw reliable conclusions about the relationships between variables in management research.

7.9 Hypothesis Testing Errors

In hypothesis testing, researchers strive to ascertain whether or not their hypotheses are substantiated by empirical evidence, thereby enabling informed conclusions about the relationships between observed variables. A critical component of this process involves understanding and managing Type I and Type II errors, as these can significantly influence the validity of research findings.

A Type I error, also known as a false positive, occurs when the null hypothesis is incorrectly rejected, despite its validity. In management research, this might manifest when a researcher erroneously concludes that a significant relationship exists between two variables. For example, if a study investigates the impact of a new marketing strategy on sales revenue and finds a significant effect where none exists, the organisation may make costly investments based on these misleading results (Stevens, 2002).

Similarly, a Type I error could arise in organisational members' performance evaluations if a manager inaccurately identifies high performers based on flawed metrics, leading to unwarranted promotions and compensation adjustments (Hanandeh et al., 2023). To illustrate a more general Type I error, consider a situation where the null hypothesis is posited as "This man is pregnant" despite the biological impossibility. Concluding that the null hypothesis is true would constitute a false positive, highlighting a fundamental flaw in the hypothesis rather than an actual finding. Whilst such an error might not lead to immediate jeopardy, it underscores the importance of formulating valid hypotheses and avoiding erroneous conclusions based on flawed premises.

Conversely, a Type II error, or false negative, arises when the null hypothesis is not rejected despite being false. This error transpires when research findings imply that there is no significant relationship between variables, even though a true relationship exists. For instance, if a study assessing the impact of organisational members' training programmes on different levels of productivity fails to detect a genuine positive effect, the organisation might forgo beneficial training programmes that could enhance overall performance (Fey et al., 2023). A more general illustration of a Type II error could be a scenario where the null hypothesis states, "This woman is not pregnant", whilst in reality, she is. Failing to detect the actual pregnancy represents a false negative, which could be detrimental by leading to the neglect of necessary prenatal care, thereby jeopardising the health of both the mother and the unborn child (Hanandeh et al., 2023). This example accentuates the critical importance of accurate detection and the potential consequences of failing to identify true conditions.

Understanding and managing Type I and Type II errors is paramount for confirming the robustness and validity of research findings. Type I errors are represented by alpha (α), whilst Type II errors are denoted by beta (β). As stressed above, Type I errors reflect the risk of detecting a non-existent effect, and Type II errors indicate the risk of failing to identify a genuine effect. Researchers must utilise rigorous study designs, ensure adequate sample sizes, and utilise thorough data analysis methods in order to minimise these errors, thereby bolstering sound, evidence-based decisions (Gelman et al., 1995; Wasserstein & Lazar, 2016).

7.10 Enhancing Research Creativity with AI

AI is transforming how researchers develop creative hypotheses. Instead of starting with a pre-existing theory, researchers can now utilise AI as a powerful assistant to explore immense amounts of data first. By analysing thousands of documents such as customer reviews or internal reports, AI can reveal surprising patterns and hidden connections, contributing to the generation of more innovative and data-driven research questions (Keding, 2021).

To illustrate, in studying rates of organisational members' turnover, a researcher might traditionally guess that salary is the main factor and test it in SPSS. An AI-augmented approach is more insightful. The AI can analyse not just salary data, but also thousands of written comments from exit interviews and performance reviews. It might discover that the tone of an organisational members' annual review is a more powerful predictor of them leaving than their salary. The AI acts as an intelligent filter, categorising the few most important factors from a huge pool of information. The researcher then takes these crucial factors into SPSS to perform a rigorous and focused statistical test, like a logistic regression. This makes the final analysis much stronger because it is based on evidence discovered in the data itself (Iyer et al., 2024).

Ultimately, AI does not replace traditional tools like SPSS; it makes them more effective. AI handles the broad, exploratory work of finding the most promising clues, whilst SPSS provides the established methods for careful, confirmatory testing. This partnership can even extend to creating "virtual companies" to simulate the impact of management decisions, allowing researchers to test creative "what-if" scenarios before they are applied in the real world (Shrestha et al., 2021). This synergy between AI's discovery power and the rigour of conventional statistics enables the development of richer and more robust management theories.

7.11 Chapter Summary

This chapter scrutinised hypothesis formulation and testing in the discipline of management research. It explained Type I errors (false positives) and Type II errors (false negatives) with practical examples. It emphasised the requirement for rigorous research design in order to avoid possible errors and certify reliable research findings.

7.12 Questions for Future Reflection

1. A management researcher wishes to investigate the effect of remote working on organisational members' productivity. Based on a preliminary literature review that suggests a positive effect, formulate a specific null hypothesis (H_0) and a directional (one-tailed) alternative hypothesis (H_a) for this study.
2. In the context of pharmaceutical research, a company is testing a new drug for a life-threatening illness. H_0 is that the drug has no effect. Explain the real-world consequences of making a Type I error versus a Type II error in this specific scenario. Which error would be more dangerous to commit, and why?
3. The chapter explains how to test hypotheses but does not distinguish between one-tailed and two-tailed tests. When would it be appropriate for a researcher to utilise a directional (one-tailed) hypothesis, and what is the primary statistical advantage of doing so?
4. A study comparing two different sales training programmes finds a statistically significant difference in performance ($p = 0.04$), but the actual difference in average sales between the two groups is very small. Why might relying solely on the p-value be misleading in this instance, and what other statistical information (e.g., effect size) would be crucial for making a sound business decision?
5. The chapter presents reductionism as a key characteristic of the quantitative approach. Using the example of studying 'organisational innovation', discuss one major advantage and one significant disadvantage of a reductionist approach. What aspects of innovation might be lost when it is broken down into measurable variables?
6. The Vietnamese SME study cited in the chapter found a strong correlation between quality of management and organisational members' loyalty. Does this finding, on its own, prove that greater management causes higher loyalty? Explain your reasoning, outlining what additional evidence would be required to make a stronger causal claim.
7. A researcher tests the hypothesis that a new performance management system enhances organisational members' engagement. The analysis yields a p-value of 0.21, with a pre-set significance level (alpha) of 0.05. State the correct conclusion in both formal statistical language (referencing the null hypothesis) and in plain English for a manager.

8. The chapter links the quantitative approach to hypothesis testing. Explain the vital role that a comprehensive literature review and established management theories play before the hypothesis testing stage even begins.
9. A researcher conducts an in-depth study on the leadership styles of managers within the Bangkok technology start-up scene and finds, counter-intuitively, that a directive, autocratic style is associated with higher team performance and faster project completion. To what extent can these findings be generalised to technology start-up scenes in other major Southeast Asian metropolitan hubs, such as Singapore, Jakarta, and Ho Chi Minh City?
10. The chapter uses a memorable example for a Type I error involving a "pregnant man". A Type I error is defined as incorrectly rejecting a true null hypothesis. Formulate the correct null hypothesis for this scenario and explain precisely how one would commit a Type I error. Does the chapter's original explanation accurately reflect this definition?

References

Aldrich, J. O. (2018). *Using IBM SPSS statistics: An interactive hands-on approach.* Sage Publications.

Argyrous, G. (2011). *Statistics for research: With a guide to SPSS.* Sage Publications.

Bernardo, A. L. D., Lacap, J. P. G., Talon, C. T., Bolante, P. S., Capalao, Z. J. T., Llado, M. C. E. A., & Dubrea, E. M. F. (2023). The mediating role of employee engagement on the link between person-organization fit and turnover intention: evidence from business process outsourcing companies in the Philippines. *Journal of Entrepreneurship & Business, 11*(2), 69–94.

Cartwright, E., & Igudia, E. (2023). The case for mixed methods research: Embracing qualitative research to understand the (informal) economy. *Review of Development Economics, 28*(4), 1947–1970. https://doi.org/10.1111/rode.13069

Creamer, E. G. (2023). Building theoretical insight through joint displays in mixed methods research. *School Psychology, 38*(6), 399–409. https://doi.org/10.1037/spq0000574

Cronk, B. C. (2016). *How to use IBM SPSS statistics: A step-by-step guide to analysis and interpretation.* Routledge.

Dai Quang, T., & Vo-Thanh, T. (2025). Vietnam Tourism Post-COVID-19: Overview and Current Challenges. *Routledge Handbook of Tourism and Hospitality Development in Vietnam*, 3–16.

Decuypere, A., & Schaufeli, W. (2021). Exploring the leadership–engagement nexus: A moderated meta-analysis and review of explaining mechanisms. *International Journal of Environmental Research and Public Health, 18*(16), 8592. https://doi.org/10.3390/ijerph18168592

Fey, C. F., Hu, T., & Delios, A. (2023). The measurement and communication of effect sizes in management research. *Management and Organization Review, 19*(1), 176–197. https://doi.org/10.1017/mor.2022.2

Field, A. (2024). *Discovering statistics using IBM SPSS statistics* (6th ed.). Sage Publications.

Gelman, A., Carlin, J. B., Stern, H. S., & Rubin, D. B. (1995). *Bayesian data analysis.* Chapman and Hall/CRC.

Ghauri, P. N., Grønhaug, K., & Strange, R. (2020). *Research methods in business studies.* Cambridge University Press.

Goel, D. (2023). *Performance appraisal and compensation management: A modern approach.* PHI Learning Pvt.

Hanandeh, A., Altaher, A., Halim, M., Rezk, W., Mahfoudh, N., Hammouri, Q., & Darawsheh, S. (2023). The effects of digital transformation, digital leadership, and entrepreneurial motivation on business decision making and business process performance: Evidence from greater Amman municipality. *International Journal of Data and Network Science, 7*(2), 575–582.

Iyer, V. H., Gupta, U., Somani, P. P., Behare, N., Mahajan, R., & Singh, M. (2024). The rise and rise of artificial intelligence in the world of finance. In *Risks and challenges of AI-driven finance: Bias, ethics, and security* (pp. 35–56). IGI Global.

Judge, T. A., Thoresen, C. J., Bono, J. E., & Patton, G. K. (2001). The job satisfaction–job performance relationship: A qualitative and quantitative review. *Psychological Bulletin, 127*(3), 376. https://doi.org/10.1037/0033-2909.127.3.376

Keding, C. (2021). Understanding the interplay of artificial intelligence and strategic management: Four decades of research in review. *Management Review Quarterly, 71*(1), 91–134.

Keith, T. Z. (2019). *Multiple regression and beyond: An introduction to multiple regression and structural equation modeling*. Routledge.

Kinnear, P. R., & Gray, C. D. (2019). *SPSS 26 made simple*. Psychology Press.

Kline, R. B. (2023). *Principles and practice of structural equation modeling* (5th ed.). Guilford Publications.

Rose, S., Spinks, N., & Canhoto, A. I. (2023). *Management research: Applying the Principles of Business Research Methods*. Taylor & Francis.

Sekaran, U., & Bougie, R. (2019). *Research methods for business: A skill-building approach* (7th ed.). Wiley.

Shrestha, Y. R., He, V. F., Puranam, P., & von Krogh, G. (2021). Algorithm supported induction for building theory: How can we use prediction models to theorise? *Organisation Science, 32*(3), 856–880.

Stevens, J. (2002). *Applied multivariate statistics for the social sciences* (4th ed.). Lawrence Erlbaum Associates.

Wasserstein, R. L., & Lazar, N. A. (2016). The ASA statement on p-values: Context, process, and purpose. *The American Statistician, 70*(2), 129–133. https://doi.org/10.1080/00031305.2016.1154108

Chapter 8
Quantitative Method Design and Data Analysis

8.1 Introduction

This chapter illustrates a variety of statistical techniques for testing research hypotheses, introducing both parametric and non-parametric inferential statistics. To provide practical examples pertinent to the management discipline, all statistical demonstrations were conducted using IBM Corp. (2022) under an authorised license from Khon Kaen University and are proposed strictly for academic purposes.

8.2 Quantitative Data Analysis

Quantitative data analysis employs statistical techniques to interpret numerical data, with academic management research involving several crucial steps. Initially, data cleaning is essential. This process involves identifying and addressing errors, missing values, and outliers in order to ensure data accuracy and integrity (Sürücü et al., 2023).

Following cleaning, descriptive statistics are applied to summarise the data, calculating measures such as mean, median, mode, standard deviation, and variance. This provides an overview of data distribution and central tendencies (Denis, 2018). Data exploration then uses visualisation tools, like scatter plots and histograms, to reveal patterns and relationships between variables.

Next, hypothesis testing occurs, employing statistical tests such as t-tests or one-way analysis of variance (ANOVA) to assess whether observed differences or relationships are statistically significant (Cohen et al., 2022). For more complex analyses involving multiple variables, multivariate techniques like multiple regression analysis (MRA) are applied to examine interactions and predict outcomes (Mertler et al., 2021).

Subsequently, interpretation of the results involves contextualising research findings within the research framework, drawing meaningful conclusions, and correlating

© The Author(s), under exclusive license to Springer Nature Singapore Pte Ltd. 2025

V. Zumitzavan, *Social Science Methodologies for Management Research*,
https://doi.org/10.1007/978-981-95-4318-2_8

results with the existing literature (Bryman, 2023). Finally, validation of the findings is crucial, involving checks for inconsistencies and seeking feedback from peers or experts to ensure robustness and reliability.

These steps are iterative and may overlap as researchers deepen their understanding of the data. The specific methods and techniques employed can vary depending on the research questions, data types, and overall research approach.

8.2.1 *Advantages of Quantitative Data Analysis*

Quantitative research is frequently esteemed for its objectivity compared to qualitative research. This is a result of its reliance on numerical data and statistical techniques. This reliance helps to minimise the influence of researcher bias, thereby enhancing the impartiality of the research findings (Cohen et al., 2022). A significant strength of quantitative research is its potential for generalisability. By using a greater number of sample sizes than typically utilised in qualitative research method, quantitative studies can extend their research findings to broader populations. For instance, a survey administered to a sizeable cohort of organisational members within an organisation can provide results that are indicative of the entire organisational members' population within that organisation (Fiandini et al., 2024).

In addition, another notable advantage is the replicability of quantitative research. The utilisation of standardised procedures and measurement tools allows for the replication of studies across different settings. This consistency not only aids in verifying the validity and reliability of the research findings but also supports the generalisation of results across numerous contexts (Field, 2024; Pallant, 2020).

8.2.2 *Disadvantages of Quantitative Data Analysis*

Quantitative research is often critiqued for providing less complex detail compared to qualitative approaches, which can mean the complexities of human behaviour and attitudes remain unrevealed. For example, a survey asking organisational members to rate their level of job satisfaction on a scale from 1 to 6 may not capture the deeper reasons behind their levels of satisfaction or dissatisfaction (Fink, 2015).

In addition, another limitation of quantitative research is its inflexibility. The reliance on standardised measures can restrict the adaptability of research methods, making it challenging to adjust the approach as new insights emerge (Johnson & Christensen, 2024).

Moreover, despite its reputation for objectivity, quantitative research can still be prone to bias in its design or analysis. For instance, if a sample is not representative or if imperfect statistical techniques are employed, the validity of the research findings may be compromised. For a study examining the relationship between levels of education (years of schooling) and salary (monthly income), a diverse sample is crucial for accurately assessing the impact of education on salary. The Pearson correlation coefficient, suitable for ratio scale data, is an appropriate statistical method for this analysis (George & Mallery, 2019).

Ultimately, the choice of research approach depends on the research question, the type of data, and available resources. Whilst quantitative research provides valuable insights into broad patterns and is often more objective and replicable than qualitative methods, it can be limited by its lack of detail and its methodological rigidity (Mertler et al., 2021).

8.2.3 *Augmenting Quantitative Analysis with Artificial Intelligence*

AI and machine learning improve quantitative analysis in management research by extending predictive capability and allowing the discovery of complex patterns beyond the reach of traditional statistical methods such as t-tests or ANOVA. Rather than substituting these techniques, AI complements them, ever-changing research from solely testing predefined hypotheses to generating novel, data-driven ones.

- Hypothesis Generation—AI can analyse large datasets to categorise unexpected but significant predictors. For instance, in customers' satisfaction research, it might reveal non-linear effects arising from specific combinations of marketing channels and support services, contributing to richer hypotheses for subsequent testing (Davenport & Ronanki, 2018).
- Predictive Modelling—Whilst Multiple Regression Analysis (MRA) captures linear relationships, AI methods such as neural networks or random forests can model complex, non-linear interactions. In sales projecting, AI may indicate that key drivers such as advertising spend and salesperson experience are effective only under certain economic conditions, offering managers with more precise, actionable insights (Rane et al., 2024).

By revealing these subtleties, AI reinforces quantitative research, cultivating question formulation and enhancing the strategic value of findings.

8.3 Inferential Parametric Statistics for the Quantitative Approach

8.3.1 *Paired Sample t-Test*

The paired sample t-test is a statistical technique used to analyse the relationship between two continuous variables measured from the same source. This method is particularly useful for comparing measurements taken at two different times, such as before and after an event. For instance, the paired sample t-test can assess changes in organisational members' scores on a Microsoft Applications test administered before and after a training workshop.

By comparing these pre- and post-training scores, the test determines whether there is a statistically significant difference, indicating whether the training had an effect on the employees' performance (Vieira Jr., 2017; Privitera, 2023).

8.3.1.1 Fundamental Assumptions

1. Both variables are in the forms of either interval or ratio scales.
2. Samples must be randomly collected.
3. Data are normally distributed.

8.3.1.2 Test of Normality

Fundamentally, for the paired sample t-test technique, the data must be distributed normally, so firstly the data need to be test for normal distribution.

8.3.1.3 Hypothesis Testing for Normal Distribution

H_0: The data are normally distributed.
H_a: The data are not normally distributed (Figs. 8.1, 8.2, 8.3, 8.4, 8.5, 8.6, 8.7, 8.8, 8.9, and 8.10).

There are two set of data: (1) pre-score and (2) post-score. As shown in Figs. 8.11, 8.12, 8.13, 8.14, 8.15 and 8.16, firstly the pre- and post-scores must be subtracted, and then the new variable (known as Diff) should be added into the descriptive statistics box to test the normality distribution. For testing the normality distribution test, firstly go to 'Analyse', 'Descriptive Statistics', and then 'Explore'. The 'Diff' variable must be added into the 'Dependent Variable Box', then select 'Plots'. The Explore Plots Box will pop up, and then select 'Normality Plots with Test', and on the 'Box Plots' select 'Factor Level Together', and in 'Descriptive Box' select 'Stem-and-Leaf' and 'Histogram', then select 'Continue' and 'OK' at the end.

In addition, the shape of the variable will appear, as shown in Fig. 8.7 and Fig. 8.8 As shown in Table 8.1, there will be two different results, which are Kolmogorov-Smirnov, and Shapiro-Wilk. If the dataset is composed of 50 or more cases, see the results at the Kolmogorov-Smirnov box. If it is composed of less than 50, see the results at the Shapiro-Wilk box. For this example, the dataset is less than 50; hence, look at the results in the Shapiro-Wilk box, i.e., 0.66, which is greater than 0.05. Therefore, the null hypothesis has been accepted, and it can be concluded that the data are normally distributed.

For example; is there a relationship between the leadership performance of managers and training before and after attending a leadership workshop for Small to

Fig. 8.1 Test of normality

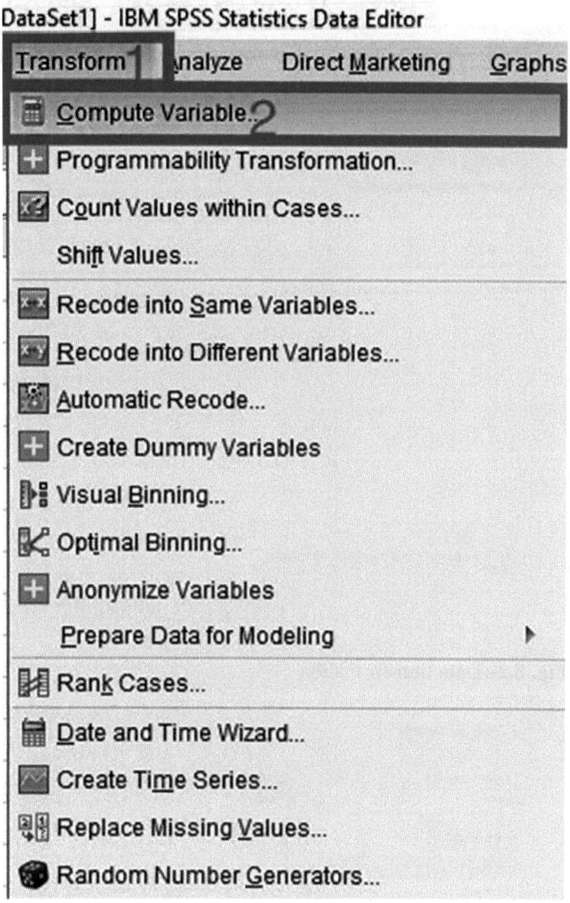

Medium Enterprises: SMEs in Northeast Thailand? The data of the 30 respondents who are SMEs managers were collected by providing a multiple-choice test to all the respondents before and after attending the workshop. Hence, the pre- and post-scores of the test are analysed by using the paired sample t-test technique (confidence interval = 95%, $\alpha = 0.05$).

8.3.1.4 Hypothesis Testing

H_0: $\mu_{\text{Pre-test scores}} = \mu_{\text{Post-test scores}}$ There is no statistical difference between the pre-test and post-test scores.

H_a: $\mu_{\text{Pre-test scores}} \neq \mu_{\text{Post-test scores}}$ There is a statistical difference between the pre-test and post-test scores.

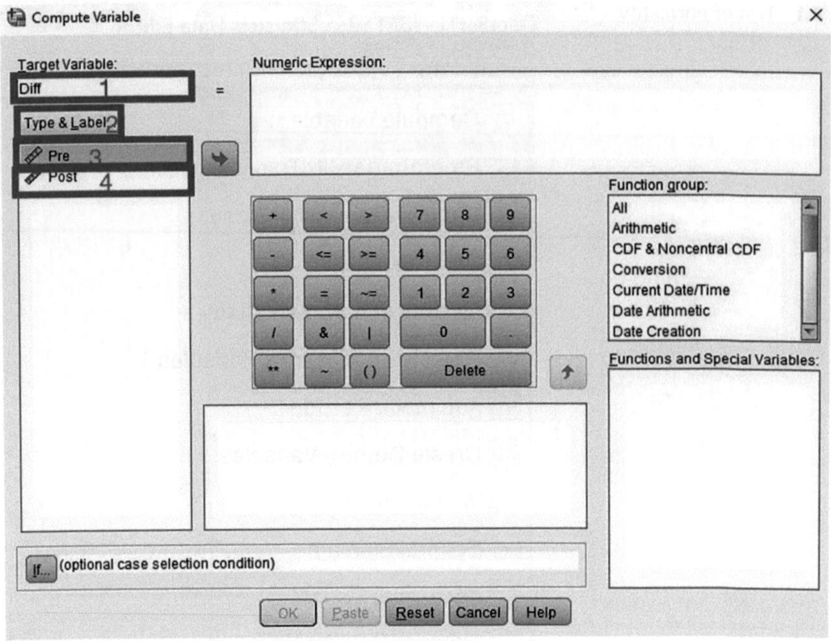

Fig. 8.2 Data transformation

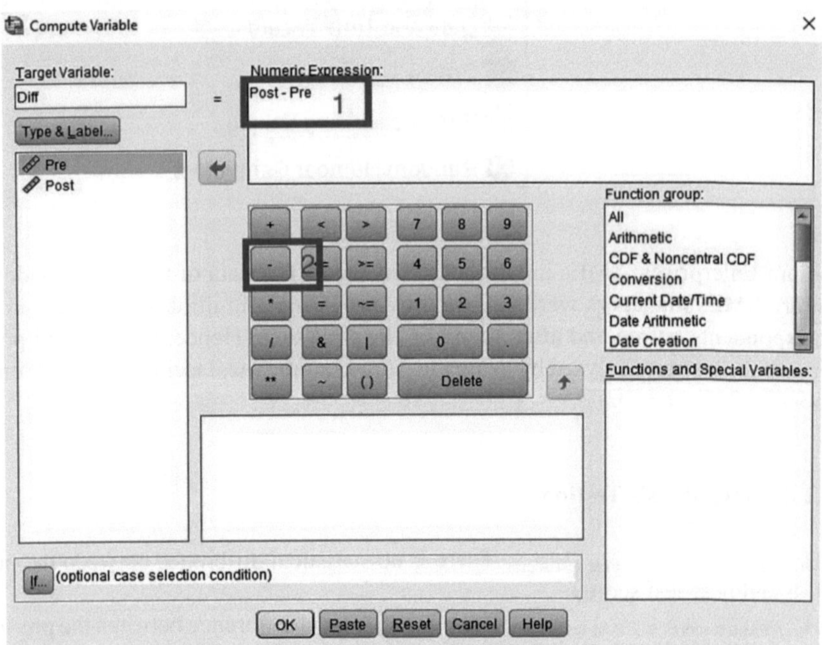

Fig. 8.3 Compute variable

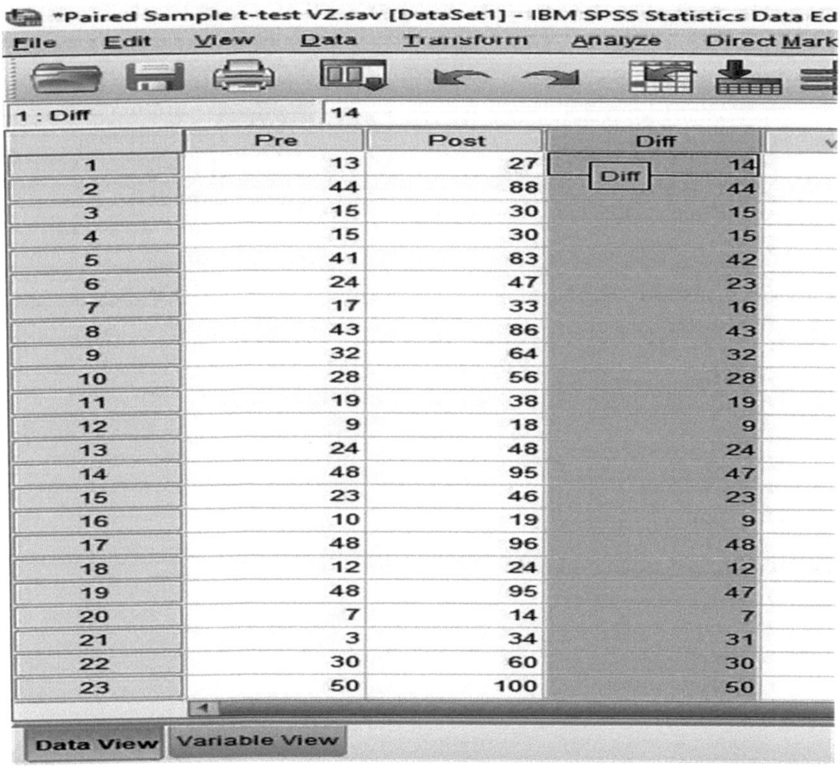

	Pre	Post	Diff
1	13	27	14
2	44	88	44
3	15	30	15
4	15	30	15
5	41	83	42
6	24	47	23
7	17	33	16
8	43	86	43
9	32	64	32
10	28	56	28
11	19	38	19
12	9	18	9
13	24	48	24
14	48	95	47
15	23	46	23
16	10	19	9
17	48	96	48
18	12	24	12
19	48	95	47
20	7	14	7
21	3	34	31
22	30	60	30
23	50	100	50

Fig. 8.4 Paired sample t-test

As indicated in Fig. 8.10, the *p*-value = 0.000 is lower than 0.05; hence, the null hypothesis is rejected. This means that there is a statistical difference between the pre-test and post-test scores, when considering the mean differences of the pre-test and post-test scores, which is equivalent to 28.400.

Hence, the mean score of the post-test is greater than the mean of the pre-test score, meaning that when the managers were attending the leadership workshop, their leadership skills developed.

8.3.2 Independent Sample t-Test

The independent-sample t-test is a statistical method used to investigate the relationship between two variables where the independent variable is categorical and the dependent variable is continuous. This test compares the means of two unrelated groups.

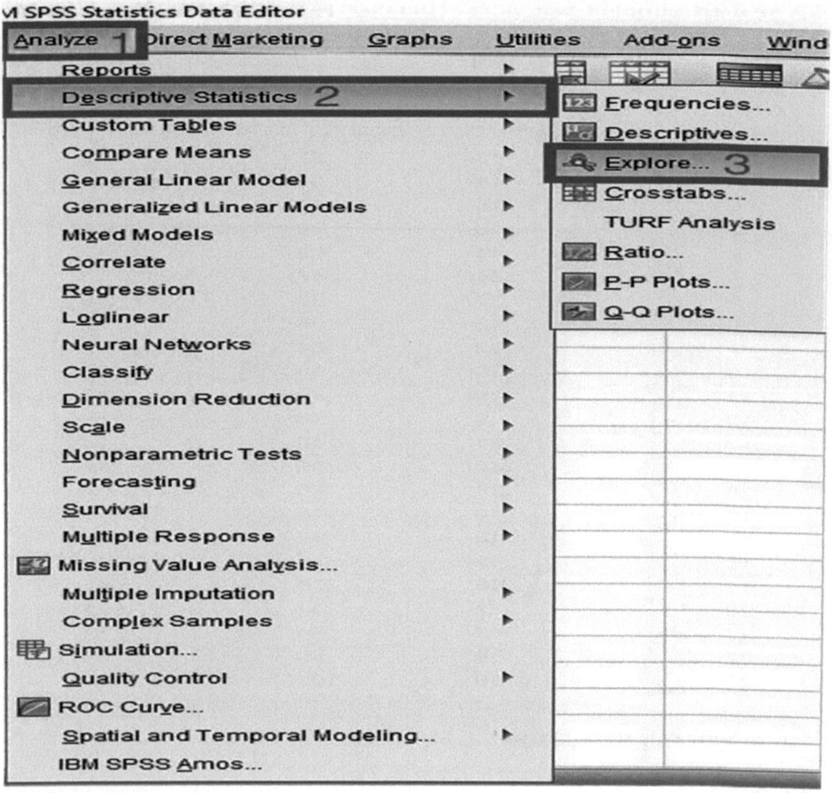

Fig. 8.5 Statistics data editor

For example, the independent-sample t-test can be employed to compare exam scores between male and female students in the same class, with males coded as 0 and females as 1. The test determines whether there is a statistically significant difference in exam scores between the two groups (Laerd Statistics, 2021; Spencer, 2013).

8.3.2.1 Fundamental Assumptions

1. The two groups of independent variables are not related and they are in the form of either nominal or ordinal scales whilst the dependent variable is the ratio scale.
2. Samples must be randomly collected.
3. Data are normally distributed.

Firstly, the dependent variable must be tested to clarify that it is normally distributed. After that, the hypothesis testing can be performed.

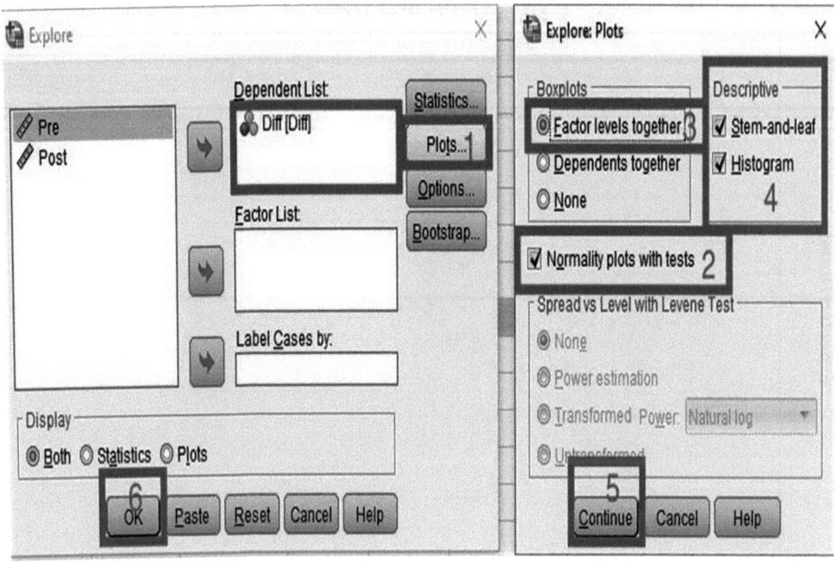

Fig. 8.6 Normality plots with tests

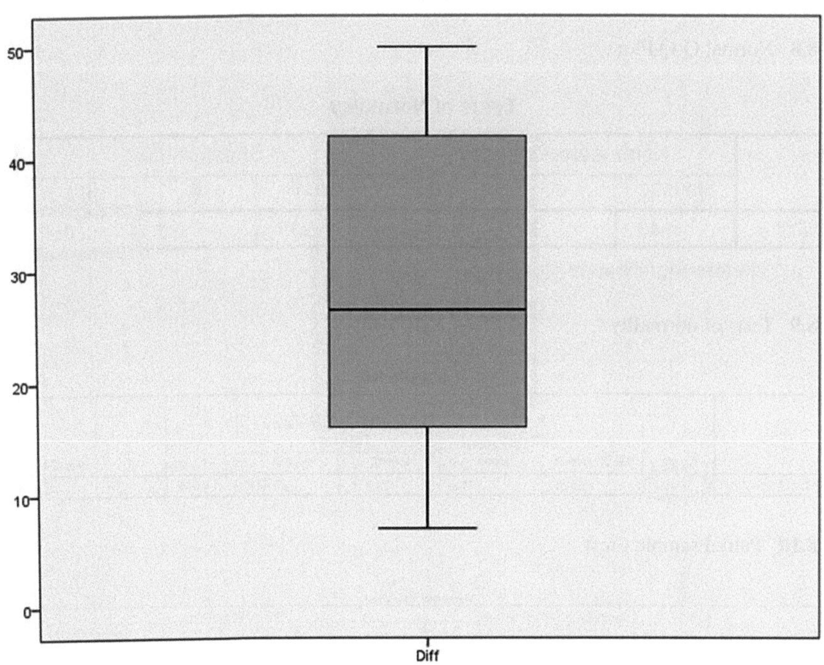

Fig. 8.7 Box Plot

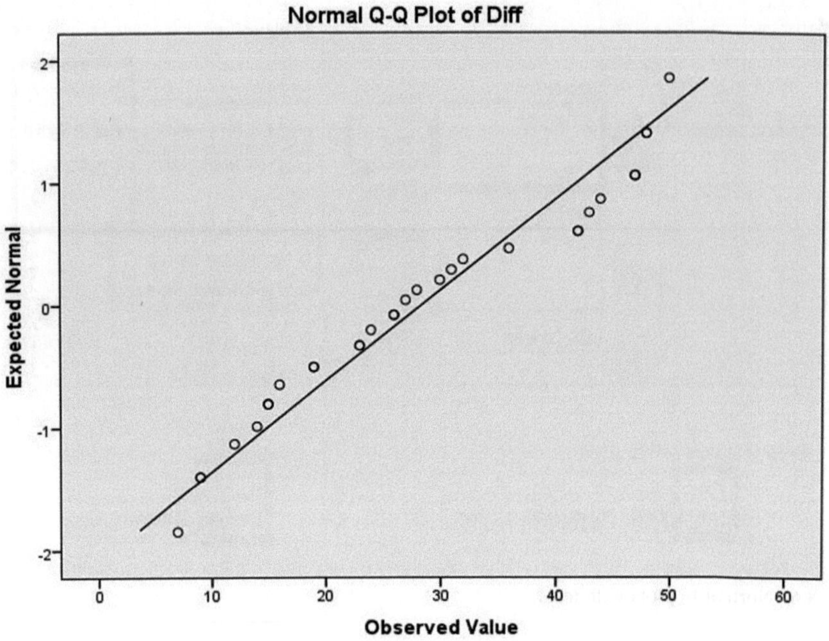

Fig. 8.8 Normal Q-Q Plot

Tests of Normality

	Kolmogorov-Smirnov[a]			Shapiro-Wilk		
	Statistic	df	Sig.	Statistic	df	Sig.
Diff	.143	30	.122	.935	30	.066

a. Lilliefors Significance Correction

Fig. 8.9 Tests of normality

Paired Samples Test

	Paired Differences					t	df	Sig. (2-tailed)
				95% Confidence Interval of the Difference				
	Mean	Std. Deviation	Std. Error Mean	Lower	Upper			
Pair 1 Post - Pre	28.400	13.520	2.468	23.351	33.449	11.505	29	.000

Fig. 8.10 Paired sample t-test

Independent Samples Test

		Levene's Test for Equality of Variances		t-test for Equality of Means						
			1			2	3		95% Confidence Interval of the Difference	
		F	Sig.	t	df	Sig. (2-tailed)	Mean Difference	Std. Error Difference	Lower	Upper
Score of the test	Equal variances assumed	.019	.891	2.830	28	.009	27.833	9.836	7.686	47.981
	Equal variances not assumed			2.854	24.423	.009	27.833	9.751	7.727	47.939

Fig. 8.11 Results of the independent sample t-test

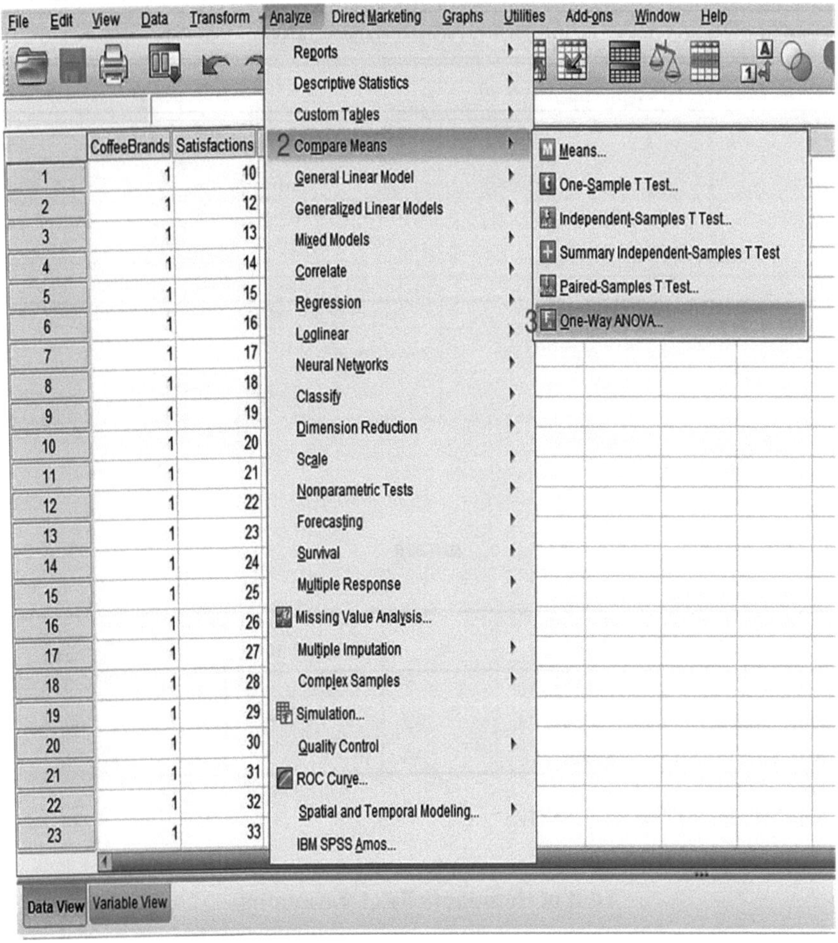

Fig. 8.12 One-Way ANOVA[1]

Example: To what extents is there a relationship between the diligent and not diligent groups of students in the Master of Public Administration programme, and what is the hypothesis testing for the variances of the two groups?

H_0: $\sigma^2_{\text{Diligent Group}} = \sigma^2_{\text{Undiligent Group}}$ = The variances of the two groups of independent variables are not statistically different.
H_1: $\sigma^2_{\text{Diligent Group}} = \sigma^2_{\text{Undiligent Group}}$ = The variances of the two groups of independent variables are statistically different.

As indicated in Fig. 8.11, the *p*-value = 0.891, which is greater than 0.05; hence, the null hypothesis or H_0 is accepted. This suggests that the variances of the two groups of independent variables are not statistically different (see Number 1 in Fig. 8.11).

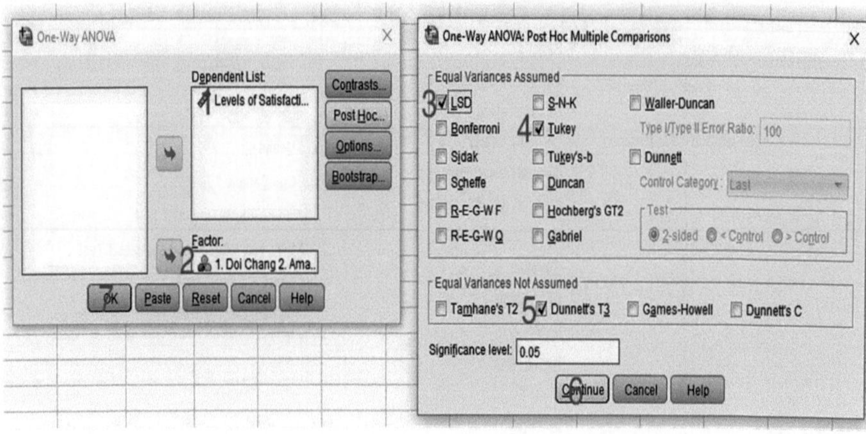

Fig. 8.13 One-Way ANOVA[2]

ANOVA

Levels of Satisfaction

	Sum of Squares	df	Mean Square	F	Sig.
Between Groups	53659.336	2	26829.668	417.681	.000
Within Groups	6230.774	97	64.235		
Total	59890.110	99			

Fig. 8.14 Results of One-Way ANOVA

Test of Homogeneity of Variances

Levels of Satisfaction

Levene Statistic	df1	df2	Sig.
4.056	2	97	.020

Fig. 8.15 Results of homogeneity of variances

8.3.2.2 Hypothesis Testing for the Independent Sample t-Test

H_0: $\sigma^2_{\text{Diligent Group}} = \sigma^2_{\text{Undiligent Group}}$ = There is no statistical difference between the diligent and not diligent groups of students for the different levels of scores.
H_1: $\sigma^2_{\text{Diligent Group}} = \sigma^2_{\text{Undiligent Group}}$ = There is a statistical difference between the diligent and not diligent groups of students for the different levels of scores.

Post Hoc Tests

Multiple Comparisons

Dependent Variable: Levels of Satisfaction

	(I) 1. Doi Chang 2. Amazon 3. Starbucks	(J) 1. Doi Chang 2. Amazon 3. Starbucks	Mean Difference (I-J)	Std. Error	Sig.	95% Confidence Interval	
						Lower Bound	Upper Bound
Tukey HSD	1	2	-30.697*	1.973	.000	-35.39	-26.00
		3	-56.560*	1.959	.000	-61.22	-51.90
	2	1	30.697*	1.973	.000	26.00	35.39
		3	-25.863*	1.959	.000	-30.52	-21.20
	3	1	56.560*	1.959	.000	51.90	61.22
		2	25.863*	1.959	.000	21.20	30.52
LSD	1	2	-30.697*	1.973	.000	-34.61	-26.78
		3	-56.560*	1.959	.000	-60.45	-52.67
	2	1	30.697*	1.973	.000	26.78	34.61
		3	-25.863*	1.959	.000	-29.75	-21.98
	3	1	56.560*	1.959	.000	52.67	60.45
		2	25.863*	1.959	.000	21.98	29.75
Dunnett T3	1	2	-30.697*	2.087	.000	-35.82	-25.57
		3	-56.560*	2.078	.000	-61.66	-51.46
	2	1	30.697*	2.087	.000	25.57	35.82
		3	-25.863*	1.716	.000	-30.06	-21.66
	3	1	56.560*	2.078	.000	51.46	61.66
		2	25.863*	1.716	.000	21.66	30.06

*. The mean difference is significant at the 0.05 level.

Fig. 8.16 Results of multiple comparisons

Table 8.1 Number of samples

Brand of Coffee Shop	*N*
1. Doi Chang	33
2. Amazon	33
3. Starbucks	34

As shown in Fig. 8.11, *p*-value = 0.009, which is lower 0.05; hence, the H_0 or null hypothesis is rejected. This means that there is a statistical difference between the diligent and not diligent groups of students for the different levels of scores (see Number 2 in Fig. 8.11).

In addition, to understand the different levels of the scores, the mean difference provides more details. The mean difference of the group of students who are diligent is greater than the group of students who are not diligent and is equivalent to 27.833. This suggests that the average scores of the diligent group is greater than those of the not diligent group by 27.833 or approximately 28 points (see Number 3 in Fig. 8.11).

8.3.3 *One-Way Analysis of Variance (ANOVA)*

A one-way analysis of variance (ANOVA) is a statistical technique employed to examine the relationship between an independent variable, which consists of two or more groups (categorical variables of either nominal or ordinal scale), and a dependent variable measured on a ratio scale (Montgomery, 2017). Specifically, a one-way ANOVA investigates whether the means of the dependent variable differ significantly across the k groups of the independent variable (Howell, 2013). This method is used to determine if the k groups exert different degrees of influence on the dependent variable (Privitera, 2023).

8.3.3.1 Fundamental Assumptions

1. Independent variable: The independent variable should consist of two or more groups which are categorical in nature and can be classified as nominal or ordinal scales. These groups, denoted ask, must be at least two in number.
2. Dependent variable: The dependent variable must be measured on an interval or ratio scale. It is essential that the dependent variable is not categorical but rather continuous in nature.
3. Sample collection: The samples must be collected randomly and independently to ensure the validity of the results.
4. Homogeneity of variances: It is assumed that the populations from which the samples are drawn have equal variances (homoscedasticity).

   Before performing hypothesis testing using a one-way ANOVA, it is crucial to test the dependent variable to ensure it is normally distributed. Once this condition is verified, hypothesis testing can proceed.

Example 3.To determine whether there is a relationship between customers' satisfaction levels across different coffee shop brands in Thailand, namely, Doi Chang (coded as 1), Amazon (coded as 2), and Starbucks (coded as 3), and to identify which brand achieves the highest customer satisfaction score (with a maximum score of 100), you would employ a one-way ANOVA. This statistical method will assess whether or not there are significant differences in customers' satisfaction levels across the three brands.

As shown in Figs. 8.12 and 8.13, firstly, go to 'Analyse', 'Compare Means', and then select 'One-Way ANOVA'. On the box of the 'Dependent List' place the dependent variable (Level of Satisfaction of the customers), and on the box of 'Factor', select the independent variables: brands of coffee shops: (1) Doi Chang, (2) Amazon, and (3) Starbucks.

8.3.3.2 Hypothesis Testing for One-Way ANOVA

H_0: $\mu_1 = \mu_2 = \mu_3 = \ldots = \mu_k$; The mean customer satisfaction scores for Doi Chang ($\mu 1$), Amazon ($\mu 2$), and Starbucks ($\mu 3$) are all equal.
H_a: At least one of the mean customer satisfaction scores for Doi Chang, Amazon, or Starbucks is different from the others.

As indicated in Fig. 8.14, the *p*-value is equal to 0.000, which is less than 0.05; hence, the null hypothesis is rejected. This suggests that at least one of the mean customer satisfaction scores for Doi Chang, Amazon, or Starbucks is different from the others.

8.3.3.3 Hypothesis Testing for Variances

H_0: ${\sigma^2}_1 = {\sigma^2}_2 = {\sigma^2}_3$ There is no significant difference between the variances of the three different groups.
H_a: At least one variance of the three different groups is different from the others.

Subsequently, as shown in Fig. 8.15, the results of the homogeneity of variances test explains that *p*-value is equal to 0.02, which is lower than 0.05; therefore, the null hypothesis is rejected. There is a significant difference between the variances of the different groups of coffee shops. As a result, the Dunnett T3 test is used to verify the mean difference.

Next, as demonstrated in Fig. 8.16, Results of Multiple Comparisons, Starbucks achieved higher levels of satisfaction than Doi Chang when considering the mean difference, which is 56.560, and Starbucks is also greater than Amazon, with the mean difference being 25.863, and Amazon is greater than Doi Chang, with the mean difference being 30.697. This suggests that in terms of level of customer satisfaction, Starbucks is the best, followed by Amazon, and finally, Doi Chang.

8.3.4 One-Way Analysis of Covariances (ANCOVA)

A one-way analysis of covariance (ANCOVA) is a statistical method used to examine the impact of one or more categorical independent variables on a continuous dependent variable, whilst controlling for the effects of additional continuous covariates. A one-way ANCOVA adjusts the dependent variable's means for differences in the covariates, allowing for a more precise comparison of the group means.

To fully comprehend a one-way ANCOVA, it is essential to first understand a one-way ANOVA (see above). A one-way ANOVA is employed to determine whether there are statistically significant differences between the means of two or more independent groups. It tests the null hypothesis that all group means are equal, assessing whether the observed differences in means are greater than what would be expected due to random variation alone (Gravetter & Wallnau, 2017).

For example, to what extent are the means of different study techniques and exam scores for a Negotiation Skills workshop for local administrators different? The workshop is randomly divided into three groups. Each group uses a different study technique for one month to prepare for an exam. At the end of the month, all of the local administrators take the same exam. To discover whether or not the mean of different studying techniques influences exam scores, a one-way ANOVA is applied, which should help identify if there is a statistically significant difference between the mean scores of the three groups.

A one-way ANCOVA is an extension of a one-way ANOVA in which the aim is to test if there is a statistically significant difference between two or more independent categories after accounting for one or more covariates. A covariate is a continuous variable which co-varies with the response variable.

For example, whether or not different brands of coffee shop have an influence on level of satisfaction is the response variable, but the brand image of the coffee shop is also related to the different levels of satisfaction that the respondents perceive once they have been using the services of the coffee shop. The level of the brand image of the coffee shop is considered to be a covariate, and a one-way ANCOVA is conducted to determine if there is a statistically significant difference between the mean of the three different brands of the coffee shop and different levels of satisfaction. The sample is 100 respondents, namely customers experiencing the services of the three different brands of coffee shop, i.e., 1. Doi Chang, 2. Amazon, and 3. Starbucks. The covariate variable is the different levels of brand image that the customers rate (full score is 100 points) whilst the dependent variable is different levels of satisfaction (full score is 100 points).

8.3.4.1 Fundamental Assumptions

1. The covariate(s) and the factor variable(s) are independent: The covariate and the factor variable should be independent of each other, since adding a covariate term into the model only makes sense if the covariate and the factor variable act independently on the response variable.
2. The covariate(s) is/are continuous data, i.e., either interval or ratio data.
3. Homogeneity of variances: The variances among the groups should be roughly equal.
4. Independence: The observations in each group should be independent.
5. Normality: The data should be normally distributed in each group.
6. No extreme outliers: There should be no extreme outliers in any of the groups that could significantly affect the results of the ANCOVA.

More importantly, before applying the ANCOVA to test the relationship between the Independent (X = Categorical Scale), Covariate (Z = Ratio Scale), and Dependent Variables (Y = Ratio Scale), the relationship between Z and Y must be tested by applying the Pearson correlation statistical technique to see whether there is a statistically significant difference between the two variables. If so, the ANCOVA can be applied. The main reason to use the ANCOVA is that it would help control for the intervening or covariate variable.

As illustrated in Figs. 8.17 and 8.18, to analyse the relationship between Z (covariate variable) and Y (dependent variable), the Pearson correlation coefficient is applied. Firstly, select 'Analyse', 'Correlate', and then 'Bivariate'. Then select 'Brand Image' (Z = Covariate Variable), and 'Levels of Satisfactions' (Y = Dependent Variable), and finally choose 'OK'.

As shown in Figs. 8.19 and 8.20, to analyse the relationship between the Independent, Covariate, and Dependent Variables by using ANCOVA, firstly, select 'Analyse', 'General Linear Model', and then 'Univariate'. Choose 'Levels of Satisfactions' and place into 'Dependent Box', select 'Brands of Coffeeshop' and place

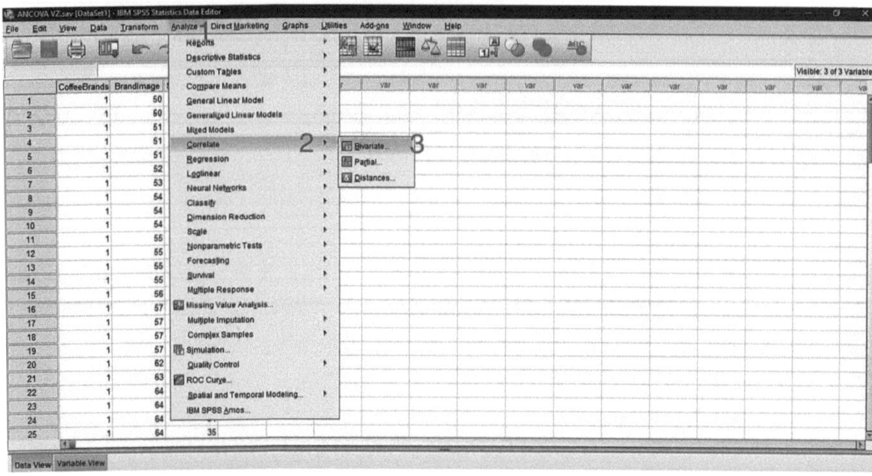

Fig. 8.17 Pearson correlation[1]

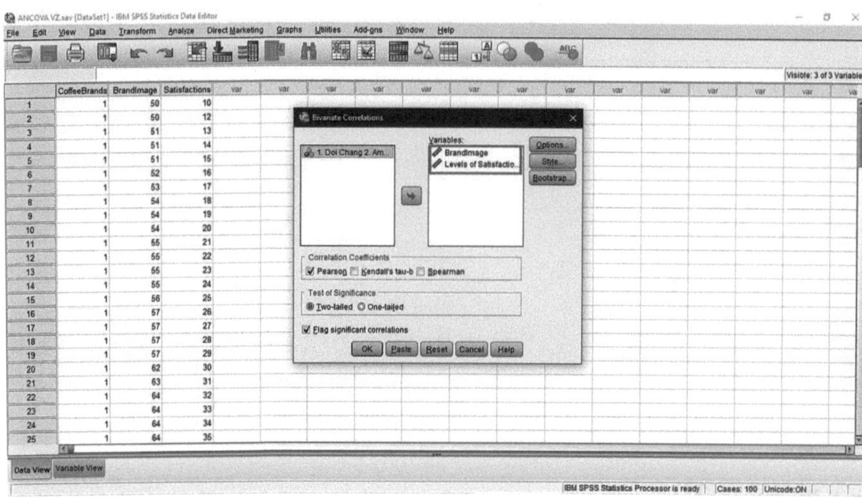

Fig. 8.18 Pearson correlation[2]

into 'Fixed Factor(s)', and select 'Brand Image' and place into 'Covariate Box', and then click 'Options', and finally click 'OK' (Table 8.2) (Fig. 8.21).

H_0: There is not a statistically significant difference in the relationship between Brand Image and Level of Satisfaction.
H_a: There is a statistically significant difference in the relationship between Brand Image and Level of Satisfaction.

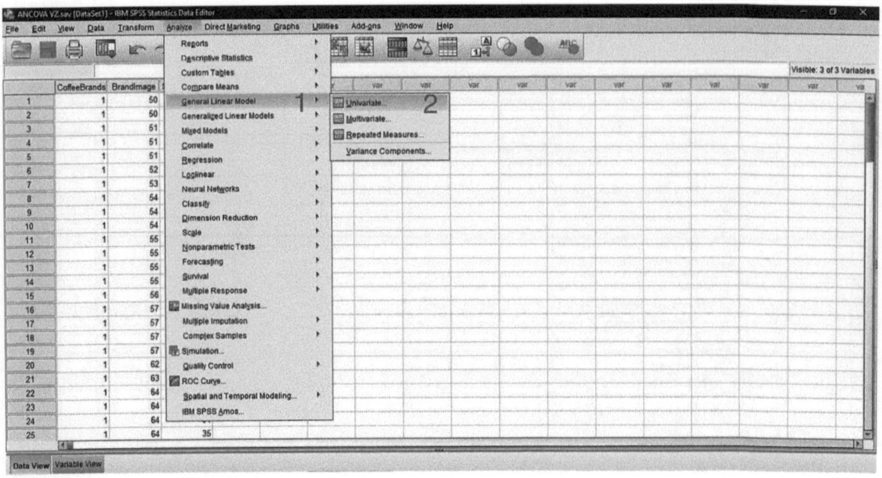

Fig. 8.19 ANCOVA[1]

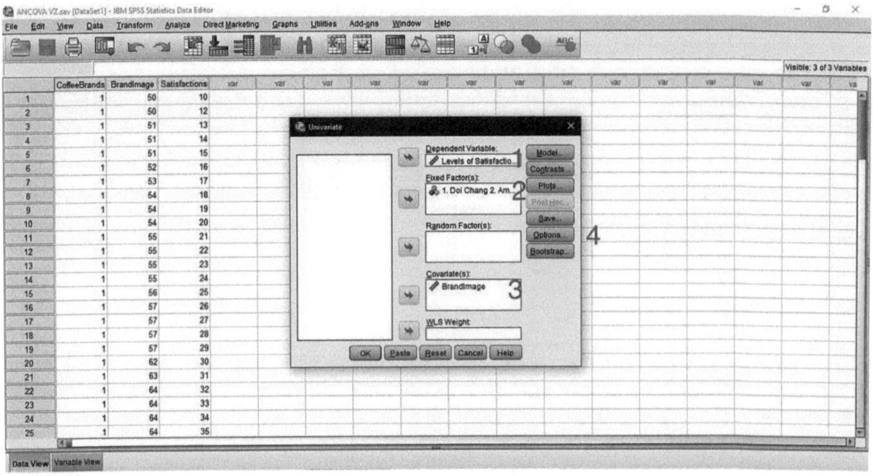

Fig. 8.20 ANCOVA[2]

Table 8.2 Descriptive statistics

Brand of Coffee Shop	Mean	Std. Deviation
1. Doi Chang	26.97	9.723
2. Amazon	57.67	7.016
3. Starbucks	83.53	7.029
Total	56.33	24.596

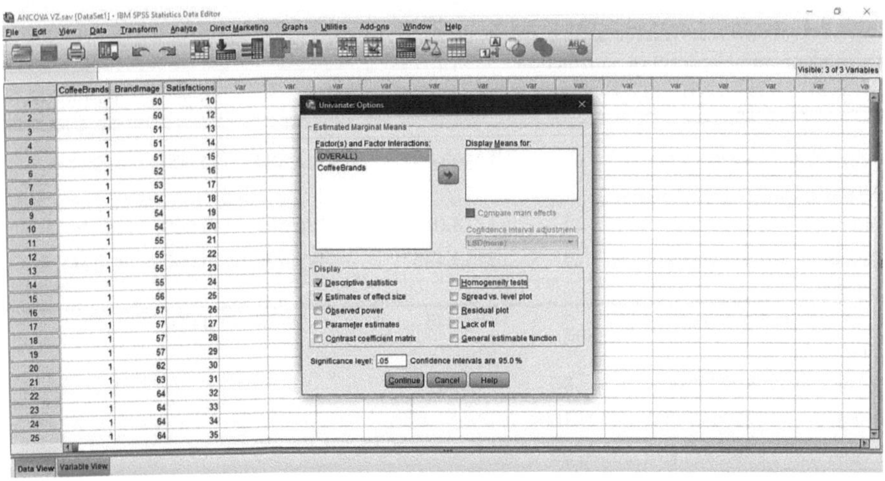

Fig. 8.21 ANCOVA[3]

As indicated in Table 8.3, the *p*-value is 0.000, which is less than 0.050. Hence, the null hypothesis is rejected. This means that there is a statistically significant difference in the relationship between Brand Image and Level of Satisfaction. This means that Brand Image has an impact on the different levels of satisfactions; hence, Brand Image is acting as an intervening variable covariate and needs to be controlled in order to see the actual impact on the different brands of coffee shop. Hence, a one-way ANCOVA is applied to test the relationship between the variables.

H_0: There is no relationship between the three brands of coffee shop and level of satisfaction, controlling for brand image. The means of the brands of coffee shop are not statistically different.
H_a: There is a relationship between the three groups of brands of coffee shop and level of satisfaction, controlling for brand image. At least one of the mean of the brands of coffee shop is statistically different from the others.

As indicated in Table 8.4, the *p*-value is 0.000, which is less than 0.050; hence, the null hypothesis is rejected. This means that there is a relationship between the three brands of coffee shop and level of satisfaction, controlling for brand image. At least one of the mean of brands of coffee shop is statistically different from the

Table 8.3 Results of correlations between brand image and level of satisfaction ($N = 100$)

Variables		Brand Image	Levels of Satisfactions
Brand Image	Pearson Correlation	1	0.989*
	Sig. (2-tailed)		0.000

*Correlation is significant at the 0.010 level (2-tailed)

Table 8.4 Results of tests of between-subjects effects

Dependent variable: level of satisfaction

Source	Type III sum of squares	df	Mean square	F	Sig.	Partial Eta squared
Corrected Model	58792.772[a]	3	19597.591	1714.484	0.000	0.982
Intercept	1218.052	1	1218.052	106.561	0.000	0.526
Brand Image	5133.435	1	5133.435	449.096	0.000	0.824
Coffee Brands	208.686	2	104.343	9.128	0.000	0.160
Error	1097.338	96	11.431			
Total	377197.000	100				
Corrected total	59890.110	99				

[a] R Squared = 0.982 (Adjusted R Squared = 0.981)

others. Moreover, the results suggest that when controlling for the covariate (Brand Image), at least the mean of one brand of coffee shop is different from the others.

8.3.5 *Two-Way Analysis of Variance (ANOVA)*

The two-way ANOVA is a statistical technique applied to compare the mean differences between groups that have been split on two independent variables (so-called 'factors'). The primary purpose of a two-way ANOVA is to understand to what extent there is an interaction between the two independent variables (at least 2 different groups) on the dependent variable.

For instance, a two-way ANOVA could be utilised when researchers want to investigate whether or not there is an interaction between gender and teaching method on the examination score of graduate students, where gender (male/female) and teaching method (project-based/lecture-based teaching) are independent variables, and examination score is the dependent variable.

The interaction term in a two-way ANOVA informs researchers whether or not the effects of one of the independent variables on the dependent variable is the same for all values of the other independent variable (and vice versa).

8.3.5.1 Fundamental Assumptions

1. There are two independent variables which are either nominal or ordinal scales.
2. The covariate(s) are continuous data, i.e., either interval or ratio data.

Table 8.5 Matrix of independent variables

Teaching Method	Gender	
	Male	Female
Project-Based Method	μ Project-Based Method Males	μ Project-Based Method Females
Lecture-Based Method	μ Lecture-Based Method Males	μ Lecture-Based Method Females

3. Homogeneity of variances: The variances among the groups should be roughly equal.
4. Independence: The observations in each group should be independent.
5. Normality: The data should be normally distributed in each group.

For example, are the effects of gender (male/female) on examination score influenced by teaching method (project-based/lecture-based teaching)? In addition, if there is no significant difference for the interaction, this is known as the random block design (RBD). Researchers need to explain the findings by considering the 'Main Effects' by reviewing the descriptive results of the groups of the independent variables. More importantly, in case there is a significant difference for the interaction, known as 'factorial design', researchers could explain this by illustrating the effects of the independent variables on the dependent variables via graphs (Auamnoy, 2002) (Table 8.5).

8.3.5.2 Three Hypotheses

Hypothesis 1; Main effect 1 (X_1) = Teaching Methods = H_0: μProject-Based Method = μLecture-Based Method.
Hypothesis 2; Main effect 2 (X_2) = Gender = H_0: μMales = μFemales.
Hypothesis 3; Interaction = Gender = μProject-Based Method Males = μProject-Based Method Females = μLecture-Based Method Males = μLecture-Based Method Females.

As illustrated in Fig. 8.22 Two-Way ANOVA, firstly select 'Analyse', and then select 'General Linear Models', and finally select 'Univariate'.

As indicated in Fig. 8.23, Two-Way ANOVA, firstly select 'Examination Scores' and place it into the 'Dependent Variable' box. and then select 'Gender' and 'Teaching Methods' into the 'Fixed Factor(s)' box, and finally click 'OK'.

As indicated in Fig. 8.24 Descriptive Results, the sample comprises 100 people, comprising 47 males, and 53 females, 55 project-based, and 45 lecture-based methods.

As illustrated in Fig. 8.25 Results of Test of Between-Subjects Effects, the *p*-value is equal to 0.000, suggesting that at least one mean group of the independent variables is statistically different from the others. Hence, the null hypothesis is rejected. The *p*-value of the interaction is equal to 0.154, which is greater than 0.05, meaning that an interaction between Gender and Teaching Methods is not found. Moreover,

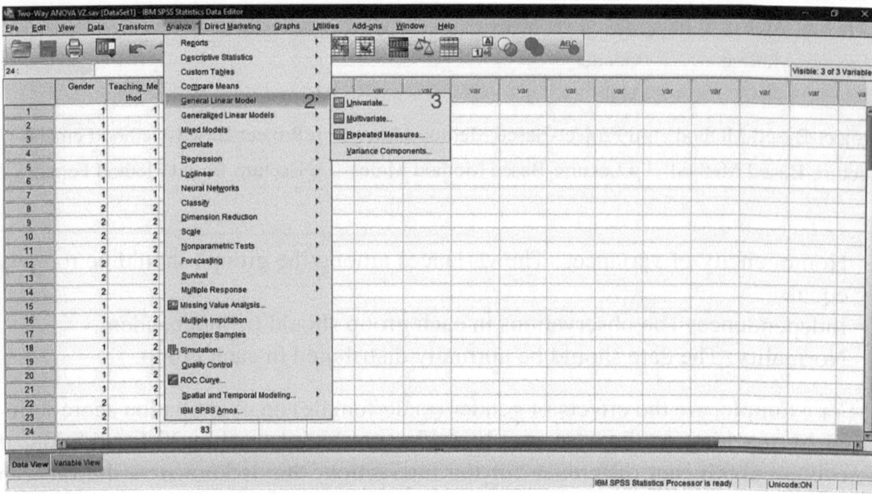

Fig. 8.22 Two-Way ANOVA[1]

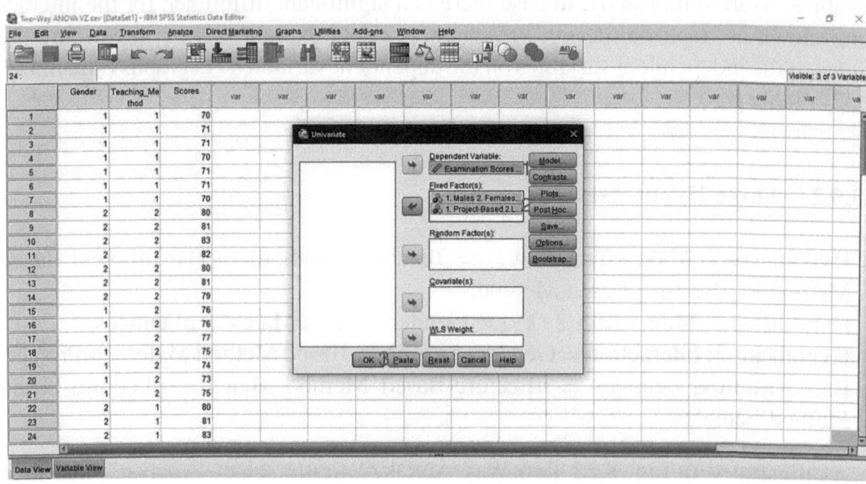

Fig. 8.23 Two-Way ANOVA[2]

Fig. 8.24 Descriptive results

Between-Subjects Factors

Independent Variables		N
Males	1	47
Females	2	53
Project-Based	1	55
Lectur-Based	2	45

the *p*-value of Gender and Teaching Methods is equal to 0.000 which is less than 0.05, suggesting that there is a statistically significant difference between males and females on examination scores. Also, there is a statistically significant difference between project-basted and lectured-based methods on examination scores.

More importantly, if there is an interaction, the relationship of the independent variables and dependent variable can be explained through graphs.

As indicated in Fig. 8.26, the graph showing that there is an interaction between gender and teaching methods suggests that males are more likely to be keen on the project-based method whilst females are more likely to be good on the lecture-based method. This is considered to be a breakthrough discovery.

Tests of Between-Subjects Effects

Dependent Variable: Examination Scores

Source	Type III Sum of Squares	df	Mean Square	F	Sig.
Corrected Model	1838.329[a]	3	612.776	26.835	.000
Intercept	561680.789	1	561680.789	24597.133	.000
Gender	1162.261	1	1162.261	50.898	.000
Teaching_Method	576.679	1	576.679	25.254	.000
Gender * Teaching_Method	47.201	1	47.201	2.067	.154
Error	2192.181	96	22.835		
Total	572999.000	100			
Corrected Total	4030.510	99			

a. R Squared = .456 (Adjusted R Squared = .439)

Fig. 8.25 Results of test of between-subjects effects

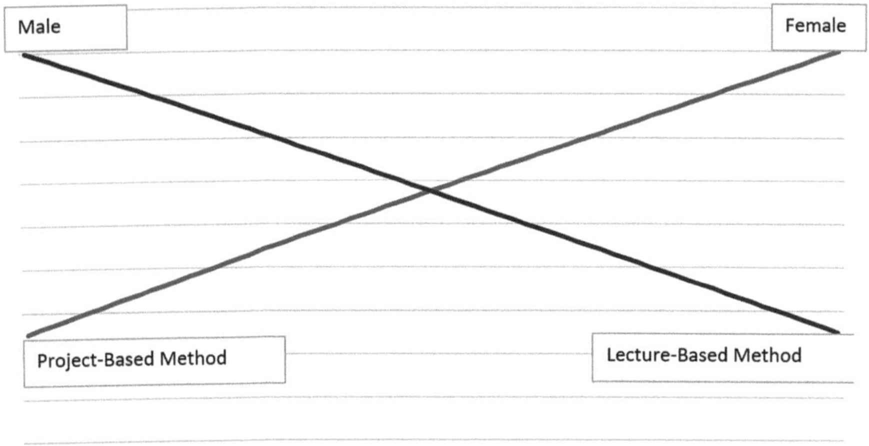

Fig. 8.26 Results of interaction between independent variables

8.3.6 *Repeated Measures ANOVA*

A repeated measures one-way ANOVA is a robust statistical technique employed to analyse data where subjects or participants are measured multiple times under varying conditions or treatments. This method is particularly useful for comparing the means of three or more related groups, such as measurements taken at different time points, under different experimental conditions, or across various treatment interventions. The repeated measures one-way ANOVA enables researchers to investigate within-subject effects, thereby assessing changes within the same individuals across different conditions or time points (Knapp, 2013; Siebert & Siebert, 2017).

In addition, a repeated measures one-way ANOVA can account for individual differences, thereby enhancing statistical power. By employing a factorial design, this technique examines multiple independent variables (factors) and their levels, revealing intricate interactions between factors and their effects on the dependent variable. Key within-subject effects illustrate how the dependent variable changes across different levels of independent variables within the same subjects, providing nuanced insights into how responses evolve over time or under varying conditions.

However, adherence to assumptions such as normality, homogeneity of variances, and sphericity is crucial for ensuring valid results. The output of a repeated measures one-way ANOVA includes F-values, degrees of freedom, and *p*-values for both main and interaction effects. Post-hoc tests are conducted to identify significant differences between conditions. Essentially, a repeated measures ANOVA offers a comprehensive method for understanding within-subject dynamics across various fields, facilitating detailed insights and supporting empirical research (Howell, 2013; Khojasteh, 2022).

8.3.6.1 Fundamental Assumptions

1. Normality: The dependent variable should follow a normal distribution within each combination of the levels of the within-subjects factor(s).
2. Homogeneity of Variances: The variance of the dependent variable should be approximately equal across all levels of the within-subjects factor(s).
3. Sphericity: Sphericity assumes that the variances of the differences between all possible pairs of within-subject conditions are equal. Violation of sphericity can lead to inflated Type I error rates. Mauchly's test is typically used to test for sphericity.
4. Independence of Observations: Observations within each level of the within-subjects factor(s) should be independent of each other. This assumption is typically met if the measurements are made without any systematic bias or influence from previous measurements.
5. Interval or Ratio Data: The dependent variable should be measured at the interval or ratio level.

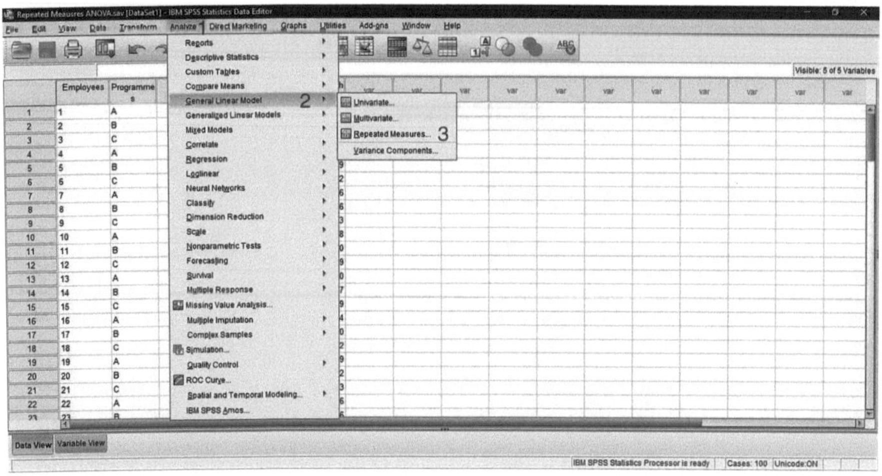

Fig. 8.27 Repeated measures ANOVA[1]

For example, a company seeks to assess the effectiveness of three different leadership training programmes over three different periods of time: before, immediately after, and three months after the training. The company measures the leadership skills of participants using a standardised 'Transformational Leadership' assessment tool.

H_0: All group means of different periods of time of training in 'Transformational Leadership' skills are not statistically different.
H_1: At least one group mean is statistically different from the others.

As depicted in Fig. 8.27, firstly, select 'Analyse', and then select 'General Linear Model'. Finally, select 'Repeated Measures'.

As depicted in Fig. 8.28, firstly, 'With in Subject Factor Name' place 'Times' into the blank since in this example, there are two times of training and the levels of effectiveness were collected before and after the training programmes were completed. So, in the 'Number of Level' fill in '2'. Next, click on 'Add'. Finally, select 'Define'.

As illustrated in Fig. 8.29, on the left box, select all three variables of Before, Immediately After and Three-Month After Training 'Within-Subjects Variables (Times)', Next, select 'Options'.

As shown in Fig. 8.30, on the 'Factor(s) and Factor Interactions:', select 'OVERALL' and 'Times' and place them into 'Display Means for'. Next, select 'Compare main effects'. For the 'Confidence Interval Adjustments', as suggested by Auamnoy (2002) select 'Bonferroni'. On the 'Display' select 'Descriptive statistics, Estimates of effect size, and Homogeneity tests'. Next, select 'Continue' and lastly select 'OK'.

As indicated in Table 8.6, the results show the average scores and their standard deviations for the variables Before Training, Immediately After Training, and Three Months After Training. The mean score for Before Training was 40.78, which increased to 63.57 for Immediately After Training and further to 72.07 for Three

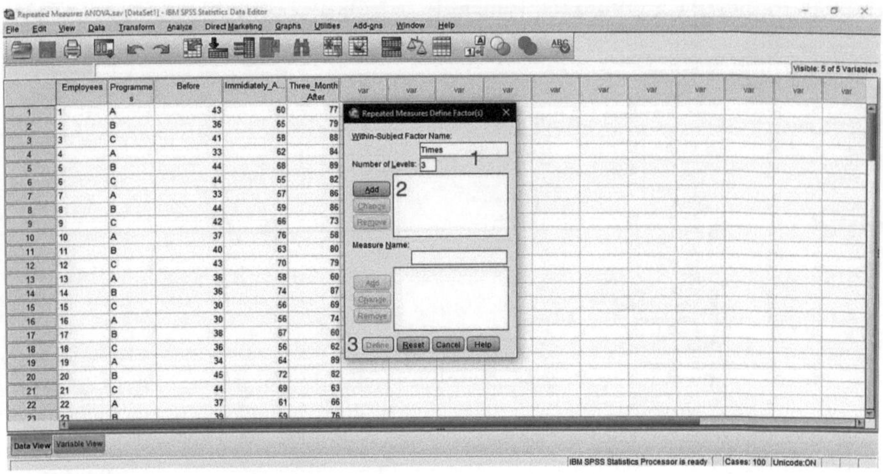

Fig. 8.28 Repeated measures ANOVA[2]

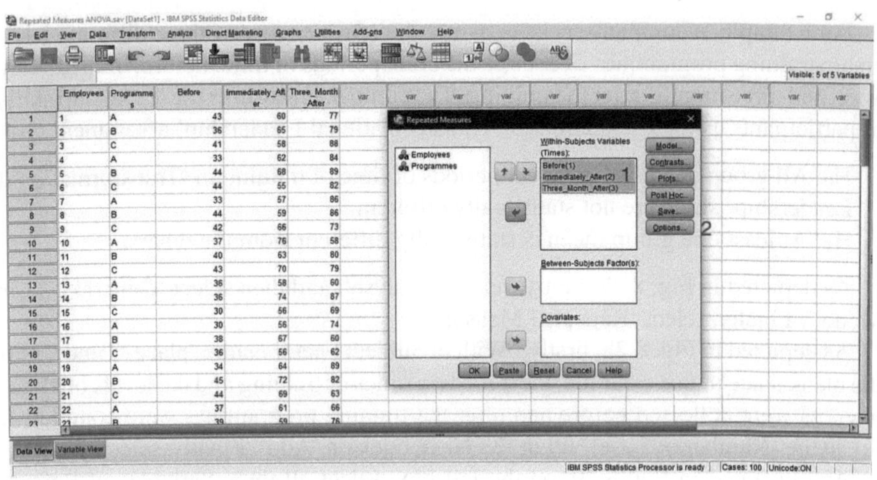

Fig. 8.29 Repeated measures ANOVA[3]

Months After Training. The standard deviations indicate the variability or spread of scores around the mean for each time point.

As indicated in Table 8.7, the results suggest that the 'Times' factor has a significant impact on the dependent variables. This means that there is a relationship between the different time points and the measured outcomes (Transformational Leadership Skills).

More importantly, the *p*-values, which indicate the likelihood of observing such results by random chance, were extremely small. This strongly suggests that the

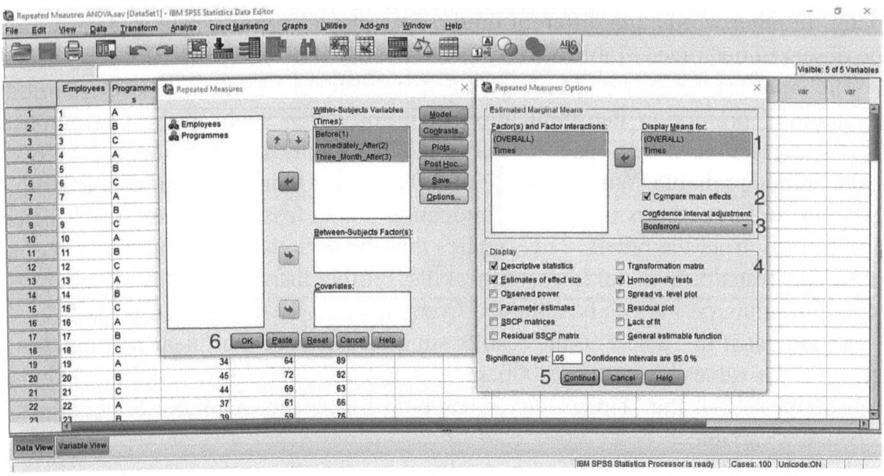

Fig. 8.30 Repeated measures ANOVA[4]

Table 8.6 Descriptive statistics ($n = 100$)

Variables	Mean	Std. Deviation
Before Training	40.78	5.382
Immediately After Training	63.57	9.450
Three-Month After Training	72.07	12.761

Table 8.7 Multivariate tests[a]

Effect		Value	F	Hypothesis df	Error df	Sig.	Partial Eta squared
Times	Pillai's Trace	0.846	269.996[b]	2.000	98.000	0.000	0.846
	Wilks' Lambda	0.154	269.996[b]	2.000	98.000	0.000	0.846
	Hotelling's Trace	5.510	269.996[b]	2.000	98.000	0.000	0.846
	Roy's Largest Root	5.510	269.996[b]	2.000	98.000	0.000	0.846

[a]Design: Intercept
Within-Subjects Design: Times
[b]Exact statistic

'Times' factor truly has an effect and that the observed results are not just due to random variation.

In addition, the large partial Eta squared values (0.846) indicate that a substantial amount of the variability in the dependent variables can be explained by the 'Times' factor. In other words, the different time points played a major role in determining the observed outcomes (Table 8.8).

The significant result of Mauchly's test indicates a violation of the sphericity assumption, prompting the application of a correction such as the Greenhouse-Geisser correction with an epsilon value of 0.877. Despite this violation, the ANOVA results remain reliable. With a *p*-value of 0.001, lower than the significance level of 0.05, the null hypothesis is rejected, indicating that at least one group mean differs significantly from the others. This implies that the periods of training have distinct effects on Transformational Leadership skills. Further insights into the effectiveness of each training period can be obtained from the Pairwise Comparisons Table.

As indicated in Table 8.9, the results suggest that both the linear and quadratic terms have *p*-values lower than 0.000, indicating that both types of relationship exist. This suggests that the 'Times' factor has both linear and quadratic effects on the dependent variable.

As indicated in Table 8.10, the results show that the intercept term is highly significant, with a very small *p*-value (*p*-value is equivalent to 0.000).

The partial eta squared value (0.987) indicates that a vast majority of the variance in the dependent variable is explained by the intercept.

These results suggest that the intercept term significantly explains the variability in the dependent variable.

The results from Table 8.11, suggesting pairwise comparisons between different time periods of training, reveal statistically significant differences across all time periods. Notably, the Three-Month After (3) period emerges as the most effective training phase for enhancing levels of Transformational Leadership skills, with mean differences notably higher compared to both the Immediately After (2) and Before (1) periods. Following closely, the Immediately After (2) period also demonstrates a significant improvement compared to the baseline Before (1) period. These findings, supported by Bonferroni-adjusted *p*-values and confidence intervals, underscore the varying impacts of timing on the effectiveness of training interventions in fostering Transformational Leadership skills.

8.3.7 *Multivariate Analysis of Variance (MANOVA)*

Multivariate Analysis of Variance (MANOVA) is a statistical technique used to determine whether multiple levels of independent variables, either individually or in combination, have an effect on several dependent variables. MANOVA examines how these independent variables influence multiple dependent variables simultaneously, thereby allowing for the assessment of complex relationships among them (Harlow, 2014).

For MANOVA to be appropriately applied, the dependent variables must meet certain parametric assumptions. Additionally, MANOVA is suitable only when the dependent variables are statistically correlated with one another and when the pattern

Table 8.8 Mauchly's test of sphericity[a]

Within-subjects effect	Mauchly's W	Approx. Chi-Square	Df	Sig.	Epsilon[b]		
					Greenhouse-Geisser	Huynh-Feldt	Lower-bound
Times	0.860	14.772	2	0.001	0.877	0.892	0.500

This tests the null hypothesis that the error covariance matrix of the orthonormalised transformed dependent variables is proportional to an identity matrix
[a]Design: Intercept
Within-Subjects Design: Times
[b]May be used to adjust the degrees of freedom for the averaged tests of significance. Corrected tests are displayed in the Tests of Within-Subjects Effects table

Table 8.9 Results of linear and quadratic

Source	Times	Type III Sum of Squares	df	Mean Square	F	Sig.	Partial Eta squared
Times	Linear	48953.205	1	48953.205	480.395	0.000	0.829
	Quadratic	3403.402	1	3403.402	73.219	0.000	0.425
Error (Times)	Linear	10088.295	99	101.902			
	Quadratic	4601.765	99	46.482			

Table 8.10 Tests of between-subjects effects

Source	Type III Sum of squares	df	Mean Square	F	Sig.	Partial Eta squared
Intercept	1037467.213	1	1037467.213	7817.652	0.000	0.987
Error	13138.120	99	132.708			

Table 8.11 Pairwise comparisons

(I) Times	(J) Times	Mean Difference (I-J)	Std. Error	Sig.[a]	95% Confidence Interval for Difference[a]	
					Lower Bound	Upper Bound
Before (1)	Immediately After (2)	−22.790*	1.111	0.000	−25.495	−20.085
	Three-Month After (3)	−31.290*	1.428	0.000	−34.767	−27.813
Immediately After (2)	Before (1)	22.790*	1.111	0.000	20.085	25.495
	Three-Month After (3)	−8.500*	1.086	0.000	−11.146	−5.854
Three-Month After (3)	Before (1)	31.290*	1.428	0.000	27.813	34.767
	Immediately After (2)	8.500*	1.086	0.000	5.854	11.146

Based on estimated marginal means
*The mean difference is significant at the 0.05 level
[a] Adjustment for multiple comparisons: Bonferroni

of group differences expected across all dependent variables is consistent in direction (Backhaus et al., 2021).

8.3.7.1 Fundamental Assumptions

1. There are two independent variables which are either nominal or ordinal scales.
2. The dependent variables are continuous data, i.e., either interval or ratio data.
3. Homogeneity of variances: The variances among the groups should be equal.

4. Independence: The observations in each group should be independent.
5. Normality: The data should be normally distributed in each group.
6. There is homogeneity of the variance-covariance matrices. Box's M test of equality of covariance can help analyse this relationship.
7. There should be a statistical association between the different dependent variables.

For example, is there a relationship between different types of restaurants (1. Japanese, 2. French, and 3. Thai) and different levels of satisfactions of the customers perceived in terms of service (highest score is 100) and taste (highest score is 10) from the customers' perspectives? (confident interval is 95 per cent or $\alpha = 0.05$)

H_0: $\mu_1 = \mu_2 \ldots = \mu_k$ (All of the dependent variable means are equal).
H_a: At least one of the groups' means $\mu_1, \mu_2, \ldots, \mu_k$ is not equal (one or more of the dependent variables' means differ between the groups).

As illustrated in Table 8.12, the data suggests that the respondents to the three different groups of restaurants are moderately similar: Japanese = 33, French = 33, and Thai = 34.

As shown in Table 8.13, the *p*-value equals 0.527, which is less than 0.05. Therefore, the null hypothesis is accepted. It can be concluded that all of the dependent variable means are equal or that all of the means of the different groups of restaurants are not statistically different.

Table 8.12 Descriptive statistics

	1. Japanese 2. French 3. Thai	Mean	SD.	*n*
Levels of Satisfaction of Services	1	27.88	9.968	33
	2	56.48	8.661	33
	3	82.71	8.16	34
	Total	55.96	24.232	100
Levels of Satisfaction of Taste	1	3.52	1.439	33
	2	6.09	1.011	33
	3	8.38	1.231	34
	Total	6.02	2.348	100

Table 8.13 Box's test of equality of covariance matrices

Box's M	5.291
F	0.856
df1	6
df2	233257.676
Sig.	0.527

H_0: There is no statistically significant difference between the mean groups of levels of satisfaction in terms of service and taste of different groups of restaurants.
H_1: There is a statistically significant difference between the mean groups of levels of satisfaction in terms of service and taste of different groups of restaurants.

As illustrated in Table 8.14, the *p*-value of Wilks' Lambda is equivalent to 0.000, which is less than 0.05. Hence, it can be concluded that there is a statistically significant difference between the mean groups of levels of satisfaction in terms of service and taste of different groups of restaurants.

H_0: There is no statistically significant difference between the variance of levels of satisfaction in terms of service and taste of different groups of restaurants.
H_1: There is a statistically significant difference between the variance of levels of satisfaction in terms of service and taste of different groups of restaurants.

As indicated in Table 8.15, the *p*-value of levels of satisfaction of service and taste are 0.190 and 0.227, which are greater than 0.05. Hence, the null hypothesis is accepted, and it can be concluded that there is no statistically significant difference between the mean groups' level of satisfaction in terms of the service and tastes of different groups of restaurants. Hence, the results of the multi-comparison between the different groups of restaurants can be seen in Tukey's results, in Table 8.14.

As indicated in Table 8.16, the *p*-value is 0.000, which is less than 0.05 for all the relationships between the pair of all independent and dependent variables. In terms of level of satisfaction of services, there is a statistically significant difference between the relationship of Thai, French, and Japanese, showing that the mean difference

Table 8.14 Results of Wilks' Lambda

Effect		Value	F	Hypothesis df	Error df	Sig.	Partial Eta squared
Intercept	Pillai's Trace	0.979	2257.941[a]	2.000	96.000	0.000	0.979
	Wilks' Lambda	0.021	2257.941[a]	2.000	96.000	0.000	0.979
	Hotelling's Trace	47.040	2257.941[a]	2.000	96.000	0.000	0.979
	Roy's Largest Root	47.040	2257.941[a]	2.000	96.000	0.000	0.979
Restaurants	Pillai's Trace	0.875	37.700	4.000	194.000	0.000	0.437
	Wilks' Lambda	0.125	87.509[a]	4.000	192.000	0.000	0.646
	Hotelling's Trace	6.968	165.502	4.000	190.000	0.000	0.777
	Roy's Largest Root	6.968	337.961[b]	2.000	97.000	0.000	0.875

[a]Exact statistic
[b]The statistic is an upper bound on F that yields a lower bound on the significance level

Table 8.15 Levene's test of equality of error variances

Variables	F	df1	df2	Sig.
Levels of Satisfaction of Service	1.689	2	97	0.190
Levels of Satisfaction of Taste	1.505	2	97	0.227

between Thai and French is 26.22*, between Thai and Japanese is 54.83*, and between French and Japanese is 28.61*. This suggests that the customers perceive that the Thai restaurant has attained the highest level of satisfaction in terms of services when compared to the others, followed by the French restaurant.

In addition, in terms of level of satisfactions of taste, there are statistically significant differences between the relationships of the Thai, French, and Japanese restaurant, showing that the mean difference between Thai and French is 2.29*, between Thai and Japanese is 4.87*, and between French and Japanese is 2.58*. This suggests that the customers perceive that the Thai restaurant has attained the highest level of satisfaction in terms of taste when compared to the others, followed by the French restaurant.

Table 8.16 Results of Tukey's test

Dependent variable				Mean Difference (I-J)	Std. Error	Sig.	95% Confidence interval	
							Lower bound	Upper bound
Level of Satisfaction of Service	Tukey HSD	1	2	−28.61*	2.204	0.000	−33.85	−23.36
			3	−54.83*	2.188	0.000	−60.04	−49.62
		2	1	28.61*	2.204	0.000	23.36	33.85
			3	−26.22*	2.188	0.000	−31.43	−21.01
		3	1	54.83*	2.188	0.000	49.62	60.04
			2	26.22*	2.188	0.000	21.01	31.43
Level of Satisfaction of Taste	Tukey HSD	1	2	−2.58*	0.305	0.000	−3.30	−1.85
			3	−4.87*	0.303	0.000	−5.59	−4.15
		2	1	2.58*	0.305	0.000	1.85	3.30
			3	−2.29*	0.303	0.000	−3.01	−1.57
		3	1	4.87*	0.303	0.000	4.15	5.59
			2	2.29*	0.303	0.000	1.57	3.01

*The mean difference is significant at the 0.05 level

1. Japanese, 2. French, and 3. Thai Restaurants

8.3.8 *Multivariate Analysis of Covariances (MANOVA)*

Multivariate analysis of covariance (MANCOVA) is an extension of analysis of covariance (ANCOVA). It is utilised to assess the statistical significance of the effects of one or more independent variables on a set of two or more dependent variables, whilst controlling for the influence of covariates (Gonzalez, 2003).

Covariates are variables that impact the dependent variables but are not the primary focus of the analysis. In experimental design, covariates are typically variables that are not directly controlled by the experimenter but still exert an influence on the dependent variables. MANCOVA adjusts for these covariate effects, thereby allowing for a clearer evaluation of the relationships between the independent variables and the dependent variables (Warner, 2020).

8.3.8.1 Fundamental Assumptions

1. Independent variables are categorical.
2. Independence of variables: The variables do not influence each other.
3. Covariates and dependent variables are continuous or ratio but at least variables are supposed to be in a form of ordinal measure.
4. Homogeneity of variance (population variances of groups are equal).
5. Normal distribution of dependent variables.
6. Relationships between independent and dependent variables are linear.
7. Covariate variables and independent variables are not related.
8. There should be an absence of multicollinearity—the dependent variables should not be statistically associated.

Example 6. Is there a relationship between the different types of restaurants (1. Japanese, 2. French, and 3. Thai) and different levels of satisfaction of the customers perceived in terms of service (highest score is 100) and taste (highest score is 10), and the covariate variable is the firms' length of time in business, from the customers' perspectives after controlling for the covariate variable (confidence interval is 95 per cent or $\alpha = 0.05$)?

H_0: $\mu_1 = \mu_2 \ldots = \mu_k$: All of the dependent variable means are equal.
H_a: At least two of the group means μ_1, μ_2, …, μ_k are not equal. One or more of the dependent variables' means differ between the groups.

As illustrated in Fig. 8.31, firstly select 'Analyse', and then select 'General Linear Models', and finally select 'Multivariate'

As illustrated in Fig. 8.32, firstly select 'Dependent Variables', and then select 'Independent Variables', next select 'Covariate', and finally select 'Options'.

As shown in Fig. 8.33, once the box of multivariate options shown up, firstly select 'Independent Variable: Restaurants' to the box of 'Display Mean for:', and then select 'Descriptive Statistics, Estimate of Effect Size, and Homogeneity Tests', and finally select 'Continue'.

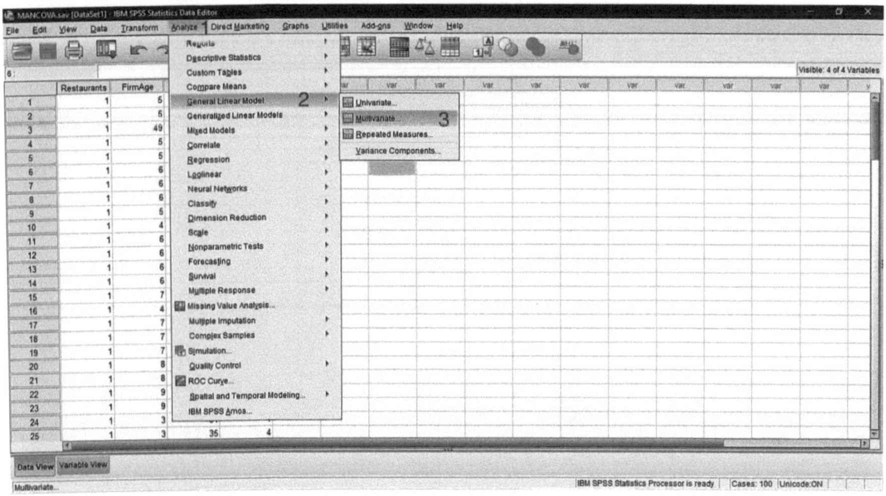

Fig. 8.31 MANCOVA[1]

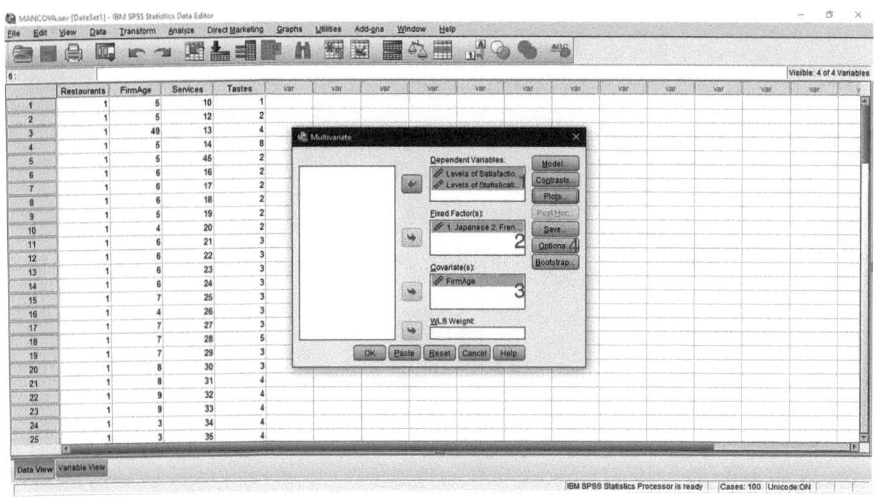

Fig. 8.32 MANCOVA[2]

As shown in Fig. 8.34, select 'Model', and then the box for 'Multivariate Model' will pop up.

As shown in Fig. 8.35, once the box for 'Multivariate Model' pops up, firstly select 'Independent Variable: Restaurants', 'Covariate: Firm Ages' to the box of 'Model', and then hold the cursor to select both 'Restaurants' and 'Firm Ages' and move them to the box of 'Model', and finally select 'Continue'.

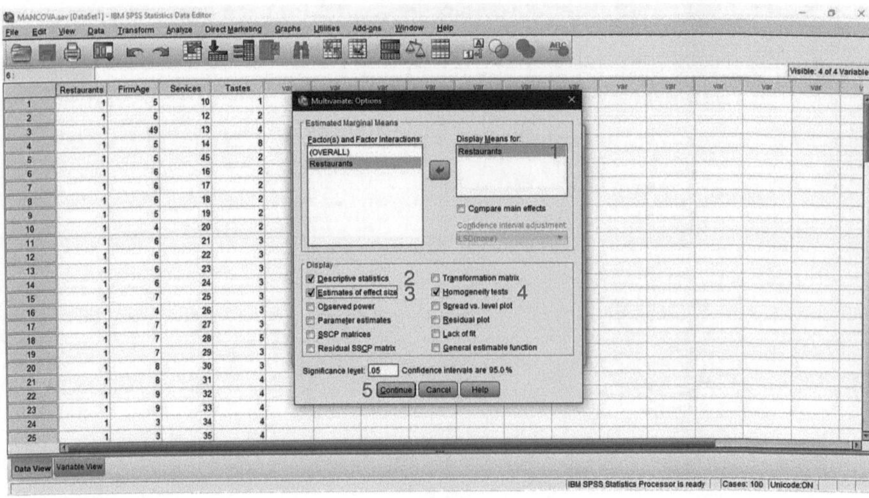

Fig. 8.33 MANCOVA[3]

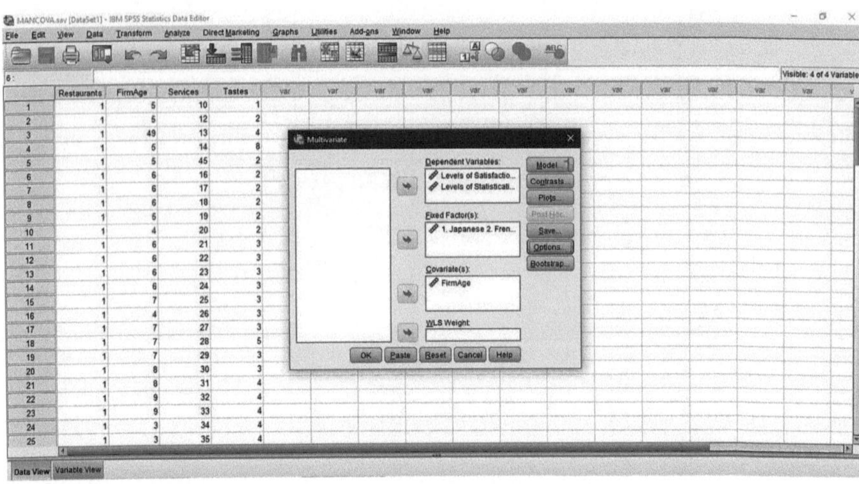

Fig. 8.34 MANCOVA[4]

As depicted in Fig. 8.36, review the *p*-value of the relationship between the Moderator (Independent Variable: Restaurants*Covariate: Firm Ages) and Dependent Variables: Levels of Satisfactions: Services and Tastes. In case that there is no statistically significant difference between the relationship of the Moderator and Dependent Variable, the MANCOVA test should be carried out (see Table 8.14, the *p*-value is 0.278, which is greater than 0.05; accept null hypothesis). Next, the researcher can select 'Full factorial' and then select 'Continue'. The results can be seen in Table 8.15, where the *p*-value (Wilks' Lambda) of the relationship between the different groups

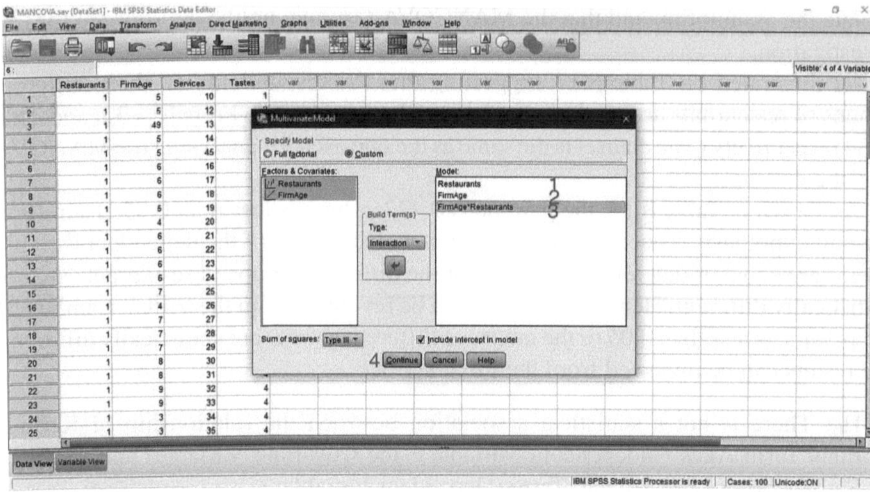

Fig. 8.35 MANCOVA[5]

of Restaurants and different Levels of Satisfaction of Service and Taste is equivalent to 0.000, which is less than 0.05; hence, reject the null hypothesis. This suggests that at least one group of the Restaurants is different from the others in term of different Levels of Satisfaction of Service and Taste when controlling for Firm Age.

However, if there is a statistically significant difference between the relationship of the Moderator and Dependent Variable. This suggests that there is an association between the Independent Variable and the Covariate, suggesting that this would

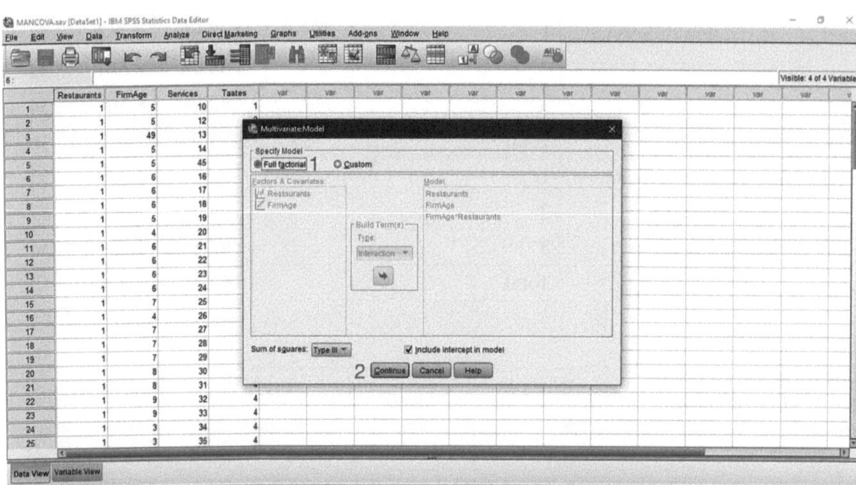

Fig. 8.36 MANCOVA[6]

violate the assumption and that the MANCOVA test may not be appropriate for this investigation.

As illustrated on Table 8.17 suggesting that the respondents on three different groups of restaurants are moderately similar; Japanese = 33, French = 33, and Thai = 34 respectively (The dataset is the same as the one used for analysing the MANOVA statistical technique).

As shown in Table 8.18, the p-value is 0.422, which is less than 0.05. Therefore, the null hypothesis is accepted. It can be concluded that all of the dependent variable means are equal or that all of the means of the different groups of restaurants are not statistically different. Hence, the results can be reviewed from the Wilks' Lambda. If the p-value is less than 0.05 or the means of different groups are statistically different, the results can be reviewed from the Pillai's Trace.

H_0: There is not a statistical association between the relationship of Restaurants*Firm Ages (Independent Variable * the Covariate Variable) and Level of Satisfaction of Service and Taste (Dependent Variables).
H_1: There is a statistical association between the relationship of Restaurants*Firm Ages (Independent Variable * the Covariate Variable) and Level of Satisfaction of Service and Taste (Dependent Variables).

As shown in Table 8.19, the *p*-value is equivalent to 0.278, which is greater than 0.05. Hence, the null hypothesis is accepted, suggesting that there is no statistical association between the relationship of Restaurants*Firm Ages (Independent Variable * the Covariate Variable) and Level of Satisfaction of Service and

Table 8.17 Descriptive statistics

	1. Japanese 2. French 3. Thai	Mean	SD.	*n*
Level of Satisfaction of Service	1	27.88	9.968	33
	2	56.48	8.661	33
	3	82.71	8.16	34
	Total	55.96	24.232	100
Level of Satisfaction of Taste	1	3.52	1.439	33
	2	6.09	1.011	33
	3	8.38	1.231	34
	Total	6.02	2.348	100

Table 8.18 Box's test of equality of covariance matrices[a]

Box's M	6.194
F	1.002
df1	6
df2	233257.676
Sig.	0.422

Taste (Dependent Variables), and this suggests that the findings do not violate the assumption.

> H_0: There is no statistical association between the relationship of Restaurants (Independent Variable) and Level of Satisfaction of Service and Taste (Dependent Variables) when controlling for Firm Age (Covariate Variable).
> H_1: There is a statistical association between the relationship of Restaurants (Independent Variable) and Level of Satisfaction of Service and Taste (Dependent Variables) when controlling for Firm Age (Covariate Variable).

Table 8.19 Multivariate tests[1]

Effect		Value	F	Hypothesis df	Error df	Sig.	Partial Eta squared
Intercept	Pillai's Trace	.951	905.091[a]	2.000	93.000	0.000	0.951
	Wilks' Lambda	.049	905.091[a]	2.000	93.000	0.000	0.951
	Hotelling's Trace	19.464	905.091[a]	2.000	93.000	0.000	0.951
	Roy's Largest Root	19.464	905.091[a]	2.000	93.000	0.000	0.951
Restaurants	Pillai's Trace	0.751	28.233	4.000	188.000	0.000	0.375
	Wilks' Lambda	0.250	46.434[a]	4.000	186.000	0.000	0.500
	Hotelling's Trace	2.991	68.786	4.000	184.000	0.000	0.599
	Roy's Largest Root	2.989	140.506[b]	2.000	94.000	0.000	0.749
FirmAge	Pillai's Trace	0.028	1.319[a]	2.000	93.000	0.272	0.028
	Wilks' Lambda	0.972	1.319[a]	2.000	93.000	0.272	0.028
	Hotelling's Trace	0	1.319[a]	2.000	93.000	0.272	0.028
	Roy's Largest Root	0.028	1.319[a]	2.000	93.000	0.272	0.028
Restaurants * Firm Ages	Pillai's Trace	0.053	1.284	4.000	188.000	0.278	0.027
	Wilks' Lambda	0.947	1.285[a]	4.000	186.000	0.278	0.027
	Hotelling's Trace	0.056	1.284	4.000	184.000	0.278	0.027
	Roy's Largest Root	0.053	2.479[b]	2.000	94.000	0.089	0.050

[a]Exact statistic
[b]The statistic is an upper bound on F that yields a lower bound on the significance level

Table 8.20 Multivariate tests[2]

Effect		Value	F	Hypothesis df	Error df	Sig.	Partial Eta squared
Intercept	Pillai's Trace	.953	961.015[b]	2.000	95.000	0.000	0.953
	Wilks' Lambda	.047	961.015[b]	2.000	95.000	0.000	0.953
	Hotelling's Trace	20.232	961.015[b]	2.000	95.000	0.000	0.953
	Roy's Largest Root	20.232	961.015[b]	2.000	95.000	0.000	0.953
Firm Age	Pillai's Trace	0.015	0.745[b]	2.000	95.000	0.478	0.015
	Wilks' Lambda	0.985	0.745[b]	2.000	95.000	0.478	0.015
	Hotelling's Trace	0.016	0.745[b]	2.000	95.000	0.478	0.015
	Roy's Largest Root	0.016	0.745[b]	2.000	95.000	0.478	0.015
Restaurants	Pillai's Trace	0.874	37.251	4.000	192.000	0.000	0.437
	Wilks' Lambda	0.127	85.570[b]	4.000	190.000	0.000	0.643
	Hotelling's Trace	6.838	160.688	4.000	188.000	0.000	0.774
	Roy's Largest Root	6.836	328.141[c]	2.000	96.000	0.000	0.872

[a]Design: Intercept + Firm Ages + Restaurants
[b]Exact statistic
[c]The statistic is an upper bound on F that yields a lower bound on the significance level

As indicated in Table 8.20, the *p*-value is equivalent to 0.000, which is lower than 0.05. Hence, the null hypothesis is rejected. This suggests that there is a statistical association between the relationship of Restaurants (Independent Variable) and Level of Satisfaction of Service and Taste (Dependent Variables) when controlling for Firm Ages (Covariate Variable). It can be concluded that the customers perceive that different groups of restaurants have statistical differences on the different levels of satisfaction of service and taste.

8.3.9 *Pearson Correlation*

Correlation is a statistical measure that quantifies the extent to which two variables are correlated. This relationship can be either positive or negative. The strength of this correlation is expressed through the Pearson Correlation Coefficient (r), which ranges from -1.0 to $+1.0$ (Pallant, 2020). A positive correlation indicates that as one variable increases, the other variable also increases, whereas a negative correlation suggests that as one variable increases, the other variable decreases. The degree of correlation can be categorised as weak or strong.

When assessing the significance of this correlation, if the *p*-value is less than or equal to 0.05 and the correlation coefficient is positive, it indicates a statistically significant positive correlation between the two variables. Conversely, a negative correlation suggests a statistically significant inverse relationship. The symbol 'ρ' (rho) is commonly used to represent the correlation coefficient in statistical contexts (Cohen et al., 2013; Gravetter et al., 2021).

8.3.9.1 Fundamental Assumptions

1. Variables must be in the form of interval or ratio scales.
2. Both variables should be normally distributed.
3. There is a linear relationship between the two variables.

For example, are there relationships between the lengths of experiences and levels of salary per month? The sample consists of 202 respondents, namely the employees of a hi-technology firm. The dataset is collected in the form of ratio scales, composed of length of experience and level of salary per month of the respondents. Hence, the Pearson correlation is applied to test whether or not there are correlations between 'Experience' and 'Salary' (confidence interval = 95%, $\alpha = 0.05$).

8.3.9.2 Hypothesis

Hypotheses (2-Tails)

- H_0: $\rho = 0$ (There is no correlation between variables).
- H_1: $\rho \neq 0$ (There is a correlation between variables).

Or, the hypotheses could be rewritten as:

- H_0: $\rho = 0$ (experience and salary are not statistically correlated).
- H_1: $\rho \neq 0$ (experience and salary are statistically correlated).

As illustrated in Fig. 8.37 Pearson Correlation, firstly select 'Analyse', and then select 'Correlate', next select 'Bivariate', and then select variables 'Experience' and 'Salary' in the box of Variables, and finally click 'OK'.

As depicted in Table 8.21, the *p*-value equals 0.000, which is lower than 0.05. Hence, the null hypothesis is rejected; this suggests that Experience and Salary are statistically correlated. Next, as indicated in Fig. 8.38 Strength of Association of the Pearson Correlation, the Pearson Correlation is observed; the strength of association is 0.420, considered to be a medium level. Hence, the longer the experience, the higher the level of salary that employees can acquire.

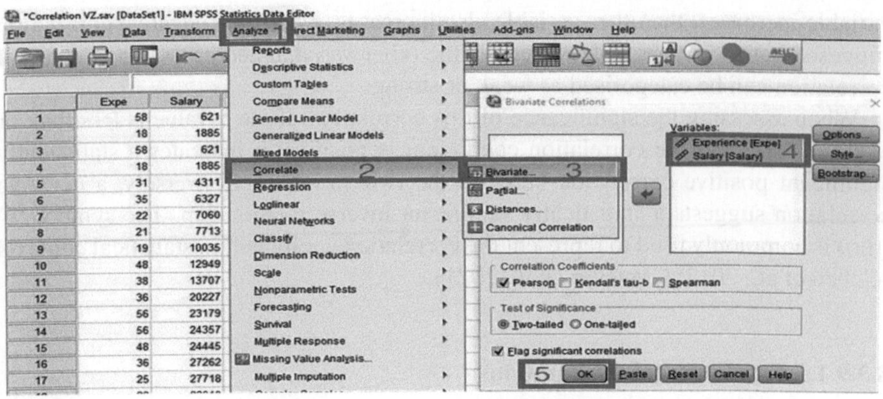

Fig. 8.37 Pearson correlation

Table 8.21 Strength of Association of the Pearson correlation

Coefficient (r)	Direction of relationships	
Strength of Association	Positive	Negative
Small	0.10 to 0.30	−0.10 to −0.30
Medium	0.30 to 0.50	−0.30 to −0.50
Large	0.50 to 1.00	−0.50 to −1.00

Tabachnick and Fidell (2019)

		Experience	Salary
Experience	Pearson Correlation	1	.420**
	Sig. (2-tailed)		.000
	N	202	202
Salary	Pearson Correlation	.420**	1
	Sig. (2-tailed)	.000	
	N	202	202

**. Correlation is significant at the 0.01 level (2-tailed).

Fig. 8.38 Results of Pearson correlation

8.3.10 Multiple Regression Analysis (MRA)

Multiple regression analysis (MRA) is a statistical method utilised to examine the relationships between a dependent variable and multiple independent variables. Unlike Simple Linear Regression Analysis, which involves only one predictor, multiple regression allows for the simultaneous consideration of several predictors to understand their collective impact on the dependent variable (Hair et al., 2019).

The primary aim of multiple regression is to assess the extent to which a set of independent variables can predict the dependent variable. This method estimates the regression coefficients for each predictor, which reflect the strength and direction of their individual relationships with the dependent variable, whilst controlling for the influence of other predictors (Mertler et al., 2021). This approach is particularly useful for exploring complex relationships and for making predictions based on multiple variables.

In addition to hypothesis testing and prediction, multiple regression can reveal interactions between predictors and identify potential issues, such as multicollinearity, where independent variables are highly correlated with each other (Aguinis, 2019). This comprehensive approach enables a nuanced understanding of how various predictors contribute to the dependent variable and provides insights into the structure of the data.

8.3.10.1 Fundamental Assumptions

1. The independent variables (xi) and dependent variable (y) should be the continuous variable, or the independent variables should be interval or ratio scale, for instance, weight, height, salary, age, score, level of satisfaction, net profits and so forth. If the independent variable is a nominal or ordinal scale, the variable must be transformed into the dummy, dichotomous, or binary variables, which is equivalent to 0 and 1, before calculating one of the set of predictors. The dummy variables should not be in the set of predictors greater than 20%; for instance, in case there are 10 IDVs, there should be only 2 dummy variables in the equation).
2. There is a linear relationship between independent and dependent variables.
3. There should not be a correlation coefficient greater than 80 per cent between the independent variables to avoid the multicollinearity problem, leading to the overvaluing of (R^2).
4. Variable should be normally distributed.
5. Variance of Y and X should not be inequivalent.

For example, how much does it cost for a taxi to travel from Central Plaza in Khon Kaen to Khon Kaen University? The charge rate starts at 35 baht ($a = 35$ baht). For each kilometre, the charge in 5 baht ($b = 5$ baht) The length of transportation is 10 kilometres ($x = 10$ kilometres). How much does it cost?

$$y_i = \beta_0 + \beta_i x_i$$

$y =$ Dependent Variable (y_i)
$x =$ Independent Variables (x_i)
$a =$ Constant (β_0)
$b =$ Slope (β_i)

where;

$y =$ Dependent Variable (y_i)
$x =$ 10 (x_i)
$a =$ 35 (β_0)
$b =$ 5 (β_i)

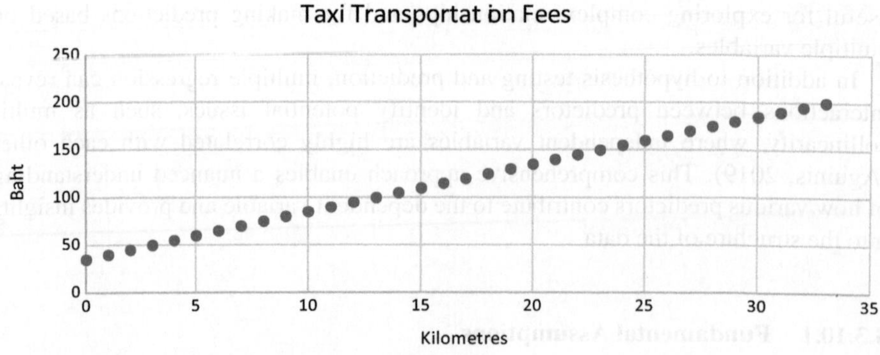

Fig. 8.39 Results of Linear Regression Analysis

$$y = 35 + 5(10)$$

$$y = 85 \text{ Baht}$$

Hence, the total charge is 85 baht.

As shown in Fig. 8.39, the starting point is 35 baht, and with each kilometre, the cost of the taxi increases by 5 baht. When travelling 10 kilometres, the total charge is 85 baht.

In addition, for example, to what extent are there relationships between the set of predictors composed of Gender, Learning Styles, and Marketing Mix (4Ps) (confidence interval = 95%, $\alpha = 0.05$) for Gender: Male, and Female; Learning Styles: Activist, Pragmatist, Reflector, and Theorist; and Marketing Mix (4Ps): Product, Price, Place, and Promotion, and the dependent variable, the sale volumes?

8.3.10.2 Hypothesis

- H_0: $\beta_1, = \beta_2 \ldots = \beta_k = 0$: There is no significant linear relationship between the set of predictors and the dependent variable.
- H_1: $\beta_i \neq 0, i = 1, 2\ldots k$: There is a significant linear relationship between the set of predictors and the dependent variable.

As illustrated in Table 8.22, there are no statistically significant correlations between the set of predictors exceeding 0.80, or 80 per cent. As recommended by Hair et al. (2019), multicollinearity may be a concern when the predictors exhibit strong statistical correlations, with Pearson's correlation coefficient exceeding 0.80 or 80 per cent. Therefore, it can be concluded that there is no evidence of multicollinearity among this set of predictors.

Table 8.22 Pearson correlation coefficient

	Activist	Pragmatist	Reflector	Theorist	Product	Price	Place	Promotion
Activist	1							
Pragmatist	−0.064	1						
Reflector	−0.136**	−0.077*	1					
Theorist	−0.092**	−0.072*	−0.089*	1				
Product	0.105**	0.215**	0.204**	0.150**	1			
Price	0.230**	0.202**	0.170**	0.063	−0.173**	1		
Place	0.179**	0.220**	0.149**	0.222**	−0.005	−0.035	1	
Promotion	0.209**	0.197**	0.110**	0.178**	−0.019	−0.014	−0.055	1

**Correlation is significant at the 0.01 level (2-tailed)
*Correlation is significant at the 0.05 level (2-tailed)

As shown in Figs. 8.40 and 8.41, the dependent variable appears to be normally distributed.

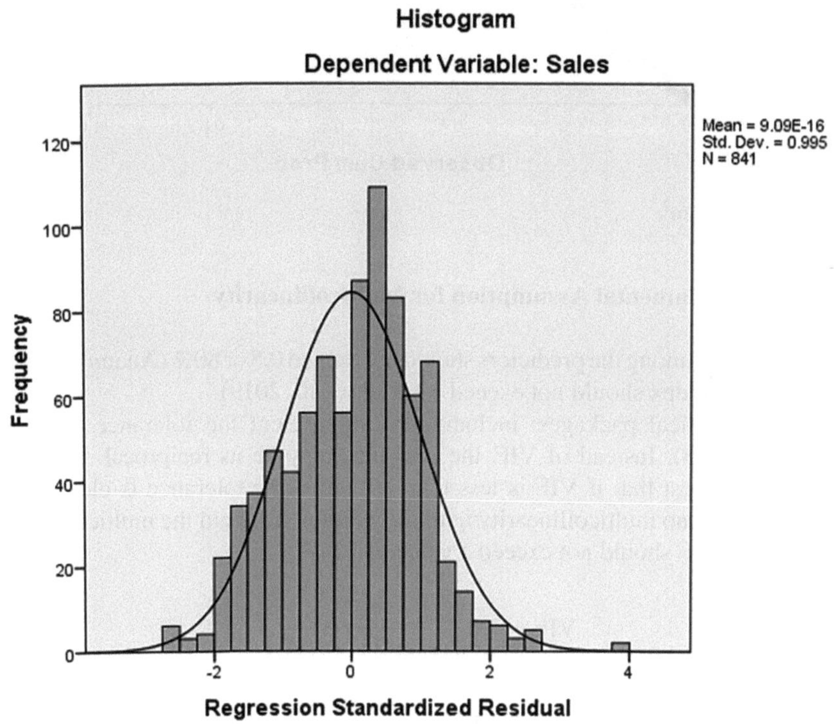

Fig. 8.40 Histogram[1]

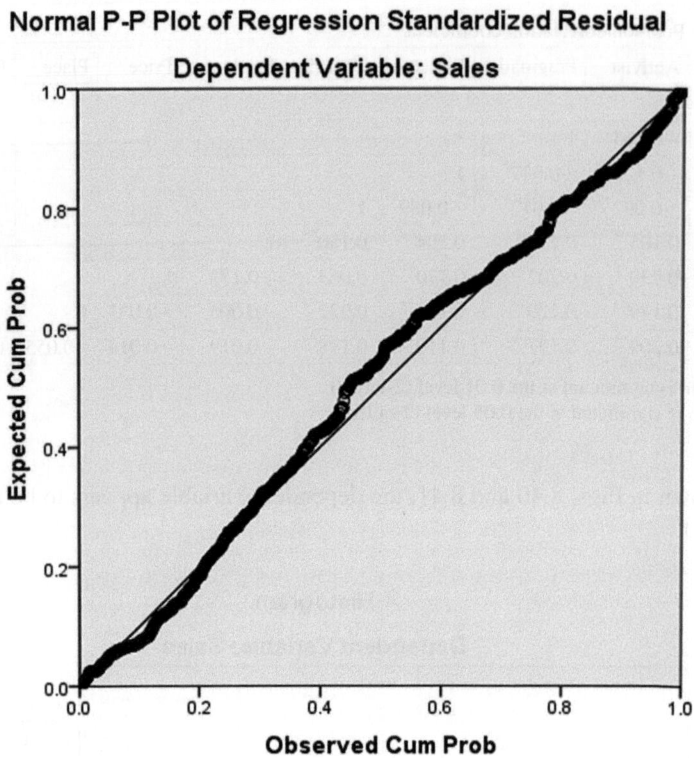

Fig. 8.41 Histogram[2]

8.3.10.3 Fundamental Assumption for Multicollinearity

1. Correlation among the predictors should not exceed 0.8 or 80% (Auamnoy, 2002).
2. Condition Index should not exceed 30 (Hair et al., 2019).
3. Some statistical packages, including SPSS, present the tolerance (Gunst & Mason, 2018). Instead of VIF, the tolerance may be its reciprocal. Hair et al. (2019) suggest that if VIF is less than 10 whilst the tolerance is close to 1.0, then there is no multicollinearity in this condition. To avoid the multicollinearity problem, VIF should not exceed a value of 10.

$$\text{VIF} = \frac{1 \quad = \quad 1}{\text{Tolerance } \left(1 - R^2 X_i\right)}$$

$R^2 =$ Coefficient of Determination
$X =$ Independent Variables

As shown in Table 8.18 Correlation, to detect the multi collinearity problem, there is no statistically significant difference between the independent variables where each pair has a greater level of Pearson correlation than 0.80 or 80 per cent (Auamnoy, 2002). Hence, it can be concluded that there is no multicollinearity problem. Moreover, in the case that there is a pair of independent variables has a statistically significant relationship and if the Pearson correlation is greater than 0.80 or 80 per cent, the researcher needs to further investigate the variance inflation factor (VIF) and tolerance in order to understand whether or not the value of VIF is greater than 10 and if the value of tolerance is high, then the chance of having a multicollinearity problem is low.

In addition, if there is a statistically significant difference between the relationship of the independent variables, the research could reduce the chance to detect the multicollinearity by deciding to remove either one or more independent variables from the set of predictors. All in all, this is dependent upon the previous review of literature of the theoretical framework and on which perspectives the researcher aims to investigate to answer the research question.

As depicted in Fig. 8.42, firstly, select 'Analyse', secondly, 'Regression', and finally select 'Linear'.

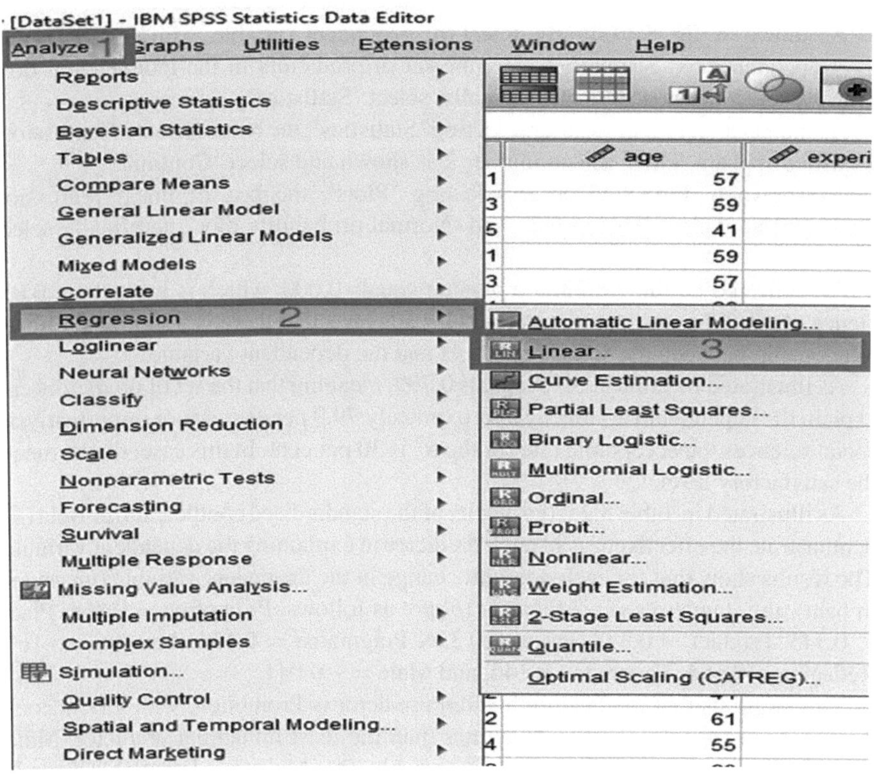

Fig. 8.42 Multiple Regression Analysis[1]

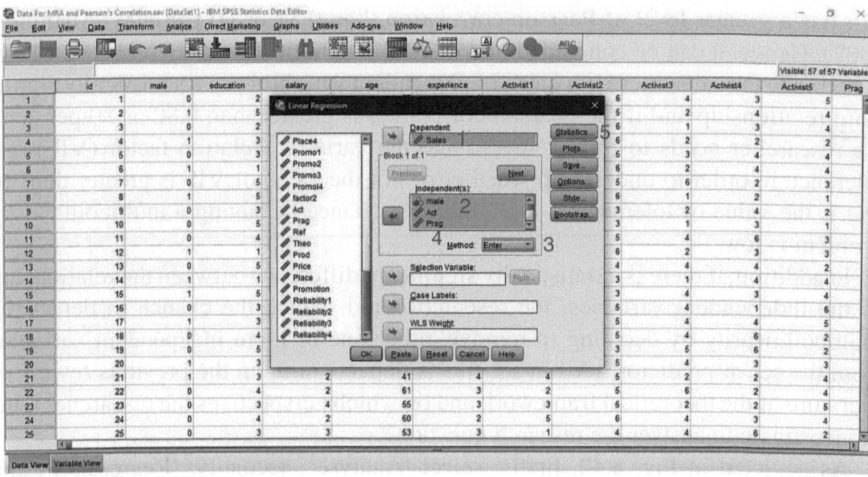

Fig. 8.43 Multiple Regression Analysis[2]

As shown in Fig. 8.43, firstly, select the dependent variable, which is 'Sales', in the Dependent box. Secondly, select the set of predictors in the independent box. Thirdly, select method as 'Enter'. Finally, select 'Statistics'.

As indicated in Fig. 8.44, after selecting 'Statistics', the box of Linear Regression; Statistics appears. Then, select number 2 as shown and select 'Continue'.

As shown in Fig. 8.45, after selecting 'Plots', the box of linear regression plots appears. Select 'Histogram', and 'Normal probability plot', and finally select 'Continue'.

As indicated in Table 8.23, the *p*-value equals 0.000, which is lower than 0.05. Hence, the null hypothesis is rejected. This suggests that there is a significant linear relationship between the set of predictors and the dependent variable.

As illustrated in Table 8.24 R^2 equals 0.799, meaning that the set of predictors can explain the dependent variable by approximately 79.9 per cent. More importantly, in social sciences the acceptable rate for the R^2 is 30 per cent. In this case, the R^2 meets the satisfactory level.

As illustrated in Table 8.25, the results of the standardised coefficients, or Beta (β), demonstrate the effectiveness of each predictor in explaining the dependent variable. The results show that for each one-unit change in the dependent variable (measured in baht), the standardised coefficients (β) are as follows: Promotion = 0.364, Place = 0.345, Product = 0.338, Price = 0.326, Pragmatist = 0.170, Activist = 0.169, Reflector = 0.164, Theorist = 0.146, and Male = −0.041.

This suggests that the most influential predictor is Promotion, with a Beta coefficient approximately nine times greater than the least influential predictor, Male. Specifically, Male is coded as a dummy variable (0 = Male, 1 = Female). This indicates that, when the dependent variable changes by one unit (baht), being Male is associated with a more significant increase in sales compared to being Female.

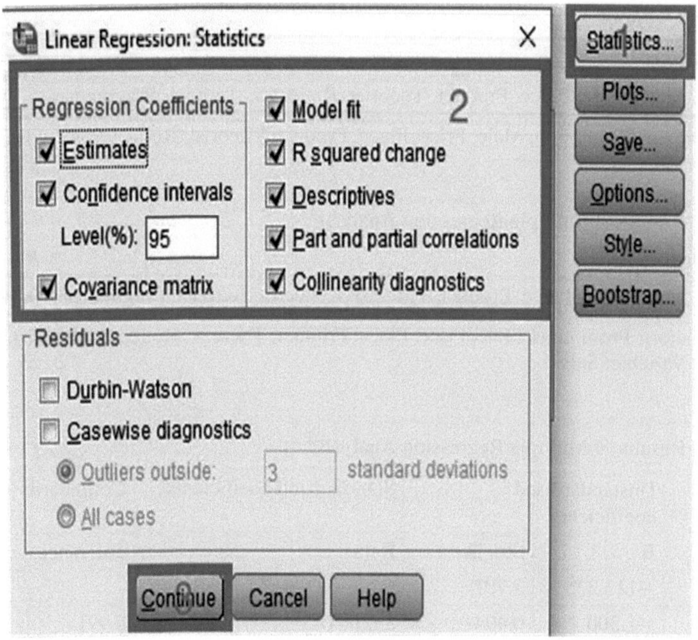

Fig. 8.44 Multiple Regression Analysis[3]

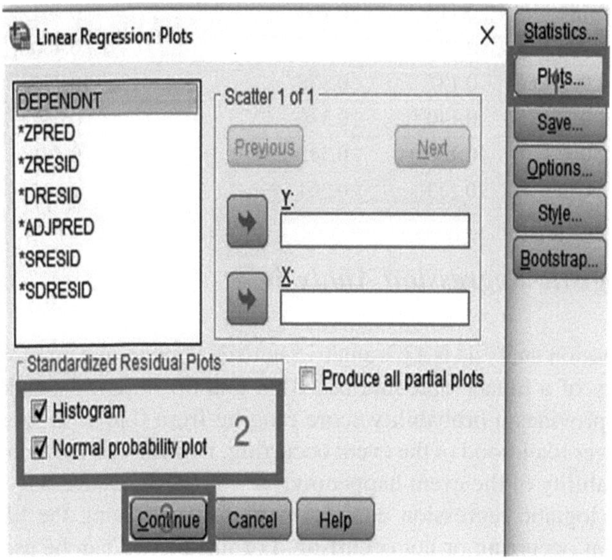

Fig. 8.45 Multiple Regression Analysis[4]

Table 8.23 ANOVA[a]

Set of Predictors	Sig.
Promotion, Male, Price, Place, Product, Theorist, Reflector, Activist, Pragmatista	0.000

[a]Set of Predictors: Promotion, Male, Price, Place, Product, Theorist, Reflector, Activist, Pragmatist

Table 8.24 Results of Multiple Regression Analysis[1]

Set of Predictors	*R*	R^2
Promotion, Male, Price, Place, Product, Theorist, Reflector, Activist, Pragmatist[a]	0.894[b]	0.799

[a]Set of Predictors: Promotion, Male, Price, Place, Product, Theorist, Reflector, Activist, Pragmatist
[b]Dependent Variable: Sales

Table 8.25 Results of Multiple Regression Analysis[2]

Model	Unstandardised coefficients		Standardised coefficients	Collinearity statistics	
	B	Std. Error	Beta	Tolerance	VIF
(Constant)	−113.335	3.701			
Male	−1.300	0.494	−0.041	0.991	1.009
Activist	0.764	0.110	0.169	0.410	2.442
Pragmatist	0.762	0.111	0.170	0.395	2.530
Reflector	0.781	0.112	0.164	0.441	2.267
Theorist	0.703	0.108	0.146	0.480	2.081
Product	2.006	0.137	0.338	0.455	2.196
Price	1.955	0.140	0.326	0.442	2.262
Place	2.047	0.136	0.345	0.461	2.171
Promotion	2.052	0.123	0.364	0.505	1.979

8.3.11 Logistic Regression Analysis

Logistic regression analysis is a parametric statistical technique employed to predict the probability of a binary outcome based on one or more independent variables. This method provides a probability score ranging from 0 to 1. A score closer to 0 indicates a lower likelihood of the event occurring, whilst a score nearer to 1 suggests a higher probability of the event happening.

Moreover, logistic regression analysis is akin to assessing the likelihood of a particular event occurring or not occurring. For instance, it can be used to evaluate the chances of a firm's success or failure based on various factors, such as learning opportunities, leadership styles, organisational culture, and other relevant variables (Hosmer et al., 2013; Menard, 2002).

8.3.11.1 Fundamental Assumptions

1. Binary Outcome: The dependent variable is binary (two possible outcomes).
2. Independence: Observations are independent of each other.
3. Linearity: There is a linear relationship between the logit of the outcome and the independent variables.
4. No Multicollinearity: Independent variables should not be highly correlated with each other.
5. Large Sample Size: A sufficient number of observations is needed for stable estimates, especially with rare events.
6. Homoscedasticity: Whilst not a strict requirement, logistic regression assumes that the variance of errors is constant.

For example, a small business firm seeks to determine the factors influencing the likelihood of a firm increasing its levels of productivity. By collecting data from 120 managers, within the model three independent variables are included: training hours (ratio scale), levels of employees' engagement (1 = the least, and 6 = the highest level of employee engagement), and level of employees' education (bachelor's degree = 1, master's degree = 2, and doctoral degree = 3). The dependent variable is the level of productivity of the firms. The respondents were asked to evaluate the level of productivity, ranging from 1 to 100. The mean is 50; hence, the least productive firm = 0, and the most productive firm = 1.

The logistic regression equation for three independent variables can be represented as:

$$\left(\frac{P(Y=1)}{1-P(Y=1)}\right) = B_0 + B_1X_1 + B_2X_2 + B_3D_{\text{Master}} + B_4D_{\text{PhD}}$$

In this equation:

- $P(Y = 1)$ is the probability of productivity being 1 (i.e., successful) given the values of the independent variables.
- B_0 is the intercept from the regression analysis.
- B_1, B_2, B_3, and B_4 are the coefficients (parameters) of the logistic regression model.
- X_1 is the training hours.
- X_2 is the level of employees' engagement.
- D_{Master} is a dummy variable where $D_{\text{Master}} = 1$ if the employees have a master's degree and 0 otherwise.
- D_{PhD} is a dummy variable where $D_{\text{PhD}} = 1$ if the employees have a master's degree and 0 otherwise.
- y is the levels of productivity (the dependent variable is the binary coded as 0 = lowest level of productivity and 1 = highest level of productivity.
- Remarks: bachelor's degree is the baseline category variable.

The B coefficients represent the effects of each independent variable on the log odds of the dependent variable being 1. These coefficients are estimated from the data during the model fitting process.

8.3.11.2 Hypotheses

H_0: There is no significant relationship between the predictor variables (Training Hours, Level of Employee Engagement, and Level of Employee Education) and the likelihood of a small business firm being productive.

H_1: There is a significant relationship between the predictor variables (Training Hours, Level of Employee Engagement, and Level of Employee Education) and the likelihood of a small business firm being productive.

As shown in Fig. 8.46, firstly, select 'Analyse'. Secondly, select 'Regression'. Thirdly, select 'Binary Logistic'.

As illustrated in Fig. 8.47, firstly, select dependent variable 'Levels of Productivity' in the dependent box. Secondly, select independent variables into the covariates box 'Training Hours, Levels of Employees' Engagement, Levels of Employees' Education'. Thirdly, choose 'Categorical'.

As depicted in Fig. 8.48, firstly, select the baseline category 'Levels of Employee Education' in the categorical covariates. Secondly, select 'First'. Thirdly, select 'Change'. Finally, select 'Continue'. On the Change Contrast, the 'Indicator' is selected as default.

As indicated in Fig. 8.49, firstly, select 'Save'. Secondly, in the predicted values box, select 'Probabilities' and 'Group Membership'. Also, in the Influence Box, select 'Cook's, Leverage values, and DfBeta(s)', and in the residuals box, select 'Standardised'. Finally, select 'Continue'. In the Export model information to XML file, the 'Include the covariance matrix' setting is selected by default.

As suggested in Fig. 8.50, firstly select 'Options'. Secondly, in the 'Statistics and Plots Box', select 'Hosmer-Lemeshow goodness-of-fit' and CI for exp.(B) 95%. Finally, select 'Continue'.

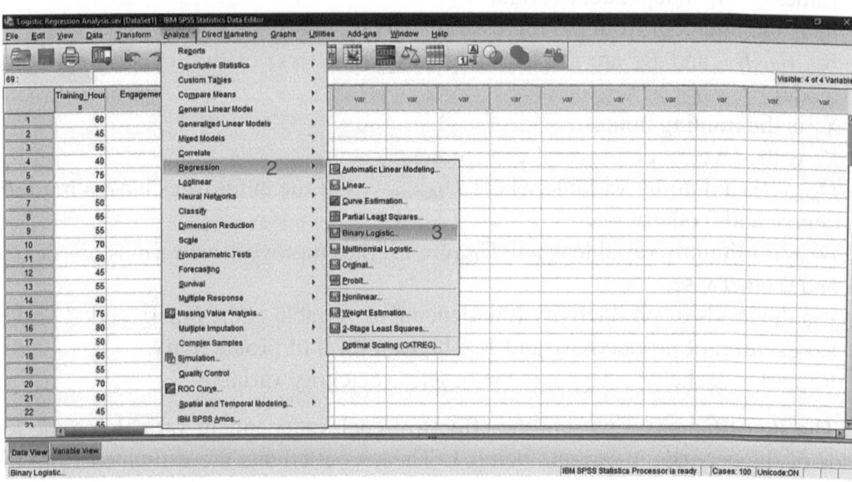

Fig. 8.46 Logistic Regression[1]

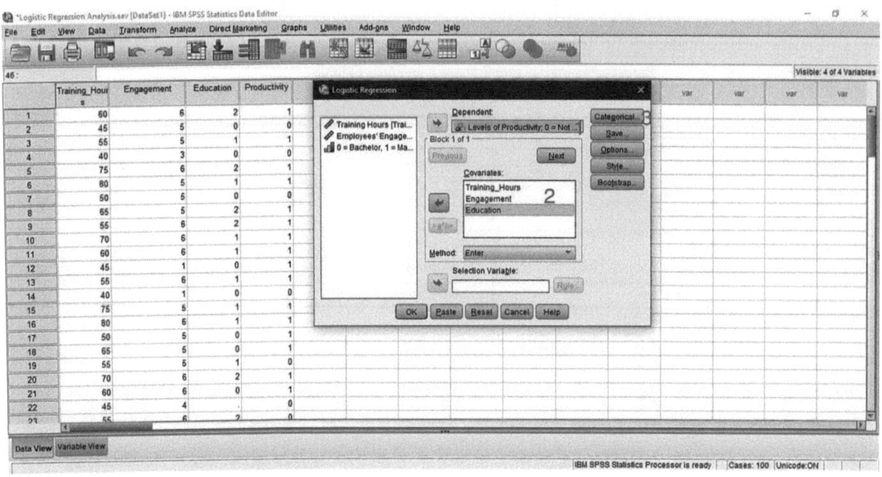

Fig. 8.47 Logistic Regression[2]

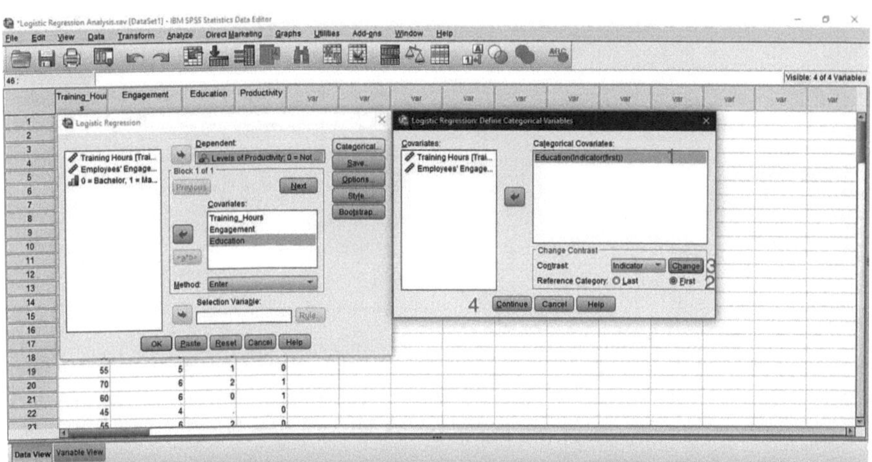

Fig. 8.48 Logistic Regression[3]

As indicated in Fig. 8.51, select 'OK'.

As indicated in Table 8.26, the logistic regression model was statistically significant, $X^2 = 58.640$, *p*-value equals 0.000, which is lower than 0.050. Hence, the null hypothesis is rejected. This suggests that there is a significant relationship between the predictor variables (training hours, levels of employees' engagement, and level of employees' education) and the likelihood of a small business firm being productive.

As indicated in Table 8.27, the model was explained between 38.7 per cent (Cox & Snell *R* Square), and 57.2 per cent (Nagelkerke *R* Square) of the variance in the level of productivity of the firms, demonstrating model fit.

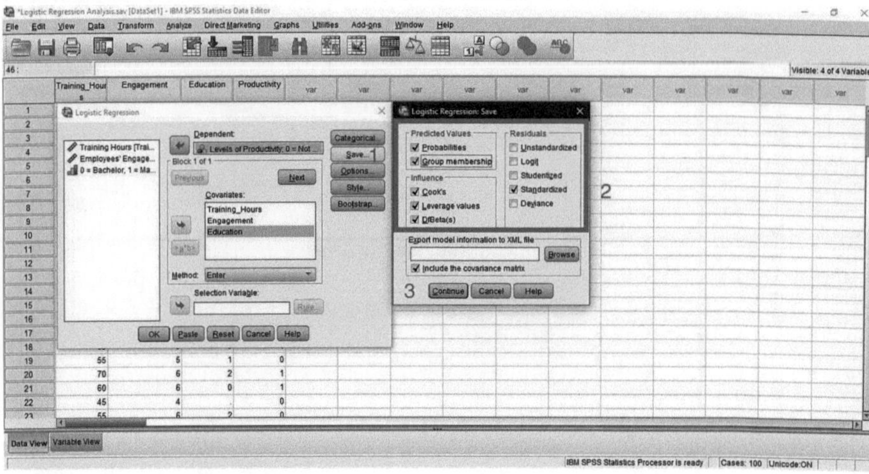

Fig. 8.49 Logistic Regression[4]

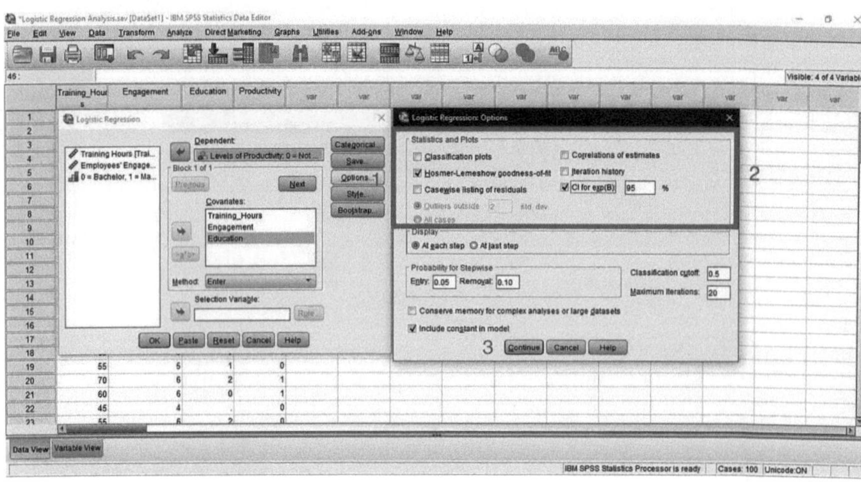

Fig. 8.50 Logistic Regression[5]

As shown in Table 8.28, the Hosmer and Lemeshow's Test shows a chi-square of 5.814 with a significance level of 0.668, indicating a good fit between the model and the observed outcomes.

The logistic regression equation with three independent variables can be represented as:

$$\left(\frac{P(y=1)}{1-P(y=1)}\right) = \mathrm{B}_0 + \mathrm{B}_1(\text{Training Hours}) + \mathrm{B}_2$$

$$(\text{Levels of Employee Engagement})$$

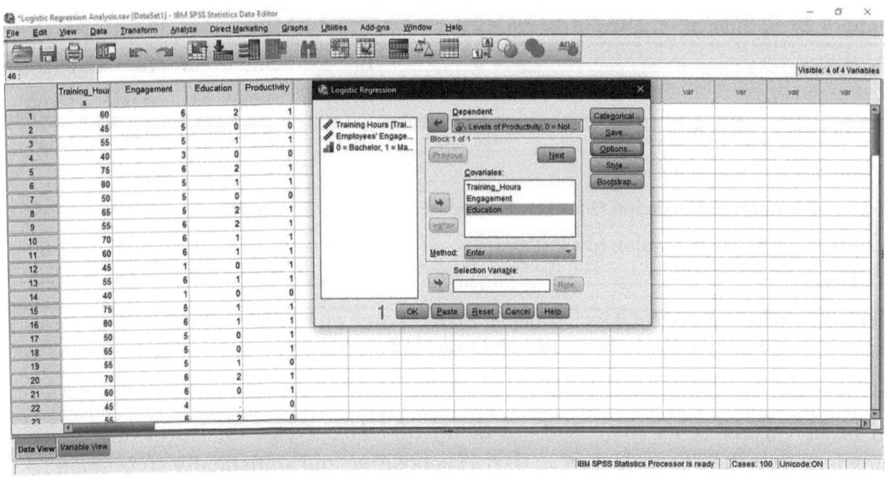

Fig. 8.51 Logistic Regression[6]

Table 8.26 Results of Omnibus tests of model coefficients

		Chi-square	df	Sig.
Step 1	Step	58.640	5	0.000
	Block	58.640	5	0.000
	Model	58.640	5	0.000

Table 8.27 Results of model summary

Step	−2 Log likelihood	Cox & Snell *R* Square	Nagelkerke *R* Square
1	**76.320**	**0.387**	**0.572**

Table 8.28 Results of Hosmer and Lemeshow's Test

Step	Chi-square	df	Sig.
	5.814	**8**	**0.668**

$$+ B_3\left(\text{Master's Degree}\right) + B_4(\text{PhD})$$

The values in the equation can be represented as:

$$\left(\frac{P(y=1)}{1-P(y=1)}\right) = -8.015 + (0.097)(\text{TrainingHours}) + (0.614)$$
$$(\text{Level of Employee Engagement}) + (1.591)(\text{Master's Degree}) + (2.487)(\text{Doctorate})$$

As shown in Table 8.29, for Training Hours, the coefficient ($B = 0.097$) is positive and statistically significant ($p = 0.001$). For each additional hour of training, the odds

Table 8.29 Results of variables in the equation

Variables	B	S.E.	df	Sig.	Exp(B)
Training Hours	0.097	0.030	1	0.001	1.102
Level of Employee Engagement	0.614	0.214	1	0.004	1.848
Level of Employee Education			2	0.013	
Level of Employee Education (Master's Degree = 1)	1.591	0.675	1	0.018	4.910
Level of Employee Education (doctorate = 2)	2.487	1.122	1	0.027	12.025
Constant	−8.015	2.021	1	0.000	0.000

Remarks: Independent Variables: Training Hours, Level of Employee Engagement, Level of Employees Education; Dependent Variable: Levels of Productivity

of higher productivity increase by a factor of 1.102. Next, for Level of Employee Engagement: the coefficient ($B = 0.614$) is positive and statistically significant ($p = 0.004$). Higher levels of employee engagement are associated with increased odds of higher productivity (Exp(B) = 1.848).

Finally, since the Level of Employee Education is collected in the form of an ordinal measure, to interpret the results of the variable, it is important to compare each variable with the baseline reference category. For the master's degree, the coefficient ($B = 1.591$) indicates the change in the log odds of higher productivity associated with employees holding a master's degree compared to those having a bachelor's degree. The p-value equals 0.000, suggesting that the coefficient is statistically significant. The odds ratio (Exp(B) = 4.910) indicates an increase in the odds of higher productivity for employees with a master's degree compared to those with a bachelor's degree.

Next, for the PhD, the coefficient ($B = 2.487$) indicates the change in the log odds of higher productivity associated with employees holding a doctorate compared to those having a bachelor's degree. The p-value equals 0.000, indicating that the coefficient is statistically significant. The odds ratio (Exp(B) = 12.025) suggests an increase in the odds of higher productivity for employees with a PhD compared to those with a bachelor's degree.

8.3.12 Discriminant Analysis

Discriminant analysis is a statistical technique utilised to classify observations into two or more distinct categories based on a set of predictor variables. The principal purpose of discriminant analysis is to classify the linear combination of predictor variables that best separates the groups under consideration. This method is widely applied across various fields, such as psychology, biology, marketing, finance, and management, to understand and predict group membership (Huberty & Morris, 1989; Green & Salkind, 2016).

The primary objective of discriminant analysis is to categorise observations into predefined groups based on their attributes or characteristics. These groups may represent different categories, classes, or outcomes of interest. To achieve this, one or more predictor variables are utilised to differentiate between the groups. These predictor variables can be continuous, categorical, or a combination of both. The dependent variable in discriminant analysis is a categorical variable that defines the groups or categories into which the observations are categorised. This variable is often referred to as the dependent variable or grouping variable (Kleinbaum et al., 2007; Stevens, 2002).

Central to discriminant analysis is the discriminant function, a mathematical equation that combines the predictor variables to achieve optimal separation between the groups. This function is derived from the differences in means and variances between the groups and acts as a critical tool in the classification process (Raykov & Marcoulides, 2008; Mardia et al., 1979).

In summary, discriminant analysis is a valuable statistical technique for classification and prediction tasks. It provides insights into the relationships between predictor variables and group membership, thereby assisting researchers in making informed decisions by identifying the factors that distinguish between different groups or categories.

8.3.12.1 Fundamental Assumptions

1. The predictor variables within each group should be normally distributed.
2. The variance-covariance matrices of the predictor variables should be equal across all groups.
3. Dependent variables or observations used in the analysis should be independent of each other. In other words, there should be no systematic relationship or dependency between observations.
4. The relationship between the predictor variables and group membership should be linear. Discriminant analysis assumes that the discriminant functions are linear combinations of the predictor variables.

For example, a dataset is collected from 102 managers of the small firms to find out how to increase levels of productivity (Dependent Variable is coded as 0 = Less Productive Firms, and 1 = More Productive Firms). Dependent Variables are composed of: 1. Experience of Employees, 2. Number of Employees, and 3. Amount of Funding for Training per Year (USD).

Note: In this example, all independent variables are collected in the form of ratio measures.

8.3.12.2 Hypotheses

H_0: There are no significant differences in the mean values of the predictors (Experience of Employees, Number of Employees, Amount of Funding for Training per Year) between More Productive and Less Productive Firms.

H_a: There are significant differences in the mean values of the predictors between More Productive and Less Productive Firms.

As indicated in Fig. 8.52, firstly, select 'Analyse'. Next, select 'Classify'. Finally, select 'Discriminant'.

As indicated in Fig. 8.53, firstly, select 'Dependent Variable; Levels of Productivity' as 'Grouping Variable'. Next, select 'Define Range', then define Minimum as '0' and Maximum as '1'. Next, select 'Continue'. Furthermore, select all independent variables as 'Independents: 1) Experience of Employees, 2) Number of Employees, and 3) Funding for Training per year'. Lastly, select 'Statistics'.

As indicated in Fig. 8.54, firstly, on the Discriminant Analysis Statistics, select 'Means, Univariate ANOVAs, Box's M' under the 'Descriptives'. Next, select 'Fisher's, and Unstandardised' under the 'Function Coefficients'. Next, select 'Within-groups correlation' under the Matrices. Finally, select 'Continue'.

As indicated in Fig. 8.55, firstly, select 'Save'. Next, on the 'Discriminant Analysis Save', select 'Predicted group membership', and 'Probabilities of group membership'. Next, select 'Continue'. Finally, select 'OK'.

As shown on Table 8.30, the correlation between the independent variables, namely Experience of Employees, Number of Employees, and Funding for Training per Year are not greater than 0.80 or 80 per cent. Hence, there is no multicollinearity (Auamnoy, 2002).

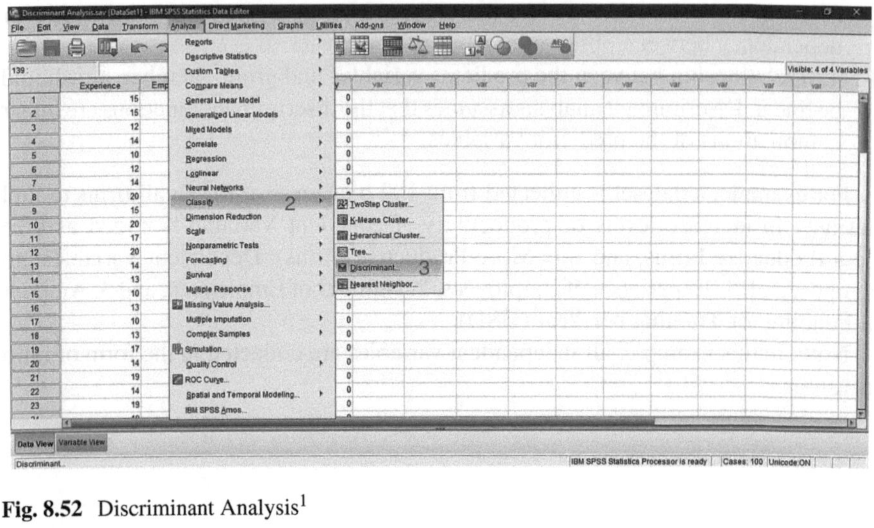

Fig. 8.52 Discriminant Analysis[1]

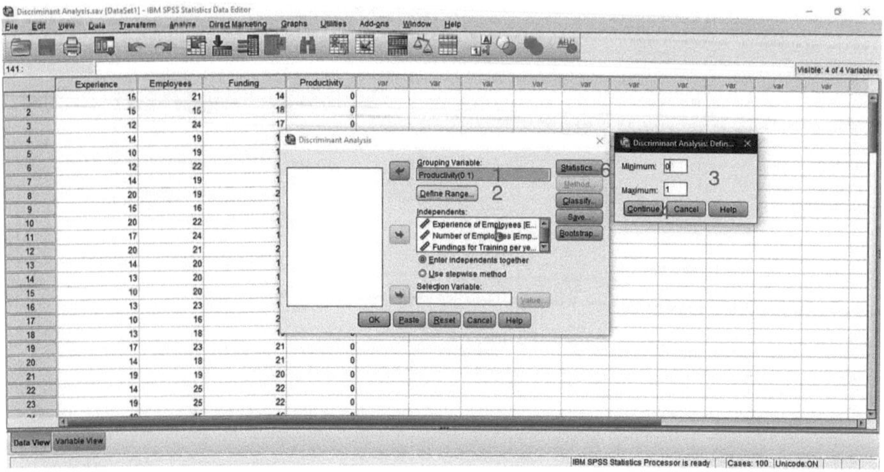

Fig. 8.53 Discriminant Analysis[2]

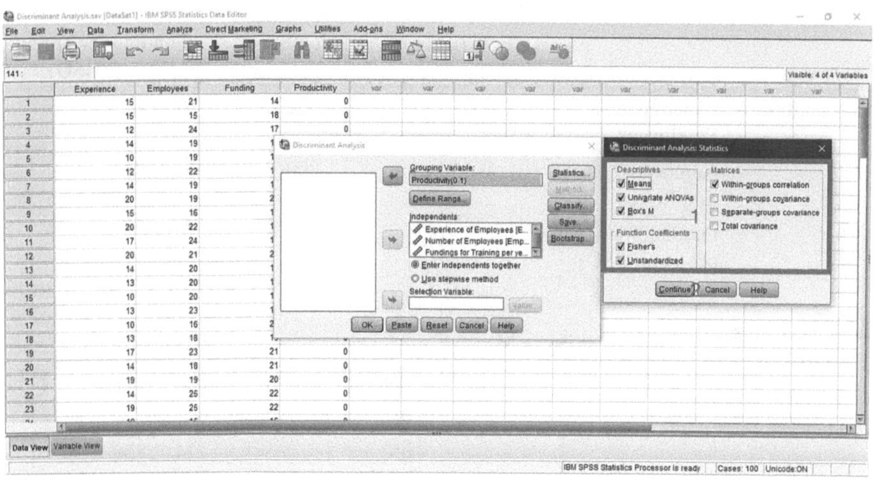

Fig. 8.54 Discriminant Analysis[3]

As indicated in Table 8.31, the *p*-value equals 0.438, which is greater than 0.01. Hence, the null hypothesis cannot be rejected. This means that it does not violate the fundamental assumptions of discriminant analysis. So, discriminant analysis can satisfactorily be applied to test this dataset.

As indicated in Table 8.32, there are 102 cases in the sample. The first group, of 51 respondents, is categorised as 'Less Productive Firms', and the latter group of 51 is classified as 'More Productive Firms'.

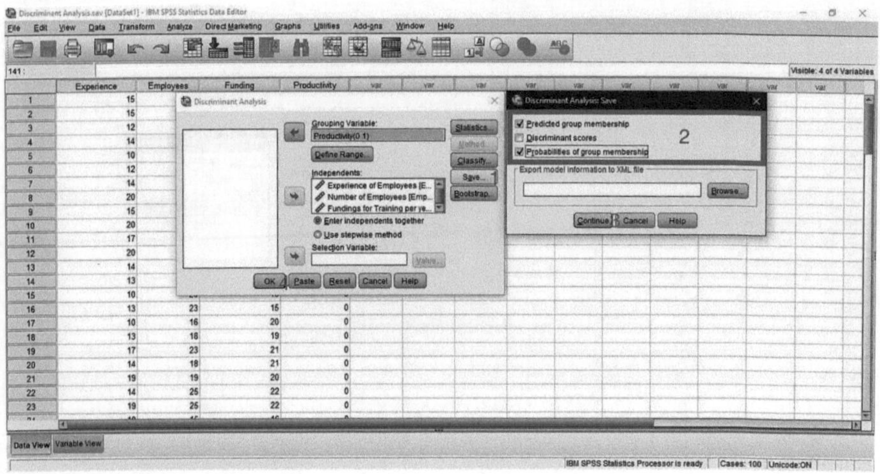

Fig. 8.55 Discriminant Analysis[4]

Table 8.30 Results of correlation; Pooled within-groups matrices

		Experience of employees	Number of employees	Funding for Training per year (USD)
Correlation	Experience of Employees	1.000	0.062	0.219
	Number of Employees		1.000	0.315
	Funding for Training per year (USD)		.	1.000

Table 8.31 Test results of Box's M

Box's M		6.067
F	Approx.	0.978
	df1	6
	df2	72452.830
	Sig.	0.438

Table 8.32 Prior Probabilities for Groups ($n = 102$)

Firm Productivity 0 = Less Productive Firms, 1 = More Productive Firms	Prior	Cases used in analysis	
		Unweighted	Weighted
0	0.500	51	51.000
1	0.500	51	51.000
Total	1.000	102	102.000

Table 8.33 Classification function coefficients

	Firm Productivity 0 = Less Productive Firms, 1 = More Productive Firms	
	0	1
Experience of Employees	1.096	1.538
Number of Employees	1.738	1.841
Funding for Training per Year (USD)	1.556	1.685
(Constant)	−40.513	−52.704

Fisher's linear discriminant functions

As shown in Table 8.33, the Fisher's linear discriminant functions shows the coefficients of each independent variable in different categorisations, namely Less Productive Firms and More Productive Firms.

As indicated in Table 8.34, the canonical correlation equals 0.623, or that the set of predictors can explain the dependent variable by 62.3 per cent. Thus, the levels of prediction are considered to be moderately accurate.

In Table 8.35, all the *p*-values of the independent variables, namely Experience of Employees, Number of Employees, and Funding for Training per Year (USD), are lower than 0.05. Hence, the null hypotheses is rejected. This suggests that all the independent variables or the set of predictors are statistically significant when tested with the dependent variable, Level of Productivity.

H_0: There are no significant differences in the mean values of the predictors (Experience of Employees, Number of Employees, Amount of Funding for Training per Year) between More Productive Firms and Less Productive Firms.
H_1: There are significant differences in the mean values of the predictors between More Productive Firms and Less Productive Firms.

As indicated in Table 8.36, the *p*-value is lower than 0.05. Hence, the null hypothesis is rejected. This suggests that there are significant differences in the mean

Table 8.34 Results of canonical correlation

Function	Eigenvalue	% of Variance	Cumulative %	Canonical correlation
1	0.634	100.0	100.0	0.623

Table 8.35 Tests of equality of group means

	Wilks' Lambda	F	df1	df2	Sig.
Experience of Employees	0.640	56.293	1	100	0.000
Number of Employees	0.938	6.620	1	100	0.012
Funding for Training per year (USD)	0.874	14.431	1	100	0.000

values of the predictors between More Productive Firms and Less Productive Firms (Tables 8.37 and 8.38).

$$z = w0 + w1 \cdot px1 + w2 \cdot px2 + w3 \cdot px3$$

The discriminant analysis equation values of unstandardised coefficients can be written as:

$$z = -7.729 + 0.281\ (\text{Experience of Employees}) + 0.066\ (\text{Number of Employees}) + 0.082\ (\text{Funding for Training per year (USD)})$$

$$z = w1 \cdot px1 + w2 \cdot px2 + w3 \cdot px3$$

The discriminant analysis equation values can be written as:

$$z = 0.881\ (\text{Experience of Employees}) + 0.199\ (\text{Number of Employees}) + 0.221\ (\text{Funding for Training per year (USD)})$$

When the z changes one unit, the most powerful predictor is the Experience of Employees (0.881) which is greater than Number of Employees (0.199), and Funding for Training per year (USD) (0.221) approximately four times. This suggests that in order to increase the level of productivity of the firms, senior management needs to consider recruiting highly experienced employees, increasing the number of employees, and investing in a greater amount of funding for training for training per year.

Table 8.36 Results of Wilks' Lambda

Test of Function(s)	Wilks' Lambda	Chi-square	df	Sig.
1	0.612	48.388	3	0.000

Table 8.37 Results of canonical discriminant function coefficients (unstandardised coefficients)

	Function
	1
Experience of Employees	0.281
Number of Employees	0.066
Funding for Training per year (USD)	0.082
(Constant)	−7.729

Table 8.38 The standardised canonical discriminant function coefficients

	Function
	1
Experience of Employees	0.881
Number of Employees	0.199
Funding for Training per year (USD)	0.221

8.4 Non-Parametric Statistics

8.4.1 Chi-square and Fisher's Exact Statistical Tests

Chi-square (χ^2) is regarded as a non-parametric statistical test used to analyse categorical variables, including those measured on nominal or ordinal scales. This statistical technique is advantageous as it does not require assumptions about the distribution of the data, making it a distribution-free approach (Leech, 2022). The chi-square test is applied when dealing with categorical data and is frequently used to determine whether or not there is a significant association between two categorical variables (Agresti, 2018).

When analysing the association between two 2×2 variables, Fisher's Exact Test serves as an alternative to the chi-square test. This statistical test is used to examine whether or not there are non-random associations between two categorical variables and is particularly valuable when dealing with small sample sizes, where the chi-square test might not be appropriate (Fisher, 1922). Fisher's Exact Test is typically employed in 2×2 contingency tables, where each variable has two categories (Sokal & Rohlf, 1995).

8.4.1.1 Fundamental Assumptions

1. Variables are in the form of categorical scales (nominal, ordinal).
2. The samples are distribution free.
3. The variance of the group of samples can be statistically different.

For example, is there a statistical relationship between people wearing or not wearing masks and a COVID-19 infection?

As indicated in Table 8.39, if the number of *a*, *b*, *c*, and *d*, are lower than 5, the *p*-value can be calculated using Fisher's Exact Test. If the number of *a*, *b*, *c*, and *d*, are greater than 5, the *p*-value can be calculated using Pearson's Chi-Square Test.

Example: Is there a statistical relationship between people wearing or not wearing masks and a COVID-19 infection?

Table 8.39 Crosstabulations[1]

		Wearing masks		
		(Observed Frequency)		
		Not infected	Infected	
Not wearing masks	Not infected	**a**	**b**	m1
(Expected frequency)	Infected	**c**	**d**	m2
		n1	n2	

8.4.1.2 Hypotheses

H_0: There is no association between groups of people wearing or not wearing masks and a COVID-19 infection.
H_1: There is an association between groups of people wearing or not wearing masks and a COVID-19 infection.

As depicted in Fig. 8.56, firstly select 'Analyse', then select 'Descriptive Statistics', next choose 'Crosstabs'.

As shown in Fig. 8.57, once the box of Crosstabs pops up, select variable (COVID: not infected = 0, infected = 1) for Row(s), and select variable (Masks: not wearing = 0, wearing = 1) to Column. Then select 'Statistics', and once the box of 'Crosstabs Statistics' appears, select 'Chi-square', 'Risk', and 'Continue', and finally select 'OK'.

As shown in Fig. 8.58, there are no numbers which are lower than 5. Hence, the results of the *p*-value can be reviewed using the Pearson's Chi-square tests.

As indicated in Fig. 8.59, the *p*-value equals 0.003, which is lower than 0.05. Hence, the null hypothesis is rejected. This suggests that there is an association

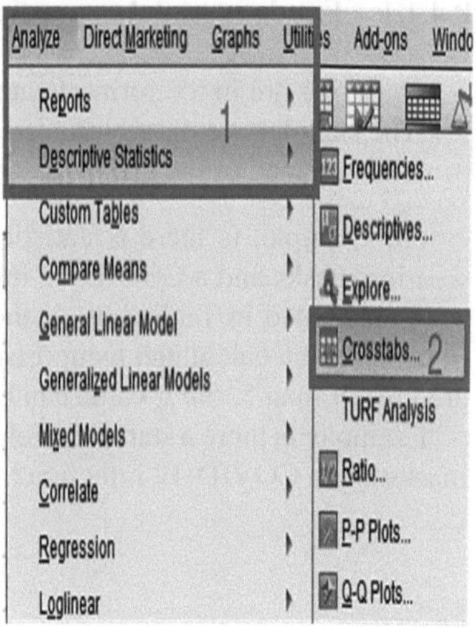

Fig. 8.56 Ch-square and Fisher's exact tests[1]

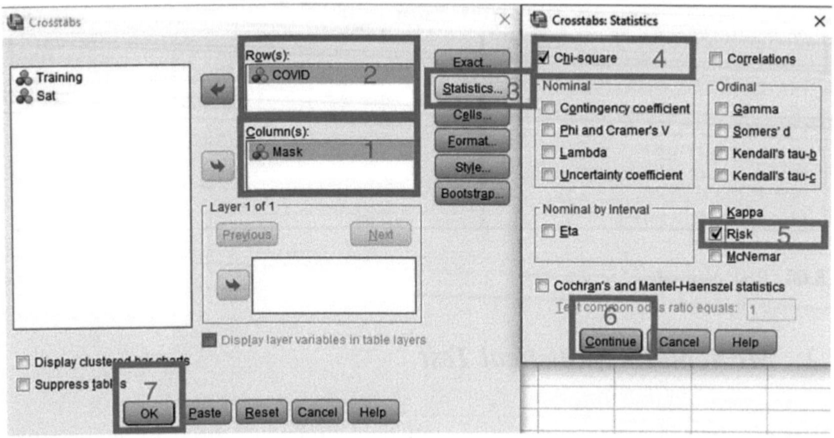

Fig. 8.57 Chi-square and Fisher's exact tests[2]

COVID * Mask Crosstabulation

Count

		Mask		
		Wearing mask	Not wearing mask	Total
COVID	Not infected	12	5	17
	Infected	5	17	22
Total		17	22	39

Fig. 8.58 Crosstabulations[2]

between the groups of people wearing and not wearing masks and a COVID-19 infection.

As illustrated in Fig. 8.60, the odds ratio value equals 8.160. This suggests that the group of people not wearing masks are 8.160 times more likely to be infected than the group of people wearing masks.

Chi-Square Tests

	Value	df	Asymptotic Significance (2-sided)	Exact Sig. (2-sided)	Exact Sig. (1-sided)
Pearson Chi-Square	8.934[a]	1	.003		
Continuity Correction[b]	7.093	1	.008		
Likelihood Ratio	9.243	1	.002		
Fisher's Exact Test				.004	.004
Linear-by-Linear Association	8.705	1	.003		
N of Valid Cases	39				

a. 0 cells (0.0%) have expected count less than 5. The minimum expected count is 7.41.

b. Computed only for a 2x2 table

Fig. 8.59 Chi-square tests

Risk Estimate

	Value	95% Confidence Interval	
		Lower	Upper
Odds Ratio for COVID (Not infected / Infected)	8.160	1.927	34.549
For cohort Mask= Wearing mask	3.106	1.355	7.118
For cohort Mask= Not wearing mask	.381	.176	.822
N of Valid Cases	39		

Fig. 8.60 Risk estimate

8.4.2 *McNemar's Statistical Test*

McNemar's Test is a non-parametric statistical procedure used to analyse paired nominal data. It is specifically designed for scenarios involving two related categorical variables, with the goal of determining whether or not there are significant differences between the marginal frequencies (the totals in each category) for these variables (Lachin, 2014).

McNemar's Test is commonly applied in 2 × 2 contingency tables with dichotomous (binary) outcomes, where the objective is to assess whether or not there is a significant difference in the distribution of outcomes between the two related groups (Pett, 2015). This type of statistical test is often utilised in fields such as medical research, psychology, management, and other social sciences where researchers aim to compare proportions or frequencies within a paired context (Gilbert, 2016).

8.4.2.1 Fundamental Assumption

1. Variables are in the form of categorical scales (nominal, ordinal), and the data should be organised into pairs, where each pair consists of two related observations or measurements.
2. The samples are distribution free.
3. Variance of the groups of samples can be statistically different.
4. relationship between people wearing or not The outcomes being compared should be dichotomous or binary, meaning there are only two possible categories or responses.
5. The observations within each pair should be dependent, reflecting some form of connection or relationship. This dependence is crucial in order for McNemar's statistical test to be appropriate.

For example, suppose a company is implementing a new management training programme to enhance the leadership skills of its employees. There are 30 managers (attendants) attending the training programme. All managers are requested to take the test before and after the training programme. The test is out of 100; 50 points and over is considered to be a pass; not pass = 0, whilst pass = 1. Hence, the relationship between the pre- and post-tests are analysed by using McNemar's statistical test.

8.4.2.2 Hypothesis

H_0: There is no association between the pre- and post-tests of the results of the managers' tests.

H_1: There is an association between the pre- and post-tests of the results of the managers' tests.

As depicted in Fig. 8.61, firstly select 'Analyse', then select 'Nonparametric Tests', and next choose 'Related Samples'.

As indicated in Fig. 8.62, firstly select 'Fields', then select 'Both Variables; Before and After' for 'Test Fields'.

As illustrated in Fig. 8.63, firstly select 'Settings', then select 'McNemar Tests (2 samples)', and next choose 'Run'.

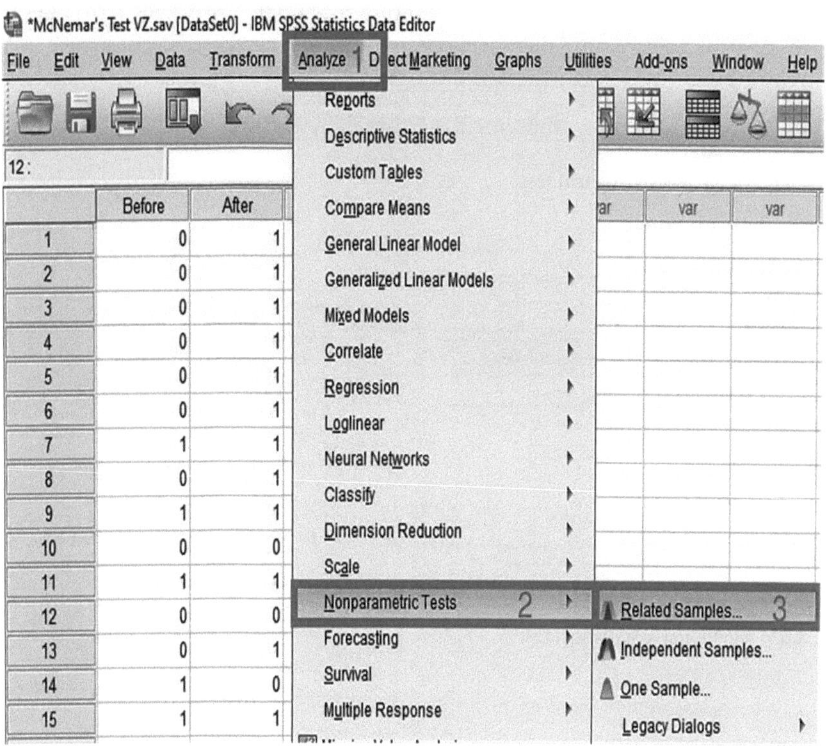

Fig. 8.61 McNemar's statistical test[1]

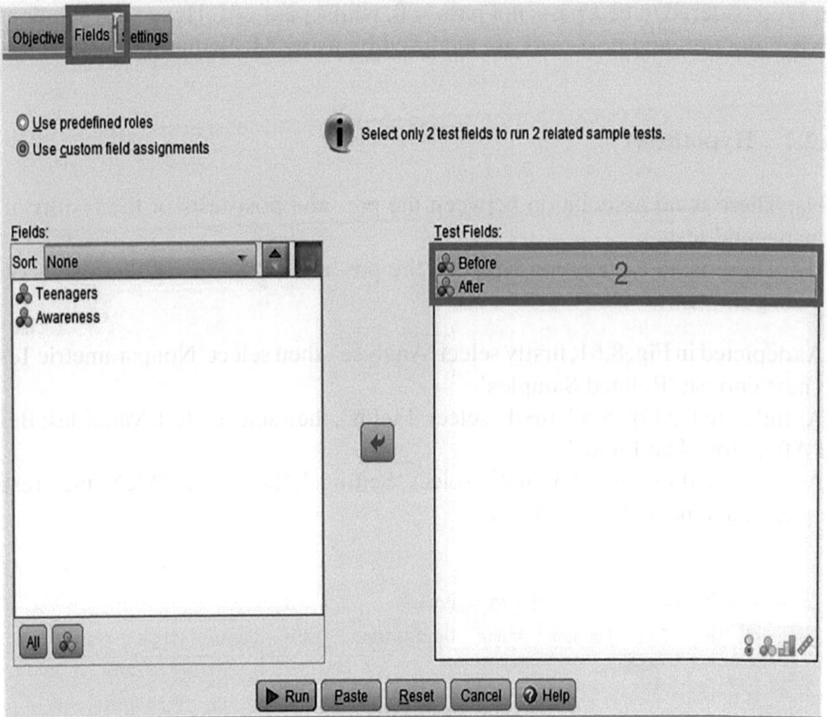

Fig. 8.62 McNemar's statistical test[2]

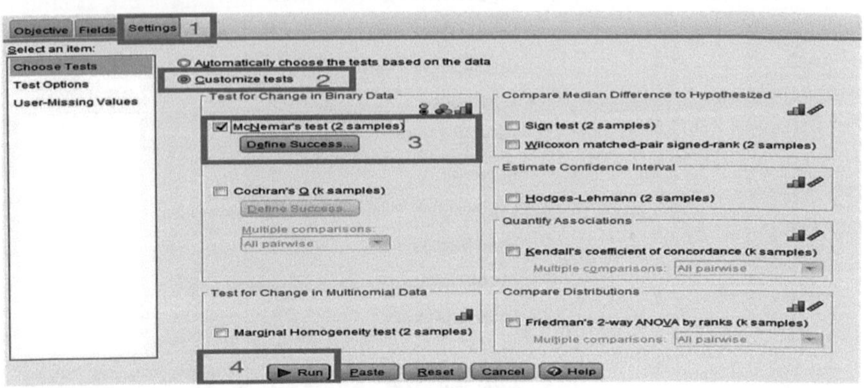

Fig. 8.63 McNemar's statistical test[3]

Hypothesis Test Summary

	Null Hypothesis	Test	Sig.	Decision
1	The distributions of different values across Before and After are equally likely.	Related-Samples McNemar Test	.039[1]	Reject the null hypothesis.

Asymptotic significances are displayed. The significance level is .05.

[1]Exact significance is displayed for this test.

Fig. 8.64 Results of McNemar's statistical test

As indicated in Fig. 8.64, the *p*-value equals 0.39, which is lower than 0.05. Hence, the null hypothesis is rejected. It can be concluded that there is an association between the pre- and post-tests of the results of the managers' tests.

8.4.3 Sign Statistical Test

The sign test is a non-parametric statistical technique utilised to appraise the difference between two dependent samples, particularly when the assumptions required for other tests, such as the paired samples t-test, are not satisfied. This test is especially useful when the data do not adhere to a normal distribution or when the sample size is too small to reliably assess the distribution (Gibbons & Chakraborti, 2010).

The sign test is often applied in scenarios involving matched pairs of subjects or repeated measurements on the same subjects, as it does not require the data to meet specific distributional assumptions (Siegel & Castellan, 1988). It is a straightforward approach for assessing whether there is a significant median difference between paired observations.

8.4.3.1 Fundamental Assumptions

1. Dependent Samples: The samples must be dependent (paired or matched). This typically means the data consist of paired observations, such as measurements before and after a treatment on the same subjects, or measurements from matched subjects in two different conditions.
2. Ordinal Scale or Higher: The data should be ordinal, interval, or ratio. Whilst the sign test does not require the assumption of normality or specific distributional forms, it does assume that it is meaningful to talk about one measurement being higher or lower than another. Thus, the test is appropriate for data that can be ranked.
3. Symmetry of the Distribution of Differences: Under the null hypothesis, it is assumed that the distribution of differences (post-treatment minus pre-treatment, for example) is symmetric around the median. This assumption is important

Table 8.40 Number of sales before and after attending the training programme

Employee	Before Training	After Training
1	9	20
2	4	12
3	3	8
4	5	15
5	14	14
6	6	19
7	7	12
8	5	16
9	3	6
10	10	18

because the sign test evaluates only the direction of changes (positive or negative), not their magnitude. The assumption of symmetry ensures that the median difference is a meaningful measure of central tendency.

4. Random Selection: The pairs or matched subjects should be randomly selected from the population. This is a common assumption for most statistical tests, ensuring that the results are generalisable to the larger population.

For example, a car dealer company has introduced a new training programme to improve the productivity of the sales representatives. Top management would like to evaluate the effectiveness of this programme. To do this, they record the number of sales each of 10 sales staff made in the month before the training and then compare it to the number of sales made in the month after the training.

As indicated in Table 8.40, by obtaining data from the ten sales representatives, the number of sales before and after attending the training programme is identified.

8.4.3.2 Hypotheses

H_0: There is no statistically significant difference between the number of sales before and after attending the training programme.

H_a: There is a statistically significant difference between the number of sales before and after attending the training programmes.

As depicted in Fig. 8.65, firstly select 'Analyse', then select 'Nonparametric Tests', and next choose 'Related Samples'.

As indicated in Fig. 8.66, firstly, select 'Customise Analysis'. Secondly, select 'Fields'.

As indicated in Fig. 8.67, firstly select 'Fields', then select 'Both Variables; Before and After' for 'Test Fields'.

As illustrated in Fig. 8.68, firstly select 'Settings', then select 'Customise Tests'. Next, select 'Sign Tests (2 samples)', then select 'Run'.

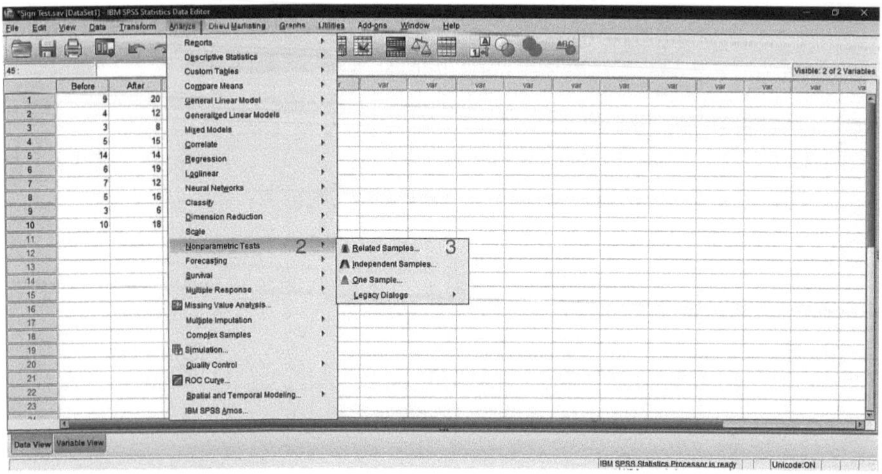

Fig. 8.65 Sign statistical test[1]

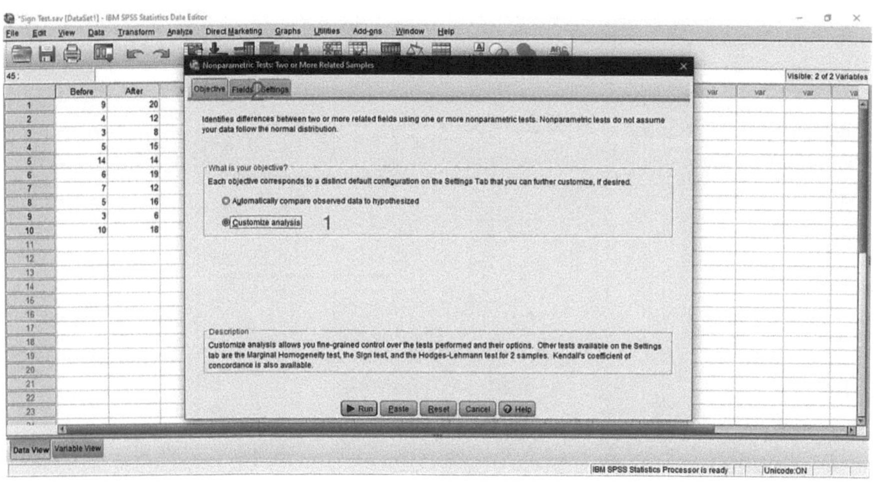

Fig. 8.66 Sign statistical test[2]

As indicated in Fig. 8.69, the p-value equals 0.04, which is lower than 0.05. Hence, the null hypothesis is rejected. It can be concluded that there is a statistically significant difference between the number of sales before and after attending the training programme.

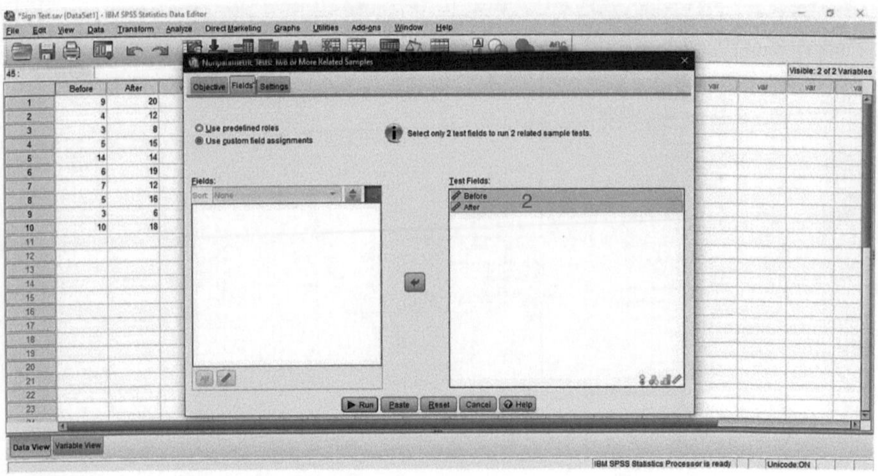

Fig. 8.67 Sign statistical test[3]

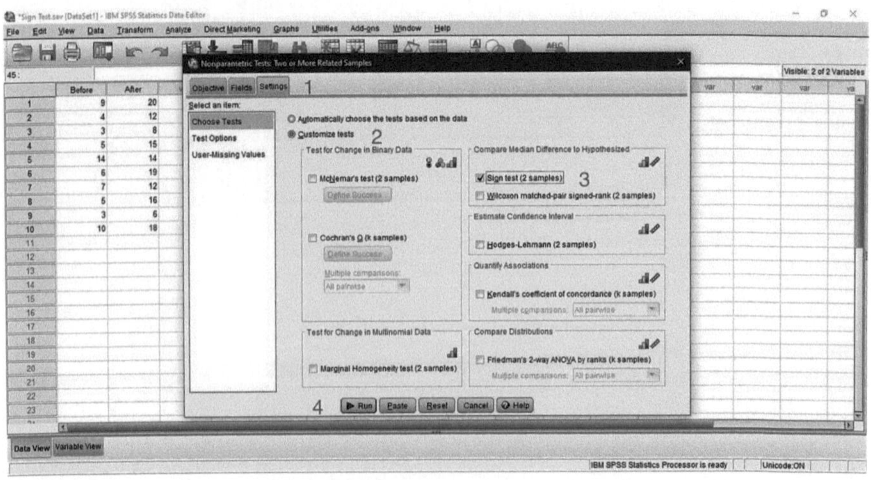

Fig. 8.68 Sign statistical test[4]

Hypothesis Test Summary

	Null Hypothesis	Test	Sig.	Decision
1	The median of differences between Before and After equals 0.	Related-Samples Sign Test	.004[1]	Reject the null hypothesis.

Asymptotic significances are displayed. The significance level is .05.

[1] Exact significance is displayed for this test.

Fig. 8.69 Results of sign statistical test

8.4.4 Wilcoxon Rank Sum Test, Mann-Whitney Test, and Mann Whitney U Test

The Wilcoxon rank sum test, Mann-Whitney test, and Mann-Whitney U test are non-parametric statistical methods employed to analyse differences between two independent groups with respect to a continuous dependent variable.

Notably, the Wilcoxon rank sum test is commonly known as both the Mann-Whitney test and the Mann-Whitney U test. This statistical test was independently developed by Frank Wilcoxon in thc United States and Henry Mann in Australia, though their work was fundamentally equivalent (Wilcoxon, 1992; Lü & Zhou, 2011). Consequently, the test is often referred to by either name, and these terms are used interchangeably across various contexts (Aumanoy, 2002).

8.4.4.1 Fundamental Assumptions

1. Independent variables (X) are in the form of categorical scales (nominal, ordinal), and the independent variable comprises only two groups.
2. Dependent variable (Y) is in the form of continuous scales (interval or ratio).
3. The samples are distribution free.

For example, a company has applied a new management strategy, and senior management wishes to assess its impact on levels of employees' satisfaction. The organisational members of the production department (variable is coded as 0) experienced the new strategy whilst the organisational members of the accounting department continued with the existing method (variable is coded as 1). The company collected satisfaction scores from both departments after the implementation (full marks is 100).

8.4.4.2 Hypotheses

H_0: There is no significant difference in employee satisfaction between the organisational members of the production department and the organisational members of the accounting department.
H_1: There is a significant difference in employee satisfaction between the organisational members of the production department and the organisational members of the accounting department.

As depicted in Fig. 8.70, firstly select 'Analyse', then select 'Nonparametric Tests', and next choose 'Independent Samples'.

As depicted in Fig. 8.71, firstly select 'Fields', then select Independent Variable for 'Groups' (Team 0 and 1), and next choose Dependent Variable for 'Test Fields' (score).

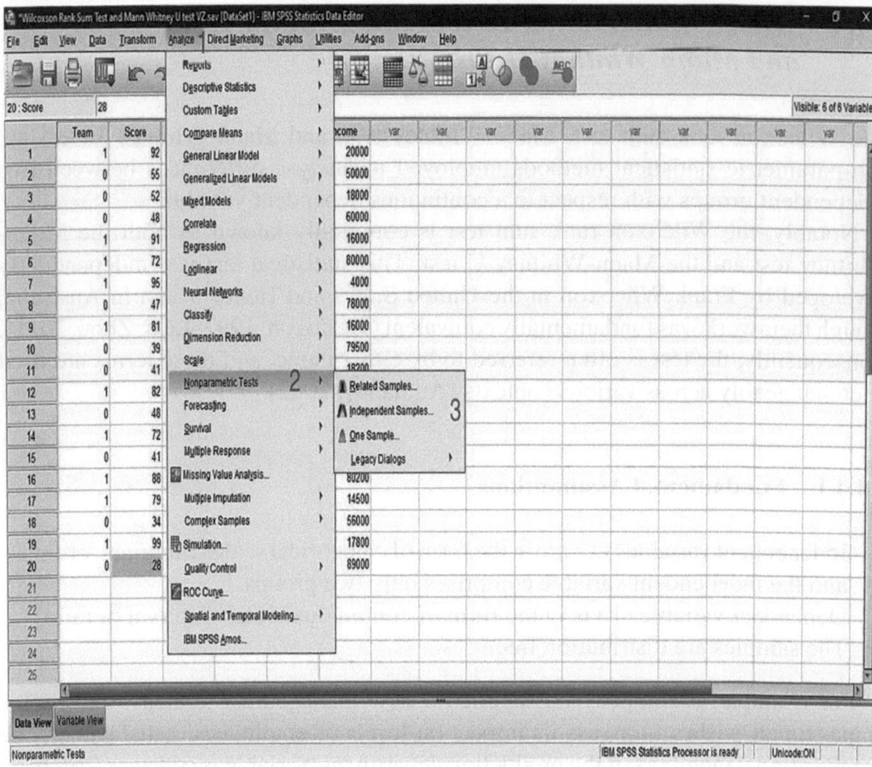

Fig. 8.70 Wilcoxon Rank Sum Test, Mann-Whitney Test, and Mann Whitney U Test[1]

As shown in Fig. 8.72, the *p*-value equals 0.000, which is lower than 0.05. Hence, the null hypothesis is rejected. This means that there is a significant difference in employee satisfaction between the organisational members of the production department and the organisational members of the accounting department.

8.4.5 The Cochran Q Statistical Test

The Cochran Q test is a non-parametric statistical method used to evaluate whether or not there are significant differences between three or more matched groups with dichotomous outcomes. This test is particularly valuable when the assumptions required for parametric tests, such as a repeated measures ANOVA, are not met (Bower et al., 2023).

Essentially, the Cochran Q test extends the McNemar test to accommodate more than two related groups. It allows for the comparison of multiple related samples by assessing whether or not the proportion of successes or failures differs significantly

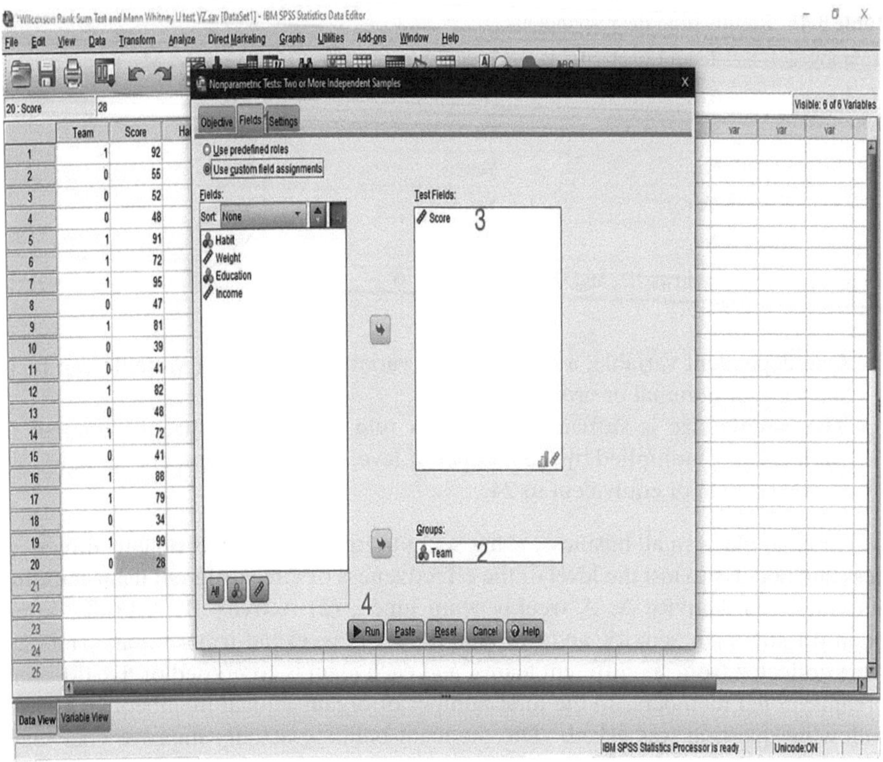

Fig. 8.71 Wilcoxson Rank Sum Test, Mann-Whitney Test, and Mann Whitney U Test[2]

Hypothesis Test Summary

	Null Hypothesis	Test	Sig.	Decision
1	The distribution of Score is the same across categories of Team.	Independent-Samples Mann-Whitney U Test	.000[1]	Reject the null hypothesis.

Asymptotic significances are displayed. The significance level is .05.

[1] Exact significance is displayed for this test.

Fig. 8.72 Wilcoxson Rank Sum Test, Mann-Whitney Test, and Mann Whitney U Test

across these groups (Cochran, 1950). This makes it a valuable tool for testing data from repeated measures or matched groups where traditional parametric assumptions cannot be satisfied.

8.4.5.1 Fundamental Assumptions

1. Independent variable with three groups or levels.

Table 8.41 Results from the respondents

Employee	Team Lunch (A)	Friday Activity (B)	Weekend Meeting (C)
1	Yes	No	No
2	Yes	Yes	No
3	No	Yes	No
4	Yes	Yes	Yes
5	No	No	No

Remark: 'Yes' is coded as '1', and 'No' is coded as '0'

2. One dependent variable, a dichotomous variable. Dependent variable can be in the form of nominal or ordinal measures.
3. The sample size is sufficiently large. A rule of thumb is that the number of subjects, '*n*', multiplied by the number of levels in the independent variable, '*k*', is greater than or equivalent to 24.

For example, a small business owner seeks to improve the level of team effectiveness and decides to test the level of the effectiveness of three different team-building activities: (1) Activity A: A weekly team lunch, (2) Activity B: A Friday afternoon off-site team activity, and (3). Activity C: A weekend-trip seminar. The data were collected from six different teams, and each team is composed of five different organisational members, so the total number of organisational members is 30. The following question was asked: "Did the team-building activity improve your team effectiveness?" (all the organisational members participated in all three activities) (Table 8.41).

Objective: To determine which team-building activity, if any, leads to a significant increase in team effectiveness.

8.4.5.2 Hypotheses

H_0: There is no difference in the level of effectiveness of the three team-building activities. In other words, the proportion of 'Yes' responses (indicating improved team effectiveness) is the same across all three activities: (P(Activity A) = P(Activity B) = P(Activity C)).

H_1: There is a difference in the level of effectiveness of at least one of the team-building activities in compared to the others. This means that at least one activity leads to a different proportion of 'Yes' responses, indicating a variance in how each activity affects team effectiveness: at least one P(Activity) is different from the others.

As depicted in Fig. 8.73, firstly select 'Analyse', then select 'Nonparametric Tests', and next choose 'Related Samples'.

As depicted in Fig. 8.74, firstly select 'Fields', then select the independent variable for 'Test Field' (Activity A, B, and C).

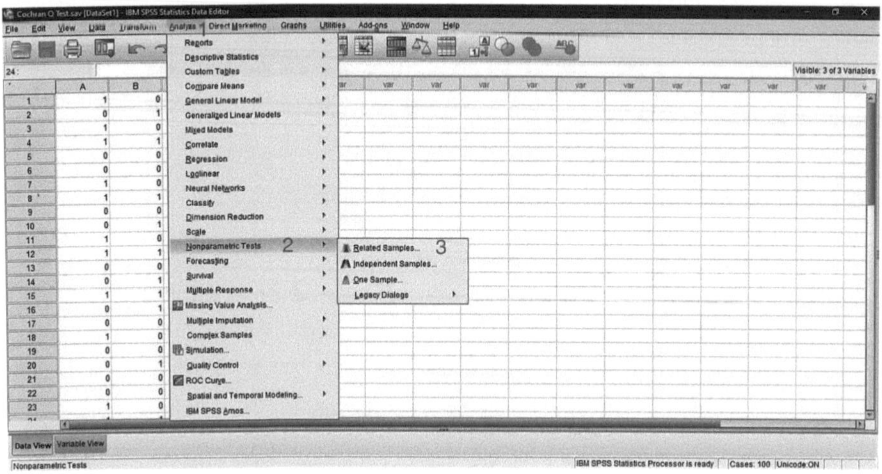

Fig. 8.73 Cochran Q statistical test[1]

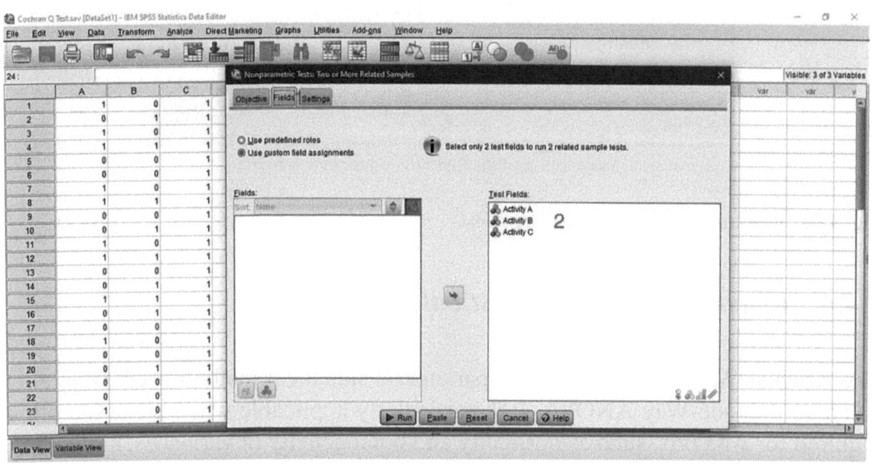

Fig. 8.74 Cochran Q statistical test[2]

As depicted in Fig. 8.75, firstly select ‘Settings’, then select ‘Customised Tests’. Next, select ‘Cochran Q (k samples)’. Finally, select ‘Run’.

As shown in Fig. 8.76, the *p*-value equals 0.000, which is lower than 0.05. Hence, the null hypothesis is rejected. This suggests that there is a difference in the level of the effectiveness of at least one of the team-building activities compared to the others. This means that at least one activity leads to a different proportion of ‘Yes’ responses, indicating a variance in how each activity affects team effectiveness: at least one P(Activity) is different from the others.

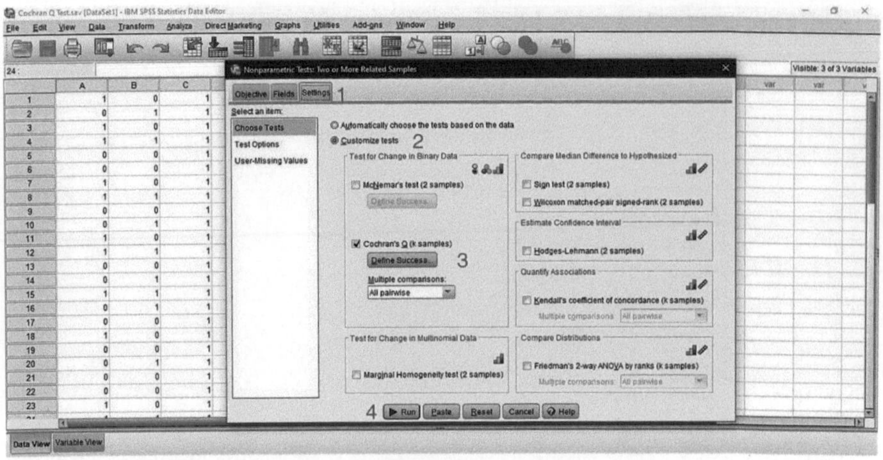

Fig. 8.75 Cochran Q statistical test[3]

Hypothesis Test Summary

	Null Hypothesis	Test	Sig.	Decision
1	The distributions of Activity A , Activity B and Activity C are the same.	Related-Samples Cochran's Q Test	.000	Reject the null hypothesis.

Asymptotic significances are displayed. The significance level is .05.

Fig. 8.76 Results of Cochran Q statistical test

8.4.6 Kruskal-Wallis H Statistical Test

The Kruskal-Wallis H Test is a non-parametric statistical method used as an alternative to the One-Way ANOVA. It is particularly applicable when the assumptions required for ANOVA, such as normality and homogeneity of variances, are not met. This situation commonly arises when the data do not follow a normal distribution or when sample sizes are too small to reliably assess the distribution's normality (Conover, 1999; Kruskal & Wallis, 1952).

The Kruskal-Wallis H test is employed to determine whether or not there are statistically significant differences between two or more independent groups with respect to a continuous or ordinal dependent variable. The test operates by ranking the data across all groups and then evaluating whether or not the distributions of these ranks differ significantly between the groups (Sprent & Smeeton, 2016). This method is effective for analysing data that do not meet the parametric test assumptions.

8.4.6.1 Fundamental Assumptions

1. The dependent variable should be at least ordinal (i.e., it can be ranked), and the independent variable should be categorical with two or more levels/groups.
2. The groups being compared should be independent of each other.
3. There is no strict minimum, but each group should ideally have at least 5 cases. Smaller groups could lead to issues with the reliability of the test results.
4. The test can handle different sample sizes across groups but performs better when group sizes are not extremely unequal.
5. Normality: Unlike parametric tests like ANOVA, the Kruskal-Wallis H test does not assume a normal distribution of the dependent variable within each group.
6. Homogeneity of Variances: The test is also less sensitive to the assumption of equal variances across groups compared to ANOVA, but extreme differences in variances can still affect the test's performance.

For example, a company wants to understand if there is a significant difference in job satisfaction levels among employees in three departments: Production (coded as 1), Marketing (coded as 2), and Finance (coded as 3). The company distributes the survey questionnaire to its employees, asking them to evaluate their level of job satisfaction on a scale from 1 (Very Dissatisfied) to 6 (Very Satisfied).

8.4.6.2 Hypothesis

H_0: There are no statistically significant differences in job satisfaction across the Production, Marketing, and Finance departments.
$H_{a:}$ There are statistically significant differences in job satisfaction across the Production, Marketing, and Finance departments.

As depicted in Fig. 8.77, firstly select 'Analyse', then select 'Nonparametric Tests', and next choose 'Independent Samples'.

As depicted in Fig. 8.78, firstly select 'Customised Analysis', then select 'Fields'.

As depicted on Fig. 8.79, firstly select 'Independent Variable: Departments (Production (1), Marketing (2), and Finance (3))' for 'Groups', then select 'Dependent Variable: Levels of Satisfaction' for 'Test Fields'. Finally, select 'Settings'.

As depicted in Fig. 8.80, firstly select 'Customised Tests'., then select 'Kuskal-Wallis 1-way ANOVA (*k*samples)'. Finally, select 'Run'.

As shown in Fig. 8.81, the *p*-value equals 0.002, which is lower than 0.05. Hence, the null hypothesis is rejected. This means that there are statistically significant differences in job satisfaction levels across the Production, Marketing, and Finance departments. Since the test does not specify where the differences lie (i.e., which specific departments differ from each other), a post-hoc analysis would be necessary to determine the exact differences.

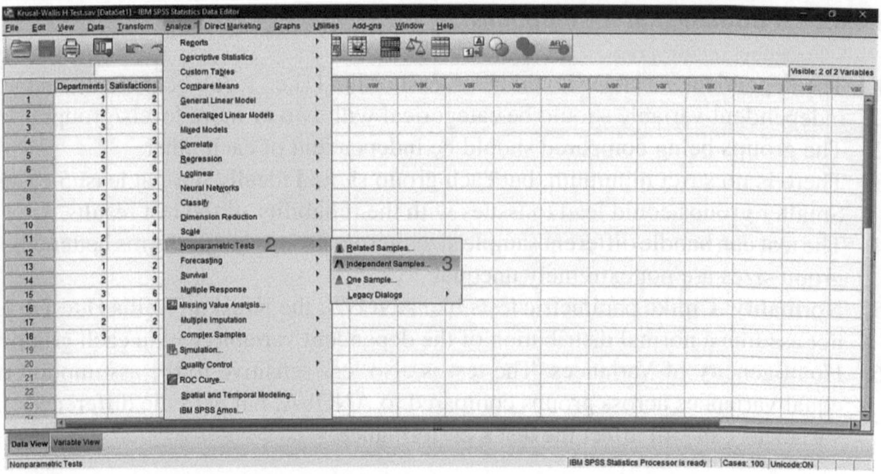

Fig. 8.77 Kruskal-Wallis H statistical test[1]

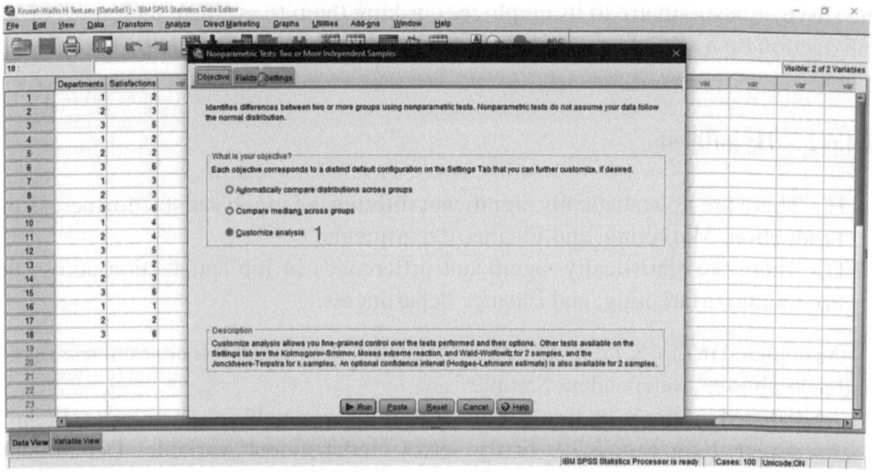

Fig. 8.78 Kruskal-Wallis H statistical test[2]

This straightforward example establishes how to apply the Kruskal-Wallis H statistical test in the management discipline by using SPSS, allowing for the analysis of differences in ordinal data across more than two groups when the data do not meet the assumptions required for ANOVA.

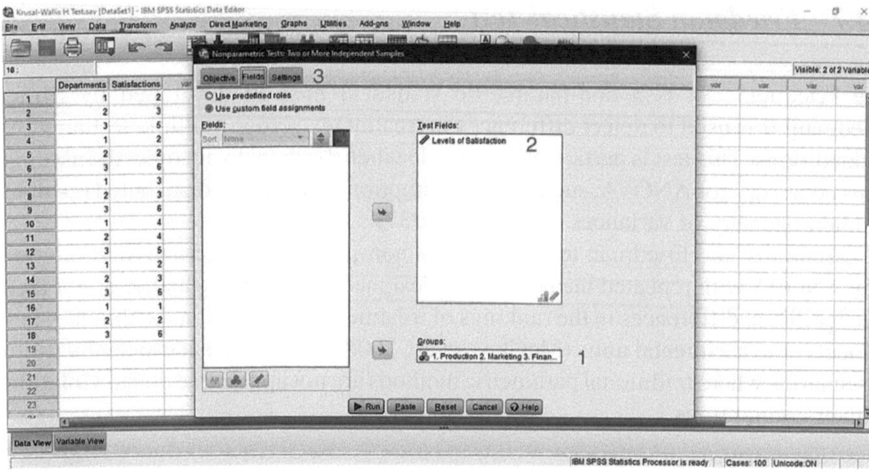

Fig. 8.79 Kruskal-Wallis H statistical test[3]

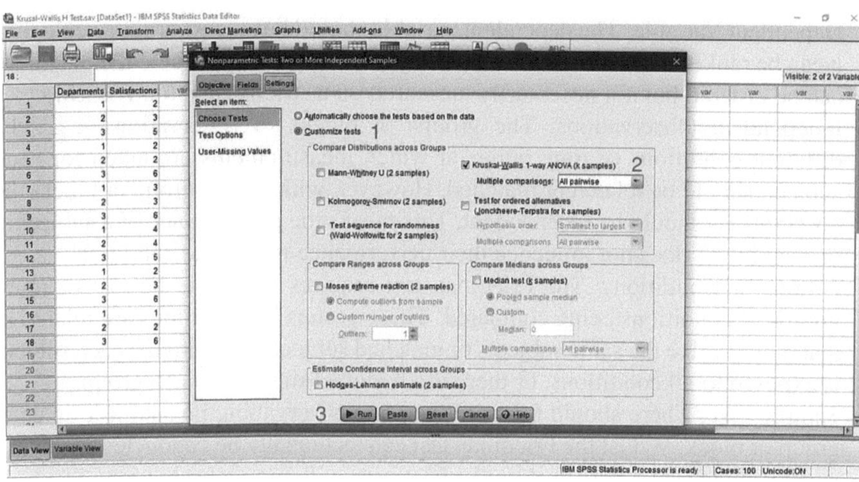

Fig. 8.80 Kruskal-Wallis H statistical test[4]

Hypothesis Test Summary

	Null Hypothesis	Test	Sig.	Decision
1	The distribution of Levels of Satisfaction is the same across categories of 1. Production 2. Marketing 3. Finance.	Independent-Samples Kruskal-Wallis Test	.002	Reject the null hypothesis.

Asymptotic significances are displayed. The significance level is .05.

Fig. 8.81 Kruskal-Wallis H statistical test

8.4.7 *Friedman Statistical Test*

The Friedman test is a non-parametric statistical method developed by Milton Friedman. It is used to detect differences in treatments across multiple test attempts or conditions. This test is particularly valuable when the data do not meet the assumptions necessary for ANOVA, such as the assumption of normally distributed residuals and homogeneity of variances (Friedman, 1937).

Essentially, the Friedman test serves as a non-parametric alternative to the one-way ANOVA with repeated measures. It is designed to evaluate whether or not there are significant differences in the rankings of treatments or conditions within the same subjects or experimental units (McClave et al., 2008). This makes it especially useful in scenarios where traditional parametric methods are not applicable due to violations of their assumptions.

8.4.7.1 Fundamental Assumptions

1. Dependent Variable: The dependent variable should be at least ordinal scale, i.e., it can be ranked. This means the test is applicable to datasets where the outcomes can be ordered but not necessarily measured on a strictly quantitative scale.
2. Independent Observations: The groups or blocks of observations, e.g., the different conditions or time points at which measurements are taken for each subject, should be related or matched. However, within each group or block, the observations should be independent. This means the performance of a subject in one condition does not influence their performance in another condition.
3. Groups or Conditions: The Friedman test requires that there be two or more groups or conditions being compared. These groups or conditions are related in that they involve the same subjects or matched subjects. Essentially, each subject is exposed to all conditions, or there is a matched subject in each group.
4. Sample Size: There should be more than one observation, i.e., subject, in each group or block. Whilst the Friedman test can technically be conducted with very small sample sizes, statistical power increases with more observations.
5. Missing Data: The test assumes that there is no missing data, meaning that every subject has a score for every condition or treatment. If there are missing observations, the Friedman test might not be appropriate without some form of imputation to handle the missing data.
6. Shape of the Distribution: Although the Friedman statistical test does not assume that the data are normally distributed (one of its main advantages over parametric tests), it does assume that the shape of the distribution of the observations is the same for each group. This means that whilst the central tendencies (means, medians) of the groups can differ, the overall shape (e.g., skewness, kurtosis) should be similar across them.

For example, a retail franchise store has three stores in different neighbourhoods—Store A, Store B, and Store C. Senior management would like to evaluate to what

Table 8.42 Data of Friedman statistical test

Customer	Store A	Store B	Store C
1	8	7	9
2	7	6	8
3	8	7	9
4	9	8	10
5	7	7	8
6	8	9	10
7	9	8	9
8	7	6	8
9	8	7	9
10	9	8	10

extents are there the levels of customers' satisfaction are consistent across these stores or if some stores are performing greater than others in terms of customers' satisfaction. Hence, to determine if there are statistically significant differences in customers' satisfaction levels across the three stores.

In addition, the company surveys 10 customers from each store about their satisfaction on a scale of 1 to 10, where 10 indicates the highest level of satisfaction. For illustration, here are the scores:

As shown in Table 8.42, ten customers are asked to rate the level of customer satisfaction with all three stores.

8.4.7.2 Hypotheses

H_0: There is no difference in the median satisfaction scores across the three stores. In other words, customer satisfaction is consistent across Stores A, B, and C (median satisfaction score of Store A = median satisfaction score of Store B = median satisfaction score of Store C).

H_1: At least one store's customer satisfaction level is significantly different from the others.

As seen in Fig. 8.82, firstly select 'Analyse', then select 'Nonparametric Tests', next choose 'Legacy Dialogs', and finally select 'K Related Samples'.

As shown in Fig. 8.83, firstly select all variables (Store A, B, and C) for the 'Test Variables Box', then select 'OK'. By default, the Friedman test is already selected.

As depicted in Table 8.43, the results show that Store C has the highest mean rank, of 2.95, with Store A equalling 1.90 and Store B equalling 1.15.

As shown in Table 8.44, the *p*-value equals 0.000, which is lower than 0.05. Hence, the null hypothesis is rejected. This suggests that at least one store's customer satisfaction level is significantly different from those of the others (at least one store's median satisfaction score differs from those of the others). The results also indicate

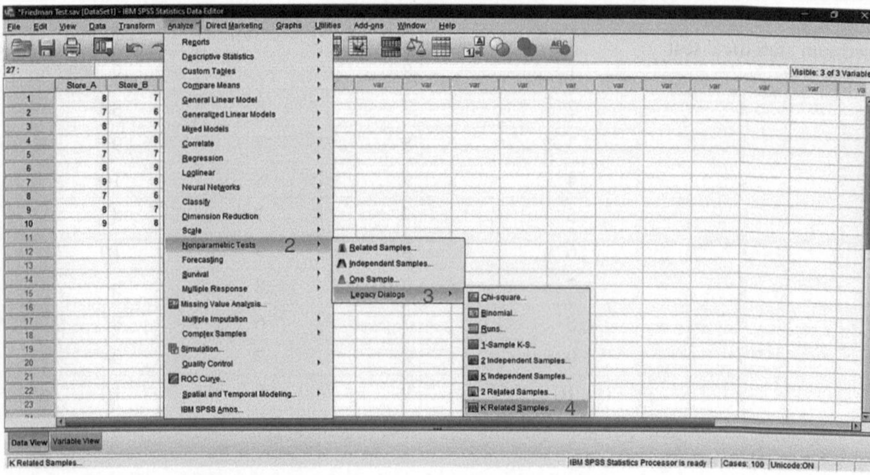

Fig. 8.82 Friedman statistical test[1]

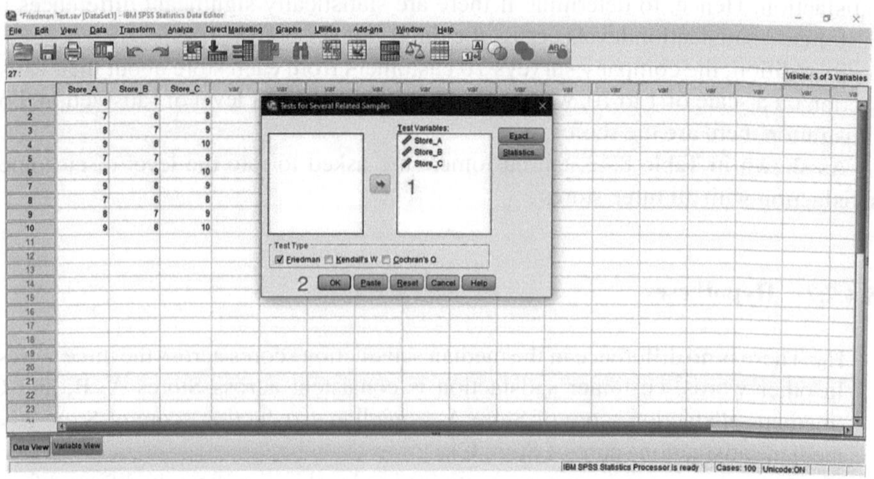

Fig. 8.83 Friedman statistical test[2]

Table 8.43 Results of Friedman statistical test ranks

Stores	Mean Rank
Store A	1.90
Store B	1.15
Store C	2.95

Table 8.44 Results of Friedman statistical test

$n = 10$	
Chi-Square	17.211
Df	2
Asymp. Sig.	0.000

that there is a statistically significant difference in level of customer satisfaction across the stores. More specifically, the results show that whilst there is a difference, the Friedman statistical test does not offer the feature to determine where the difference lies. Researchers need to further conduct post-hoc tests for pairwise comparisons to determine which stores significantly differ from each other in terms of customer satisfaction.

To evaluate post-hoc comparisons, the Wilcoxon signed-rank test is a commonly used statistical technique. This non-parametric test is applied to assess the differences between two related samples or repeated measurements on the same subjects. It is particularly useful in situations where the assumptions required for parametric tests, such as normality, are not met (Jhun et al., 2007). The Wilcoxon signed-rank test evaluates whether or not the median differences between paired observations are significantly different from zero. This makes it a suitable choice for post-hoc analysis when comparing multiple conditions or treatments after an initial analysis reveals significant differences (Conover, 1999).

Firstly, the number of pairwise comparisons needs to be calculated. For k groups, the number of comparisons is $k(k - 1)/2$. With three stores, this would be equivalent to $3(3–1)/2 = 33(3–1)/2 = 3$ comparisons (Store A vs. Store B, Store A vs. Store C, Store B vs. Store C). Next, to adjust for multiple comparisons using the Bonferroni correction, divide the usual alpha level (e.g., 0.05) by the number of comparisons. For three comparisons, you would use $0.05/3 = 0.0167$ as the new alpha level.

As shown in Fig. 8.84, firstly select 'Analyse', then select 'Nonparametric Tests', then choose 'Legacy Dialogs', and finally select '2 Related Samples'.

As shown in Fig. 8.85, firstly select 'Variables (Store A and Store B, Store A and Store C, and Store B and Store C)' respectively into 'Test Pairs', then select 'Wilcoxon', and finally select 'OK'.

H_0: There is no statistically significant difference between Store A and Store B in terms of customer satisfaction.

H_1: There is a statistically significant difference between Store A and Store B in terms of customers satisfaction.

As indicated in Table 8.45, the *p*-value is 0.02, which is greater than 0.0167. Hence, the null hypothesis is accepted. This means that there is no statistically significant difference between Store A and Store B in terms of customer satisfaction.

H_0: There is no statistically significant difference between Store A and Store C in terms of customer satisfaction.

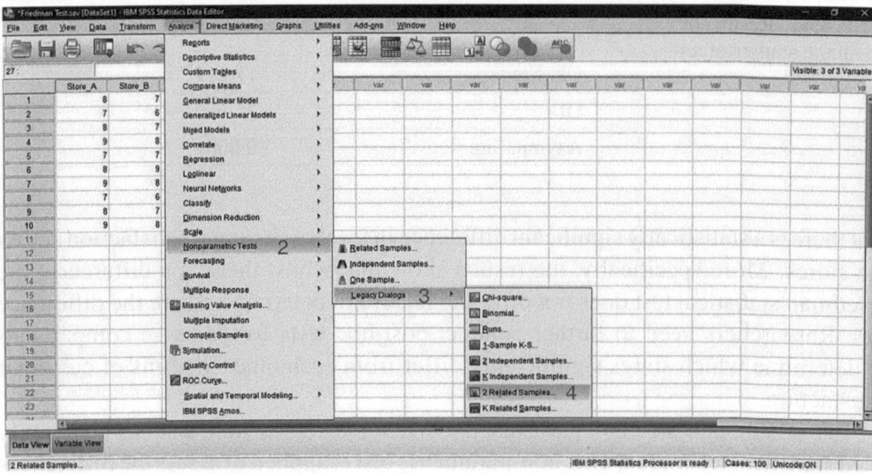

Fig. 8.84 Wilcoxon Signed-Rank Test[1]

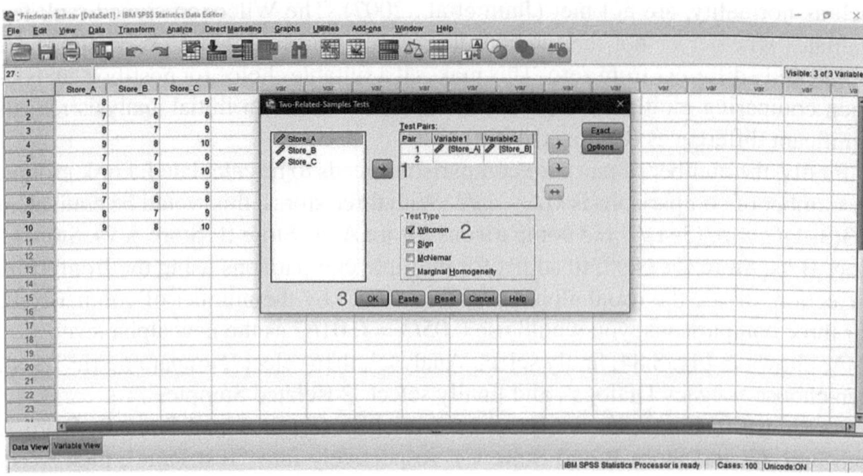

Fig. 8.85 Wilcoxon Signed-Rank Test[2]

Table 8.45 Results of Store A and Store B

	Store_A—Store_B
Z	2.333
Asymp. Sig. (2-tailed)	0.020

Table 8.46 Results of Store A and Store C

	Store_A—Store_C
Z	2.887
Asymp. Sig. (2-tailed)	0.004

Table 8.47 Results of Store B and Store C

	Store_B—Store_C
Z	2.919
Asymp. Sig. (2-tailed)	0.004

H_1: There is a statistically significant difference between Store A and Store C in terms of customer satisfaction.

As indicated in Table 8.46, the *p*-value is 0.004, which is lower than 0.0167. Hence, the null hypothesis is rejected. This means that there is a statistically significant difference between Store A and Store C in terms of customer satisfaction. It can be concluded that Store A has a higher level of customer satisfaction than store C.

H_0: There is no statistically significant difference between Store B and Store C in terms of customer satisfaction.
H_1: There is a statistically significant difference between Store B and Store C in terms of customer satisfaction.

As indicated in Table 8.47, the *p*-value is 0.004, which is lower than 0.0167. Hence, the null hypothesis is rejected. This means that there is a statistically significant difference between Store B and Store C in terms of customer satisfaction. It can be concluded that Store B has a higher level of customer satisfaction than Store C.

In summary, top management should focus on strengthening customer service at Store C and learn from the successful approaches at Store A and Store B to further improve overall customer satisfaction.

8.4.8 Spearman Rank Order Correlation

Spearman rank order correlation, often simply referred to as Spearman's correlation, is a non-parametric statistical measure used to assess the strength and direction of the association between two ranked variables. This method is particularly advantageous in fields such as management due to its flexibility and robustness (Spearman, 2010).

The Spearman rank order correlation is especially useful because it does not require the assumption of a normal distribution for the dataset. This makes it suitable for analysing ordinal data, where variables can be ranked but do not necessarily conform to a standard scale (Cohen et al., 2013). By evaluating the monotonic relationship between two variables, Spearman's correlation provides insights into how well the rankings of one variable correspond to the rankings of another.

Table 8.48 Levels and directions of relationship between variables

Spearman's Correlation Coefficients ($\|\rho\|$)	Interpretations
$\|\rho\|$ 0.00 to 0.30	Weak
Greater than $\|\rho\|$ 0.30 to 0.70	Moderate
Greater than $\|\rho\|$ 0.70 to 1.00	Strong

In Table 8.48, the levels and directions of the relationship between variables have been recommended by Auamnoy (2002). The relationship between variables can be either positive or negative, whilst the *sign of* ρ or rho (positive or negative) represents the direction of the relationship, not the strength.

8.4.8.1 Fundamental Assumptions

1. Ordinal Data: Both variables should be ranked (ordinal) or can be continuous data that is not normally distributed.
2. Monotonic Relationship: There must be a consistent, one-directional relationship between the two variables (either both increase together or as one increases, the other decreases).
3. Independence of Observations: Each pair of variables is independent from other pairs.
4. Data can be distribution free.

For example, the senior management of a retail company with several stores of varying size wants to determine whether or not the size of the store influences customer satisfaction. The company collects data from customers rating their satisfaction on a 6-point Likert scale (1 = Very Dissatisfied, 6 = Very Satisfied) and categorises store size similarly (1 = Very Small, 6 = Very Large).

As shown in Table 8.49, the customers were asked to rank the varying size of the stores and levels of satisfaction.

Table 8.49 Data of Spearman rank order correlation

Store ID	Store Lengths (Rank)	Customers' Satisfaction (Rank)
1	1	2
2	2	1
3	3	4
4	4	3
5	5	6
6	6	5

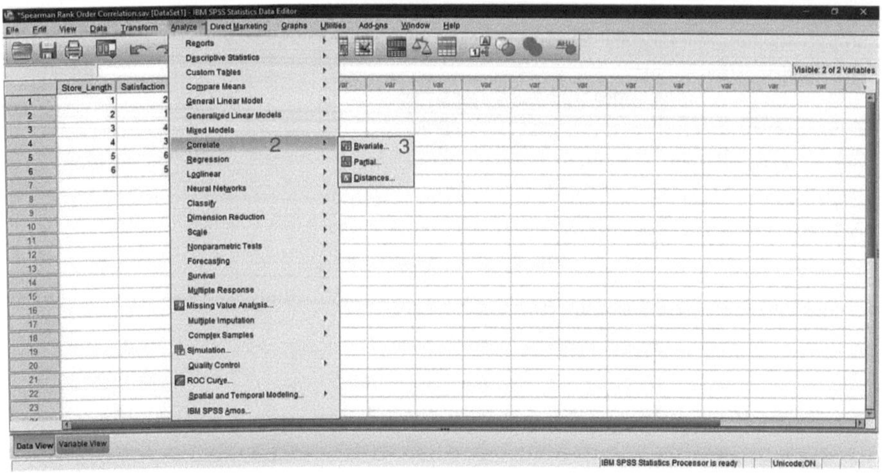

Fig. 8.86 Spearman rank order correlation[1]

8.4.8.2 Hypotheses

H_0: There is no statistical correlation between store size and customer satisfaction.
H_1: There is a statistical correlation between store size and customer satisfaction.

As shown in Fig. 8.86, firstly select ‘Analyse’, then select ‘Correlate’, and lastly, choose ‘Bivariate’.

As seen in Fig. 8.87, firstly select all variables (Store Length, and Satisfaction) for the ‘Variables Box’, then select ‘Spearman’, and lastly, select ‘OK’. By default, the ‘Pearson’s correlation’, ‘two-tailed’, and ‘flag significant correlations’ settings are already selected.

As indicated in Table 8.50, the *p*-value equals 0.042, which is lower than 0.05. Hence, the null hypothesis is rejected. This suggests that there is a statistical correlation between store size and customer satisfaction. The results also show a moderate positive correlation between size of store and level of customer satisfaction. This suggests that in this scenario, larger shops are associated with a higher level of customer satisfaction. Senior management could consider this insight when planning the layout or location of future stores, focussing on larger spaces in order to potentially enhance customer satisfaction.

8.5 Chapter Summary

This chapter explored statistical techniques for testing research hypotheses, focussing on both parametric and non-parametric methods. It provided an overview of inferential statistics and illustrated these concepts with practical examples drawn from

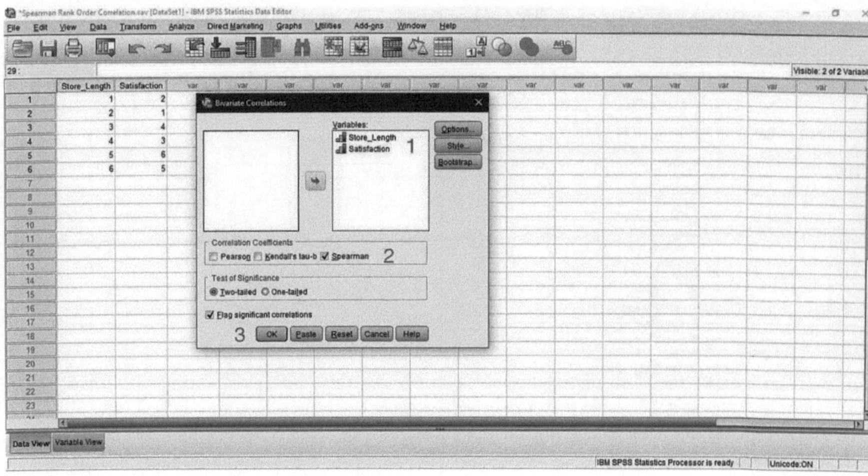

Fig. 8.87 Spearman rank order correlation[2]

Table 8.50 Results of Spearman rank order correlation ($n = 6$)

			Store Length	Customers' Satisfaction
Spearman's rho	Store Length	Correlation Coefficient	1.000	0.829*
		Sig. (2-tailed)		0.042

*Correlation is significant at the 0.05 level (2-tailed)

research in the management discipline, demonstrating effective data analysis and interpretation. The next chapter addresses methods for applying qualitative data analysis.

8.6 Questions for Future Reflection

1. A researcher wants to determine if there is a difference in the annual performance ratings (measured on a scale of 1–100) among organisational members from three different departments: Sales, Marketing, and Operations. The data are found to be non-normally distributed. From the tests explained in this chapter, which is the most appropriate statistical test to use, and why? Justify your choice by explaining why a One-Way ANOVA would be inappropriate in this case.
2. A study investigates the impact of both 'Management Style' (Factor 1: Democratic vs. Autocratic) and 'Work Setting' (Factor 2: Office-based vs. Remote) on 'Organisational Members' Engagement' (the dependent variable). The analysis reveals a statistically significant interaction effect ($p = 0.012$) between the two

factors. What does this interaction effect signify, and why must the researcher now be cautious when interpreting the main effects of 'Management Style' and 'Work Setting' independently?

3. A researcher plans to utilise a One-Way ANOVA to test the effect of three different training programmes on different levels of organisational members' productivity scores. A senior colleague suggests that 'prior years of experience' might influence productivity and recommends utilising a One-Way ANCOVA instead. In simple terms, explain the purpose of including 'prior years of experience' as a covariate in this analysis. What would be the main benefit of using ANCOVA over ANOVA here?
4. A study measures organisational members' morale scores before and after a corporate merger. What is the key statistical assumption that would lead a researcher to select a Paired Sample t-test over a non-parametric alternative such as the Wilcoxon Signed-Rank Test? If that assumption were violated, what would be the risk of proceeding with the t-test?
5. In the Multiple Regression Analysis (MRA) example (Table 8.34), the unstandardised coefficient (B) for 'Promotion' is 2.052, and its standardised coefficient (Beta) is 0.364. Explain in plain English what each of these two numbers informs a manager about the relationship between promotional activities and sales. Why is the Beta coefficient more useful for comparing the relative importance of different predictors in the model?
6. A researcher produces a Pearson's correlation matrix for five variables. They find a correlation of $r = 0.15$ between 'job satisfaction' and 'salary', with a p-value of $p = 0.04$. How would you advise the researcher to interpret this finding, considering both its statistical significance and the strength of the association (as per Table 8.30)?
7. In the Logistic Regression example (Table 8.38), the odds ratio (Exp(B)) for 'Level of Employee Engagement' is 1.848. Provide a clear, non-technical explanation of what this odds ratio means for a manager trying to improve the firm's productivity.
8. The One-Way ANOVA example on coffee shops (Table 8.4) shows a significant result ($p = 0.000$). Why is this result insufficient on its own to conclude that Starbucks has the highest customer satisfaction? Explain the necessary role of post-hoc tests (such as the Dunnett T3 test used in Table 8.6) in this analysis.
9. A researcher wants to investigate if a new leadership programme impacts several employee outcomes simultaneously: job satisfaction, organisational commitment, and intent to leave. Why would a MANOVA be a more appropriate statistical approach than running three separate One-Way ANOVAs (one for each dependent variable)?
10. You are asked to investigate whether there is an association between an employee's 'generation' (classified as Gen Z, Millennial, Gen X) and their preferred 'communication method' (classified as Email, Instant Messaging, Face-to-Face). What is the most appropriate statistical test from this chapter to analyse this relationship? State the null hypothesis for this test.

References

Agresti, A. (2018). *Statistical methods for the social sciences* (5th ed.). Pearson.

Aguinis, H. (2019). *Regression analysis for categorical moderators*. Guilford Press.

Auamnoy, T. (2002). *Statistics and SPSS for 21st century research*. Chulalongkorn University.

Backhaus, K., Erichson, B., Gensler, S., Weiber, R., & Weiber, T. (2021). *Multivariate analysis*. Springer Gabler Wiesbaden.

Bower, R., Hager, J., Cherniakov, C., Gupta, S., & Cipolli, W., III. (2023). A case for nonparametrics. *The American Statistician, 77*(2), 212–219. https://doi.org/10.1080/00031305.2022.2141858

Bryman, A. (2023). *Social research methods* (6th ed.). Oxford University Press.

Cochran, W. G. (1950). The comparison of percentages in matched samples. *Biometrika, 37*(3/4), 256–266. https://doi.org/10.1093/biomet/37.3-4.256

Cohen, J., Cohen, P., West, S. G., & Aiken, L. S. (2013). *Applied multiple regression/Correlation analysis for the behavioral sciences*. Routledge.

Cohen, L., Manion, L., & Morrison, K. (2022). *Research methods in education*. Routledge.

Conover, W. J. (1999). *Practical nonparametric statistics* (3rd ed.). Wiley.

Davenport, T. H., & Ronanki, R. (2018). Artificial intelligence for the real world. *Harvard Business Review, 96*(1), 108–116.

Denis, D. J. (2018). *SPSS Data analysis for univariate, bivariate, and multivariate statistics*. John Wiley & Sons.

Fiandini, M., Nandiyanto, A. B. D., Al Husaeni, D. F., Al Husaeni, D. N., & Mushiban, M. (2024). How to calculate statistics for significant difference test using SPSS: Understanding students comprehension on the concept of steam engines as power plant. *Indonesian Journal of Science and Technology, 9*(1), 45–108. https://doi.org/10.17509/ijost.v9i1.64035

Field, A. (2024). *Discovering statistics using IBM SPSS statistics* (6th ed.). Sage Publications.

Fink, A. (2015). *How to conduct surveys: A step-by-step guide*. Sage Publications.

Fisher, R. A. (1922). On the interpretation of $\chi 2$ from contingency tables, and the calculation of P. *Journal of the Royal Statistical Society, 85*(1), 87–94. https://doi.org/10.2307/2340521

Friedman, M. (1937). The use of ranks to avoid the assumption of normality implicit in the analysis of variance. *Journal of the American Statistical Association, 32*(200), 675–701. https://doi.org/10.2307/2279372

George, D., & Mallery, P. (2019). *IBM SPSS statistics 26 step by step: A simple guide and reference*. Routledge.

Gibbons, J. D., & Chakraborti, S. (2010). *Nonparametric statistical inference* (5th ed.). CRC Press.

Gilbert, N. (2016). *Researching social life* (4th ed.). Sage Publications.

Gonzalez, R. (2003). *Applied multivariate statistics for the social sciences*. The American Statistician.

Gravetter, F. J., & Wallnau, L. B. (2017). *Introduction to the practice of statistics* (10th ed.). Cengage Learning.

Gravetter, F. J., Wallnau, L. B., Forzano, L. A. B., & Witnauer, J. E. (2021). *Essentials of statistics for the behavioral sciences*. Cengage Learning.

Green, S. B., & Salkind, N. J. (2016). *Using SPSS for windows and Macintosh: Analyzing and understanding data* (8th ed.). Pearson.

Gunst, R. F., & Mason, R. L. (2018). *Regression analysis and its application: a data-oriented approach*. CRC Press.

Hair, J. F., Black, W. C., Babin, B. J., Anderson, R. E., & Tatham, R. L. (2019). *Multivariate data analysis* (8th ed.). Pearson Education.

Harlow, L. L. (2014). *The Essence of multivariate thinking: Basic themes and methods* (2nd ed.). Routledge.

Hosmer, D. W., Lemeshow, S., & Sturdivant, R. X. (2013). *Applied logistic regression* (3rd ed.). Wiley.

Howell, D. C. (2013). *Statistical methods for psychology* (8th ed.). Cengage Learning.

Huberty, C. J., & Morris, J. D. (1989). Multivariate analysis versus multiple univariate analyses. *Psychological Bulletin, 105*(2), 302–308. https://doi.org/10.1037/0033-2909.105.2.302

IBM Corp. (2022). *IBM SPSS Statistics (Version 29)* [Computer software]. https://software.kku.ac.th/data/software-etc.php

Jhun, M., Jeong, H. C., & Bahng, J. S. (2007). Simultaneous confidence intervals for the mean of multivariate Poisson distribution: A comparison. *Communications in Statistics—Simulation and Computation®, 36*(1), 151–164. https://doi.org/10.1080/03610910601096569

Johnson, R. B., & Christensen, L. B. (2024). *Educational research: Quantitative, qualitative, and mixed approaches*. Sage Publications.

Khojasteh, J. (2022). Review of A Beginner's Guide to Structural Equation Modeling: by Whittaker, TA & RE.

Kleinbaum, D. G., Kupper, L. L., & Muller, K. E. (2007). *Applied regression analysis and other multivariate methods* (4th ed.). Duxbury Press.

Knapp, H. (2013). *Introductory statistics using SPSS*. Sage Publications.

Kruskal, W. H., & Wallis, W. A. (1952). Use of ranks in one-criterion variance analysis. *Journal of the American Statistical Association, 47*(260), 583–621. https://doi.org/10.2307/2280779

Lachin, J. M. (2014). *Biostatistical methods: The assessment of relative risks*. John Wiley & Sons.

Laerd Statistics. (2021). Independent samples t-test using SPSS Statistics. *Laerd Statistics*. https://statistics.laerd.com/spss-tutorials/independent-samples-t-test-using-spss-statistics.php

Leech, N. L. (2022). Using IBM SPSS statistics for integration in mixed methods research. In J. H. Hitchcock & A. J. Onwuegbuzie (Eds.), *The Routledge handbook for advancing integration in mixed methods research* (pp. 527–539). Routledge.

Lü, L., & Zhou, T. (2011). Link prediction in complex networks: A survey. *Physica A: Statistical Mechanics and its Applications, 390*(6), 1150–1170. https://doi.org/10.1016/j.physa.2010.11.027

Mardia, K. V., Kent, J. T., & Bibby, J. M. (1979). *Multivariate analysis*. Academic Press.

McClave, J. T., Benson, P. G., & Sincich, T. (2008). *Statistics for business and economics*. Pearson Education.

Menard, S. (2002). *Applied logistic regression analysis*. Sage Publications. https://doi.org/10.4135/9781412983433

Mertler, C. A., Vannatta, R. A., & LaVenia, K. N. (2021). *Advanced and multivariate statistical methods: Practical application and interpretation*. Routledge.

Montgomery, D. C. (2017). *Design and analysis of experiments*. John Wiley & Sons.

Pallant, J. (2020). *SPSS survival manual: A step by step guide to data analysis using IBM SPSS*. Routledge. https://doi.org/10.4324/9781003117452

Pett, M. A. (2015). *Nonparametric statistics for health care research: Statistics for small samples and unusual distributions*. Sage Publications.

Privitera, G. J. (2023). *Statistics for the behavioral sciences*. Sage Publications.

Rane, N. L., Paramesha, M., Choudhary, S. P., & Rane, J. (2024). Artificial intelligence, machine learning, and deep learning for advanced business strategies: A review. *Partners Universal International Innovation Journal, 2*(3), 147–171.

Raykov, T., & Marcoulides, G. A. (2008). *An introduction to applied multivariate analysis*. Routledge.

Siebert, C. F., & Siebert, D. C. (2017). *Data analysis with small samples and non-normal data: Nonparametrics and other strategies*. Oxford University Press.

Siegel, S., & Castellan, N. J. (1988). *Nonparametric statistics for the behavioral sciences* (2nd ed.). McGraw-Hill Education.

Sokal, R. R., & Rohlf, F. J. (1995). *Biometry: The principles and practice of statistics in biological research* (3rd ed.). W. H. Freeman and Co.

Spearman, C. (2010). The proof and measurement of association between two things. *International Journal of Epidemiology, 39*(5), 1137–1150. https://doi.org/10.1093/ije/dyq191

Spencer, N. H. (2013). *Essentials of multivariate data analysis*. CRC Press.

Sprent, P., & Smeeton, N. C. (2016). *Applied nonparametric statistical methods*. CRC Press.

Stevens, J. (2002). *Applied multivariate statistics for the social sciences* (4th ed.). Lawrence Erlbaum Associates.

Sürücü, L., Şeşen, H., & Maslakçı, A. (2023). *Regression, mediation/moderation, and structural equation modeling with SPSS, AMOS, and PROCESS Macro*. Livre de Lyon.

Tabachnick, B. G., & Fidell, L. S. (2019). *Using multivariate statistics* (7th ed.). Pearson.

Warner, R. M. (2020). *Applied statistics II: Multivariable and multivariate techniques*. Sage Publications.

Wilcoxon, F. (1992). Individual comparisons by ranking methods. In S. Kotz & N. L. Johnson (Eds.), *Breakthroughs in statistics* (pp. 196–202). Springer. https://doi.org/10.1007/978-1-4612-4380-9_16

Chapter 9
Qualitative Method Design and Data Analysis

9.1 Introduction

This chapter illustrates various instruments for qualitative data analysis. It also introduces different types of data collection methods, such as interviews and focus groups, and presents examples relevant to research within the management discipline.

9.2 Qualitative Data Analysis

The qualitative approach is fundamentally grounded in the philosophy of interpretivism, which asserts that knowledge is inherently subjective and can only be comprehended through the interpretation of the meanings individuals ascribe to their experiences, perceptions, and attitudes. This philosophical stance asserts that reality is intricate and multifaceted, and thus cannot be simplified to objective, quantitative data (Bryman, 2023).

Within the realm of management research, the qualitative method strives to establish and understand the experiences, perspectives, and behaviours of individuals or groups. This approach relates to the collection of non-numerical data through techniques such as in-depth interviews, focus groups, and observational studies. The qualitative analysis is employed to interpret and make sense of the phenomena under investigation (Saunders et al., 2024).

9.2.1 Key Characteristics of the Qualitative Approach

The qualitative approach is rooted in the philosophy that knowledge is inherently subjective, constructed through the researchers' personal experiences, perceptions,

© The Author(s), under exclusive license to Springer Nature Singapore Pte Ltd. 2025

V. Zumitzavan, *Social Science Methodologies for Management Research*,
https://doi.org/10.1007/978-981-95-4318-2_9

and interpretations (Lichtman, 2023). Researchers are thus required to engage in reflexivity, critically examining their own biases and assumptions to mitigate their impact on the research process (Mason, 2002).

The qualitative approach highlights significant emphasis on contextuality, aiming to understand the social, cultural, and historical dimensions that shape individuals' experiences (Gould & Taylor, 2017). It recognises the complexity of these experiences, aiming to reflect their richness and depth rather than reducing them to numerical data (Silverman, 2024). Consequently, the phenomena under investigation may be perceived differently by various individuals. Rather than merely summarising these phenomena by counting frequencies, the qualitative approach requires a detailed exploration of the sophisticated and insightful information about the phenomena being studied. This depth of analysis provides a more comprehensive perspective of the experiences in question.

Furthermore, qualitative research is characterised by an inductive approach. Researchers develop theories and hypotheses grounded in the data rather than test pre-existing hypotheses (Braun & Clarke, 2023).

Whilst the qualitative approach offers significant advantages, such as its ability to capture the intricate and multidimensional nature of individual experiences, it also has limitations. It may be susceptible to researcher bias and its findings may not always be generalisable to diverse populations (Tracy, 2024).

In essence, the qualitative methodology is deeply anchored in the belief that knowledge is both subjective and interconnected, highlighting the need for a consideration of the connotations that individuals ascribe to their experiences to truly understand this complexity.

For example, in academic management research utilising the qualitative research approach, initially, researchers endeavour to comprehend the experiences of organisational members who have recently undergone a restructuring process within a large organisation. This type of research typically encompasses conducting in-depth interviews with a purposive sample of organisational members requested to articulate their experiences and emotional responses throughout the restructuring process (Kelly, 2023). As individuals face different experiences, they may develop varying insights, which can lead to varied perspectives. Following data collection, the researcher undertakes a thorough analysis to identify and categorise recurring themes and patterns in the organisational members' narratives (Braun et al., 2023). This method allows for a distinguished understanding of the impact of restructuring on organisational members' experiences.

Secondly, a business school purposes to investigate the factors that influence consumers' decision-making processes when purchasing luxury items. Typically, this research involves conducting focus groups with a sample of customers who have recently acquired a luxury item. During these sessions, participants are encouraged to discuss their decision-making processes and the various factors that impacted their choices (Alazzam et al., 2024). The researchers then analyse the qualitative data to discern and categorise the principal themes and factors that shape consumers' purchasing decisions (Gibbs, 2018).

Thirdly, a research team could study the purchasing decisions of young Muslim women in Brunei and Malaysia regarding Halal-certified cosmetics. The study would involve conducting in-depth interviews to discover their understanding of Halal principles, the significance of certification, brand trust, and the impact of social circles. Thematic analysis of the data would then reveal key drivers such as 'religious obligation,' 'purity and safety,' and 'modern Muslim identity,' providing valuable insights for cosmetic companies targeting this market (Rahim et al., 2025).

Fourthly, researchers endeavour to attain insights into the organisational culture of a small start-up enterprise. This typically contains a combination of observational approaches and interviews with organisational members. Researchers attend team meetings and observe the day-to-day manoeuvres within the organisation to obtain a comprehensive view of its organisational culture (Engel & Schutt, 2016). Subsequently, they analyse the collected data to identify and elucidate the fundamental values, norms, and practices that characterise the organisational culture (Braun et al., 2023).

Fifthly, the researchers aim to understand the experiences of entrepreneurs who have successfully established and extended their businesses. This generally comprises conducting in-depth interviews with a sample of entrepreneurs, where they are encouraged to discuss their experiences, motivations, and challenges (Creswell & Poth, 2016). The researchers then analyse the data to identify and categorise recurring themes and factors contributing to the success of these enterprises (Flick, 2023).

In summary, the qualitative approach is utilised to explore and attain insights into individuals' experiences and perspectives. Researchers collect rich, comprehensive, and refined data through methods such as interviews, observations, and focus groups. They then employ qualitative analysis to interpret and classify the data into a range of themes, ultimately providing a detailed synthesis of the findings.

9.2.2 Process of Qualitative Approach

Qualitative data analysis involves the meticulous examination and interpretation of non-numerical data, such as texts, images, or videos. This analytical process typically unfolds in numerous critical phases, each integral to academic management research. Initially, data organisation is essential, encompassing the transcription of audio or video recordings and the systematic typing of written notes, ensuring that the data is well-structured and readily accessible (Miles et al., 2014).

In the next phase, data familiarisation requires researchers to immerse themselves in the data through repeated reviews or listening sessions, thereby deepening their understandings and aids in the identification of emerging themes (Lester et al., 2020). The subsequent phase, data coding, comprises the process of identifying and labelling significant themes within the data. Researchers may utilise coding schemes or qualitative data analysis software to facilitate this task, thus structuring the data into coherent categories.

More elaborately, qualitative data analysis software simplifies the process of coding, organising, and interpreting qualitative data by providing systematic and visual tools. NVivo is one of the most widely utilised options, known for its versatility, such as its ability to organise mixed-methods research and visualisation features, such as word clouds and network maps, which reveal relationships between themes. Atlas.ti is another widely utilised software programme, particularly valuable for coding multimedia data, such as audio and video, whilst its network mapping functionalities allow researchers to identify conceptual connections and patterns effectively. Then, MAXQDA combines qualitative and mixed-methods analysis with strong visualisation capabilities, including charts and graphs, and offers multilingual support, making it ideal for cross-cultural studies. These tools streamline the coding process, support collaborative research, and offer intuitive visual insights, helping researchers to classify themes, patterns, and relationships in their data efficiently (Saldaña, 2021). In the data analysis phase, researchers examine relationships between codes, classify sub-themes, and scrutinise into the underlying meanings, striving to reveal patterns and insights and thus contributing a comprehensive understanding of the data (Flick, 2023).

The subsequent phase, data interpretation, is where researchers draw conclusions based on their analyses and relate these findings back to the research questions, thus elucidating the implications and significance of the results (Savin-Baden & Major, 2023).

Finally, the validation phase involves scrutinising the findings for inconsistencies or errors and seeking feedback from peers or research participants. This stage may also embrace peer review to endorse that the data has been accurately classified and interpreted (Faulkner & Faulkner, 2018). These steps, though outlined linearly, often involve iterative processes as researchers hone their understandings. More importantly, the specific methods and techniques utilised can vary depending on the research question, data type, and methodological approach (Poth et al., 2024b).

All in all, qualitative data analysis involves organising data, coding to identify themes, and interpreting these themes in relation to research questions. Researchers validate findings through feedback and peer review to ensure accuracy. This process often requires iterative refinement as researchers deepen their understanding. The specific methods may vary based on the research question and data type.

9.2.3 Advantages of the Qualitative Approach

Qualitative research offers a profound understanding of complex phenomena such as human behaviour and attitudes, which are often elusive to quantitative methods. For instance, when a researcher seeks to explore how organisational members perceive their organisational culture, qualitative techniques including interviews or focus groups can provide rich, detailed data, leading to a deep comprehension of these intricate dynamics (Fryer, 2022).

Furthermore, qualitative research is notably more flexible than quantitative approaches, allowing researchers to adapt their methods and questions as new insights emerge from the data. This flexibility is especially beneficial in exploratory studies where research questions may not be fully defined; for example, open-ended questions in interviews can reveal unexpected themes as they arise during the sessions (Lungu, 2022).

Additionally, qualitative research excels in contextualisation, providing an in-depth understanding of the social, cultural, or historical factors influencing the phenomena under study. Ethnographic methods, for instance, can be employed to investigate how an organisation operates within a specific cultural or geographical context, presenting comprehensive insights into its environment (Liamputtong, 2023).

9.2.4 Disadvantages of the Qualitative Approach

Qualitative research is frequently critiqued for its subjectivity, as the interpretation of data can be influenced by the researcher's own biases and assumptions, which complicates the evaluation of validity and reliability. For example, different researchers might interpret the same interview data differently due to their personal perspectives or biases. If one researcher focuses on emotional responses whilst another emphasises behavioural responses, the conclusions drawn about the same subject may vary significantly (Taylor et al., 2015). For example, due to numerous customers' complaints, an organisation commissions a researcher to discover ways to improve the levels of customers' satisfaction with the services provided by the customer relationship management officers. In this case, in-depth interviews are conducted to collect data. If the research solely focuses on the emotional responses of the officers, the data may fail to capture the behavioural responses. Although the officers may not display overt emotional reactions, their behaviour may not improve in response to customers' complaints on the issue.

Additionally, qualitative research typically employs small sample sizes, which can limit the generalisability of findings. For instance, interviewing a small number of employees about their workplace experiences may provide deep insights but may not reflect the experiences of the broader workforce, making it challenging to generalise the results to a larger population (Poth et al., 2024a).

Furthermore, qualitative research can be time-consuming, requiring considerable resources for data collection and analysis. For example, transcribing lengthy interviews and coding complex textual data can be labour-intensive and may necessitate the use of specialised software like Atlas.ti or NVivo to manage and analyse the data effectively (Flick, 2023). Despite such challenges, qualitative research remains invaluable for acquiring a distinguished understanding of complex phenomena, although it is important to be aware of its limitations regarding subjectivity, sample size, and time constraints (Hennink et al., 2020; Linneberg & Korsgaard, 2019).

In summary, qualitative research is generally critiqued for its subjectivity, as different researchers may interpret the same data in varying ways, which could compromise its validity. It frequently involves small sample sizes, thereby limiting generalisability, and can be time-consuming, demanding considerable resources for processes, such as transcription and coding. Despite these limitations, qualitative research remains invaluable for acquiring insights into complex phenomena.

9.2.5 *Research Instruments for Qualitative Approach (Types of Interview Techniques)*

In qualitative research, in-depth interviews are typically classified into three categories of techniques: unstructured, structured, and semi-structured. Firstly, unstructured interviews are characterised by their absence of a fixed set of questions or a pre-arranged script, thus allowing interviewees to express their thoughts and experiences freely. This approach enables the interviewer to probe for additional details and so obtain rich, narrative insights into complex phenomena, such as a chief executive officer's leadership style and decision-making processes (Bhattacharya, 2017). Secondly, structured interviews, on the other hand, involve a strict adherence to a predetermined set of questions delivered in a specific order. This format often uses closed-ended questions to elicit specific information, thereby ensuring data standardisation and comparability, as seen in surveys assessing customer satisfaction with products or services (Foroudi & Dennis, 2023).

Thirdly, semi-structured interviews offer a combination of flexibility and structure. Whilst they use a prepared set of questions or themes, the interviewer can adapt the conversation to explore emerging topics. This method, involving both closed and open-ended questions, is particularly useful for understanding organisational members' experiences with new organisational strategies, thus providing a balanced approach between detailed exploration and structured data collection (Silverman, 2021). Ultimately, the choice of interview type should be guided by the research question, data needs, and available resources. Unstructured interviews provide in-depth insights but can be time-consuming and complex to analyse, whereas structured interviews offer standardised data with limited depth. Semi-structured interviews strike a balance, facilitating comprehensive exploration within a structured framework (Hammersley & Atkinson, 2019; Mason, 2017) (Table 9.1).

Table 9.1 Comparison of the advantages and disadvantages of unstructured, structured, and semi-structured interviews

Interview type	Advantages	Disadvantages
Unstructured Interviews (Harding, 2018)	- Facilitate interviewees to express themselves without restrictions and provide rich, detailed information. - Provide ability to explore unanticipated themes and areas of interest. - Enable the interviewer to build affinity with the interviewees.	- Time-consuming and difficult to analyse. - May lack structure and standardisation, making it more difficult to compare responses across interviewees' data. - May be dominated by interviewer bias.
Structured Interviews (Khoa et al., 2023)	- Enable standardised data collection, making it simpler to compare responses across interviewees. - Could be effortlessly analysed applying quantitative methods. - May be less dominated by interviewer bias.	- May not allow interviewees to express themselves fully or provide more detailed data. - May be restricted in their capability to capture confounding phenomena. - May lack the flexibility to explore unforeseen themes or areas of interests.
Semi-Structured Interviews (Lester et al., 2020)	- Enable in-depth exploration of definite topics whilst providing a framework for data collection and analysis. - Enable a balance between flexibility and structure. -May provide rich, detailed data.	- May be time-consuming and tough to analyse. - May still be dominated by interviewer bias. - May require additional training and skills for the interviewer to effectively balance flexibility and structure.

9.2.6 *The Art and Evolving Science of Qualitative Interpretation*

Whilst qualitative research depends on the systematic processes that form its 'science', it is vital to distinguish the profound role of interpretive 'art' in generating knowledge. This relationship between art and science is not a conflict but a foundational strength of the qualitative method, a strength now being redefined by advancements in AI.

Qualitative research fundamentally sees the researcher as the primary analytical tool. More than simply applying coding schemes, the researcher performs a creative and interpretive act, weaving data into a coherent and meaningful narrative. This process is an art form, where the researcher's unique perspective and self-awareness are not just biases to be removed, but lenses that can reveal unique and deep insights (Leavy, 2014). The 'art' of qualitative analysis is the capability to realise patterns others may miss, construct compelling stories from wide-ranging data, and communicate the complex distinctions of human experience. This view line up with a growing movement in management studies to utilise creative research approaches—such as photo-elicitation or poetic inquiry—which value personal interpretation and aesthetic expression as valid ways of understanding the world (Denzin & Lincoln, 2011).

At the same time, the 'science' of qualitative analysis is undergoing a significant evolution through the integration of AI, particularly Large Language Models (LLMs). Going beyond the organisational functions of software such as NVivo, generative AI tools provide new possibilities for both efficiency and depth. For instance, AI can help in the early stages of analysis by quickly identifying potential themes and summarising large amounts of text, enabling researchers to handle larger datasets than ever before (Brigham et al., 2022).

More significantly, AI can function as an analytical 'thought partner'. By recommending different interpretations, emphasising overlooked connections between themes, or challenging a researcher's hidden biases, AI can enhance the rigour and creativity of the analysis (Hsu, 2023). However, utilising these powerful tools requires careful and critical thought. Researchers must be aware of AI's limitations, such as its potential to repeat biases from its training data and its lack of true contextual and cultural understanding (Owoahene Acheampong & Nyaaba, 2024). The final ethical responsibility for interpretation always rests with the human researcher, who must critically evaluate, refine, and deliver context for any AI-generated output.

Finally, the future of rigorous and impactful qualitative management research is not about selecting between art and science, but skilfully incorporating them. The researcher's creative interpretation and deep contextual understanding—the 'art'—can be improved and confronted by the systematic power and new capabilities of AI—the 'evolving science'. This partnership promises to produce richer, more sophisticated, and more trustworthy insights into the complexities of management phenomena.

9.3 Data Analysis of Qualitative Approaches

9.3.1 Thematic Analysis

Thematic analysis is a robust qualitative method extensively utilised across numerous disciplines for the extraction and interpretation of patterns of meaning within documentary or interview-based data. This methodological approach facilitates the systematic organisation and distillation of qualitative data, thereby enabling an in-depth exploration of the themes emerging from participants' or interviewees' narratives. Rooted in the traditions of grounded theory and phenomenology, thematic analysis presents researchers with a flexible yet rigorous framework for investigating the complexities of human experiences and social phenomena (Braun et al., 2023; Terry et al., 2017).

Originally extracted from the principles of grounded theory and phenomenology, thematic analysis has evolved to become a versatile tool in qualitative research.

It provides a structured approach to identifying, analysing, and reporting patterns (or themes) within data, permitting researchers to understand and interpret various dimensions of their subjects' experiences (Braun et al., 2023). This method not only assists in organising data systematically but also facilitates uncovering deeper insights into the narrative content, making it an invaluable technique for exploring intricate social and psychological constructs (Terry et al., 2017).

For instance, in research examining organisational members' motivation within organisations, thematic analysis can be employed to scrutinise qualitative data from interviews with employees. This approach may uncover various themes, such as the distinctions between intrinsic and extrinsic motivation, the impact of different leadership styles on motivational levels, and how organisational culture affects motivation (Nowell et al., 2017). By identifying and analysing these themes, researchers can develop a more sophisticated understanding of the drivers influencing organisational members' motivation and the interplay between various organisational elements (Dusi & Stevens, 2022).

To ensure the richness and relevance of the data, participants should be selected purposively. In this context, researchers might choose individuals who have direct experience with the motivational dynamics being investigated, whilst also ensuring diversity in terms of the roles, departments, and lengths of service within the organisation. This focused approach facilitates capturing a wide array of perspectives and experiences, thus improving the depth and validity of the thematic analysis (Clarke & Braun, 2017).

9.3.1.1 Process of Thematic Analysis Approach

Initial Steps and Data Familiarisation

The preliminary stage of thematic analysis involves a thorough immersion in the data to achieve a profound comprehension of its contents. This phase necessitates multiple readings and close engagement with transcripts or documentary sources, enabling the researcher to familiarise themselves with the variations and subtleties embedded within the dataset. Such immersion is crucial, as it facilitates the identification of prominent features and establishes a foundation for the subsequent systematic coding process (Braun & Clarke, 2022). This initial engagement ensures that the researcher is well-acquainted with the data, thus enhancing the rigour and depth of the thematic analysis (Majumdar, 2022).

Systematic Coding and Theme Development

A central component of thematic analysis is the development of coding, where segments of data are systematically labelled to discover significant concepts or ideas. This comprises assigning codes based on recurring patterns or notable features within the data. Codes can vary from descriptive labels which represent specific phenomena to interpretive or conceptual codes that probe underlying meanings

For instance, in a research study exploring organisational members' motivation, codes might include 'Intrinsic Rewards', 'Leadership Impact', and 'Organisational Culture', each representing different aspects of the motivational experience. Through iterative coding, related codes are aggregated to form preliminary themes, thereby laying the groundwork for more profound thematic exploration (Braun & Clarke, 2022). This methodical approach ensures a thorough analysis of the data, facilitating the development of rich and intricate themes reflecting the complexity of the research subject (Braun et al., 2023).

Furthermore, during the early stages of technological change or strategic planning, when investigating technology adoption and its effect on organisational performance, codes might comprise 'Digital Transformation', 'Organisational Members' Training Programs', and 'Technological Readiness', each addressing key factors influencing the successful implementation of technological change. The process of aggregating these codes into themes such as 'Technology Integration Capacity' or 'Organisational Readiness for Change' can shed light on how technology adoption bolsters competitive advantages and strengthens operational efficiency improvements (Braun et al., 2023; Salamzadeh et al., 2022).

Lastly, in a research study exploring market orientation and its relationship with organisational performance, codes might include 'Customer-Centric Strategies', 'Competitor Analysis', and 'Innovation Focus', each representing distinct strategic approaches underpinning market orientation practices. These codes could cluster into broader themes, such as 'Strategic Market Responsiveness' or 'Alignment with Customer Needs', offering insights into how organisations achieve performance improvements by adapting strategies to market trends and consumers' preferences (Chahal & Sharma, 2006; Khanagha et al., 2017).

Theme Refinement and Verification

As themes begin to take shape, a critical phase encompasses refining and structuring them to ensure coherence and relevance to the research questions and objectives. This procedure requires the iterative review and revision of themes, probing the relationships between codes and themes, and ensuring that each theme encapsulates a distinct yet cohesive pattern within the dataset.

For example, in a research study investigating consumers' attitudes towards sustainable fashion, themes such as 'Environmental Impact', 'Ethical Production', and 'Brand Loyalty' must be distinct whilst collectively providing a comprehensive understanding of consumers' behaviour. Themes are further validated through the ongoing evaluation of the original data and cross-referencing among themes, thereby enhancing the robustness and reliability of the analysis (Saldaña, 2021; Maguire & Delahunt, 2017).

Documenting and Reporting Findings

After the themes have been finalised, the researcher constructs a narrative that synthesises the research findings into a coherent and compelling argument. This narrative not only elaborates on each theme in detail but also elucidates their significance in relation to the more extensive research questions or theoretical framework. By incorporating illustrative quotes or excerpts from the data, the narrative supports the researcher's interpretations and offers profound insights into the themes revealed through the analysis.

For example, if the research is on the level of organisational members' engagement, the narrative might weave together themes like 'Job Satisfaction', 'Work-life Balance', and 'Career Development' to demonstrate their interconnections and the implications for organisational practice. Additionally, researchers can apply strategies such as member checking, peer debriefing, and maintaining an audit trail to bolster the credibility and trustworthiness of their interpretations (Braun & Clarke, 2022; Tufford & Newman, 2012).

Applications in Academic Management Contexts

In academic management contexts, thematic analysis proves invaluable support for exploring diverse phenomena such as consumers' behaviour, organisational culture, leadership dynamics, and organisational members' experiences. For instance, within management research studies, thematic analysis can illuminate themes related to workplace satisfaction, leadership effectiveness, or organisational change strategies, providing actionable insights for managerial decision-making and policy formulation.

In conclusion, thematic analysis exemplifies a multi-purpose and vivid methodological approach for making sense of qualitative data. By systematically detecting and interpreting patterns of meaning, this method not only enriches our understanding of human experiences and social phenomena but also contributes to the enhancement of knowledge across various academic and professional realms. Through its structured yet flexible framework, thematic analysis empowers researchers to explore the complexities of qualitative data and produce meaningful insights that inform theories, practices, and policies.

9.3.2 Grounded Theory

9.3.2.1 Grounded Theory: A Systematic Approach to Theory Development from Qualitative Data

Grounded theory represents a robust qualitative research method renowned for its systematic approach to theory development directly from empirical data. Originating in the sociological research tradition through the pioneering work of Glaser and Strauss in the 1960s, and subsequently refined by Charmaz and others, Grounded theory has acquired prominence across various disciplines for its capacity to uncover new theoretical insights grounded in the complexities of human experiences and social phenomena (Charmaz & Thornberg, 2021; Glaser & Strauss, 2017).

In the management discipline, grounded theory has been utilised to discover intricate organisational dynamics and managerial practices. For instance, recent research utilising Grounded Theory has examined how organisations adapt to digital transformation. A research study by Kerguenne, Meisel and Meinel (2023) explored how organisations implement digital technologies in their business processes, revealing refined strategies and organisational behaviours that traditional theories may overlook.

Another relevant application of grounded theory in management is in understanding leadership styles and their impact on employee engagement. A study by Russen, Dawson, Madera, Kitterlin-Lynch, and Abbott (2023) investigated how different leadership methods influence organisational members' motivation and organisational commitment. Their research illuminated the complex interplay between leadership behaviours and organisational members' perceptions, providing a more insightful view of leadership effectiveness driving beyond established theoretical models.

9.3.2.2 The Process of Grounded Theory

Initial Steps and Data Collection

The process of grounded theory involves a systematic and rigorous approach to data collection. Researchers engage in qualitative methods, such as interviews, observations, or document analysis, to obtain rich, contextually embedded data. This initial phase is characterised by openness to exploration, allowing researchers to continue to be receptive to emerging themes and theoretical concepts as they investigate the data more deeply.

For example, in a study on organisational change management, researchers used grounded theory to understand how organisational members perceive and react to change initiatives within a multinational corporation. Through in-depth interviews and participant observations, they collected data that revealed several key themes, including resistance to change and the impact of leadership communication. This process enabled the researchers to develop and refine a theoretical framework that captured the complexity of organisational members' experiences during organisational transformations (Boccoli et al., 2023).

Another related example investigated in Myanmar, this research provides a comparative analysis of Grounded Theory (GT) and the Affinity Diagram (AD) as methods for interpreting qualitative data. The author highlights that whilst both are bottom-up approaches used to categorise information, they serve distinct purposes. GT is presented as a rigorous academic method for generating substantive theory from data, whereas the Affinity Diagram is a practical tool for organising complex ideas to facilitate group problem-solving. The analysis concludes that the choice between them should be based on whether the researcher's primary objective is theory generation or practical problem clarification (Aung et al., 2016).

In another related example, in a research project on supply chain resilience, researchers utilised grounded theory to investigate how managers observe and respond to disruptions stemming from global logistical challenges. Through comprehensive interviews and an analysis of operational reports, they collected data that highlighted several key themes, including strategies for risk qualification and the influence of leadership communication during periods of crisis. This approach allowed the researchers to develop a theoretical framework that provided insights into the intricacies of managerial decision-making and adaptive strategies in times of supply chain uncertainty (Tiwari et al., 2024).

Coding and Constant Comparison

Central to grounded theory is the iterative process of coding, in which data segments are systematically labelled with descriptive, interpretive, or theoretical codes. Initial coding comprises breaking down the data into discrete units, whilst focused coding refines these units to identify recurring patterns or themes. Through constant comparison, where data are compared and contrasted within and across codes, emerging themes naturally surface, laying the groundwork for theoretical insights.

For example, in a research project exploring organisational members' motivation in remote work surroundings, researchers utilised grounded theory to analyse interview data from various organisational members. During initial coding, they segmented the data into basic units, such as 'Flexibility', 'Work-life balance', and 'Communication Challenges'. Focused coding then refined these units by grouping them into broader categories, such as 'Organisational Members' Satisfaction' and 'Productivity'. Constant comparison of these codes exposed key themes, including the impact of flexible working hours on job satisfaction and the role of regular communication in maintaining productivity. This iterative coding process allowed the researchers to develop a theory explaining how different aspects of remote work influence organisational members' motivation (Brandhorst et al., 2023).

Theoretical Sampling and Saturation

As themes and concepts develop, grounded theory employs theoretical sampling, a strategic approach to data collection designed to refine emerging theories and validate conceptual frameworks. Researchers purposefully select new participants or data sources driven by the theoretical insights obtained from initial analyses. This process allows for a deeper understanding and leads to theoretical saturation, which is the stage at which no new data contribute additional insights or modify the emerging theory.

For example, in a research project examining innovation practices within startups, researchers initially interviewed founders and managers in order to identify key themes related to innovation strategies. As the analysis progressed and concepts began to emerge, they used theoretical sampling to include additional participants from different types of startups, such as those in varying stages of growth and across sectors. This approach helped to refine their understanding of how innovation practices vary across different contexts and validated their theoretical framework. The researchers achieved theoretical saturation when subsequent interviews yielded no new information that altered their emerging theory of innovation processes (Wang et al., 2024b).

Memoing and Theoretical Integration

Throughout the coding and analysis process, researchers engage in memoing, a reflective practice that involves detailed notes and annotations noting insights, hypotheses, and theoretical connections. Memos serve as a critical tool for theorising and refining emerging concepts, facilitating the integration of data, codes, and theoretical frameworks into a cohesive and coherent narrative.

For example, in a study probing organisational resilience, researchers utilised memoing to document their reflections and insights as they coded interview data from various organisational leaders. Memos included notes on observed patterns related to resilience strategies, such as leadership responses to crises and adaptive organisational practices. These reflections helped in developing a more nuanced theoretical framework by connecting specific codes to broader concepts of organisational resilience and by identifying gaps in the emerging theory. The iterative process of memoing ensured that the theoretical narrative remained grounded in empirical data and was logically consistent (Jackson et al., 2018).

Constructing and Validating Theory

The final stage of grounded theory comprises constructing and validating the emergent theory. Researchers articulate a theoretical framework that encapsulates the interconnected themes and conceptual relationships identified through rigorous analysis. This process involves writing theoretical memos and engaging in theoretical discussions within the research community in order to validate findings and enhance the credibility of the theory.

For example, in a study on team dynamics in agile project management, researchers reached the final stage by developing a comprehensive theoretical framework that integrated themes such as team collaboration, adaptive leadership, and iterative feedback. They wrote detailed theoretical memos to articulate how these themes interconnected and contributed to successful project outcomes. To validate their findings, the researchers presented their framework at academic conferences and engaged in discussions with peers in order to receive feedback and refine their theory. This validation process helped to ensure the robustness and applicability of the theoretical framework in multiple agile environments (AlHamad et al., 2022).

Applications in Academic and Practical Settings

In academic and practical settings, grounded theory provides profound insights into a range of phenomena, including organisational change, healthcare practices, educational processes, and social interactions. Within the discipline of management, Grounded theory can elucidate aspects such as emerging leadership styles, organisational resilience strategies, or innovation processes, thereby informing evidence-based decision-making and strategic planning.

For instance, in the domain of management with a focus on consumer behaviour, grounded theory can be applied to understand how consumers make purchasing decisions online. By employing iterative data collection and analysis, researchers can identify and theorise themes such as trust in online reviews, perceived value for money, and convenience factors. This method allows for the development of a theory grounded in empirical data that reflects the complex dynamics of online consumer decision-making. Another example would be that in a recent study on online consumers' behaviour, researchers utilised grounded theory to analyse interviews and survey data from a variety of consumers. Through this process, they identified key themes, such as the influence of online reviews on trust, the role of perceived value for money in purchase decisions, and the impact of convenience on consumer choices. Iterative analysis and theoretical sampling helped refine these themes and develop a comprehensive framework that explains how these factors interact to influence online purchasing behaviour (Azim et al., 2019).

In conclusion, grounded theory constitutes a rigorous and systematic approach to theory development from qualitative data. By grounding theory in empirical evidence and iterative analysis, this methodological approach not only advances knowledge within academic disciplines but also informs policy, practice, and intervention strategies in diverse professional contexts. Through its methodological rigour and commitment to theoretical emergence, grounded theory continues to shape and enrich qualitative research methodologies, contributing to a deeper understanding of complex social phenomena and human experiences.

9.3.3 Narrative Analysis

9.3.3.1 Narrative Analysis: Unravelling Stories and Meaning in Qualitative Research

Narrative analysis is a prominent qualitative research approach centred on the interpretation and understanding of stories and narratives shared by individuals. Based on the belief that stories are fundamental to human experiences and meaning-making, narrative analysis presents a systematic technique for realising the structures, contents, and contexts of narratives to uncover underlying themes, patterns, and significance.

For example, in a research project examining leadership effectiveness, narrative analysis could be employed to explore Chief Executive Officers' (CEOs) perceptions of overcoming challenges. By analysing the narratives provided by CEOs, researchers can identify and examine themes such as leadership styles, strategic decision-making under pressure, and personal growth through leadership experiences. This approach helps to elucidate how CEOs interpret and articulate their experiences, thereby providing deeper insights into the nature of effective leadership (Denning, 2006).

Another related example in the management discipline is that in a recent study on leadership effectiveness, researchers conducted in-depth interviews with CEOs to obtain their narratives about managing organisational crises. The analysis of these narratives revealed key themes, including adaptive leadership styles, the role of strategic decision-making in high-pressure situations, and the personal and professional growth experienced through these challenges. This narrative approach enabled a nuanced understanding of how CEOs perceive and respond to complex leadership situations (Burger et al., 2024).

9.3.3.2 Process of Narratives Analysis

Understanding Narratives and Narrative Identity

At the core of narrative analysis lies the recognition that narratives serve as vehicles through which individuals construct and communicate personal experiences, identities, and world views. Narratives are not merely descriptions of events but are elaborate constructs permeated with emotions, interpretations, and cultural meanings. Researchers engage in narrative analysis to explore the complexities of narrative identity, thereby understanding how individuals make sense of their lives and experiences through the art of storytelling.

For instance, in a research project investigating the career development of mid-level managers, narrative analysis can be used to probe into how these managers describe their professional journeys. By analysing the narratives shared by these managers, researchers can examine how they articulate their professional identities, interpret pivotal career events, and integrate personal and professional growth into their life stories. This approach reveals how emotions, cultural influences, and personal interpretations shape their understanding of career development and success (Rostron, 2022).

Approaches to Narrative Analysis

Narrative analysis encompasses various approaches, including structuralist, phenomenological, and socio-cultural perspectives, each providing unique insights into the analysis of narratives.

Structuralist methods focus on the fundamental elements of narratives, such as plot, characterisation, and setting. This approach analyses how these components interact to construct meaning and coherence within a story. For example, in a research project investigating the structure of organisational success stories, structuralist analysis might examine how narratives use plot elements like challenges and resolutions to understand an organisation's achievements (Hagebakken et al., 2024).

Phenomenological methods investigate the lived experiences and subjective realities expressed within narratives. This perspective seeks to understand how individuals interpret and make sense of their personal experiences through storytelling. For instance, in research on employee experiences of workplace transformation, phenomenological analysis might explore how organisational members narrate their emotional and psychological responses to organisational changes (Lemon, 2019).

Moving to another related example, for instance, in research on consumers' experiences of brand loyalty during the COVID-19 pandemic, phenomenological analysis might examine how customers narrate their emotional and psychological responses to the uncertainty of spending money on luxury services, such as travel or hospitality, at a time when health risks, financial instability, and restrictions disrupted their ability to access these services. This could involve exploring how customers struggled with concerns about whether investing in flights, hotels or fine dining would meet their expectations of value and satisfaction within an unpredictable economic and social climate. It would investigate how fear, uncertainty and shifting priorities influenced their decisions to either postpone spending, seek alternative options, or reinforce their loyalty to brands that reassured them through clear and transparent communication (Niros et al., 2023).

Socio-cultural approaches examine narratives within broader social and cultural contexts, considering how collective narratives shape individual identities and social practices. This perspective looks at how cultural and social factors influence the stories people tell and how these stories, in turn, reflect and perpetuate social norms and values. For example, in a research project on community responses to social movements, socio-cultural analysis could investigate how narratives about the movement are shaped by and contribute to broader societal attitudes and collective identities.

For example, in a research on the impact of organisational change on organisational members' identity, researchers might use a structuralist approach to analyse the narrative elements of employees' stories about the change process. They could use a phenomenological approach to explore the subjective experiences of these organisational members, and a socio-cultural approach to understand how broader organisational culture and societal norms influence and are influenced by these narratives (Mathew, 2019).

Methods of Narrative Analysis

The process of narrative analysis typically begins with the collection of narrative data through methods such as interviews, autobiographies, oral histories, or written accounts (Marshall & Rossman, 2014). Researchers then transcribe and analyse these narratives, categorising key themes, plot structures, verbal devices, and narrative strategies utilised by storytellers (Bolden et al., 2023). This analysis includes the close reading and interpretation of textual or audiovisual data to reveal the connotations and cultural resonances embedded within the narratives (Gill, 2014).

For instance, in a research study exploring the impact of leadership styles on organisational members' morale, researchers might collect narrative data through interviews with organisational members and managers. After transcribing the interviews, they could analyse the narratives by identifying recurring themes, such as leadership approaches, organisational members' reactions, and organisational culture. Researchers could also scrutinise plot structures and verbal devices to understand how managers and organisational members describe their experiences and interactions. This analysis could help to reveal underlying cultural meanings and the emotional characteristics of leadership experiences (Bolden et al., 2023).

Narrative Typologies and Themes

Through thematic analysis, researchers identify recurrent themes or topics emerging across narratives. These themes can encompass various aspects, such as personal growth, resilience, identity negotiation, cultural heritage, or social justice issues, depending upon the focus and context of the research (Braun & Clarke, 2022). Each theme represents a pattern of meaning that illustrates broader societal discourses or individual experiences, offering insights into how narratives create and negotiate meaning in diverse contexts (Braun & Clarke, 2006).

For instance, in a research project on the experiences of immigrants adapting to a new country, thematic analysis might reveal themes related to identity negotiation, cultural heritage, and resilience. Researchers could analyse the narratives to identify how immigrants describe their adaptation processes and the challenges they face. By probing these themes, researchers attain a deeper understanding of how immigrants shape their identities and navigate cultural transitions within their new environments (Braun et al., 2023).

Contextualisation and Interpretation

Central to narrative analysis is the contextualisation of narratives within their socio-historical, cultural, and political contexts. Researchers scrutinise how power dynamics, social norms, and discursive practices influence the production and reception of narratives. By situating narratives within their broader contexts, narrative analysis reveals how storytelling functions as a mode of sense-making and social action, thereby shaping perceptions, beliefs, and collective identities (Gee, 2014; Chabay et al., 2019).

For instance, in a research study exploring how marginalised communities narrate their experiences of systemic discrimination, researchers might explore how narratives are shaped by socio-historical factors such as historical injustices and predominant social norms. They then analyse how these narratives represent power dynamics and discursive practices that influence the communities' perceptions and responses to discrimination. This contextual analysis then assists with understanding how storytelling acts as both a reflection and a tool of social change, contributing to the formation of collective identities and influencing public discourse (Gee, 2014).

Applications in Academic and Applied Settings

In academic research, narrative analysis significantly contributes to disciplines such as psychology, sociology, anthropology, education, healthcare, and management by enriching deep insights into human experiences, identity formation, and social interactions. Essentially, narrative analysis informs therapeutic practices, policy development, and organisational change initiatives by offering rich, contextual understandings of stakeholders' experiences and perspectives.

In the management discipline, for example, narrative analysis can be instrumental in understanding how organisational members perceive and experience organisational changes. Researchers might analyse organisational members' narratives about transitions such as mergers, restructurings, or leadership changes. A relevant example is the Renault-Nissan-Mitsubishi Alliance's recent restructuring and strengthening efforts, emphasising the complexities of multi-organisational partnerships in response to technological innovation and market demands.

By probing narratives from organisational members involved in this strategic restructuring, such as organisational members, middle managers, and executives, researchers can explore how they experienced and interpreted these transitions. These experiences include adapting to shared production platforms, integrating technological innovations such as electric vehicle (EV) development, and managing cross-cultural differences between the organisations' varied corporate practices and operational goals.

By analysing these narratives, researchers can reveal themes related to organisational members' adaptation to change, resistance driven by uncertainty or differing corporate priorities, and strategies for engagement in realigning operational processes. This understanding can inform strategies for supervising change more effectively by addressing organisational members' concerns, nurturing cross-organisation collaboration, and reassuring clear and consistent communication during times of significant strategic transformation (Jango, 2024; Mladjan & Markovic, 2019).

In conclusion, narrative analysis exemplifies a powerful lens through which to explore and interpret the stories outlining human lives and societies. Through analysing narratives as intricate texts rich in personal and cultural meanings, this qualitative research method enhances our understanding of narrative identity, social practices, and the constructions of meaning in wide-ranging contexts. Through its methodological rigour and interpretive depth, narrative analysis continues to illuminate the interconnected patterns between storytelling, identity, and social change.

9.3.4 Phenomenological Analysis

9.3.4.1 Phenomenological Analysis: Exploring Lived Experience in Qualitative Research

Phenomenological analysis is a qualitative research methodology specifically aimed at investigating and elucidating the subjective experiences of individuals (van Manen, 2016). Drawing upon the phenomenological tradition established by seminal philosophers such as Edmund Husserl, Martin Heidegger, and Maurice Merleau-Ponty, this approach seeks to highlight the fundamental essences and meanings inherent in subjective perceptions, consciousness, and the lived realities of research participants (Giorgi, 2021).

For instance, in the management discipline, phenomenological analysis can be employed to explore the experience of leadership styles of middle managers. By conducting in-depth interviews with these managers, researchers can identify themes related to their daily experiences of leading teams, including aspects such as the impact of leadership practices on team dynamics, the challenges of balancing authority with empathy, and the strategies implemented to bolster team motivation and cohesion (Garrido-Moreno et al., 2024; Smith et al., 2021).

9.3.4.2 Process of Phenomenological Analysis

Fundamentals of Phenomenology

Fundamentally, phenomenological analysis concentrates on first-person perspectives and subjective experiences, designed to explicate how individuals interpret their experiences and construct their realities. Phenomenologists assert that our comprehension of the world is profoundly influenced by our lived experiences, and thus, phenomenological analysis strives to capture the rich, fine-grained textures of these experiences through qualitative inquiries (Husserl & Moran, 2012; Smith, 2017).

Epoché and Bracketing

At the heart of phenomenological analysis is the methodological principle of epoché (bracketing), wherein researchers suspend preconceived assumptions, biases, and theoretical frameworks to approach the data with openness and receptivity. By setting aside presuppositions, researchers aim to engage in a phenomenological unveiling, disentangling away layers of interpretation to access the essential structures of subjective experience as perceived by the participants themselves (Anosike et al., 2012; van Manen, 2016).

For instance, in the management discipline, phenomenological analysis could be applied to understand the individual experiences of organisational members navigating organisational change. Researchers might conduct in-depth interviews with organisational members undergoing a significant restructuring process, using epoché to bracket their own expectations and biases. This approach would enable them to uncover the core experiences and perceptions of organisational members regarding the change, including how they experience shifts in organisational culture, changes in their roles, and their emotional responses to the transformation (Cameron & Green, 2024).

In another related example, phenomenological analysis could be utilised to explore the personal experiences of consumers as they adjust to the shift towards digital-only shopping environments. Researchers might carry out in-depth interviews with consumers navigating the transition into online retail models, employing epoché to set aside their own preconceptions and assumptions. This method would allow them to analyse the primary insights and experiences of consumers during this transition, investigating how changes in shopping habits influence their emotions, how their trust and loyalty to brands are shaped by digital changes, and how these shifts influence their overall purchasing behaviours (van Manen, 2016).

Data Collection and Phenomenological Interviews

Phenomenological analysis typically begins with qualitative data collection methods, such as in-depth interviews or phenomenological observations. These methods facilitate participants in articulating their subjective experiences, perceptions, perspectives, emotions, and meanings associated with specific phenomena of interest. Through open-ended questioning and active listening, researchers encourage participants to delve deeply into the distinctions of their individual experiences (Smith & Eatough, 2019).

For example, in the context of organisational success, participants might define the concept differently based on their individual experiences and perspectives. One participant might view an organisation's success simply as its ability to remain operational in the market, whilst another might assert that success requires accomplishing a minimum net profit margin (NPM) of 20 per cent. This divergence illustrates how subjective interpretations of organisational success are shaped by personal experiences and values (Cameron & Green, 2024).

Similarly, consider how the concept of 'beauty' is defined. One individual might assess beauty based on facial symmetry, whilst another might consider body proportionality as a key criterion. These variations in defining beauty underscore the subjective nature of personal experiences and cultural perspectives (Finlay, 2011).

Likewise, the concept of 'Wealth' can be defined in various ways depending upon individual perspectives. For instance, an individual might equate wealth with the possession of expensive items such as luxury watches or supercars, whilst another might define it as the ownership of knowledge and intellectual capital. This variability illustrates how different individuals perceive, observe, and define the same concept differently based on their subjective experiences and values (Smith, et al., 2019).

In the management discipline, these subjective definitions can influence organisational practices and decision-making. For example, an organisation might define 'levels of organisational success' differently depending upon its values and objectives. One organisation might view success in terms of individual achievements and promotions whilst another might consider it in terms of team performance and collaborative results (Cameron, 2011). Such differences highlight how organisational goals and measures are shaped by diverse interpretations of success, reflecting the broader phenomenon of subjective definition.

In essence, phenomenological analysis reveals that participants' interpretations and articulations of specific phenomena are deeply informed by their personal experiences, their perceptions, and the meanings associated with those phenomena (Remenyi et al., 1998).

Transcendental Phenomenological Reduction

Transcendental phenomenological reduction is a methodological approach pioneered by Edmund Husserl to investigate the essential structures of consciousness and experience. This rigorous method challenges conventional understandings and approaches to phenomena that shape lived experience (Moran, 2002).

A fundamental aspect of transcendental phenomenological reduction is the principle of bracketing or epoché. This critical step comprises suspending the natural attitude towards the external world, essentially, everyday assumptions about its existence and properties. By engaging in bracketing, researchers are prompted to set aside preconceived notions and biases that might mask the perception of phenomena. Bracketing does not comprise disregarding the external world but serves as a methodological instrument to focus attention solely on phenomena as they present themselves within consciousness (Farrell, 2020).

In addition, following epoché, the process of phenomenological description is employed. This process involves methodically probing phenomena as they appear in consciousness. The focus is on understanding how consciousness is directed towards objects (intentionality) and exploring the layers of meaning inherent in these experiences. Through detailed phenomenological description, the aim is to uncover what is fundamental and constant in experiences, distinguishing these from elements which consist of incidental or contingent (Moran, 2013).

A practical application of phenomenological description in the management discipline might involve analysing levels of organisational success. For example, different organisational members might have diverse perceptions of what represents success. An organisational member might define success as the mere ability of the organisation to remain operational and competitive, whereas another might consider it in terms of accomplishing specific financial measures, such as a 20 per cent net profit margin (NPM). Such variations in defining different levels of organisational success reflect the subjective nature of personal experiences and organisational values (Mızrak, 2024).

Similarly, the concept of wealth can be understood in various ways within a corporate context. For instance, one manager might define organisational wealth in terms of financial assets, such as owning substantial physical assets, luxury facilities, or high-value investments. This perspective aligns with traditional financial metrics and the visible accumulation of capital. In contrast, another manager might interpret wealth through the lens of intellectual capital, valuing the organisation's human resources, innovative capabilities, and proprietary knowledge. This view focuses on intangible assets, namely organisational members' expertise, organisational culture, and innovative potential, which are increasingly recognised as critical drivers of long-term competitive advantage.

For example, in a study of technology organisations, it was found that organisations like Google and Apple emphasise the importance of intellectual capital as a key component of their success. These organisations invest heavily in research and development (R&D) and attract top talent, viewing their intellectual assets as a major driver of growth and innovation (Mızrak 2024). On the other hand, traditional manufacturing firms might place a greater emphasis on tangible assets such as production facilities and equipment, seeing these as core to their operational capabilities and financial stability.

This divergence in defining wealth underscores how personal and organisational values shape the understanding and prioritisation of key concepts in management. Whilst financial measures provide a snapshot of immediate capital and resource allocation, intellectual capital reflects a strategic approach to sustainable growth and competitive positioning (de Vaujany et al., 2023). At the heart of Husserl's method is the identification of essences. In phenomenological description, the goal is to pinpoint the fundamental characteristics defining experiences. These essences are not merely abstract concepts but are integral to how individuals perceive and interpret the world. Husserl contended that identifying these essences provides a deeper understanding of the universal patterns of consciousness shaping human experience (de Vaujany et al., 2023).

The reduction process also introduces the concept of the transcendental ego. This notion refers to the pure ego or consciousness that forms the basis for all experiences. Unlike a personal ego tied to individual identity, the transcendental ego represents the universal structure of consciousness itself. Through phenomenological reduction, it becomes apparent that all phenomena manifest within the realm of this transcendental ego, thereby determining the understanding of how consciousness interacts with the world (Dasey, 2022).

Despite the abstract and seemingly detached nature of phenomenological reduction, Husserl underscored the importance of returning to the lifeworld. The lifeworld represents the everyday realm of human experience where interactions with others and the environment occur. Phenomenology, enriched by the insights gained through reduction, seeks to illuminate and deepen the understanding of the lifeworld. By integrating the findings of phenomenological methodology back into the lifeworld, a more in-depth appreciation of the complexities and structures of lived experiences can be achieved (van Manen, 2016).

In summary, transcendental phenomenological reduction invites a reconsideration and exploration of the fundamental structures of consciousness. By suspending assumptions and engaging in meticulous phenomenological description, the essences that define experiences can be revealed. This approach provides profound insights into the universal structures of consciousness and their manifestation within the lifeworld, thereby enriching the understanding of human existence and the nature of reality itself (Moran, 2002; Farrell, 2020).

Eidetic Variation and Phenomenological Insights

Phenomenological analysis engages techniques such as eidetic variation, a method rooted in phenomenological philosophy, notably associated with Edmund Husserl. Eidetic variation involves systematically exploring variations and similarities within participants' experiences to elucidate essential themes and structures. The purpose is to illuminate the universal aspects of human experience whilst honouring the distinct perspectives and contexts of individual participants. This method is particularly effective in uncovering the fundamental characteristics or essences of phenomena by varying aspects of a phenomenon in one's imagination in order to discern what remains constant or invariant across these variations (Biggerstaff & Thompson, 2008).

In the management discipline, eidetic variation can be adopted to reveal essential characteristics or principles expressing effective leadership or organisational structure. For instance, consider the following scenarios to explore the essence of effective leadership:

Scenario 1: A hierarchical management structure with stringent top-down decision-making.
Scenario 2: A flat organisational structure with decentralised decision-making.
Scenario 3: A leadership style centred on participatory decision-making and consensus-building.

Despite these variations in management styles, what remains essential to effective leadership? Through eidetic variation, one might identify key qualities, such as clear communication, strategic vision, adaptability, and the ability to encourage and motivate teams. These qualities could be considered fundamental irrespective of the specific organisational structure or decision-making process. For example, research highlights that clear communication is critical in both hierarchical and flat structures, facilitating alignment and reducing misunderstandings (Cassell et al., 2018). Similarly, strategic vision and adaptability are universally recognised as essential traits for leaders to navigate organisational changes and challenges (Witzel, 2022).

Eidetic variation also provides insights into the fundamental principles of effective organisational structure. For example, a study by Kumar (2018) demonstrates that regardless of whether an organisation adopts a hierarchical or flat structure, the underlying principles of effective coordination, role clarity, and resource allocation remain crucial for organisational success. This approach allows researchers and practitioners to abstract from specific instances and contexts in order to identify deeper insights into what makes management practices successful and enduring.

In conclusion, eidetic variation is a valuable tool in phenomenological analysis, contributing a methodical approach to uncovering the universal essences of phenomena such as leadership and organisational structures. By systematically varying aspects of management practices or leadership styles, one can identify the core attributes that underpin effective management, furnishing a profound understanding of what drives success in diverse organisational surroundings (Smith & Jones, 2023; Gedro, 2017).

Contextualisation and Interpretive Frameworks

Phenomenological analysis highlights significant emphasis on the role of context in shaping lived experiences. This method involves situating participants' narratives within broader socio-cultural, historical, and existential frameworks in order to elucidate how these contexts intersect with and influence subjective perceptions. By contextualising experiences within their specific contexts, researchers can achieve a more insightful understanding of their meanings and implications.

In the contexts of exploring why professionals in human resource development (HRD) pursue specific career paths or developmental opportunities, contextualisation plays a crucial role. For instance, the socio-cultural context significantly impacts career decisions. An HRD professional's choice to opt for certification in training and development may be strongly influenced by societal values emphasising continuous learning and professional growth. In cultures where advanced qualifications are highly esteemed, HRD professionals might be motivated to strengthen their credentials in order to develop career prospects and professional status (Kozminski et al., 2022).

Moreover, historical contexts distribute additional layers of understanding. Historical shifts in organisational priorities, such as increased prioritise on organisational members' development or changes in industry regulations, can outline career decisions. For example, during periods of economic downturn, HRD professionals might prioritise skill development programmes as a strategy to retain talent and bolster organisational resilience. These historical trends, including the rise of remote work and changes in labour laws, significantly influence career trajectories and professional focus within the HRD discipline (Jones & Smith, 2023).

Existential contexts also play a critical role. Personal experiences and aspirations deeply steer career choices. An HRD professional's decision to specialise in talent management might stem from past experiences with recruitment challenges, a desire to contribute strategically to organisational success, or personal values aligned with fostering organisational members' growth. Understanding these personal factors provides insight into why certain developmental opportunities are pursued and how they align with individual career goals (Dhiman, 2023).

In terms of contextualisation and interpretation, embedding career development decisions within these socio-cultural, historical, and existential contexts enables researchers to uncover the deeper motivations and meanings behind HRD professionals' choices. This approach reveals underlying aspirations for professional growth, responses to industry inclinations, and personal commitments to advancing organisational effectiveness through human capital development (Proudfoot, 2023).

Furthermore, this contextual approach furnishes a comprehensive insight into how HRD professionals navigate career development opportunities. It highlights the convergence of societal expectations, industry dynamics, and personal aspirations in shaping career trajectories. By examining these intersecting factors, researchers attain insightful perspectives on professional motivations and their contributions to organisational goals (McDonald & Hite, 2023).

In summary, phenomenological analysis, by considering socio-cultural, historical, and existential contexts, enriches interpretations of career development decisions. It elucidates the complex interplay between professional aspirations, societal norms, and organisational contexts, offering a deeper understanding of HRD practices and strategies for talent development.

Applications in Academic and Applied Settings

In academic research, phenomenological analysis significantly enriches fields such as management by delivering profound insights into organisational dynamics, leadership practices, employee experiences, and organisational culture. This methodology offers a sophisticated understanding of how individuals perceive their roles, interactions, and environments within organisational contexts.

For example, in management, phenomenological analysis can bolster leadership development by revealing the underlying experiences and perceptions of leaders or managers and their team members. By examining how leaders or managers experience and interpret their roles, challenges, and successes, organisations can customise development programmes to address the real needs and aspirations of their leaders. Similarly, this approach can be applied to understand organisational members' experiences more deeply, shedding light on how organisational members distinguish organisational culture, job satisfaction, and work-life balance. Such insights are invaluable for designing more effective organisational policies and practices reflective of organisational members' lived realities and contexts (Lemon, 2019).

In practical terms, phenomenological analysis informs various aspects of management practice. For instance, it can enhance organisational development initiatives by delivering a holistic view of how organisational members' experience changes within the organisation. Understanding organisational members' subjective experiences during periods of transformation, such as mergers, restructuring, or the implementation of new technologies, can guide leaders in managing these transitions more effectively and empathetically (Kuchinke, 2023).

Additionally, in the realm of strategic management, phenomenological analysis can contribute to understanding how organisational values and cultures influence decision-making processes and strategic adoptions. By investigating how organisational members' and leaders' or managers' experience and interpret these values, organisations can develop strategies that are more in tune with their organisational realities, contexts, and external market conditions (Heil, 2008).

Phenomenological analysis is a rigorous and empathetic method for qualitative research in management, focusing on the investigation of first-hand experiences and subjective perceptions. By uncovering the essences and meanings embedded within organisational narratives, this methodological approach enhances management's understanding of human elements in the organisational settings. It clarifies the complexities of organisational life and provides transformative insights that can inspire more effective management practices and strategies. Through its commitment to capturing the rich texture of human experiences and reducing biases, phenomenological analysis continues to offer valuable perspectives in the study and practice of management.

9.3.5 Ethnographic Analysis

9.3.5.1 Ethnographic Analysis: Understanding Social Practices and Cultural Dynamics

Ethnographic analysis is a qualitative research method deeply rooted in the tradition of ethnography. It is designed to enhance the understanding of social practices, cultural dynamics, and subjective experiences within specific communities or settings. Originating from anthropological research traditions, ethnographic analysis utilises immersive fieldwork and participant observation to reveal the complexities of daily life, social interactions, and cultural phenomena.

For instance, consider an ethnographic study conducted within a tech startup to investigate organisational culture. This study would typically involve extensive participant observation and in-depth interviews with employees. Through this immersive approach, ethnographic analysis might reveal key cultural norms and practices, such as the ways in which collaboration is facilitated, the methods used to foster innovation, and the nature of informal communication patterns within the organisation. By capturing these elements, researchers can acquire insights into how such cultural aspects contribute to the overall success of the organisation, providing a deeper understanding of the internal dynamics driving performance and organisational members' satisfaction (O'Reilly, 2012; Pöllänen, 2021).

Another example of ethnographic analysis in the management discipline might contain examining the integration of remote work practices within a global corporation. An ethnographic research study could include both field and remote observations of various teams working at different sites. Through detailed observations and interviews, researchers could determine how remote work practices are implemented in different cultural contexts, how organisational members interact across various time zones, and how organisational culture is maintained in a virtual environment. This analysis might reveal insights into the challenges and adaptations required for effective remote collaboration, as well as the impact on levels of team cohesion and productivity (Gutiérrez-Crocco et al., 2024)

Ethnographic analysis stands out for providing a rich, context-driven understanding of social and cultural life. By incorporating participants' experiences and observations within their natural environments, this method delivers insights informing both academic research and practical applications, particularly in organisational studies. Understanding the complexities of organisational culture and remote work dynamics can lead to more effective management and organisational strategies.

9.3.5.2 Process of Ethnographic Analysis

Foundations of Ethnographic Analysis

Ethnographic analysis is founded on the understanding that culture shapes, and is shaped by, human behaviour, beliefs, and social structures. It highlights the need to explore social phenomena within their natural contexts, recognising that the dynamic interplay between culture and individual actions is best captured through immersive engagement.

Researchers utilising ethnographic analysis undertake prolonged, immersive fieldwork within the research setting to accomplish a comprehensive understanding of the values, norms, rituals, and symbolic meanings that define community life. This methodological approach prioritises the contexts in which social practices occur, aiming to reveal the depths and complexities of social phenomena as they naturally unfold.

By embedding themselves in the daily lives of participants, researchers utilising this approach are capable of capturing the sophisticated customs generated when cultural contexts influence and are influenced by human behaviour. This immersion enables a richer and more detailed exploration of how individuals navigate and interpret their social worlds, offering insights into the underlying structures and meanings forming their experiences and interactions (Hammersley & Atkinson, 2019; Goffman, 2023).

For example, consider an ethnographic research study within a multinational corporation aiming to explore the impact of organisational culture on organisational members' engagement and organisational performance. Researchers might spend extended periods observing various teams, attending meetings, and conducting informal interviews with organisational members across different levels of the organisation. This immersive approach would permit researchers to discern how organisational values and practices are internalised by organisational members, how they influence conventional interactions, and how they contribute to overall organisational performance. Insights obtained from such a research study could inform strategies for enhancing organisational members' engagement and nurturing a cohesive organisational culture (van Maanen, 2011).

Another example could involve examining the implementation of sustainable practices within a manufacturing firm. An ethnographic approach might encompass researchers working alongside organisational members to observe how sustainability initiatives are integrated into daily operations. This could reveal how different levels of the organisation adapt to and interpret these initiatives, uncovering challenges and successes in aligning environmental goals with operational practices. Such insights could help refine sustainability strategies and improve their effectiveness within the organisational contexts (Verbuyst & Galazka, 2023).

In sum, ethnographic analysis provides a robust framework for understanding the intricacies of social phenomena within authentic contexts. By immersing in the environments which they study, researchers can illuminate the rich, multidimensional aspects of culture and behaviour, offering valuable insights that inform both theoretical understanding and practical applications in various fields, including management.

Immersion and Participant Observation

At the core of ethnographic analysis lies participant observation, a pivotal methodological approach in which researchers deeply immerse themselves in the day-to-day activities and routines of research participants. This technique involves both direct observation and active interaction, permitting researchers to acquire first-hand insights into the social interactions, behavioural patterns, communication styles, and cultural practices that influence and define community dynamics (Malinowski, 2013).

By engaging in participant observation, researchers have the opportunity to witness and document the subtle manners of social life as it clarifies in real time. This immersive engagement provides a window into how individuals and groups navigate their social environments, contributing a comprehensive understanding of the context-specific meanings and practices forming their experiences. For instance, in an organisational context, participant observation might comprise a researcher working alongside organisational members in order to perceive how they interact with each other and with management, how organisational norms and values are enacted in day-to-day responsibilities, and how informal communication channels function within the organisation (Dyer et al., 2024).

In a different context, an ethnographic research study of a community celebrating a significant cultural festival might involve the researcher participating in the event, engaging with organisational members, and observing the rituals, celebrations, and social interactions that characterise the festival. This immersive method allows the researcher to understand the cultural significance of the cultural practice and its implications on organisational unity and identity (Holloway et al., 2010).

Participant observation thus offers a rich, detailed perspective on the subjective experiences of individuals and groups. It enables researchers to reveal the implicit rules and meanings that govern social behaviour, yielding insights often concealed in more superficial or detached research methods. This methodological technique is integral to ethnographic analysis, facilitating a deeper understanding of the complex interplay between culture and human behaviour within their natural contexts.

Data Collection and Ethnographic Techniques

Ethnographic analysis adopts a variety of data collection techniques, including field notes, interviews, visual documentation, and artefact analysis. Each technique plays an integral role in capturing the rich, intricate details of social life and organisational environments.

Firstly, field notes are essential for recording observations, conversations, and reflections during fieldwork. These notes provide a comprehensive account of the day-to-day interactions and activities within the research setting. For example, in a research project studying organisational culture within a multinational corporation, field notes might document informal interactions between organisational members and managers, the physical layout of office spaces, and the dynamics of team meetings. These observations can reveal insights into how organisational culture is enacted and experienced by different organisational members (Harvey, 2021). Additionally, the field notes could support the researcher in revisiting and cross-checking the collected data at any time, ensuring that no essential details are disregarded.

Secondly, interviews complement participant observation by contributing deeper insights into participants' perspectives on cultural beliefs, values, and experiences. In the management context, interviews with organisational members and managers can provide valuable information on perceptions of leadership styles, organisational change, and organisational members' satisfaction. For instance, an ethnographic research study exploring the impact of new leadership on team morale might involve in-depth interviews with organisational members to understand their experiences and attitudes towards the changes employed by the new leadership (Batista-Foguet et al., 2021).

Thirdly, visual documentation, such as photographs or video recordings, can further enrich ethnographic analysis by documenting visual aspects of the research setting. In a study of corporate branding, for instance, visual documentation might include photographs of office spaces, marketing materials, and organisational members' uniforms. These images can help demonstrate how the organisational brand identity is expressed and perceived within the organisation (Pera et al., 2022).

Fourthly, artefact analysis involves examining physical items or documents relevant to the research topic. In a research study of innovation practices within a technology firm, artefact analysis might include reviewing internal reports, project plans, and prototypes. This examination can provide insights into the processes and tools utilised by organisational members to drive innovation and how these practices align with the organisational strategic goals (Thompson & Green, 2024).

Finally, by integrating these data collection techniques, ethnographic analysis facilitates a holistic view of organisational life, documenting both the tangible and intangible elements shaping organisational dynamics and culture.

Cultural Interpretation and Thick Description

Ethnographic analysis places significant emphasis on the production of thick description, a methodologically rigorous approach entailing a comprehensive and contextualised interpretation of social practices and cultural phenomena observed during fieldwork. This approach seeks to probe deeper into surface-level observations, illustrating the intricate meanings, symbols, and implicit understandings embedded within cultural practices and social interactions (Geertz, 1973; Edwards, 2020).

Thick description comprises contributing a detailed and comprehensive account of the contexts and significances of observed behaviours and practices. For example, in the management discipline, an ethnographic research study investigating the implementation of agile methodologies within a software development team would not simply document the procedural aspects of these methodologies. Instead, it would scrutinise how team members understand and adapt these practices, the symbolic meanings attached to agile rituals, and the cultural shifts that arise from adopting agile principles. Agile methodologies, which prioritise flexibility, iterative development, and team collaboration, focus on continuous improvement and responsiveness to change. The research would thus endeavour to discover not only the procedural details but also the deeper ways in which these principles influence team dynamics and organisational culture (Hutasuhut et al., 2021).

Similarly, in a research project focusing on corporate social responsibility (CSR) initiatives within a multinational corporation, thick description would go beyond documenting CSR activities. It would involve analysing how organisational members and stakeholders perceive and engage with these initiatives, the cultural and symbolic meanings attached to the corporation's CSR efforts, and the impact of these initiatives on organisational identity and community relations (Evans & Patel, 2024).

By focusing on thick description, researchers are able to offer in-depth, sophisticated interpretations bringing to light the deeper, often unarticulated, layers of meaning within social practices. This technique facilitates a more profound understanding of the ways in which cultural practices and organisational behaviours are rooted in and shaped by their specific contexts (Geertz, 2008; Edwards, 2020).

Reflexivity and Positionality

Ethnographic analysis encourages reflexivity, i.e., an awareness of the researchers' roles, biases, and subjectivity in influencing data collection and interpretation. Reflexivity comprises researchers critically acknowledging on their own positionality and reflecting on how their background, beliefs, and identities may affect their interactions with participants and influence their interpretations within the research contexts (Clifford & Marcus, 2022; Madison, 2011).

By engaging in reflexivity, researchers can obtain a more comprehensive understanding of how their personal experiences and perspectives influence the research process. For instance, in ethnographic research study on consumers' behaviour within a luxury retail environment, a researcher's own socio-economic background and purchasing habits may impact how they interpret customers' interactions and brand perceptions. If the researcher derives from a background familiar with luxury goods, they may unintentionally focus on aspects of consumers' behaviour associated with their own experiences, potentially overlooking alternative viewpoints of customers from different socio-economic backgrounds. Recognising such biases allows the researcher to present their findings with greater transparency and adopt strategies to address potential distortions in data collection and analysis (Nanjundeswaraswamy, 2023).

In another context, consider an ethnographic research study of organisational diversity initiatives within a global corporation. Reflexivity helps researchers recognise how their own beliefs and experiences regarding diversity and inclusion might influence their interpretation of organisational members' responses and the effectiveness of these initiatives. For example, if a researcher has a strong personal commitment to diversity and has previously worked in diverse environments, they may be more likely to view the organisational diversity endeavours positively and may interpret organisational members' feedback through this lens. By acknowledging these potential biases, the researcher can adopt a more balanced approach to data analysis, guaranteeing a more accurate and comprehensive understanding of the impact of diversity initiatives on different groups of organisational members (Janssens & Zanoni, 2021).

In conclusion, reflexivity plays a critical role in ethnographic analysis by enhancing transparency and rigour. It allows researchers to systematically address potential biases and assumptions, leading to more nuanced and credible interpretations of social phenomena (Geertz, 2008; Hammersley & Atkinson, 2019).

Applications in Academic and Applied Settings

In academic management research, Ethnographic Analysis significantly contributes to disciplines such as anthropology, sociology, education, healthcare, and organisational studies by providing profound insights into cultural diversity, social structures, and community dynamics. For instance, in the discipline of healthcare, ethnographic approaches can illuminate how different communities navigate and experience health services, thus informing the development of culturally sensitive care practices (Kiaos, 2024). Similarly, in organisational studies, ethnographic analysis can provide a deep understanding of organisational culture and organisational members' interactions, aiding in the design of more effective organisational change strategies (Gellner & Hirsch, 2020).

Practically, ethnographic analysis informs various applied settings, including policy development, cultural competency training, community development initiatives, and organisational change efforts. By providing sophisticated understandings of stakeholders' perspectives and social contexts, ethnographic analysis allows policymakers and practitioners to create more informed and contextually relevant strategies. For example, in community development, ethnographic insights can help customise interventions to more effectively address the unique needs and values of different community groups, thus improving the effectiveness of such initiatives (Mauksch et al., 2017).

In conclusion, ethnographic analysis is a rigorous and immersive method to a qualitative research, dedicated to investigating and interpreting social practices, cultural dynamics, and lived experiences within specific communities or settings. Through extensive fieldwork and participant observation, this methodological approach deepens our understanding of cultural diversity, social interactions, and the complex interplay between individuals and their environments. By emphasising cultural interpretation and thick description, Ethnographic Analysis continues to shed light on the intricacies of human behaviour and cultural meaning-making across diverse contexts (Susen, 2024; Hammersley & Atkinson, 2019).

9.3.6 Content Analysis

9.3.6.1 Content Analysis: Uncovering Patterns and Insights in Textual and Visual Data

Content analysis is an advanced qualitative research methodology utilised to meticulously scrutinise textual and visual data in order to distinguish patterns, themes, and underlying meanings. Originally perceived within the realms of communication and media studies, it has since extended into the social sciences and psychology, and it is increasingly utilised within management research. Content analysis offers a robust framework for investigating the substance and context of messages, documents, and artefacts, all the whilst considering their socio-cultural and historical milieus (Morse, 2016b).

For instance, in the management domain, content analysis can be applied to evaluate organisational communication such as internal reports, corporate social media posts, or organisational members' feedback surveys. By analysing internal communications, researchers can reveal themes associated with organisational culture, leadership effectiveness, and organisational members' engagement (Hsieh & Shannon, 2005). Additionally, content analysis can be utilised to measure corporate marketing materials, such as advertisements and promotional content, in order to understand brand positioning and customers' perceptions of organisational market strategies (Bluhm et al., 2011).

Another related example is from Singapore, this study investigated the Singaporean public's primary concerns during the initial phase of the COVID-19 pandemic.

Utilising qualitative content analysis, the researchers analysed comments posted on the Facebook pages of six local news publications between January and April 2020. The analysis identified five main themes, with the most prevalent being 'fear and concern' (35%), which appeared to drive other behaviours like 'panic buying and hoarding' (21%). The study concludes that clear, timely communication and supportive measures from the government are essential for managing public anxiety and maintaining social cohesion during a national health crisis (Shorey et al., 2020).

Another related example is analysing customer feedback on social media regarding a new product launch. Qualitative content analysis in this context can reveal insights into levels of customer satisfaction, product strengths and weaknesses, and emerging trends in consumers' preferences. This method can also be applied to study organisational members' performance reviews in order to identify prevalent themes in feedback, which can inform talent management and development strategies (Bengtsson, 2016).

9.3.6.2 Process of Content Analysis

Fundamentals of Content Analysis

Content analysis starts with the systematic scrutiny and interpretation of textual or visual data. Researchers utilise a methodical method to categorising, coding, and analysing data in order to discover recurring themes, patterns of communication, and inherent meanings embedded within the contents. This methodological precision ensures the reliability and validity of the findings, contributing to robust, evidence-based interpretations and insights (Forman & Damschroder, 2007; Mayring, 2015).

In the realm of management, content analysis can be adopted into multitudinous contexts. For instance, analysing internal corporate communications, such as emails or meeting minutes, can reveal insights into organisational culture, leadership styles, and organisational members' engagement (Forman & Damschroder, 2007). Investigating corporate social media posts and marketing materials can provide an understanding of brand positioning and customers' perceptions of organisational strategies (Myers, 2019). In addition, content analysis can be applied to evaluate organisational members' performance reviews, identifying common feedback themes that can inform human resource practices and talent management strategies (Myers, 2019).

To ensure the reliability of content analysis, researchers can utilise strategies such as inter-coder reliability, where multiple analysts independently code the same data and compare results to certify consistency. Furthermore, establishing clear coding schemes and maintaining comprehensive documentation of the coding process helps achieve consistent analysis across different datasets (Mayring, 2015). Validity can be enhanced by triangulating data from multiple sources assisting in cross-verifying findings and ensuring that the analysis captures the true essence of the data. Providing detailed examples and maintaining a rigorous audit trail further bolster the credibility and accuracy of the findings, guaranteeing a robust and transparent research process (Forman & Damschroder, 2007).

Types of Content Analysis

Content analysis encompasses various types, including manifest and latent analysis. Manifest content analysis emphasises the explicit, observable elements within texts or visuals, such as identifiable themes and topics, and their frequency of occurrence. For instance, in a management context, manifest content analysis might involve analysing corporate communication materials, such as company newsletters or annual reports, to quantify mentions of key topics, including corporate social responsibility, financial performance, or organisational members' engagement (Stake, 2013). This approach allows for a clear and straightforward examination of surface-level content (Krippendorff, 2018).

In contrast, latent content analysis explores the deeper meanings, motivations, and implicit messages conveyed through symbols, metaphors, and cultural references (Vaismoradi et al., 2013). For example, analysing organisational culture through internal documents and organisational members' feedback might reveal underlying attitudes towards leadership styles or organisational change. Latent content analysis can reveal subtle patterns in how organisational members perceive management strategies or corporate values, such as implicit messages about innovation and risk-taking present in leadership communications or strategic planning documents (Kuckartz & Rädiker, 2023). This method aims to shed light on the more complex and often hidden aspects of content.

Data Collection and Sampling

In content analysis, non-probability sampling methods are often used when researchers need to select participants or samples in accordance with specific criteria rather than random selection. Three notable non-probability sampling techniques are purposive sampling, accidental sampling, and quota sampling.

Purposive sampling involves selecting samples using specific characteristics or criteria relevant to the research. For instance, in a research study examining the effectiveness of leadership communication within an organisation, researchers might use the purposive sampling technique to select only high-level executives' speeches and internal memos. This targeted method ensures that the analysis focuses on communications from key decision-makers, which are critical for understanding leadership strategies and their impact on organisational culture (Gummesson, 2000).

Accidental sampling, also referred to as convenience sampling, involves selecting samples in accordance with ease of accessibility and availability. For example, if researchers are analysing customers' feedback on a new product through social media, they might use accidental sampling technique by selecting the most recent and readily available customer reviews. This method is practical when time or resource constraints prevent a more systematic approach but may limit the generalisability of the findings (Musa et al., 2024).

Quota sampling is a method where researchers ensure that specific subgroups within the population are represented in the sample according to predetermined quotas. For example, if a research aims to analyse organisational members' opinions on an organisation's new HR policies, researchers might set quotas to include feedback from organisational members across numerous departments and levels of seniority. This guarantees that the sample reflects the diversity of perspectives within the organisation, providing a comprehensive view of the policies' impact (Nicmanis, 2024).

By utilising these non-probability sampling methods, researchers can customise their data collection to specific needs and contexts, although it is important to acknowledge that these approaches may bring about certain biases and limit the generalisability of the findings.

Coding and Categorisation

Central to content analysis is the systematic coding and categorisation of data. Researchers begin by developing a coding scheme, essentially a set of rules or categories suggesting the identification and classification of content foundations. This coding scheme is designed to systematically organise and interpret the data in line with the specific research objectives and questions.

Codes in content analysis can be descriptive, involving categorising content based on observable features such as topics or themes. For example, in a research study analysing corporate social media posts, descriptive codes might include categories including 'Customers' Service', 'Product Promotion', and 'Brand Engagement' (Neuendorf, 2017).

Interpretive codes in content analysis extend beyond surface-level content to reveal underlying attitudes and emotions. For example, when analysing organisational members' opinions on new policies, interpretive codes might identify sentiments such as 'Satisfaction', 'Frustration', or 'Indifference'. These codes provide a sophisticated understanding of organisational members' responses, revealing deeper insights into how individuals perceive and react to organisational changes (Rua, 2013). By applying interpretive codes, researchers can investigate the subtler aspects of the data, moving beyond mere descriptions to discover the emotional and psychological dimensions of the contents. This approach enables a more comprehensive analysis of the data, improving the depth and relevance of the research findings.

Evaluative codes assess content in line with certain value judgments, such as distinguishing between desirable and undesirable interpretations. For example, in an analysis of customers' reviews for a new product, evaluative codes might classify feedback as 'Positive', 'Neutral', or 'Negative', providing a measure for assessing overall product reception and areas for improvement (Johnson & Duberley, 2003).

The development and application of these coding schemes guarantee that data is organised in a manner that aligns with the research objectives, facilitating a structured analysis yielding insightful and actionable findings (Vaismoradi et al., 2013).

Reliability and Validity

Content analysis places significant emphasis on both reliability and validity to ensure the robustness of research findings. Reliability relates to the consistency and reproducibility of the results, whilst validity pertains to the accuracy and credibility of the interpretations. Researchers apply different strategies to improve these aspects, including the use of coding manuals, inter-coder reliability tests, and triangulation.

Coding manuals provide a comprehensive guide for categorising and interpreting data, ensuring that the coding process is systematic and consistent across different analysts (Armborst, 2017). Inter-coder reliability tests involve multiple researchers independently coding the same data and comparing their results to assess consistency. This approach strengthens the reliability of the findings by ensuring that the coding scheme is applied uniformly. High inter-coder reliability indicates that the results are reliable and consistent (Alston, 2020).

Triangulation, another critical technique, includes comparing and cross-validating findings across different data sources or methods in order to corroborate interpretations. For instance, researchers might use triangulation by comparing insights from in-depth interviews with those attained from documentary analysis. This approach helps verify whether similar themes or patterns emerge across various sources, thus improving the credibility of the findings (Lerigo-Sampson, 2022). By cross-checking results from multiple perspectives, researchers guarantee that their conclusions are strongly supported and provide a wide-ranging understanding of the data.

These methodological approaches, comprising triangulation and consistency checks, significantly contribute to the reliability and validity of content analysis, providing a robust foundation for drawing meaningful and credible conclusions from the data (Leso et al., 2023).

Interpretation and Reporting Findings

Upon completion of coding and analysis, content analysis culminates in the interpretation and reporting of findings. Researchers synthesise the coded data in order to discern overarching themes, patterns, and trends within the content. This synthesis encompasses integrating the identified codes into larger categories or concepts, revealing significant insights into the data. The findings are then contextualised within relevant theoretical frameworks or existing literature, aiding in understanding the implications of the results in relation to broader social phenomena, cultural discourses, communication dynamics, or public opinion (Creswell & Poth, 2016).

For instance, if a research study examines organisational communication regarding new policies, researchers might identify recurring themes such as 'Organisational Members' Resistance', 'Levels of Management Transparency', and 'Policy Effectiveness'. These themes are then analysed in the context of organisational theory or communication models to understand their implications for organisational members' relations and organisational change (Kuckartz, 2023). By framing the findings within established theoretical frameworks, researchers provide a richer interpretation of how these themes influence or reflect organisational dynamics and organisational members' attitudes (Tesch, 2013).

The final reporting phase comprises articulating these insights in a manner that highlights their relevance and contributions to the field. This comprises discussing how the findings align with or challenge existing theories, how they contribute to understanding specific phenomena, and what practical implications they might have for stakeholders, such as policymakers, organisational leaders, or the public (Bazeley, 2023). Through this comprehensive interpretation and reporting, content analysis not only elucidates distinct content features but also advances knowledge within the field by linking empirical data with theoretical and practical considerations.

Applications in Academic and Applied Settings

In academic research, content analysis provides valuable insights across various disciplines, including communication, media studies, sociology, political science, marketing research, and management. This methodological approach systematically examines textual and visual representations to reveal underlying patterns and themes. By applying rigorous coding and categorisation techniques, content analysis reveals audience perceptions, preferences, and the socio-cultural influences embedded within communication materials.

As an illustration, in policy analysis, content analysis can assess public opinion on legislative changes by analysing media coverage and public discourse. In market research, it helps identify consumer attitudes towards products by examining customer reviews and advertisements. Similarly, in management research, it can evaluate internal communications in order to understand employees' engagement and organisational culture (Mayring, 2015; Krippendorff, 2018).

In conclusion, content analysis is a robust and systematic approach to qualitative research. Its methodological principles of coding, categorisation, and interpretation facilitate a comprehensive understanding of communication dynamics, cultural representations, and societal discourses across various contexts. By maintaining a commitment to reliability and validity, content analysis not only improves scholarly inquiry but also guides practical applications in communication, social sciences, and beyond, making it an indispensable tool for both academic research and practical applications (Fox & King, 2020; Wilson, 2016).

9.3.7 *Case Study Analysis:*

9.3.7.1 Case Study Analysis: Exploring Complex Phenomena in Context

Case study analysis is a qualitative research method used to discover complex phenomena within their real-life contexts, with the goal of providing comprehensive insights and understandings of specific cases or situations. This methodology is widely utilised across disciplines such as social sciences, business, psychology, education, and management, and it employs a holistic approach in order to examine unique instances, events, or individuals. Through detailed exploration of contextual factors, processes, and outcomes, case study analysis offers a deep understanding of how different elements interact within particular environments (May & Perry, 2022; Schwartz-Shea & Yanow, 2013).

The value of case study analysis lies in its ability to present profound insights into intricate phenomena generally missed by broader quantitative studies. It allows for a thorough examination of intricacies and complexities, thereby providing a richer understanding of the subject matter (Cherkaoui & Oudrhough, 2024). By focusing on real-life contexts, case studies reveal how numerous factors operate and influence outcomes within specific settings (Kumar, 2024). In particular, they are useful for exploring new or inadequately understood phenomena, aiding in the development of theories and hypotheses for future research (Schwartz-Shea, 2021). For practitioners, case studies offer actionable recommendations and solutions based on real-world analysis, making them highly relevant for addressing specific challenges (Hunziker & Blankenagel, 2024).

The methodology of case study analysis encompasses several key steps. The selection of cases is fundamental, often based on their uniqueness, their representativeness, or the insights they provide. For example, a retail chain experiencing difficulties might be selected to analyse its turnaround strategies (Yin, 2018). Data collection is typically multifaceted, including interviews with stakeholders, such as senior management, organisational members, and customers, to obtain diverse perspectives (Schwartz-Shea, 2021).

Additionally, documents, including financial reports and internal memos, as well as observations of operations or customers' interactions, are used to provide a comprehensive view (Cherkaoui & Oudrhough, 2024). Data analysis involves identifying patterns and themes through techniques, such as thematic analysis or pattern matching, in order to derive meaningful conclusions (Braun & Clarke, 2022). Contextualisation is also essential, involving the understanding of the environment where the case is positioned, including industry trends, organisational culture, and external factors (Perry, 2015). Findings are then presented in a detailed narrative that includes background information, methodology, results, and conclusions, illustrating the complexities and nuances of the case (Hartley et al., 2023)

For instance, consider a case study investigating a retail chain that has faced declining levels of organisational performance. The objective is to evaluate the effectiveness of its turnaround strategies. Data sources might include interviews with management to understand strategic decisions, financial reports to track organisational performance measures, and historical data to identify trends (Eisenhardt, 2021). The analysis would focus on leadership decisions, operational changes, and customers' engagement initiatives in order to assess their impact on the turnaround (Yin, 2018). Findings from such a case study would provide valuable lessons and practical insights applicable to similar situations, illustrating the utility of case studies in both academic research and practical implications (Hunziker & Blankenagel, 2024).

9.3.7.2 Process of Case Study Analysis

Fundamentals of Case Study Analysis

At the core of case study analysis is a thorough examination of specific cases, regarded as comprehensive entities within their natural contexts. Researchers engage in an in-depth exploration of qualitative data, such as interviews, observations, documents, or archival records, to develop sophisticated, contextualised understandings of the cases under investigation. This methodological approach prioritises depths over breadths, emphasising the intricate complexities and dynamics inherent to each case (Saldaña & Omasta, 2016; Strijker et al., 2020).

In case study analysis, the focus is on understanding the case in its entirety, recognising it as a complex and multifaceted phenomenon influenced by various contextual factors. Researchers aim to reveal profound insights and patterns through meticulous examination of qualitative data. This approach enables a thorough appreciation of how different elements interact, contributing to a holistic understanding encapsulating the complexities and interactions specific to the phenomenon under investigation (Hancock et al., 2021; Morgan, 2022).

By concentrating on depth, case study analysis provides a rich, contextualised account that underscores the specific complexities and dynamics of the case, thereby enhancing the understanding of broader implications and contributing to theory development and practical applications (Stake, 2013; Strijker et al., 2020).

Types of Case Studies

Case study analysis encompasses various types, each serving particular aims and approaches to research. Intrinsic case studies focus on understanding the unique qualities and intricacies of a specific case of interest, aiming to attain insight into the particularities of that individual case. For instance, an intrinsic case study in management might examine the distinctive leadership style of a CEO within a high-tech startup in order to understand how their unique approach influences organisational culture and levels of organisational innovation (Simons, 2014).

Instrumental case studies are designed to illuminate a broader phenomenon or theory through an in-depth examination of a particular case. In the management discipline, this could involve a research study of an organisation that successfully established a new organisational structure in order to shed light on how such structural changes can affect overall business performance and employee satisfaction. For example, an instrumental case study might analyse the reorganisation of a multinational corporation in order to understand how it impacts global operations and strategic alignment (Tight, 2017).

Collective case studies entail the analysis of multiple cases within a shared framework, often referred to as cross-case studies. This approach is advantageous for comparing and contrasting numerous instances in order to draw broader conclusions. In the management discipline, a collective case study might investigate several organisations adopting remote working policies in order to assess how different organisational cultures and business models influence the success and challenges of remote work arrangements (Proudfoot, 2023).

Holistic case studies, also known as single-case studies, deliver comprehensive analyses of intricate situations or systems. In management, a holistic case study could focus on the comprehensive evaluation of an organisational entire supply chain management system to understand how it affects operational efficiency and competitiveness. For instance, a holistic case study might explore a retail organisational supply chain from procurement to distribution in order to assess the integration of new technologies and their impact on overall organisational performance (Merriam & Tisdell, 2015).

Data Collection and Analysis

The process of case study analysis begins with the meticulous collection of data from a diverse array of relevant sources. Case studies may be selected guided by extreme examples, such as best or worst practices within a specific category, in order to highlight significant contrasts and insights. For instance, an intrinsic case study might investigate a highly successful company like Amazon in order to understand best practices in e-commerce and customer service (Mansar & Reijers, 2007; Zumitzavan, 2011). The data analysis process for Amazon could involve thematic analysis of customers' feedback and reviews, content analysis of marketing materials, and comparative analysis of operational measures in order to identify the key factors driving their success.

Conversely, a study might scrutinise an organisation facing significant failure, such as Yahoo's decline in the tech industry, to explore lessons from worst practices in strategic decision-making and market positioning (Phillips & Klein, 2023). The data analysis process for Yahoo could include a historical analysis of strategic decisions, a trend analysis of market share over time, and a qualitative analysis of interviews with former executives in order to discover the factors leading to their decline.

Researchers adopt diverse methods, including interviews, observations, surveys, and document analysis, to obtain comprehensive qualitative data that reflects a broad spectrum of perspectives and dimensions of the case (Given, 2015; Naeem et al., 2023). This data collection process is typically iterative, allowing researchers to refine their understanding and explore emerging themes and patterns throughout the study.

For example, a research study on Amazon's management practices might encompass interviews with key executives, observations of operational strategies, and analyses of market and performance data. The data analysis would include coding interview transcripts to identify recurring themes, mapping out operational strategies against performance metrics, and using comparative analysis in order to evaluate Amazon's strategies against industry benchmarks (Mansar & Reijers, 2007).

Conversely, analysing Yahoo's strategic missteps might involve reviewing business decisions through the examination of documents, conducting interviews with former executives, and analysing market trends. The data analysis could include a historical comparative analysis of strategic decisions versus market outcomes, a thematic analysis of interviews to reveal strategic weaknesses, and a trend analysis of market position relative to competitors (Phillips & Klein, 2023).

Thick Description and Contextualisation

Central to case study analysis is the production of thick description, i.e., a comprehensive and refined interpretation of the case that captures its contexts, processes, and interactions. Researchers aim to contextualise the case within its socio-cultural, historical, and organisational settings, meticulously scrutinising how both external factors and internal dynamics influence the case's development, outcomes, and overall significance.

For instance, consider a case study focusing on the turnaround strategies of General Electric (GE) under CEO Jack Welch. Researchers could produce a thick description by detailing GE's strategic initiatives, organisational restructuring, and leadership approaches. This entails examining how GE's internal dynamics, such as Welch's management philosophy and corporate culture, interacted with external factors such as economic conditions and competitive pressures to drive the company's transformation and success. Researchers could contextualise these elements within the broader socio-economic environment of the late 20th and early 21st centuries, exploring how these factors contributed to GE's growth and to eventual challenges (Grove, 2023).

In contrast, a case study investigating the deterioration of Sears might involve producing a thick description of the organisational strategic missteps, organisational issues, and market interactions which contributed to its decline. Researchers could explore Sears' historical context, including its initial market dominance and subsequent struggles with adapting to changing consumers' preferences and e-commerce. They could also analyse internal dynamics, such as management decisions and organisational structure, and external pressures, such as market competition and technological advancements, to understand the factors contributing to Sears' difficulties (David, 2011).

Finally, through thick description, case study analysis can deliver a rich, contextually grounded understanding of the case, highlighting the intricate interplay of factors influencing on its outcomes and significance.

Analytical Techniques and Pattern Recognition

Researchers can employ various analytical techniques, such as pattern recognition, thematic analysis, and cross-case comparison, to reveal recurring themes, causal relationships, and theoretical insights within case studies. By systematically organising and interpreting qualitative data, case study analysis generates evidence-based interpretations and theoretical propositions that contribute to scholarly knowledge and understanding.

For example, in management research, cross-case comparison is a valuable analytical technique for refining themes and highlighting theoretical insights, as illustrated by Shultz, Whitney, and Zickar (2020). Consider a hypothetical study exploring effective strategies for managing organisational change. This research focuses on three distinct companies: Organisation A, a technology firm; Organisation B, a manufacturing enterprise; and Organisation C, a retail business, each of which has recently undergone significant restructuring.

Data Collection and Initial Thematic Analysis: The research begins with comprehensive data collection from each company. For Organisation A, data includes interviews with managers and employees, internal documents detailing the change processes, and customer feedback. Organisation B's data comprises observations from restructuring meetings, employee surveys, and financial performance reports. Meanwhile, Organisation C's data is obtained through focus groups with organisational members, analysis of marketing and sales data, and interviews with executives (Silverman, 2016).

With the data collected, researchers perform an initial thematic analysis. Preliminary themes identified might include 'Leadership style', 'Organisational Members' Engagement', 'Communication Strategies', and 'Impact on Performance', reflecting several dimensions of change management observed within each case (Liamputtong, 2020).

Applying Cross-Case Comparison: The next step is cross-case comparison, which allows researchers to identify patterns and contrasts across the cases. For instance, the analysis might reveal that a transformational leadership style is present in all three companies but manifests differently in each context. Similarly, the level of organisational members' engagement varies: Organisation A and C exhibit high engagement levels, whereas Organisation B shows comparatively lower engagement. Communication strategies also differ, with Organisation A using frequent updates, Organisation B adopting a formal approach, and Organisation C employing a mixed strategy (Bartlett & Vavrus, 2016).

By comparing these patterns, researchers refine their understanding of the themes. They observe that transformational leadership consistently associates with positive organisational members' responses and improved performance measures. This refined theme highlights that whilst leadership style is crucial, its effectiveness is influenced by other factors, such as communication and engagement (Shultz et al., 2020).

Developing Theoretical Insights: Through this refined analysis, researchers develop theoretical propositions. For instance, one proposition might suggest that transformational leadership positively influences organisational change success across different industries. Another proposition could be that transparent and frequent communication is a key driver of organisational members' engagement during restructuring. These insights offer a deeper understanding of how various elements interact to affect levels of organisational performance (Clark et al., 2021).

Evidence-Based Interpretation and Recommendations: The refined themes and theoretical propositions are supported by evidence from the case studies. Researchers compile this evidence to substantiate their findings, presenting a comprehensive view of effective change management strategies. The research's recommendations are customised to a variety of types of organisation, reflecting the distinctiveness observed across the cases.

In conclusion, cross-case comparison is an invaluable technique in organisational management research. By systematically comparing cases and refining themes, researchers develop robust theoretical insights and evidence-based recommendations. This approach not only improves the depth of understanding but also provides practical guidance applicable across diverse organisational contexts.

Generalisation and Transferability

Case study analysis prioritises in-depth and context-specific understanding, with findings potentially informing broader theoretical frameworks, hypotheses, or policy implications. Researchers consider principles such as generalisation, i.e., drawing more general implications from specific cases, and transferability, that is, applying findings to similar contexts or settings, in orderto enhance the relevance and applicability of their analyses beyond individual cases (Yanow & Schwartz-Shea, 2006; Hancock et al., 2021).

However, when addressing generalisation and transferability, researchers must recognise that findings from single or cross-case studies may not be directly applicable across different norms, cultures, or settings. Limitations, in terms of the characteristics, types, and periods of data collection of the unit of analysis, can constrain the applicability of the findings. For example, a case study focused on a tech start-up's innovation practices may offer valuable insights into similar tech organisations but might not fully apply to organisations in traditional manufacturing sectors or different cultural contexts (Geertz, 2017). More specifically, the matrix organisational structure may be well-suited to tech firms that require a diversity of ideas for innovation, whereas the traditional vertical organisational structure may be more appropriate for organisations in the manufacturing sector that demand a high degree of responsibility for specialised tasks.

Thus, whilst case study analysis can provide a rich understanding of specific phenomena within a particular time and organisational context, researchers and practitioners need to exercise caution when generalising findings. For instance, a case study of a successful digital transformation initiative at a large, multinational financial services organisation might highlight effective strategies for integrating new technologies and processes. However, the findings may not directly apply to a small, family-owned business in the hospitality sector. The financial organisation's success could be attributed to its substantial resources, extensive IT infrastructure, and an organisational culture that supports innovation, conditions that might be absent in the smaller, less resource-intensive hospitality business (Dul & Hak, 2008).

Similarly, a case study investigating the implementation of a comprehensive diversity and inclusion programme in a global technology corporation might provide valuable insights into fostering a more inclusive workplace. Nonetheless, these insights may not be fully applicable to a mid-sized manufacturing organisation with a different organisational structure and cultural context. The technology organisational programme may benefit from sophisticated training tools and policies personalised to a highly diverse workforce, which might not be practical or appropriate for the manufacturing organisation, where the diversity challenges and organisational dynamics differ (Cassell & Kele, 2021).

Finally, in both examples, researchers must consider how the specific characteristics of the case, such as industry type, organisational size, and available resources, might affect the generalisability of the results. Therefore, whilst case study analysis provides in-depth insights, its findings should be carefully assessed before applying them to different contexts or organisations (Yin, 2009b). Hence, case study analysis offers in-depth, context-specific insights but may not be universally applicable. Researchers should carefully evaluate how specific case characteristics influence the generalisability of findings

Applications in Academic and Applied Settings

Case study analysis is a crucial methodological method within management research, offering deep insights into organisational practices, decision-making processes, and human behaviour by examining specific instances in their real-world contexts.

In the management discipline, case study analysis is instrumental in understanding complex practices and transformations. For instance, research on strategic agility in multinational corporations highlights how organisations employ agile methodologies to navigate market uncertainties and enhance competitive advantage. Case studies have demonstrated that firms implementing agile practices can enhance responsiveness and innovation, effectively managing complex projects and adapting to rapid market changes (Denning, 2021).

Similarly, the examination of corporate social responsibility (CSR) initiatives provides valuable insights into how organisations integrate ethical practices into their business models. Studies have shown that companies that actively engage in CSR can enhance their brand reputation and stakeholder relationships, as well as achieve greater levels of financial performance. These findings are crucial for organisations seeking to balance profit with social and environmental responsibilities (Kandpal et al., 2024).

Another relevant example is the analysis of change management practices in organisations undergoing digital transformation. Case studies have explored how different companies manage the shift to digital technologies, revealing that effective change management requires not only technological adoption but also a cultural shift and strong leadership. These insights are vital for organisations seeking to successfully implement digital strategies and drive sustainable growth (Mihu et al., 2023).

Furthermore, research into organisational members' engagement strategies within high-performance teams provides crucial information on how to maximise productivity and satisfaction. Case studies of companies with high levels of organisational members' engagement reveal that investing in professional development and creating a supportive work environment are key factors in achieving superior organisational performance (Kahn, 2024).

In summary, case study analysis is a powerful method for discovering diverse management phenomena, providing comprehensive insights into practices and strategies within specific contexts. Through rigorous data collection and contextual analysis, researchers can obtain a deeper understanding of organisational dynamics, contributing to effective strategy development and evidence-based decision-making. Nonetheless, the context of each case must be carefully considered to ensure the applicability of findings to different organisational settings (Yin, 2018).

9.4 Chapter Summary

This chapter presented key qualitative data analysis methodologies, including coding and thematic analysis, with a particular emphasis on their application within management research. It highlighted that data collection techniques, such as interviews and focus groups, demonstrate their efficacy in obtaining insights into management practices. The chapter provided comprehensive guidance for conducting rigorous qualitative research in the discipline of management. The following chapter addressed mixed-methods data analysis, providing an in-depth exploration of how to integrate and implement it.

9.5 Questions for Future Reflection

1. A researcher aims to develop a new, data-driven theory illuminating the process of how first-time entrepreneurs navigate the challenges of securing venture capital funding. From the methods discussed in this chapter, which would be the most appropriate: Grounded Theory or Narrative Analysis? Justify your

choice by explaining what each method searches for producing and why one is better suited to the research aim than the other.

2. An internal researcher is steering a study on the workplace culture of their own organisation. Critically discuss the concepts of reflexivity (as mentioned in Ethnography) and epoché/bracketing (as clarified in Phenomenology). How are these concepts different, and what specific practical steps could the researcher take to organise their inherent biases and pre-existing assumptions?
3. You are tasked with researching the factors influencing senior managers' strategic decision-making during a corporate crisis. Why would a semi-structured interview be more apposite for this task than a fully structured or completely unstructured interview? Outline three to five key open-ended questions you might include in your interview lead to explore this topic.
4. A researcher wants to understand how a recent, high-profile merger has affected the daily working lives and social dynamics of organisational members in the acquired company. What is the fundamental difference between approaching this study as an Ethnography versus a Case Study? Consider the researcher's level of immersion and how the 'boundaries' of the research subject would be defined in each approach.
5. You are conducting a Content Analysis of a company's public-facing Corporate Social Responsibility (CSR) reports from the last five years. Provide examples of what you might code for at the manifest level (the explicit, surface-level content) versus the latent level (the underlying, implicit meanings and assumptions).
6. Imagine you have completed a thematic analysis of interviews regarding employee burnout. A sceptic argues that your findings are "just your interpretation." What specific procedures or techniques (e.g., member checking, peer debriefing, maintaining an audit trail) could you have employed during your research process to defend the credibility and dependability of your findings?
7. In a Grounded Theory study, what is meant by 'theoretical saturation'? How does this concept guide the process of 'theoretical sampling', and what is the primary risk of a researcher concluding their data collection prematurely before saturation is accomplished?
8. The chapter notes that purposive sampling is often used in qualitative research. Explain why purposive sampling is more aligned with the goals of qualitative inquiry than the probability sampling methods (like random sampling) that are dominant in quantitative research. Use the chapter's example of studying young Muslim women's cosmetic purchases to demonstrate your point.
9. A detailed case study of Apple Inc.'s innovation processes reveals several key success factors. A critic dismisses the findings, stating that they cannot be generalised because Apple is a unique company. How can a case study researcher respond to this criticism? Discuss the concept of analytical generalisation (or transferability) as it applies to case study research.
10. What do you consider to be the primary ethical dilemma a researcher might face when conducting an immersive, long-term ethnographic study within an organisation? Discuss the challenges related to informed consent, the potential for

participants to forget they are being observed, and the researcher's responsibility to protect participant anonymity.

References

Alazzam, F. A. F., Tubishat, B. M. A. R., Storozhuk, O., Poplavska, O., & Zhyvko, Z. (2024). Methodical approach to the choice of a business management strategy within the framework of a change in commercial activities. *Business: Theory and Practice, 25*(1), 1–10. https://doi.org/10.3846/btp.2024.19676

AlHamad, A., Alshurideh, M., Alomari, K., Kurdi, B., Alzoubi, H., Hamouche, S., & Al-Hawary, S. (2022). The effect of electronic human resources management on organizational health of telecommunications companies in Jordan. *International Journal of Data and Network Science, 6*(2), 429–438. https://doi.org/10.5267/j.ijdns.2021.12.011

Alston, M. (2020). *Research for social workers: An introduction to methods.* Routledge.

Anosike, P., Ehrich, L. C., & Ahmed, P. (2012). Phenomenology as a method for exploring management practice. *International Journal of Management Practice, 5*(3), 205–224. https://doi.org/10.1504/IJMP.2012.048073

Armborst, A. (2017). Thematic proximity in content analysis. *Sage Open, 7*(2). https://doi.org/10.1177/2158244017707797

Aung, N., Yuizono, T., & Kohda, Y. (2016). Comparative analysis of grounded theory and affinity diagram.

Azim, M. T., Fan, L., Uddin, M. A., Jilani, A. K., & M. M., & Begum, S. (2019). Linking transformational leadership with employees' engagement in the creative process. *Management Research Review, 42*(7), 837–858. https://doi.org/10.1108/MRR-08-2018-0286

Bartlett, L., & Vavrus, F. (2016). *Rethinking case study research: A comparative approach.* Routledge.

Batista-Foguet, J. M., Esteve, M., & van Witteloostuijn, A. (2021). Measuring leadership an assessment of the multifactor leadership questionnaire. *Plos One, 16*(7), e0254329. https://doi.org/10.1371/journal.pone.0254329

Bazeley, P. (2023). *Qualitative data analysis: Practical strategies* (3rd ed.). Sage Publications.

Bengtsson, M. (2016). How to plan and perform a qualitative study using content analysis. *NursingPlus Open, 2*, 8–14. https://doi.org/10.1016/j.npls.2016.01.001

Bhattacharya, K. (2017). *Fundamentals of qualitative research: A practical guide.* Routledge.

Biggerstaff, D., & Thompson, A. R. (2008). Interpretative phenomenological analysis (IPA): A qualitative methodology of choice in healthcare research. *Qualitative Research in Psychology, 5*(3), 214–224. https://doi.org/10.1080/14780880802314304

Bluhm, D. J., Harman, W., Lee, T. W., & Mitchell, T. R. (2011). Qualitative research in management: A decade of progress. *Journal of Management Studies, 48*(8), 1866–1891. https://doi.org/10.1111/j.1467-6486.2010.00972.x

Boccoli, G., Gastaldi, L., & Corso, M. (2023). The evolution of employee engagement: Towards a social and contextual construct for balancing individual performance and wellbeing dynamically. *International Journal of Management Reviews, 25*(1), 75–98. https://doi.org/10.1111/ijmr.12304

Bolden, R., Gosling, J., & Hawkins, B. (2023). *Exploring leadership: Individual, organizational, and societal perspectives.* Oxford University Press.

Brandhorst, J. K., Compton, C., Solon, K., Huyler, D., McGill, C. M., & Barnhart, L. (2023). What can grounded theory do for human resource development? An approach for post-pandemic research and beyond. *Human Resource Development Review, 22*(2), 180–203. https://doi.org/10.1177/15344843221149309

Braun, V., & Clarke, V. (2006). Using thematic analysis in psychology. *Qualitative Research in Psychology, 3*(2), 77–101.

Braun, V., & Clarke, V. (2022). *Thematic analysis: A practical guide.* Sage Publications.

Braun, V., & Clarke, V. (2023). Toward good practice in thematic analysis: Avoiding common problems and be (com)ing a knowing researcher. *International Journal of Transgender Health, 24*(1), 1–6. https://doi.org/10.1080/26895269.2022.2129597

Braun, V., Clarke, V., Hayfield, N., Davey, L., & Jenkinson, E. (2023). Doing reflexive thematic analysis. In *Supporting research in counselling and psychotherapy: Qualitative, quantitative, and mixed methods research* (pp. 19–38). Cham: Springer International Publishing.

Brigham, R., Orr, S. A., Wilson, L., Frost, A., Strlič, M., & Grau-Bové, J. (2022). Using citizen heritage science to monitor remote sites before and during the first COVID-19 lockdown: a comparison of two methods. *Conservation and Management of Archaeological Sites, 24*(4–6), 127–142.

Bryman, A. (2023). *Social research methods* (6th ed.). Oxford University Press.

Burger, M., Coun, M. J., Stoffers, J., Van Den Heuvel, S., Vanderstukken, A., & Van Waeyenberg, T. (2024). Positive leadership and worker well-being in dynamic regional contexts. *Frontiers in Psychology, 14*, 1349522. https://doi.org/10.3389/fpsyg.2023.1349522

Cameron, R. (2011). Mixed methods in business and management: A call to the 'first generation'. *Journal of Management & Organization, 17*(2), 245–267. https://doi.org/10.1017/S1833367200001644

Cameron, E., & Green, M. (2024). *Making sense of change management: A complete guide to the models, tools, and techniques of organisational change* (6th ed.). Kogan Page.

Cassell, C., & Kele, J. (2021). Managing diversity and inclusion. In A. Wilkinson, T. Dundon, & T. Redman (Eds.), *Contemporary human resource management: Text and cases* (6th ed., pp. 278–298). Sage Publications.

Cassell, C., Cunliffe, A. L., Grandy, G., Piekkari, R., & Welch, C. (2018). The case study in management research: Beyond the positivist legacy of Eisenhardt and Yin? In C. Cassell, A. L. Cunliffe, & G. Grandy (Eds.), *The SAGE handbook of qualitative business and management research methods: History and traditions* (pp. 345–358). Sage Publications. https://doi.org/10.4135/9781526430212

Chabay, I., Koch, L., Martinez, G., & Scholz, G. (2019). Influence of narratives of vision and identity on collective behavior change. *Sustainability, 11*(20), 5680. https://doi.org/10.3390/su11205680

Chahal, H., & Sharma, R. D. (2006). Implications of corporate social responsibility on marketing performance: A conceptual framework. *Journal of Services Research, 6*(1), 205.

Charmaz, K., & Thornberg, R. (2021). The pursuit of quality in grounded theory. *Qualitative research in psychology, 18*(3), 305–327.

Cherkaoui, A., & Oudrhough, Y. (2024). Case study methodology in business management: A systematic review. In B. Bentalha & L. Alla (Eds.), *Applying qualitative research methods to management science* (pp. 53–74). IGI Global.

Clark, T., Foster, L., Bryman, A., & Sloan, L. (2021). *Bryman's social research methods.* Oxford University Press.

Clarke, V., & Braun, V. (2017). Thematic analysis. *The Journal of Positive Psychology, 12*(3), 297–298. https://doi.org/10.1080/17439760.2016.1262613

Clifford, J., & Marcus, G. E. (2022). *Writing culture: The poetics and politics of ethnography.* University of California Press.

Creswell, J. W., & Poth, C. N. (2016). *Qualitative inquiry and research design: Choosing among five approaches* (5th ed.). Sage Publications.

Dasey, S. (2022). *Phenomenology and the transcendental Ego.* Routledge.

David, F. R. (2011). *Strategic management concepts and cases.* Prentice Hall.

De Vaujany, F. X., Aroles, J., & Pérezts, M. (Eds.). (2023). *The Oxford handbook of phenomenologies and organization studies.* Oxford University Press.

Denning, S. (2006). Effective storytelling: Strategic business narrative techniques. *Strategy & leadership, 34*(1), 42–48. https://doi.org/10.1108/10878570610637885

Denning, S. (2021). *The age of agile: How smart companies are transforming the way work gets done.* AMACOM.

Denzin, N. K., & Lincoln, Y. S. (Eds.). (2011). *The Sage handbook of qualitative research.* Sage Publications.

Dhiman, S. K. (Ed.). (2023). *The Routledge companion to leadership and change.* Taylor & Francis.

Dul, J., & Hak, T. (2008). *Case study methodology in business research.* Routledge.

Dusi, D., & Stevens, P. A. (2022). Thematic analysis: An analytical method in its own right. *Qualitative Data Analysis: Key Approaches*, 293–316.

Dyer, S., Hurd, F., Kenworthy, A., Hedges, P., Wall, T., Shankaran, S., & Jones, D. R. (2024). A collaborative autoethnographic journey of collective storying: Transitioning between the 'I', the 'We' and the 'They'. *Management Learning, 55*(3), 432–450. https://doi.org/10.1177/13505076241236319

Edwards, M. (2020). Ethnography in applied health research. In C. Walshe & S. Brearley (Eds.), *Handbook of theory and methods in applied health research* (pp. 88–106). Edward Elgar Publishing.

Eisenhardt, K. M. (2021). What is the Eisenhardt Method, really? *Strategic Organization, 19*(1), 147–160. https://doi.org/10.1177/1476127020982866

Engel, R. J., & Schutt, R. K. (2016). *The practice of research in social work.* Sage Publications.

Evans, S., & Patel, R. (2024). *Corporate social responsibility: Cultural and symbolic dimensions.* Palgrave Macmillan.

Farrell, E. (2020). Researching lived experience in education: Misunderstood or missed opportunity? *International Journal of Qualitative Methods, 19.* https://doi.org/10.1177/1609406920942066

Faulkner, S. S., & Faulkner, C. A. (2018). *Research methods for social workers: A practice-based approach.* Oxford University Press.

Finlay, L. (2011). *Phenomenology for therapists: Researching the lived world.* Wiley-Blackwell.

Flick, U. (2023). *An introduction to qualitative research* (7th ed.). Sage Publications.

Forman, J., & Damschroder, L. (2007). Qualitative content analysis. In *Empirical methods for bioethics: A primer* (pp. 39–62). Emerald Group Publishing Limited.

Foroudi, P., & Dennis, C. (Eds.). (2023). *Researching and analysing business: Research methods in practice.* Taylor & Francis.

Fox, R. G., & King, B. J. (Eds.). (2020). *Anthropology beyond culture.* Routledge.

Fryer, T. (2022). A critical realist approach to thematic analysis: Producing causal explanations. *Journal of Critical Realism, 21*(4), 365–384. https://doi.org/10.1080/14767430.2022.2076776

Garrido-Moreno, A., Martín-Rojas, R., & García-Morales, V. J. (2024). The key role of innovation and organizational resilience in improving business performance: A mixed-methods approach. *International Journal of Information Management, 77.* https://doi.org/10.1016/j.ijinfomgt.2024.102777

Gedro, J. (2017). *Identity, meaning, and subjectivity in career development: Evolving perspectives in human resources.* Springer.

Gee, J. P. (2014). *An introduction to discourse analysis: Theory and method.* Routledge.

Geertz, C. (1973). *The interpretation of cultures: Selected essays.* Basic Books.

Geertz, C. (2008). Thick description: Toward an interpretive theory of culture. In T. Oakes & P. L. Price (Eds.), *The cultural geography reader* (pp. 41–51). Routledge.

Geertz, C. (2017). *The interpretation of cultures.* Basic Books.

Gellner, D., & Hirsch, E. (Eds.). (2020). *Inside organizations: Anthropologists at work.* Routledge.

Gibbs, G. R. (2018). *Analysing qualitative data.* Sage Publications.

Gill, M. J. (2014). The possibilities of phenomenology for organizational research. *Organizational Research Methods, 17*(2), 118–137. https://doi.org/10.1177/1094428113518348

Giorgi, A. (2021). *The phenomenological psychology of Edmund Husserl: A critical introduction.* Routledge.

Given, L. M. (2015). *100 questions (and answers) about qualitative research.* Sage Publications.

Glaser, B., & Strauss, A. (2017). *Discovery of grounded theory: Strategies for qualitative research*. Routledge.
Goffman, E. (2023). The presentation of self in everyday life. In W. Longhofer & D. Winchester (Eds.), *Social theory re-wired* (pp. 450–459). Routledge.
Gould, N., & Taylor, I. (2017). *Reflective learning for social work: Research, theory and practice*. Routledge.
Grove, A. S. (2023). *High output management (Updated Ed.)*. Vintage Books.
Gummesson, E. (2000). *Qualitative methods in management research*. Sage Publications.
Gutiérrez-Crocco, F., Martin-Caballero, A., & Godoy, A. (2024). The impact of remote work on managerial compliance: Changes in the control regime over line managers. *Work, Employment and Society, 38*(2), 527–548. https://doi.org/10.1177/09500170221142713
Hagebakken, G., Olsen, T. H., & Solstad, E. (2024). Success or failure? Making sense of outcomes in a public sector change project. *Journal of Management & Organization, 30*(2), 287–303. https://doi.org/10.1017/jmo.2020.19
Hammersley, M., & Atkinson, P. (2023). *Ethnography: Principles in practice*. Routledge.
Hancock, D. R., Algozzine, B., & Lim, J. H. (2021). *Doing case study research: A practical guide for beginning researchers*. Teachers College Press.
Harding, J. (2018). *Qualitative data analysis: From start to finish*. Sage Publications.
Hartley, J. M., Mathieu, D., & Sørensen, J. K. (2023). Introduction: Datapublics beyond the rise and fall narrative. In J. K. Sørensen, D. Mathieu, & J. M. Hartley (Eds.), *DataPublics* (pp. 1–24). Bristol University Press.
Harvey, G. (2021). Field research and participant observation. In S. Engler & M. Stausberg (Eds.), *The Routledge handbook of research methods in the study of religion* (pp. 273–299). Routledge.
Heil, D. (2008). Strategic innovation and organisational identity: A hermeneutic phenomenological investigation. *Journal of General Management, 33*(4), 1–12. https://doi.org/10.1177/030630700803300401
Hennink, M., Hutter, I., & Bailey, A. (2020). *Qualitative research methods*. Sage Publications.
Holloway, I., Brown, L., & Shipway, R. (2010). Meaning not measurement: Using ethnography to bring a deeper understanding to the participant experience of festivals and events. *International Journal of Event and Festival Management, 1*(1), 74–85. https://doi.org/10.1108/17852951011029315
Hsieh, H. F., & Shannon, S. E. (2005). Three approaches to qualitative content analysis. *Qualitative Health Research, 15*(9), 1277–1288. https://doi.org/10.1177/1049732305276687
Hsu, H. P. (2023). Can generative artificial intelligence write an academic journal article? Opportunities, challenges, and implications. *The Irish Journal of Technology Enhanced Learning, 7*(2), 158–171. https://doi.org/10.3390/su16177677
Hunziker, S., & Blankenagel, M. (2024). Single case research design. In S. Hunziker & M. Blankenagel (Eds.), *Research design in business and management: A practical guide for students and researchers* (2nd ed., pp. 171–186). Springer Fachmedien Wiesbaden.
Husserl, E., & Moran, D. (2012). *Ideas: General introduction to pure phenomenology*. Routledge.
Hutasuhut, I., Ahmad Zaidi Adruce, S., & Jonathan, V. (2021). How a learning organization cultivates self-directed learning. *Journal of Workplace Learning, 33*(5), 334–347. https://doi.org/10.1108/JWL-05-2020-0074
Jackson, J., Vandall-Walker, V., Vanderspank-Wright, B., Wishart, P., & Moore, S. L. (2018). Burnout and resilience in critical care nurses: A grounded theory of managing exposure. *Intensive and Critical Care Nursing, 48*, 28–35. https://doi.org/10.1016/j.iccn.2018.07.002
Jango, J. (2024). Leadership and management of change: Introduction to navigating organisational change. *EuroMed Journal of Management, 6*(1), 57–71. https://doi.org/10.1504/EMJM.2024.135991
Janssens, M., & Zanoni, P. (2021). Making diversity research matter for social change: New conversations beyond the firm. *Organization Theory, 2*(2). https://doi.org/10.1177/26317877211004603

Johnson, P., & Duberley, J. (2003). Reflexivity in management research. *Journal of management studies, 40*(5), 1279–1303.

Jones, P., & Smith, J. (2023). *Understanding organisational dynamics: The impact of economic and regulatory changes*. Routledge.

Kahn, W. A. (2024). Through the narrows: The meaning and enactment of interpersonal holding. *Organization Science, 36*(1), 340–360. https://doi.org/10.1287/orsc.2023.17661

Kandpal, V., Jaswal, A., Santibanez Gonzalez, E. D. R., & Agarwal, N. (2024). Corporate social responsibility (C.S.R.) and E.S.G. reporting: Redefining business in the twenty-first century. In *Sustainable energy transition: Circular economy and sustainability* (pp. 123–145). Springer. https://doi.org/10.1007/978-3-031-52943-6_8

Kelly, G. J. (2023). Qualitative research as culture and practice. In N. G. Lederman, D. L. Zeidler, & J. S. Lederman (Eds.), *Handbook of research on science education* (pp. 60–86). Routledge. https://doi.org/10.4324/9780367855758

Kerguenne, A., Meisel, M., & Meinel, C. (2023). Opportunities and limitations of design thinking as a strategic approach for navigating digital transformation in organizations. In C. Meinel & L. Leifer (Eds.), *Design thinking research: Understanding innovation* (pp. 215–230). Springer. https://doi.org/10.1007/978-3-031-36103-6_14

Khanagha, S., Volberda, H., & Oshri, I. (2017). Customer co-creation and exploration of emerging technologies: the mediating role of managerial attention and initiatives. *Long Range Planning, 50*(2), 221–242. https://doi.org/10.1016/j.lrp.2015.12.019

Khoa, B. T., Hung, B. P., & Hejsalem-Brahmi, M. (2023). Qualitative research in social sciences: data collection, data analysis and report writing. *International Journal of Public Sector Performance Management, 12*(1–2), 187–209. https://doi.org/10.1504/IJPSPM.2023.132247

Kiaos, T. (2024). Organizational culture, cultural control, and the self: Directions for organizational ethnographers. *Organizational Cultures, 24*(2), 37. https://doi.org/10.18848/2327-8013/CGP/v24i02/37-60

Kozminski, A. K., Baczyńska, A. K., Skoczeń, I., & Korzyński, P. (2022). Towards leadership effectiveness: The role of leadership individual competencies and constraints. Introduction of the Bounded Leadership Model. *Leadership & Organization Development Journal, 43*(4), 596–611. https://doi.org/10.1108/LODJ-04-2020-0157

Krippendorff, K. (2018). *Content analysis: An introduction to its methodology*. Sage Publications.

Kuchinke, K. P. (2023). Phenomenology and human resource development: Philosophical foundations and implication for research. *Human Resource Development Review, 22*(1), 36–58. https://doi.org/10.1177/15344843221139352

Kuckartz, U. (2023). *Qualitative content analysis: A practical guide* (2nd ed.). Sage Publications.

Kuckartz, U., & Rädiker, S. (2023). *Qualitative content analysis: Methods, practice and software*. Sage Publications.

Kumar, R. (2018). Research methodology: A step-by-step guide for beginners.

Kumar, V. (2024). *International marketing research: A transformative approach*. Springer Nature.

Leavy, P. (Ed.). (2014). *The Oxford handbook of qualitative research*. Oxford University Press.

Lemon, L. L. (2019). The employee experience: How employees make meaning of employee engagement. *Journal of Public Relations Research, 31*(5–6), 176–199. https://doi.org/10.1080/1062726X.2019.1704288

Lerigo-Sampson, M. (2022). Qualitative data analysis. In S. Childe & A. Soares (Eds.), *Handbook of research methods for supply chain management* (pp. 187–201). Edward Elgar Publishing.

Leso, B. H., Cortimiglia, M. N., & Ghezzi, A. (2023). The contribution of organizational culture, structure, and leadership factors in the digital transformation of SMEs: A mixed-methods approach. *Cognition, Technology & Work, 25*(1), 151–179. https://doi.org/10.1007/s10111-022-00714-2

Lester, J. N., Cho, Y., & Lochmiller, C. R. (2020). Learning to do qualitative data analysis: A starting point. *Human Resource Development Review, 19*(1), 94–106. https://doi.org/10.1177/1534484320903890

Liamputtong, P. (2020). *Qualitative research methods* (6th ed.). Oxford University Press.

Liamputtong, P. (2023). Qualitative research in the social sciences: Setting the scene. In P. Liamputtong (Ed.), *How to conduct qualitative research in social science* (pp. 1–13). Edward Elgar Publishing.
Lichtman, M. (2023). *Qualitative research in education: A user's guide*. Routledge.
Linneberg, M. S., & Korsgaard, S. (2019). Coding qualitative data: A synthesis guiding the novice. *Qualitative Research Journal, 19*(3), 259–270. https://doi.org/10.1108/QRJ-12-2018-0012
Lungu, M. (2022). The coding manual for qualitative researchers. *American Journal of Qualitative Research, 6*(1), 232–237. https://doi.org/10.29333/ajqr/12085
Madison, D. S. (2011). *Critical ethnography: Method, ethics, and performance*. Sage Publications.
Maguire, M., & Delahunt, B. (2017). Doing a thematic analysis: A practical, step-by-step guide for learning and teaching scholars. *All Ireland Journal of Higher Education, 9*(3), 3351–3359. https://doi.org/10.62707/aishej.v9i3.335
Majumdar, A. (2022). Thematic analysis in qualitative research. In Information Resources Management Association (USA) (Ed.), *Research anthology on innovative research methodologies and utilization across multiple disciplines* (pp. 604–622). IGI Global.
Malinowski, B. (2013). *Argonauts of the Western Pacific: An account of native enterprise and adventure in the archipelagoes of Melanesian New Guinea* [1922/1994]. Routledge.
Mansar, S. L., & Reijers, H. A. (2007). Best practices in business process redesign: Use and impact. *Business Process Management Journal, 13*(2), 193. https://doi.org/10.1108/14637150710740455
Marshall, C., & Rossman, G. B. (2014). *Designing qualitative research*. Sage Publications.
Mason, J. (2002). Linking qualitative and quantitative data analysis. In A. Bryman & B. Burgess (Eds.), *Analyzing qualitative data* (pp. 89–110). Routledge.
Mason, J. (2017). *Qualitative researching*. Sage Publications.
Mathew, J. (2019). Organisational culture and effectiveness: A multi-perspective evaluation of an Indian knowledge-intensive firm. *Employee Relations, 41*(3), 538–551. https://doi.org/10.1108/ER-09-2017-0219
Mauksch, S., Dey, P., Rowe, M., & Teasdale, S. (2017). Ethnographies of social enterprise. *Social Enterprise Journal, 13*(02), 114–127. https://doi.org/10.1108/sej-03-2017-0019
May, T., & Perry, B. (2022). *Social research: Issues, methods and process*. McGraw-Hill Education.
Mayring, P. (2015). Qualitative content analysis: Theoretical background and procedures. In A. Bikner-Ahsbahs, C. Knipping, & N. Presmeg (Eds.), *Approaches to qualitative research in mathematics education* (pp. 365–380). Springer. https://doi.org/10.1007/978-94-017-9181-6_13
McDonald, K. S., & Hite, L. M. (2023). *Career development: A human resource development perspective*. Routledge.
Merriam, S. B., & Tisdell, E. J. (2015). *Qualitative research: A guide to design and implementation*. John Wiley & Sons.
Mihu, C., Pitic, A. G., & Bayraktar, D. (2023). Drivers of digital transformation and their impact on organizational management. *Studies in Business and Economics, 18*(1), 149–170. https://doi.org/10.2478/sbe-2023-0009
Miles, M. B., Huberman, A. M., & Saldaña, J. (2014). *Qualitative data analysis: A methods sourcebook* (3rd ed.). Sage Publications.
Mızrak, F. (2024). Effective change management strategies: Exploring dynamic models for organizational transformation. In *Perspectives on artificial intelligence in times of turbulence: Theoretical background to applications* (pp. 135–162). IGI Global.
Mladjan, M. M., & Markovic, D. Z. (2019). Diagrams of power and strategic decision making: The case of strategic alliances in the automotive industry. *Management: Journal of Sustainable Business and Management Solutions in Emerging Economies, 24*(3), 21–32. https://doi.org/10.7595/management.fon.2019.0015
Moran, D. (2002). *Introduction to phenomenology*. Routledge.
Moran, D. (2013). Edmund Husserl and phenomenology. In A. Bailey (Ed.), *Philosophy of mind: The key thinkers* (pp. 37–58). Bloomsbury.

Morgan, H. (2022). Conducting a qualitative document analysis. *The Qualitative Report, 27*(1), 64–77. https://doi.org/10.46743/2160-3715/2022.5044

Morse, J. M. (2016b). *Qualitative health research: Creating a new discipline*. Routledge.

Musa, H. G., Fatmawati, I., Nuryakin, N., & Suyanto, M. (2024). Marketing research trends using technology acceptance model (TAM): A comprehensive review of researches (2002–2022). *Cogent Business & Management, 11*(1). https://doi.org/10.1080/23311975.2024.2329375

Myers, M. D. (2019). *Qualitative research in business and management* (3rd ed.). Sage Publications.

Naeem, M., Ozuem, W., Howell, K., & Ranfagni, S. (2023). A step-by-step process of thematic analysis to develop a conceptual model in qualitative research. *International Journal of Qualitative Methods, 22*. https://doi.org/10.1177/16094069231205789

Nanjundeswaraswamy, T. S. (2023). The mediating role of job satisfaction in the relationship between leadership styles and employee commitment. *Journal of Economic and Administrative Sciences, 39*(2), 286–304. https://doi.org/10.1108/JEAS-02-2021-0029

Neuendorf, K. A. (2017). *The content analysis guidebook*. Sage Publications.

Nicmanis, M. (2024). Reflexive content analysis: An approach to qualitative data analysis, reduction, and description. *International Journal of Qualitative Methods, 23*. https://doi.org/10.1177/16094069241236603

Niros, M. I., Niros, A., Pollalis, Y., & Ding, Q. S. (2023). Effective marketing strategies for global FMCG brands during COVID-19 pandemic crisis. *International Marketing Review, 40*(5), 1012–1034. https://doi.org/10.1108/IMR-11-2021-0327

Nowell, L. S., Norris, J. M., White, D. E., & Moules, N. J. (2017). Thematic analysis: Striving to meet the trustworthiness criteria. *International Journal of Qualitative Methods, 16*(1). https://doi.org/10.1177/1609406917733847

O'reilly, K. (2012). *Ethnographic methods*. Routledge.

Owoahene Acheampong, K., & Nyaaba, M. (2024). Review of qualitative research in the era of generative artificial intelligence. *Matthew, Review of Qualitative Research in the Era of Generative Artificial Intelligence (January 7, 2024).*

Pera, R., Quinton, S., & Baima, G. (2022). The use of embedded visual methods in unveiling consumers' values: A digital ethnography perspective. *Psychology & Marketing, 39*(2), 309–319. https://doi.org/10.1002/mar.21596

Perry, B. (2015). Gamifying French language learning: A case study examining a quest-based, augmented reality mobile learning-tool. *Procedia-Social and Behavioral Sciences, 174*, 2308–2315. https://doi.org/10.1016/j.sbspro.2015.01.892

Phillips, J., & Klein, J. D. (2023). Change management: From theory to practice. *TechTrends, 67*(1), 189–197. https://doi.org/10.1007/s11528-022-00775-0

Pöllänen, K. (2021). Organizational culture and masculinities in a startup company in Finland. *Nordic Working Life Studies, 11*(4), 117–135. https://doi.org/10.18291/njwls.126226

Poth, C. N., Wongvorachan, T., Bulut, O., & Otto, S. J. G. (2024a). Adaptive case study-mixed methods design practices for researchers studying complex phenomena. *Journal of Mixed Methods Research, 18*(3), 292–303. https://doi.org/10.1177/15586898241250217

Poth, C., Georgiou, G., Mack, E., & Kierstead, M. (2024b). Mixed methods research teams: Leveraging integrative teamwork for addressing complex problems. *Frontiers in Education, 9*, 1356629. https://doi.org/10.3389/feduc.2024.1356629

Proudfoot, K. (2023). Inductive/deductive hybrid thematic analysis in mixed methods research. *Journal of Mixed Methods Research, 17*(3), 308–326. https://doi.org/10.1177/15586/898221126816

Rahim, S. M., Sulaiman, N. S., Muhamad, Z. S., & Jini, L. H. M. (2025). Muslim consumer attitudes in Brunei Darussalam toward current trends in cosmetics products from non-Muslim countries acquired by personal shoppers. *Journal Halal Science, Industry, and Business, 3*(1), 24–43.

Remenyi, D., Swartz, E., Money, A., & Williams, B. (1998). *Doing research in business and management: An introduction to process and method*. Sage Publications.

Rostron, A. (2022). How to be a hero: How managers determine what makes a good manager through narrative identity work. *Management Learning, 53*(3), 417–438. https://doi.org/10.1177/13505076211007275

Rua, O. L. (2013). The importance of qualitative methodology in management empirical research. *INBAM-International Network of Business and Management Journals.*

Russen, M., Dawson, M., Madera, J. M., Kitterlin-Lynch, M., & Abbott, J. L. (2023). Leadership inclusion theory: A grounded theory study on hotel executives. *International Journal of Contemporary Hospitality Management, 35*(11), 3825–3843. https://doi.org/10.1108/IJCHM-10-2022-1252

Salamzadeh, A., Hadizadeh, M., Rastgoo, N., Rahman, M. M., & Radfard, S. (2022). Sustainability-oriented innovation foresight in international new technology-based firms. *Sustainability, 14*(20), 13501. https://doi.org/10.3390/su142013501

Saldaña, J. (2021). *The coding manual for qualitative researchers* (4th ed.). Sage Publications.

Saldaña, J., & Omasta, M. (2016). *Qualitative research: Analyzing life.* Sage Publications.

Saunders, M., Lewis, P., & Thornhill, A. (2024). *Research methods for business students* (9th ed.). Pearson.

Savin-Baden, M., & Major, C. (2023). *Qualitative research: The essential guide to theory and practice.* Routledge.

Schwartz-Shea, P. (2021). Feminist use of qualitative/interpretive methods. In *The Routledge Handbook of feminist economics* (pp. 138–147). Routledge.

Schwartz-Shea, P., & Yanow, D. (2013). *Interpretive research design: Concepts and processes.* Routledge.

Shorey, S., Ang, E., Yamina, A., & Tam, C. (2020). Perceptions of public on the COVID-19 outbreak in Singapore: a qualitative content analysis. *Journal of Public Health, 42*(4), 665–671.

Shultz, K. S., Whitney, D., & Zickar, M. J. (2020). *Measurement theory in action: Case studies and exercises.* Routledge.

Silverman, D. (2016). Introducing qualitative research. *Qualitative Research, 3*(3), 14–25.

Silverman, D. (2021). *Doing qualitative research.* Sage Publications.

Silverman, D. (2024). *Interpreting qualitative data.* Sage Publications.

Simons, H. (2014). Case study research: In-depth understanding in context. In P. Leavy (Ed.), *The Oxford handbook of qualitative research* (pp. 455–470). Oxford University Press.

Smith, J. A. (2017). Interpretative phenomenological analysis: Getting at lived experience. *The journal of positive psychology*, 12(3), 303–304.

Smith, J. A., & Eatough, V. (2019). Looking forward: Conceptual and methodological developments in interpretative phenomenological analysis: Introduction to the special issue. *Qualitative Research in Psychology, 16*(2), 163–165. https://doi.org/10.1080/14780887.2018.1540620

Smith, J. A., & Jones, P. (2023). *The essence of leadership: Insights from phenomenological research.* Sage Publications.

Smith, J. A., Flowers, P., & Larkin, M. (2021). *Interpretative phenomenological analysis: Theory, method and research.* Sage Publications.

Stake, R. E. (2013). *Multiple case study analysis.* Guilford Press.

Strijker, D., Bosworth, G., & Bouter, G. (2020). Research methods in rural studies: Qualitative, quantitative and mixed methods. *Journal of Rural Studies, 78*, 262–270.

Susen, S. (2024). The Interpretation of cultures: Geertz is still in town. *Sociologica–International Journal for Sociological Debate, 18*(1), 25–63. https://doi.org/10.6092/issn.1971-8853/18664

Taylor, B. J., Killick, C., & McGlade, A. (2015). *Understanding and using research in social work.* Learning Matters.

Terry, G., Hayfield, N., Clarke, V., & Braun, V. (2017). Thematic analysis. In *The SAGE handbook of qualitative research in psychology, 2* (17–37), 25.

Tesch, R. (2013). *Qualitative research: Analysis types and software.* Routledge.

Thompson, G., & Green, H. (2024). *Innovation practices in tech firms: An ethnographic approach.* Palgrave Macmillan.

Tight, M. (2017). *Understanding case study research: Small-scale research with meaning*. Sage Publications.
Tiwari, M., Bryde, D. J., Stavropoulou, F., & Malhotra, G. (2024). Understanding the evolution of flexible supply chain in the business-to-business sector: A resource-based theory perspective. *International Studies of Management & Organisation, 54*(4), 380–406. https://doi.org/10.1080/00208825.2024.2324245
Tracy, S. J. (2024). *Qualitative research methods: Collecting evidence, crafting analysis, communicating impact*. John Wiley & Sons.
Tufford, L., & Newman, P. (2012). Bracketing in qualitative research: A typology. *Qualitative Social Work, 11*(1), 80–96. https://doi.org/10.1177/1473325010368316
Vaismoradi, M., Turunen, H., & Bondas, T. (2013). Content analysis and thematic analysis: Implications for conducting a qualitative descriptive study. *Nursing & Health Sciences, 15*(3), 398–405. https://doi.org/10.1111/nhs.12048
van Maanen, J. (2011). Ethnography as work: Some rules of engagement. *Journal of Management Studies, 48*(1), 218–234. https://doi.org/10.1111/j.1467-6486.2010.00980.x
van Manen, M. (2016). *Researching Lived Experience: Human Science for an Action Sensitive Pedagogy*. Routledge.
Verbuyst, R., & Galazka, A. M. (2023). Introducing "navigating failure in ethnography": A forum about failure in ethnographic research. *Journal of Organizational Ethnography, 12*(1), 61–75. https://doi.org/10.1108/JOE-10-2022-0027
Wang, W., Zhang, Y., & Chen, S. (2024b). The development of the sustainable innovation capabilities construct using grounded theory: Evidence from Chinese equipment manufacturers. *European Journal of Innovation Management, 27*(8), 2483–2521. https://doi.org/10.1108/EJIM-10-2022-0546
Wilson, V. (2016). Research methods: Content analysis. *Evidence-Based Library and Information Practice, 11*(1(S)), 41–43. https://doi.org/10.18438/B8CG9D
Witzel, M. (2022). *Management: The basics*. Routledge.
Yanow, D., & Schwartz-Shea, P. (Eds.). (2006). *Interpretation and Method: Empirical Research Methods and the interpretive turn*. Routledge.
Yin, R. K. (2009b). How to do better case studies: (with illustrations from 20 exemplary case studies). In L. Bickman & D. J. Rog (Eds.), *How to do better case studies: (with illustrations from 20 exemplary case studies)* (2nd ed., pp. 254–282). Sage Publications.
Yin, R. K. (2018). *Case study research and applications: Design and methods*. Sage Publications.
Zumitzavan, V. (2011). *The impact of managers' learning styles and leadership styles on the effectiveness of their organisations: A case study from small retail tyre companies in Thailand* (Doctoral dissertation, University of Birmingham).

Chapter 10
Mixed Methods Design and Data Analysis

10.1 Introduction

This chapter describes the various instruments used in the mixed methods approach, highlighting the advantages and disadvantages of each technique. It also provides examples pertinent to research within the management discipline.

10.2 Mixed-Method Data Analysis

Mixed methods research represents a research design synergistically integrating both quantitative and qualitative data collection and analysis within a single study or research programme. From a philosophical standpoint, mixed methods research is predominantly regarded as a pragmatic approach, seeking to harvest the strengths inherent in both quantitative and qualitative methodologies in order to furnish a more comprehensive and precise understanding of complex phenomena (Ghanad, 2023).

For example, a study examining the impact of leadership styles on team performance might quantify team outcomes through performance indicators and surveys (quantitative), whilst also conducting interviews with team members to investigate their perceptions of leadership and its influence on their motivation and collaboration (qualitative). This dual approach can generate richer insights into how different leadership styles affect team dynamics and performance outcomes (Harter et al., 2002).

The philosophical underpinnings of mixed methods research are influenced by several theoretical perspectives, notably pragmatism, critical realism, and constructivism. Pragmatism is a philosophical framework prioritising the practical application of knowledge, valuing empirical evidence, experimentation, and problem-solving (Rorty, 2009).

© The Author(s), under exclusive license to Springer Nature Singapore Pte Ltd. 2025
V. Zumitzavan, *Social Science Methodologies for Management Research*,
https://doi.org/10.1007/978-981-95-4318-2_10

For instance, a pragmatic approach in a management research might encompass using both financial measures (quantitative) and focus groups (qualitative) to evaluate the effectiveness of a new marketing strategy, thus strengthening a well-rounded assessment of its impact (Sweeney et al., 2023).

Critical realism focuses on the underlying structures and mechanisms that shape social phenomena, recognising the intricate and multifaceted nature of reality (Bukowska, 2021). A critical realist approach might investigate how organisational culture (qualitative) interacts with employees' performance metrics (quantitative) to yield a more comprehensive understanding of performance outcomes (Shea et al., 2023).

Constructivism emphasises the subjective nature of knowledge and underscores the importance of understanding how individuals interpret and construct their experiences (Fosnot, 2013). In management, this could manifest in research exploring how leaders' personal narratives shape their decision-making processes, combining narrative analysis (qualitative) with performance data (quantitative) (Chong & Zainal, 2024; Rich et al., 2010).

From a philosophical perspective, the mixed methods research approach endeavours to illustrate the limitations inherent in the exclusive application of a single research methodology by integrating diverse perspectives and data types. By utilising both quantitative and qualitative techniques, researchers are greater positioned to acquire a more comprehensive and sophisticated understanding of complex phenomena (Dawadi et al., 2021).

For example, a study investigating organisational change might utilise surveys to evaluate organisational members' resistance, i.e. a quantitative approach utilising survey questionnaires, alongside in-depth interviews to explore the underlying causes of that resistance, i.e. a qualitative approach employing semi-structured interviews), ultimately informing more effective change management strategies (Kurtaliqi et al., 2024; Lim, 2024). This approach acknowledges the merits of both deductive and inductive reasoning, endeavouring to synthesise these into a coherent and integrative research programme.

In conclusion, the philosophy underpinning the mixed methods research approach in management adopts a pragmatic stance, seeking to utilise multiple methodologies to achieve a thorough and accurate understanding of intricate phenomena. This approach is informed by numerous theoretical perspectives, notably pragmatism, critical realism, and constructivism, and it emphasises the significance of integrating quantitative and qualitative methodologies.

10.2.1 The Artful Science of Integration and the Role of AI

The philosophy of mixed methods research, grounded in pragmatism, inherently embodies the fusion of 'art' and 'science'. The 'science' is manifest in the structured research designs and the rigorous analysis of quantitative data. The 'art', however, resides not only in the sophisticated interpretation of qualitative findings but, most critically, in the sophisticated act of incorporating the two different data streams. This integrative process is a creative and intellectual craft, which is now being reformed by the capacities of AI. In addition, the art of synthesis the true value of mixed methods is realised in the synthesis stage, where the researcher interchanges beyond contributing parallel findings and weaves them into a single, coherent, and more insightful narrative. This is an interpretive art method. When quantitative results separate from qualitative themes, it necessitates creative reasoning and profound contextual understanding to construct a probable explanation for the discrepancy. The researcher must artfully connect the gap between numerical patterns and lived experiences, a task that demands reflexivity, theoretical sensitivity, and a capacity for holistic thinking (Leavy, 2014). This creative process is fundamental to creating the 'added value' justifying a mixed methods approach, transforming distinct data points into a richer understanding of a management phenomenon.

Furthermore, the 'science' of mixed methods is progressing meaningfully with the integration of AI tools, particularly Large Language Models (LLMs). AI can augment both strands of a study; for instance, by recognising patterns in large quantitative datasets or by performing initial thematic coding on qualitative interview transcripts. More profoundly, AI provides new pathways for the integration process itself. It can systematically categorise points of convergence and divergence between quantitative survey data and qualitative text, flagging areas that require the researcher's artistic interpretation (Combrinck, 2024). To illustrate, an AI tool could correlate low numerical scores on an organisational member's engagement survey with specific negative sentiments expressed in open-ended comments, thereby accelerating the analytical process. However, whilst AI can improve the scientific rigour and efficiency of data integration, it cannot substitute the interpretive 'art'. AI models lack the deep cultural, organisational, and contextual understanding necessary to make final sense of complex human phenomena (Zhang et al., 2023). Researchers must, hence, approach AI as a powerful analytical partner rather than an autonomous decision-maker. The ethical responsibility to critically evaluate AI-generated outputs, contextualise the findings, and craft the final interpretive narrative remains firmly with the human researcher (Aithal & Aithal, 2023).

Intrinsically, modern mixed methods research characterises a sophisticated relationship between the structured 'science' of its designs, the interpretive 'art' of human synthesis, and the computational power of AI. By skilfully steering this triad, management researchers can produce findings that are not only methodologically robust but also contextually rich and deeply insightful.

10.3 Convergent Parallel Mixed Methods Design

As illustrated in Fig. 10.1, the convergent parallel mixed methods design is one of the most well-regarded strategies in both foundational and advanced mixed methods research. For novice researchers, this approach frequently serves as an entry point, as it initially seems straightforward in its combining quantitative and qualitative

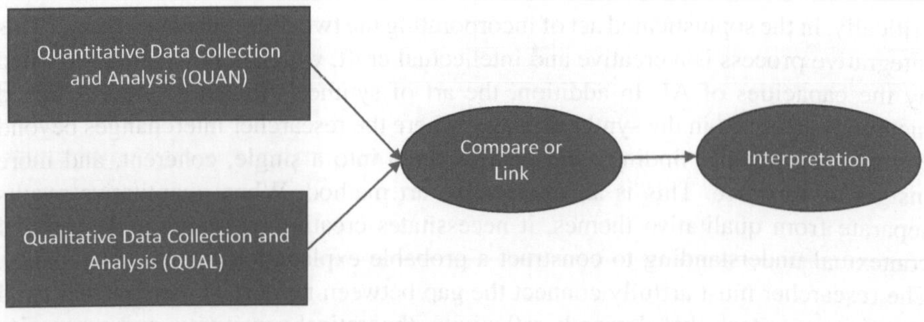

Fig. 10.1 Convergent parallel mixed methods design. (Source: Adopted from Creswell and Poth (2024) and Toledo and Shannon-Baker (2023))

data. This design entails the simultaneous collection of both data types, followed by separate analyses, ultimately leading to a comparison of the results to assess whether they complement or contradict one another.

For instance, in a study evaluating organisational members' satisfaction, a researcher might use a survey questionnaire to collect quantitative data on levels of satisfaction (e.g., using a Likert scale) whilst concurrently conducting focus group discussions to gather qualitative insights into employees' experiences and perceptions. After separately analysing the survey results and thematic content from the focus groups, the researcher would compare the findings. If the quantitative data indicate high satisfaction whilst qualitative feedback highlights specific grievances, this contrast could prompt further investigation into the reasons behind the discrepancy, leading to more sophisticated management strategies (Teng-Calleja et al., 2024).

This methodology operates on the premise that quantitative data, typically represented by scores from standardised instruments, and qualitative data, which provide rich participant insights, each contribute unique perspectives. By integrating these distinct types of data, researchers aim to achieve more comprehensive research outcomes. This approach builds upon the foundational concept of multi-method, multi-trait research introduced by Campbell and Fiske (1959), which initially emphasised the acquisition of multiple forms of quantitative data to understand psychological traits. Contemporary mixed methods researchers have since expanded this concept, advocating for the concurrent collection and analysis of both quantitative and qualitative data streams.

This design is particularly advantageous in management research because it allows for a comprehensive understanding of complex issues. By integrating diverse data sources, researchers.

can validate their findings and uncover richer insights. For example, in researching the implications of remote work on productivity, a researcher might collect performance metrics (quantitative) and employee narratives about their experiences (qualitative). This dual approach not only affirms findings through triangulation but also reveals underlying factors that quantitative data alone might overlook (Mackenzie, 2017).

10.3.1 Data Collection Convergent Parallel Mixed Methods Design

Qualitative data can manifest in various forms, including interviews, observations, and archival documents, whilst quantitative data encompasses instrument readings, checklists, and numerical records such as census data. The core principle underlying this methodology is to collect both types of data using equivalent variables, constructs, or concepts. For instance, whilst evaluating the 'Transformational Leadership' style quantitatively, researchers can explore the same concept qualitatively through open-ended interviews (Weyant, 2022).

A critical consideration in this methodological framework is sample size, which shows significant variation between qualitative and quantitative approaches. Generally, qualitative research utilises smaller sample sizes to obtain detailed insights, whereas quantitative studies necessitate larger samples to enable rigorous statistical analysis. To address this disparity in convergent mixed methods designs, researchers may adopt various strategies. Some might opt to increase the qualitative sample size to align with the quantitative one, although this could limit the depth of information obtained from each participant.

For example, in a study on organisational members' motivation, researchers might interview more people but ask fewer questions from each participant, rather than conducting detailed interviews with a smaller group (Macey & Schneider, 2008). Alternatively, researchers could adjust the number of qualitative cases to match the size of the quantitative sample, ensuring a more proportional representation in their analysis.

Despite these strategies, some mixed methods researchers argue that uneven sample sizes are not inherently problematic. They contend that qualitative and quantitative research fulfil distinct roles, providing depth of understanding versus ensuring generalisability, and that each approach can yield valuable insights within its own context (Creswell & Tashakkori, 2007).

For instance, in research aimed at enhancing organisational performance, the quantitative approach may involve distributing a survey questionnaire to organisational members across all departments, whilst the qualitative approach may comprise conducting in-depth interviews with a small group of divisional managers, such as five individuals from each department. Consequently, the depth and breadth of the information collected may differ in terms of volume, yet the perspectives provided by survey respondents and interview participants would both offer valuable insights, each contributing to a more comprehensive understanding of the issue.

As another example, in a study on customers' satisfaction, researchers might conduct extensive qualitative interviews with a select group of customers to investigate their experiences whilst simultaneously surveying a larger, more diverse population in order to distinguish predominant trends.

In addition to sample size, it is efficacious for researchers to consider which participants can offer the most pertinent insights to address the research questions. Identifying suitable groups is essential for obtaining fruitful, meaningful data. Furthermore, researchers must contemplate whether the participants in the qualitative research should overlap with those in the quantitative research. Typically, mixed methods researchers include qualitative participants within the broader quantitative sample to facilitate direct comparisons between the datasets. This strategy improves the comparability of groups, thereby refining the overall analysis (Tashakkori & Teddlie, 2002). For example, in investigating organisational change, a researcher might survey all organisational members quantitatively whilst conducting in-depth interviews with a subset of those organisational members in order to obtain deeper insights into their experiences during the transition.

10.3.2 Data Analysis in Convergent Parallel Mixed Methods Design

In a convergent mixed methods design, the primary challenge resides in effectively synthesising the collected data. This approach starts with the separate evaluation of each dataset, followed by their integration. Several methodologies facilitate this integration process.

One common method is the side-by-side comparison approach, often realised in the discussion sections of mixed methods research. In this method, researchers present the quantitative statistical findings first, followed by the qualitative insights, such as themes aligning or contradicting with the statistical results. Conversely, researchers may select to reverse this sequence, starting with qualitative findings and subsequently comparing them with the quantitative results. This method is termed 'side-by-side' because it juxtaposes findings within the same contextual framework (Lui et al., 2011; Cabrera-Tenecela, 2023). For instance, a study evaluating an organisation's customer satisfaction might present survey results representing high levels of satisfaction, together with focus group themes revealing concerns about product availability and delivery times, providing a comprehensive understanding of customers' experiences and areas for improvement (Cameron, 2011).

Another method involves converting qualitative codes or themes into quantitative variables through data transformation. During this phase, researchers quantify and categorise qualitative themes to create measurable variables. For example, the results from qualitative interviews could be collated into specific dimensions of customers' satisfaction, which can then be analysed as distinct variables in a quantitative framework. This approach not only enhances the comparability of the data but also enriches the overall analysis (Merriam & Grenier, 2019).

In summary, integrating data in mixed methods designs dependent upon methodologies such as side-by-side comparisons, data transformation, and joint displays, all aim at effectively merging findings from both qualitative and quantitative datasets. By adopting these strategies, researchers can derive richer insights and more refined understandings of the phenomena under investigation.

10.3.3 Interpretation in Convergent Parallel Mixed Methods Design

In the convergent approach, interpretation typically occurs in the discussion section of a study. Whilst the results section presents findings from both quantitative and qualitative datasets, the discussion section explores further by comparing these results to evaluate alignment convergence, or divergence between the two sources. Such comparisons often reveal differences in concepts, themes, or scales, rather than simply indicating straightforward convergence or divergence (Creswell, 2014).

When discrepancies arise, researchers must consider numerous strategies to address them. One option is to acknowledge the divergence as a limitation of the study, which may be seen as a less robust approach. Alternatively, researchers can re-analyse the datasets to explore the discrepancies further, collect additional data to reconcile differences, or critically evaluate the validity of the quantitative constructs and qualitative themes. For instance, discrepancies may emerge from unvalidated quantitative measures or misalignments between qualitative themes and participant responses. In such cases, re-reviewing and reorganising transcripts may prove beneficial in illuminating these discrepancies (Aurini et al., 2021).

An illustrative example comprises the closely related management terms of 'Empowerment' and 'Authorisation', conveying slightly different meanings depending on the research context. These terms may need to be classified into distinct constructs for the quantitative analysis process and categorised into different themes for the qualitative analysis (Hendren et al., 2023). By utilising these sophisticated methods, researchers can effectively navigate the complexities of mixed methods research, ensuring a comprehensive understanding of how quantitative and qualitative findings interact to shape the overall research outcomes.

10.3.4 Validity in Convergent Parallel Mixed Methods Design

In the convergent approach to mixed methods research, ensuring validity requires the establishment of both quantitative aspects, such as construct validity, and qualitative validity through triangulation of each dataset (Creswell & Tashakkori, 2007).

However, this approach also presents unique validity concerns that warrant additional attention. Oen critical element is the validity of the integration methodology itself, often referred to as integration validity or methodological coherence. This aspect ensures that the methods used to merge quantitative and qualitative data are robust and that the interpretive frameworks applied effectively reconcile any discrepancies between the datasets (Pedersen et al., 2023).

One specific threat to validity in this approach is the potential issue of unequal sample sizes between the quantitative and qualitative datasets. Such imbalances can affect the depth of insights sourced from qualitative data, which tends to involve smaller samples, in contrast to quantitative research, with its the larger samples. For example, in a study examining consumers' preferences for a new product, researchers might collect quantitative data through a large-scale online survey whilst obtaining qualitative data from a smaller number of focus group discussions. Ensuring integration validity in this case means that the qualitative findings must improve the understanding of the quantitative results. If the survey shows that most consumers prefer a particular feature, but the focus groups reveal concerns about the product's price, the integration of these insights should create a coherent narrative that guides product development and pricing strategies.

Another illustrative scenario involves assessing the effectiveness of a new training programme. If the quantitative analysis draws from 500 organisational members whilst only 10 are involved in qualitative interviews, the richness of the qualitative insights may be compromised. This disparity can lead to misinterpretations, as the qualitative data might not adequately reflect the broader organisational members' experience. More significantly, management must tread carefully when interpreting qualitative findings in order to ensure they are contextually grounded (May & Perry, 2022). Thus, in this scenario, researchers must recognise that subjectivity is crucial when interpreting the findings. Drawing conclusions from a small group of participants to explain the experiences of a much larger group could be misleading.

Triangulation is also crucial in this approach. For instance, when evaluating a new marketing strategy, an organisation might utilise surveys (quantitative approach) to gauge customers' satisfaction and focus groups (qualitative approach) to explore customers' attitudes in depth. Effective triangulation comprises comparing these data sources to identify contradictions or complementary insights. If survey findings indicate high levels of satisfaction whilst focus groups highlight concerns about service delivery, management needs to address these discrepancies in order to formulate a comprehensive strategy enhancing both levels of satisfaction and service quality (Kansteiner & König, 2020).

By addressing these validity concerns and implementing robust integration strategies, researchers in the management discipline can ensure that their findings are both credible and applicable in practice, ultimately leading to more informed decision-making and improved organisational performance.

10.4 Explanatory Sequential Mixed Methods Design

The explanatory sequential mixed-methods approach is particularly well-suited for individuals with a strong quantitative background or those who are new to qualitative methods. This approach consists of two distinct phases: initially, researchers collect and analyse quantitative data, which then informs and enriches a subsequent qualitative phase (Creswell, 2014) (Fig. 10.2).

Typically, this approach comprises the purposeful selection of participants founded on quantitative findings and the framing of qualitative questions in accordance with these results. The primary objective is for qualitative data to provide

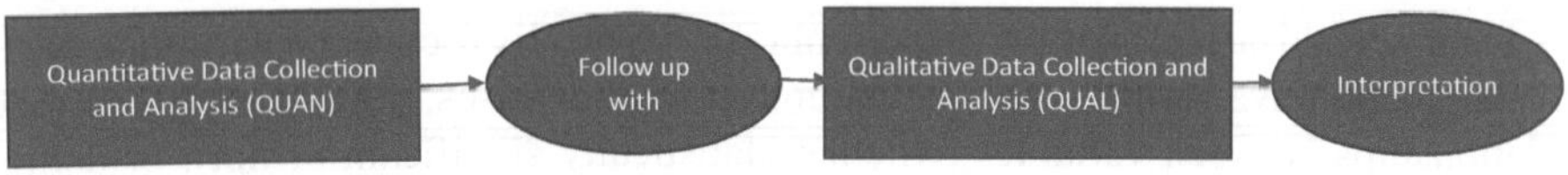

Fig. 10.2 Explanatory sequential mixed method (QUAN to QUAL)[1]. (Source: Adopted from Creswell (2014); and Taheri and Okumus (2024))

deeper insights and explanations for the initial quantitative outcomes (Taheri & Okumus, 2024).

For instance, a study may begin with the analysis of survey data, followed by qualitative interviews aimed at elucidating and contextualising the survey responses. An example of this can be seen in research that investigates the impact of managers' learning styles and leadership styles on organisational effectiveness, where initial quantitative findings are further explored through qualitative methods (Zumitzavan, 2011).

A more contemporary example in the management field could involve assessing the levels of innovation applied within for-profit firms, such as those in the airline industry. Researchers might initially collect quantitative data on different forms of organisational performance measures, such as on-time performance, customers' satisfaction scores, and revenue growth. Once this data is analysed and correlations between innovation practices and these organisational performance measures are identified, the next phase could comprise conducting focus groups with airlines' organisational members and customers to obtain insights into their perceptions of the innovative strategies being applied. This qualitative phase aims to explore how organisational members experience these innovations and what factors contribute to both operational success and customers' satisfaction, thereby enriching the understanding of the quantitative findings (Clark & Ivankova, 2015). By leveraging both quantitative and qualitative methods in this sequential manner, researchers can achieve a more comprehensive view of their subjects, leading to more sophisticated conclusions and practical applications within the management domain, particularly in terms of enhancing competitive advantages through innovation in the airline industry.

10.4.1 Data Collection in Explanatory Sequential Mixed Methods Design

The explanatory sequential mixed methods approach consists of two distinct stages of data collection, i.e., initial rigorous quantitative sampling, followed by purposeful sampling in a subsequent qualitative phase. A key challenge in this strategy is centred on effectively planning which quantitative results to further investigate and which participants to target for qualitative data collection in the second phase. The aim is for qualitative data to enhance and shed light on the quantitative findings (Creswell & Creswell, 2017; Dawadi et al., 2021; Morse, 2016a).

In the second phase, qualitative data collection typically focuses on various aspects of the quantitative results, such as extreme or outlier cases, significant predictors, relationships between variables (whether statistically significant or not), or demographic differences. For example, initial quantitative analysis may expose that individuals from different socio-economic backgrounds respond differently to certain variables. Suppose two groups are identified; those with higher and lower income levels. If the quantitative findings indicate that the higher-income group is statistically associated with purchasing product 'A', whilst the lower-income group is associated with purchasing product 'B', the researcher may then use qualitative methods to categorise respondents in light of these demographics and conduct interviews to probe the reasons behind their differing purchasing preferences (Zumitzavan, 2020).

Importantly, it is crucial to consider whether the qualitative sample should include participants from the initial quantitative phase. In an ideal circumstance, it should comprise the same individuals, thereby enabling more in-depth probing and offering explanations for the quantitative findings. The strength of this design stems from its capacity to clarify how variables interact, with qualitative methods adopted to discover these interactions in greater details (Palinkas et al., 2015).

To further enrich the analysis, especially when adopting a thematic analysis approach, researchers may compare results from different demographic groups with those that cannot be categorised, often referred to as 'Uncodable Data' or 'Uncategorisable Data'. These are pieces of information that do not fit neatly into predefined themes during the analysis process. When such data is encountered, researchers may need to reconsider their coding framework or explore additional themes to accommodate this information. Interviews with individuals from the 'Uncodable Data' group are crucial for attaining a comprehensive understanding of the phenomenon under investigation. These discussions may reveal unique perspectives that may have been overlooked by predefined themes, thereby enhancing the depths of understanding (Abisoye, 2024).

Insights obtained from these interviews also play an essential role in refining the coding framework or introducing new themes that greater capture the diversity of experiences within the dataset (Fetters et al., 2013). Moreover, comparing the perspectives of those whose data fit established themes with those in the 'uncodable data' group allows researchers to uncover significant differences in perceptions, experiences, or contexts. This comparative analysis not only enriches the findings but also strengthens the validity of the research by ensuring a greater range of experiences and perspectives is considered.

10.4.2 Data Analysis in Explanatory Sequential Mixed Methods Design

In the explanatory sequential mixed methods approach, the quantitative and qualitative datasets are analysed separately, with the quantitative findings serving as a key factor in framing the subsequent qualitative phase. A significant aspect of this design is that the quantitative findings not only influence the sampling strategy but also guide the formulation of open-ended qualitative questions for the second phase. These questions, which are vital for effective qualitative research, are broad and exploratory in nature (Gajendran & Harrison, 2007).

For instance, in a study examining the factors influencing levels of customers' satisfaction within a large retail chain, the initial quantitative phase might involve a survey questionnaire measuring levels of satisfaction across various store settings. The results could reveal that customers in urban stores report significantly higher levels of customer satisfaction than those in rural locations. Based on these findings, the researcher may decide to focus the qualitative phase on the rural locations, purposefully choosing participants from these areas for in-depth interviews. The quantitative data would further guide the formulation of qualitative questions, such as: "What specific challenges do you encounter that influence your levels of satisfaction with the store?" or "How do factors such as product availability or store layout determine your shopping experience in the rural stores?" (Shi et al., 2020).

Furthermore, analysing each phase independently affords several advantages for researchers. In the context of research on levels of customer's satisfaction, the quantitative phase facilitates the identification of tendencies and statistical relationships within a large dataset, thereby offering a robust overview of the overall level of customer satisfaction. This preliminary phase serves to highlight key areas for further inquiry. Upon commencing the qualitative phase, researchers are afforded the opportunity to investigate the identified issues in more depth, free from the potential biases inherent in the quantitative analysis. Such an independent approach enables the collection of rich, detailed narratives from customers, thereby recognising the underlying factors and contextual subtleties that quantitative data alone may fail to fully explicate (Cronin, 2016).

For example, qualitative interviews could highlight specific factors, such as how service quality or product availability contribute to varying levels of customer satisfaction. These insights would help identify key areas for improvement, providing actionable recommendations. By following this structured approach, researchers acquire a deeper understanding of the factors influencing the level of customer satisfaction, providing more comprehensive insights whilst maintaining a clear focus on each phase of the research (Ratten, 2023).

10.4.3 Interpretation in Explanatory Sequential Mixed Methods Design

In the mixed methods approach, the researcher interprets follow-up results in the research's discussion section. This comprises initially summarising the quantitative results from the first phase, followed by the qualitative findings from the second phase. However, this design takes a step further by integrating a third layer of interpretation: illuminating how the qualitative insights elucidate the quantitative findings (Stoecker & Avila, 2021).

A common mistake made by early-career researchers at this stage is to merge the two datasets. Whilst this might seem beneficial, the design's purpose is for qualitative data to enrich and deepen the understanding of the quantitative findings (Creswell, 2014). For example, in a research study probing organisational members' satisfaction in an organisation, quantitative results may indicate that overall satisfaction scores are low. Following this, qualitative interviews could reveal specific reasons behind these scores, such as inadequate management communication or a lack of career development opportunities. By merging the quantitative and qualitative results, researchers risk losing the more comprehensive insights provided by qualitative data, as the specific concerns revealed through interviews may be overshadowed by the general trends indicated by the quantitative scores.

Additionally, this combination can lead to oversimplification, reducing complex human experiences to mere numbers and failing to acknowledge the richness of individual perspectives. The two methods serve different purposes: quantitative analysis highlights trends across a large sample whilst qualitative analysis explores the 'why' behind those trends. Therefore, it is crucial to present the results separately. This practice enhances clarity, permitting readers to understand how quantitative findings inform qualitative insights, and vice versa. This approach not only deepens the understanding of the research problem but also improves the validity of the study by demonstrating how different types of data corroborate or expand upon each other. Thus, in the interpretation section, after presenting both sets of results separately, it is essential to discuss how the qualitative data contribute to expanding or explaining the quantitative findings (Matović & Ovesni, 2023).

In contrast to the convergent design, where directly comparing qualitative and quantitative datasets risks oversimplification due to their differing focuses, the method of making use of findings from both methods involves using quantitative results to support qualitative insights. For instance, if a quantitative survey illustrates that a significant percentage of organisational members feel undervalued, qualitative interviews might reveal specific practices leading to these feelings, such as limited recognition programmes. Rather than comparing the datasets directly, this method integrates them to provide a more comprehensive understanding. Essentially, the broader insights gained from the quantitative approach can illuminate and validate specific details uncovered by the qualitative approach, collectively presenting a clearer and more complete picture of the research.

10.4.4 Validity in Explanatory Sequential Mixed Methods Design

In an explanatory sequential mixed methods study, researchers are tasked with ensuring the validity of quantitative measures whilst also critically appraising the validity of qualitative findings. This approach, however, introduces additional concerns regarding validity. A significant issue is the potential compromise in the accuracy of overall findings if researchers restrict their exploration of how to follow up on quantitative results. Concentrating solely on individual demographics can obscure essential factors that require deeper scrutiny. For instance, if a research study on leadership effectiveness focuses only on the age and tenure of managers, it may fail to account for other pivotal elements, such as leadership styles or the organisational structures, which can play a far more substantial role in contributing to levels of organisational performance (Kamning, 2023; Michie & Zumitzavan, 2016).

Moreover, employing distinct samples for each phase of the study can undermine the intended continuity between phases, ultimately compromising the validity of the results. For instance, if the quantitative phase collects data from patients across various hospitals in order to assess overall levels of patient satisfaction with healthcare services, but the qualitative phase conducts interviews solely with patients from one specific hospital, the findings may lack coherence and fail to be applicable to more well-rounded healthcare contexts. This limitation might cause insights that do not reflect the diverse experiences and opinions of patients across different facilities, ultimately distorting the understanding of patients' level of satisfaction and hindering effective policy-making (Gajendran et al., 2021).

Another challenge lies in ensuring sufficient sample sizes and refining the quality of samples for both the quantitative and qualitative components. Inadequate sample sizes or poorly qualified samples can impede the research's ability to draw meaningful conclusions. For instance, in a study assessing the effectiveness of a new training programme, if the quantitative phase surveys only a handful of participants from one location, it may not accurately reflect the training's impact across different branches of the organisation. Consequently, this limited data may result in misguided assumptions about the programme's overall effectiveness and delay the development of customised improvements (Rampun et al., 2020).

To address these challenges, meticulous planning during the design phase of an explanatory sequential mixed methods study is indispensable. Researchers must thoughtfully consider how to integrate and develop further findings from each phase in order to ensure robust and valid research outcomes. Such strategic planning not only enhances the validity of the research but also guarantees that qualitative insights genuinely enhance the quantitative results, resulting in a more comprehensive understanding of the research problem (Onwuegbuzie & Collins, 2017).

10.5 Exploratory Sequential Mixed Methods Design

In an exploratory sequential mixed methods design, researchers commence their research with a qualitative phase before proceeding to a quantitative phase. This approach stands in contrast to the explanatory sequential method. Initially, the researcher investigates qualitative data and conducts an analysis, subsequently utilising these findings to inform the quantitative phase. Similar to the explanatory approach, the second phase of data collection is constructed upon the insights inferred from the initial phase (Serban & Roberts, 2016) (Fig. 10.3).

The primary objective of this strategy is to sharpen measurements utilising specific population samples and assess whether insights derived from a limited number of individuals in the qualitative phase can be generalised to a larger population in the quantitative phase.

For instance, a researcher may start by collecting and analysing focus group data, develop a measurement instrument based on these findings, and then administer this instrument to a broader sample. This method is particularly useful when existing instruments fail to adequately grasp the concepts the researcher intends to explore. For example, in studying leadership styles, researchers might start with a draft of structured questions addressing three distinct leadership styles. i.e. Transformational, Transactional, and Laissez-Faire, employing focus groups of approximately ten participants each, across three separate groups. After key themes emerge from these discussions, the researcher can develop a comprehensive questionnaire and extend these questions to a larger group in order to identify differences and draw comparisons (Jensen et al., 2020).

A pertinent example from Singapore is a study that utilised a mixed-methods approach comprising four distinct phases. The research commenced with a qualitative environmental scan (a PESTEEL analysis) to identify the key drivers of change affecting the future of work engagement in Singapore. Next, a quantitative survey was administered to 330 strategic leaders to measure their foresight, strategic thinking, and leadership styles. The study concluded in a qualitative Delphi study designed to synthesise and validate the preceding findings, which then informed the development of future scenarios for work engagement in 2030. This sequential design enabled comprehensive triangulation of the data and provided a robust foundation for effective scenario planning (Azmy, 2021).

Furthermore, a pertinent example within the management sphere involves investigating organisational members' turnover rates, presenting a multifaceted challenge. To thoroughly explore this issue, a mixed-methods approach is adopted.

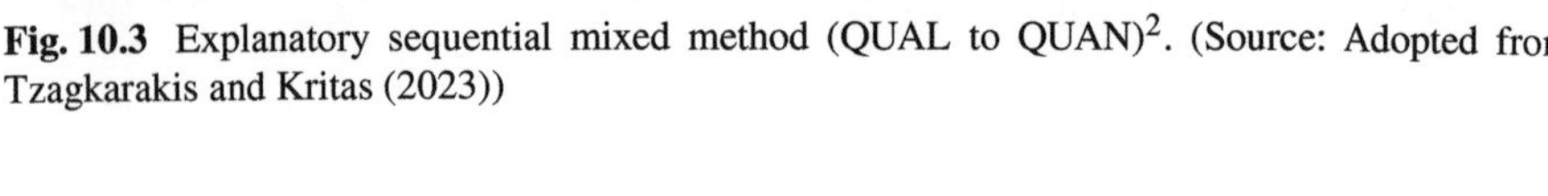

Fig. 10.3 Explanatory sequential mixed method (QUAL to QUAN)[2]. (Source: Adopted from Tzagkarakis and Kritas (2023))

Through qualitative interviews with current and former organisational members, key themes such as dissatisfaction with managerial practices, concerns regarding work-life balance, and perceived limitations in career advancement opportunities are identified. Thematic analysis of these interviews steers the creation of a structured questionnaire for subsequent quantitative data collection. The survey questions are meticulously crafted to validate and quantify the qualitative insights, scrutinising factors such as job satisfaction and intentions to leave across diverse demographic groups and job roles (Creswell and Poth, 2016).

Through careful statistical analysis of survey responses, the qualitative findings are corroborated, revealing correlations such as diminished satisfaction scores associated with managerial dissatisfaction. This integrated methodology fosters a sophisticated understanding of turnover dynamics, providing valuable insights to optimise retention strategies and enhance overall levels of organisational performance.

Ultimately, the exploratory sequential mixed methods design enriches the understanding of turnover factors by combining qualitative depth with robust quantitative validation. This methodology equips organisations with the insights needed to cultivate a supportive workplace culture and optimise employees' retention in today's competitive management landscape (Serban & Roberts, 2016).

10.5.1 Data Collection in Exploratory Sequential Mixed Methods Design

In this approach, data collection transpires across two distinct phases, commencing with qualitative data collection and followed by quantitative data collection. A pivotal challenge is effectively harnessing insights from the initial phase to inform the subsequent phase. An array of strategies are available to facilitate this transition (Min & Casselden, 2021).

Qualitative data analysis forms the substratum for developing an instrument with robust psychometric properties, including both validity and reliability. This process typically entails extracting quotes, codes, and themes from the qualitative data. For instance, in a research study investigating organisational members' engagement, quotes from focus groups might reveal concerns about management communication and recognition of effort. These quotes can be transformed into survey items, such as "I feel valued by my manager". Codes are then employed to create variables that group these items, whilst themes organise these codes into scales measuring overall levels of organisational members' engagement (Hesketh & Fleetwood, 2023). Adherence to rigorous design principles, such as item discrimination, construct validity, and reliability estimates (Wang et al., 2024a), guarantees the creation of a psychometrically sound instrument customised to the research's specific sample and population.

Researchers can utilise qualitative data analysis to discover new variables, comprehend existing scale structures, and delineate categories of information for exploration in the subsequent quantitative phase. A critical decision is whether the individuals engaged in the qualitative research should be the same as those in the quantitative research. Typically, due to the smaller sample sizes in qualitative research and the broader representation called for in quantitative studies, researchers may opt for utterly different samples for each phase (Vogt et al., 2012) In a study aimed at enhancing team collaboration, qualitative interviews with a small group of team leaders might reveal common challenges, such as unclear roles and insufficient resources. Following this, a larger quantitative survey could be performed with a broader sample of organisational members from different teams to determine if these challenges are widespread across the organisation (Saunders & Bezzina, 2015). It is imperative that both samples are derived from the same overall organisational member population whilst ensuring no overlap between participants in the two phases. Using the same individuals for both developing the survey and participating in it could inadvertently introduce bias into the research design (Fàbregues et al., 2023).

In terms of data analysis, this strategy necessitates a separate analysis of the two datasets, with findings from the exploratory qualitative phase directly informing the development of quantitative measures. This requires meticulous attention to qualitative data analysis procedures to determine which findings to incorporate. For example, if grounded theory methods are utilised, the theoretical model generated may serve as a framework for testing in the subsequent quantitative phase (Corbin & Strauss, 2015). Similarly, qualitative case studies may identify distinct cases that become focal points for key variables in the quantitative phase.

10.5.2 Data Analysis Exploratory Sequential Mixed Methods Design

In exploratory sequential mixed methods design, the analysis phase is structured to first prioritise qualitative data collection and analysis, underpinning subsequent quantitative research. This design begins with qualitative methods, such as interviews, focus groups, or observations, to explore participants' perspectives, experiences, or insights vis-à-vis a particular management phenomenon (Harrison et al., 2020). The findings from this qualitative phase serve to develop hypotheses or inform the creation of instruments for the quantitative phase.

Initially, qualitative data is analysed using thematic analysis or other qualitative techniques, allowing researchers to identify key themes, patterns, and insights. For example, in a study exploring leadership styles, qualitative interviews with managers might reveal themes related to Transformational Leadership's impact on organisational members' motivation and engagement (Jensen et al., 2020). These themes can then be used to construct a structured survey instrument that quantitatively measures the prevalence and effectiveness of various leadership styles within an organisation.

Once the qualitative phase is completed and the relevant themes have been established, researchers proceed to the quantitative phase. Here, the data collected through survey questionnaires are analysed utilising statistical techniques, such as multiple regression analysis or descriptive statistics (Crawford et al., 2013). For instance, if the qualitative data illustrate that participative leadership improves team collaboration, the quantitative analysis could measure the correlation between participative leadership practices and team performance measures across a broader sample of organisations.

One common challenge in this design is ensuring that the qualitative insights effectively influence the quantitative phase. Researchers must be diligent in linking the qualitative themes to specific survey items or variables in the quantitative research (Hendren et al., 2023). For example, if the qualitative research findings suggest that communication gaps hinder project success, the quantitative phase could include survey questions specifically measuring communication effectiveness and its relationship to project outcomes. This integration ensures that the quantitative data is rooted in the rich contextual understanding provided by the qualitative phase, resulting in more relevant and meaningful results.

Ultimately, the exploratory sequential mixed methods design is advantageous for resolving complicated management research questions, as it allows for a thorough exploration of a phenomenon before quantifying it. By capitalising on qualitative findings to guide quantitative inquiry, researchers can achieve a more comprehensive understanding of issues such as leadership effectiveness, team dynamics, and organisational culture, ultimately yielding more informed decision-making and policy development.

10.5.3 Interpretation Exploratory Sequential Mixed Methods Design

Researchers typically analyse mixed methods results in the discussion section of a research by first presenting qualitative findings. For instance, in a research project analysing the effectiveness of training programmes in a technology firm, qualitative interviews might uncover themes such as the importance of hands-on experience and peer support. These insights can then guide the creation of a quantitative survey to measure the magnitude of these themes across a larger group of organisational members, particularly within a matrix organisational structure, where team members from various departments cooperate to foster creativity and innovation (Williams & Nafukho, 2015).

Similarly, in a study investigating levels of organisational performance within a retail organisation, qualitative focus groups might identify key factors, such as the availability of organisational resources and budgets for training opportunities. These insights would then steer the development of a quantitative survey designed to measure how these factors are perceived by organisational members and their influence on overall organisational performance (Rahman et al., 2020).

The discussion finalises with the presentation of quantitative results from these final phases, summarising the survey findings. Side-by-side comparison between the two datasets is generally avoided due to potential discrepancies in the samples used. The primary objective of this approach is to measure the generalisability of qualitative themes to a more extensive population rather than making head-to-head comparisons between specific findings from each dataset (Baker & Rachman, 2023).

10.5.4 Validity Exploratory Sequential Mixed Methods Design

Researchers adopting a mixed methods strategy must maintain the validity of both qualitative data and quantitative scores, addressing specific validity concerns inherent to this design during the proposal development phase. A critical challenge is assuring the rigorous design and testing of psychometric instruments, which necessitates meticulous methodological planning and execution (Asabor et al., 2021). Additionally, there is the challenge of fully leveraging qualitative findings, particularly when the analysis is limited to thematic exploration rather than deeper investigations typical of ethnographic or grounded theory approaches (Savin-Baden & Major, 2023).

Furthermore, it is crucial to avoid participant overlap between the qualitative and quantitative phases in order to prevent redundant responses. For example, if focus group discussions reveal that organisational members are struggling with time management whilst working remotely, these insights should inform a separate, larger-scale survey administered to a different cohort of organisational members. This strategy enables the identification of broader trends and patterns throughout the organisation. In a study analysing the effectiveness of training programmes, qualitative interviews might reveal themes such as the need for more interactive elements in training sessions. Following this, a larger survey could be conducted with a different group of organisational members to evaluate how prevalent these training preferences are and their relationship to varying degrees of organisational performance (Curry et al., 2009).

Finally, in the realm of management research, the adoption of mixed methods offers distinct advantages, alongside notable challenges. These methodologies enrich knowledge development by presenting a comprehensive understanding of complex management phenomena. For instance, a study on leadership effectiveness might begin with qualitative interviews to identify key leadership styles that resonate with organisational members. The subsequent quantitative phase could involve a survey across a wider population to measure how these traits correlate with varying degrees of organisational performance, which serves as the dependent variable reflecting how different leadership styles might influence outcomes such as levels of productivity, efficiency, and organisational members' satisfaction. By integrating quantitative numerical insights with qualitative contextual distinctions and underlying meanings, researchers can achieve a holistic view that enhances the depth of analysis and explores multifaceted dimensions that would remain obscured within the limitations of a single method (Alston, 2020; Dawadi et al., 2021; Baran & Sypniewska, 2020).

10.6 Chapter Summary

This chapter described several mixed methods approaches. The next chapter explores how to interpret research findings.

10.7 Questions for Future Reflection

1. A management team wants to understand why a recently implemented performance management system is receiving negative feedback, despite initial metrics indicating a slight increase in productivity. They need to both quantify the extent of the dissatisfaction and understand the reasons behind it to make improvements. Which mixed methods design—Convergent Parallel, Explanatory Sequential, or Exploratory Sequential—would be most appropriate for this research objective, and why?
2. In a Convergent Parallel study, a researcher finds that their quantitative survey data indicates a high level of overall job satisfaction among employees. However, their concurrent qualitative interviews reveal significant frustration with a lack of autonomy and poor communication. How should the researcher interpret this divergence? What are the risks of simply concluding that the qualitative findings offer "more depth" to the quantitative results?
3. A researcher is utilising an Exploratory Sequential design to study the novel concept of 'digital leadership' in remote teams. They conduct initial interviews and identify several key themes. What are the critical steps and potential pitfalls in transforming these rich, qualitative themes into a psychometrically sound quantitative survey instrument for the second phase of the study?
4. In an Explanatory Sequential study, quantitative analysis reveals that employee engagement scores are significantly lower for employees aged over 50 compared to their younger colleagues, but there is no difference based on gender. How should these findings guide the purposeful sampling strategy for the follow-up qualitative phase? Who should the researcher aim to interview to best explain the initial quantitative results?
5. The chapter notes that mixed methods research is grounded in pragmatism. Critically discuss the potential ontological and epistemological tensions a researcher might face when attempting to integrate findings from a positivist-oriented quantitative survey with findings from an interpretivist-oriented series of in-depth interviews. How does a pragmatic stance help explain these tensions?

6. A researcher conducts an Explanatory Sequential study on customer loyalty. They survey 1000 customers in the quantitative phase but only conduct follow-up interviews with five customers from one specific store location. Critically appraise the threats to validity in this research design, paying particular attention to the generalisability of the explanatory qualitative findings.
7. In the MANCOVA section of the previous chapter, we saw how a covariate ('Firm Age') could be used to statistically control for a variable's influence. How could a qualitative component in a mixed-methods study attain a similar, though conceptually different, goal of accounting for the influence of a key contextual variable?
8. Formulate a single, overarching mixed-methods research question and two subsequent, specific sub-questions (one quantitative, one qualitative) for a study investigating the effectiveness of a corporate wellness programme on employee well-being and absenteeism.
9. The chapter mentions transforming qualitative data into quantitative variables. A researcher codes interview transcripts for 'positive,' 'neutral,' and 'negative' comments about a new software implementation, turning these codes into a numerical variable. What is gained by this data transformation, but more importantly, what crucial contextual information is potentially lost in the process?
10. Beyond the methodological and philosophical considerations, what are the primary practical challenges (e.g., time, cost, researcher skills) a PhD student or a small research team might face when undertaking a comprehensive mixed methods study compared to a single-method study?

References

Abisoye, A. (2024). A Conceptual Framework for Integrating Artificial Intelligence into STEM Research Methodologies for Enhanced Innovation. International Journal of Research and Innovation in Social Science.

Aithal, P. S., & Aithal, S. (2023). Application of ChatGPT in higher education and research–A futuristic analysis. *International Journal of Applied Engineering and Management Letters (IJAEML), 7*(3), 168–194.

Alston, M. (2020). *Research for social workers: An introduction to methods*. Routledge.

Asabor, E. N., Lett, E., Moll, A., & Shenoi, S. V. (2021). We've got our own beliefs, attitudes, myths: A mixed methods assessment of rural South African health care workers' knowledge of and attitudes towards PrEP implementation. *AIDS and Behavior, 25*(8), 2517–2532. https://doi.org/10.1007/s10461-021-03213-z

Aurini, J. D., Heath, M., & Howells, S. (2021). *The how to of qualitative research*. Sage Publications.

Azmy, W. (2021). *The possible futures of work engagement by 2030: a mixed methods study investigating strategic leadership and work engagement in Singapore* (Vol. 1). University of Southern Queensland.

Baker, L., & Rachman, A. (2023). Mixed methods research in organisational studies: Understanding training outcomes. *International Journal of Management Reviews, 25*(1), 34–50. https://doi.org/10.1111/ijmr.12245

Baran, M., & Sypniewska, B. (2020). The impact of management methods on employee engagement. *Sustainability, 12*(1), 426. https://doi.org/10.3390/su12010426

Bukowska, M. (2021). Critical realism: one of the main theoretical orientations of the social sciences in the twentieth and twenty-first centuries. *Journal of Critical Realism, 20*(4), 44–447.

Cabrera-Tenecela, P. (2023). New organization of research designs. *South American Research Journal, 3*(1), 37–51. https://doi.org/10.5281/zenodo.8050508

Cameron, R. (2011). Mixed methods in business and management: A call to the 'first generation'. *Journal of Management & Organization, 17*(2), 245–267. https://doi.org/10.1017/S1833367200001644

Campbell, D. T., & Fiske, D. W. (1959). Convergent and discriminant validation by the multitrait-multimethod matrix. *Psychological Bulletin, 56*(2), 81–105. https://doi.org/10.1037/h0046016

Chong, Y. K., & Zainal, S. R. M. (2024). Employee agility's moderating role on the link between employee vitality, digital literacy and transformational leadership with job performance: an empirical study. *Cogent Business & Management, 11*(1), 2337447. https://doi.org/10.1080/23311975.2024.2337447

Clark, V. L. P., & Ivankova, N. V. (2015). *Mixed methods research: A guide to the field* (Vol. 3). Sage Publications.

Combrinck, C. (2024). A tutorial for integrating generative AI in mixed methods data analysis. *Discover Education, 3*(1), 116.

Corbin, J., & Strauss, A. (2015). *Basics of qualitative research* (Vol. 14). Sage Publications.

Crawford, E. R., Rich, B. L., & Borman, W. C. (2013). The antecedents and consequences of job engagement: A meta-analytic review. *Personnel Psychology, 66*(4), 827–865.

Creswell, J. W. (2014). *Research design: Qualitative, quantitative, and mixed methods approaches* (4th ed.). Sage Publications.

Creswell, J. W., & Poth, C. N. (2016). Qualitative inquiry and research design: Choosing among five approaches. Sage publications.

Creswell, J. W., & Creswell, J. D. (2017). Research design: Qualitative, quantitative, and mixed methods approaches. Sage publications.

Creswell, J. W., & Poth, C. N. (2024). *Qualitative inquiry and research design: Choosing among five approaches* (5th ed.). Sage Publications.

Creswell, J. W., & Tashakkori, A. (2007). Editorial: Differing perspectives on mixed methods research. *Journal of Mixed Methods Research, 1*(4), 303–308. https://doi.org/10.1177/1558689807306132

Cronin, B. (2016). Multiple and mixed methods research for economics. In F. S. Lee & B. Cronin (Eds.), *Handbook of research methods and applications in heterodox economics* (pp. 286–300). Edward Elgar Publishing.

Curry, L. A., Nembhard, I. M., & Bradley, E. H. (2009). Qualitative and mixed methods provide unique contributions to outcomes research. *Circulation, 119*(10), 1442–1452. https://doi.org/10.1161/CIRCULATIONAHA.107.742775

Dawadi, S., Shrestha, S., & Giri, R. A. (2021). Mixed-methods research: A discussion on its types, challenges, and criticisms. *Journal of Practical Studies in Education, 2*(2), 25–36. https://doi.org/10.46809/jpse.v2i2.20

Fàbregues, S., Escalante-Barrios, E. L., Turk, S. T., Guetterman, T. C., & Fetters, M. D. (2023). Assessing quality in mixed methods research: Concepts, frameworks, and criteria. In R. Cameron & X. Golenko (Eds.), *Handbook of mixed methods research in business and management* (pp. 76–93). Edward Elgar Publishing.

Fetters, M. D., Curry, L. A., & Creswell, J. W. (2013). Achieving integration in mixed methods designs—Principles and practices. *Health Services Research, 48*(6pt2), 2134–2156. https://doi.org/10.1111/1475-6773.12117

Fosnot, C. T. (2013). *Constructivism: Theory, perspectives, and practice.* Teachers College Press.

Gajendran, R. S., & Harrison, D. A. (2007). The good, the bad, and the unknown about telecommuting: meta-analysis of psychological mediators and individual consequences. *Journal of Applied Psychology, 92*(6), 1524. https://doi.org/10.1037/0021-9010.92.6.1524

Gajendran, D., Shrestha, S., & Giri, R. A. (2021). Mixed-methods research: A discussion on its types, challenges, and criticisms. *Journal of Practical Studies in Education, 2*(2), 25–36. https://doi.org/10.46809/jpse.v2i2.20

Ghanad, A. (2023). An overview of quantitative research methods. *International Journal of Multidisciplinary Research and Analysis, 6*(8), 3794–3803. https://doi.org/10.47191/ijmra/v6-i8-52

Harrison, R. L., Reilly, T. M., & Creswell, J. W. (2020). Methodological rigor in mixed methods: An application in management studies. *Journal of Mixed Methods Research, 14*(4), 473–495. https://doi.org/10.1177/1558689819900585

Harter, J. K., Schmidt, F. L., & Hayes, T. L. (2002). Business-unit-level relationship between employee satisfaction, employee engagement, and business outcomes: A meta-analysis. *Journal of Applied Psychology, 87*(2), 268–279. https://doi.org/10.1037/0021-9010.87.2.268

Hendren, K., Newcomer, K., Pandey, S. K., Smith, M., & Sumner, N. (2023). How qualitative research methods can be leveraged to strengthen mixed methods research in public policy and public administration? *Public Administration Review, 83*(3), 468–485. https://doi.org/10.1111/puar.13528

Hesketh, B., & Fleetwood, S. (2023). Employee engagement in the workplace: Qualitative insights and quantitative measures. *Journal of Management Studies, 60*(3), 457–480.

Jensen, M., Potočnik, K., & Chaudhry, S. (2020). A mixed-methods study of CEO transformational leadership and firm performance. *European Management Journal, 38*(6), 836–845. https://doi.org/10.1016/j.emj.2020.05.004

Kamning, D. L. (2023). Exploring the impact of the COVID-19 pandemic on approaches to innovation in the consulting industry: A grounded theory pilot study. *Innovation & Management Review, 20*(4), 314–330. https://doi.org/10.1108/INMR-05-2021-0076

Kansteiner, K., & König, S. (2020). The role(s) of qualitative content analysis in mixed methods research designs. *Forum Qualitative Sozialforschung / Forum: QualitativeSocial Research, 21*(1), Article 11. https://doi.org/10.17169/fqs-21.1.3412

Kurtaliqi, F., Miltgen, C. L., Viglia, G., & Pantin-Sohier, G. (2024). Using advanced mixed methods approaches: Combining PLS-SEM and qualitative studies. *Journal of Business Research, 172*, Article 114464. https://doi.org/10.1016/j.jbusres.2023.114464

Leavy, P. (Ed.). (2014). *The Oxford handbook of qualitative research.* Oxford University Press.

Lim, W. M. (2024). What is qualitative research? An overview and guidelines. *Australasian Marketing Journal*. https://doi.org/10.1177/14413582241264619

Lui, S., Mitchell, J., & Weale, M. (2011). The utility of expectational data: Firm-level evidence using matched qualitative–quantitative UK surveys. *International Journal of Forecasting, 27*(4), 1128–1146. https://doi.org/10.1016/j.ijforecast.2010.10.003

Macey, W. H., & Schneider, B. (2008). The meaning of employee engagement. *Industrial and Organizational Psychology, 1*(1), 3–30. https://doi.org/10.1111/j.1754-9434.2007.0002.x

Mackenzie, A. (2017). *A mixed-methods research approach exploring the relationship between 'green' building performance and organizational productivity* (Doctoral dissertation).

Matović, N., & Ovesni, K. (2023). Interaction of quantitative and qualitative methodology in mixed methods research: Integration and/or combination. *International Journal of Social Research Methodology, 26*(1), 51–65. https://doi.org/10.1080/13645579.2021.1964857

May, T., & Perry, B. (2022). *Social research: Issues, methods and process.* McGraw-Hill Education.

Merriam, S. B., & Grenier, R. S. (Eds.). (2019). *Qualitative research in practice: Examples for discussion and analysis.* John Wiley & Sons.

Michie, J., & Zumitzavan, V. (2016). The impact of 'learning' and 'leadership' management styles on organizational outcomes: a study of tyre firms in Thailand. In Leadership in the Asia Pacific (pp. 165-188). Routledge.

Min, S. L. L., & Casselden, B. (2021). A case study of Singapore Management University Libraries: Adopting a mixed methods approach towards collection evaluation. *The Journal of Academic Librarianship, 47*(3). https://doi.org/10.1016/j.acalib.2021.102330

Morse, J. M. (2016a). *Mixed method design: Principles and procedures.* Routledge.

Onwuegbuzie, A. J., & Collins, K. M. T. (2017). The role of sampling in mixed methods research: Enhancing inference quality. *Kölner Zeitschrift für Soziologie und Sozialpsychologie, 69*(Suppl 2), 133–156. https://doi.org/10.1007/s11577-017-0455-0

Palinkas, L. A., Horwitz, S. M., Green, C. A., Wisdom, J. P., Duan, N., & Hoagwood, K. (2015). Purposeful sampling for qualitative data collection and analysis in mixed method implementation research. *Administration and Policy in Mental Health and Mental Health Services Research, 42*(5), 533–544. https://doi.org/10.1007/s10488-013-0528-y

Pedersen, G. A., Shrestha, P., Akellot, J., Sepulveda, A., Luitel, N. P., Kasujja, R., Contreras, C., Galea, J. T., Moran, L., Neupane, V., Rimal, D., Schafer, A., & Kohrt, B. A. (2023). A mixed methods evaluation of a World Health Organization competency-based training package for foundational helping skills among pre-service and in-service health workers in Nepal, Peru, and Uganda. *Global Mental Health (Cambridge, England), 10*, e55. https://doi.org/10.1017/gmh.2023.43

Rahman, M. S., Hossain, M. A., Abdel Fattah, F. A. M., & Akter, S. (2020). Optimising competitive performance of service firms in data-rich environment. *Journal of Service Theory and Practice, 30*(6), 681–706. https://doi.org/10.1108/JSTP-04-2020-0077

Rampun, R., Zainol, Z., & Tajuddin, D. (2020). The effects of training transfer on training program evaluation and effectiveness of training program. *Management Research Journal, 9*, 43–53. https://doi.org/10.37134/mrj.vol9.sp.4.2020

Ratten, V. (2023). *Research methodologies for business management*. Routledge.

Rich, B. L., Lepine, J. A., & Crawford, E. R. (2010). Job engagement: Antecedents and effects on job performance. *Academy of Management Journal, 53*(3), 617–635. https://doi.org/10.5465/AMJ.2010.51468988

Rorty, R. (2009). *Philosophy and the mirror of nature*. Princeton University Press.

Saunders, M. N., & Bezzina, F. (2015). Reflections on conceptions of research methodology among management academics. European management journal, 33(5), 297-304.

Savin-Baden, M., & Major, C. (2023). *Qualitative research: The essential guide to theory and practice*. Routledge.

Serban, A., & Roberts, A. J. (2016). Exploring antecedents and outcomes of shared leadership in a creative context: A mixed-methods approach. *The Leadership Quarterly, 27*(2), 181–199. https://doi.org/10.1016/j.leaqua.2016.01.009

Shea, T., Usman, S. A., Arivalagan, S., & Parayitam, S. (2023). "Knowledge management practices" as moderator in the relationship between organizational culture and performance in information technology companies in India. *VINE Journal of Information and Knowledge Management Systems, 53*(4), 719–747. https://doi.org/10.1108/VJIKMS-12-2020-0232

Shi, S., Wang, Y., Chen, X., & Zhang, Q. (2020). Conceptualisation of omnichannel customer experience and its impact on shopping intention: A mixed-method approach. *International Journal of Information Management, 50*, 325–336. https://doi.org/10.1016/j.ijinfomgt.2019.09.001

Stoecker, R., & Avila, E. (2021). From mixed methods to strategic research design. *International Journal of Social Research Methodology, 24*(6), 627–640. https://doi.org/10.1080/13645579.2020.1799639

Sweeney, G., Long, D., & Smith, K. (2023). Assessing marketing strategies: A mixed methods evaluation. *Journal of Marketing Management, 39*(1–2), 120–137.

Taheri, B., & Okumus, F. (2024). Conducting mixed methods research. *International Journal of Contemporary Hospitality Management, 36*(3), 995–1004. https://doi.org/10.1108/IJCHM-08-2023-1309

Tashakkori, A., & Teddlie, C. (2002). *Handbook of mixed methods in social & behavioural research*. Sage Publications.

Teng-Calleja, M., Mactal, M. T. D. G., & Caringal-Go, J. F. (2024). Examining employee experiences of hybrid work: An ecological approach. *Personnel Review, 53*(6), 1408–1424. https://doi.org/10.1108/PR-03-2023-0222

Toledo, C., & Shannon-Baker, P. (2023). Choosing a qualitatively oriented mixed methods research approach: Recommendations for researchers. In R. Cameron & X. Golenko (Eds.), *Handbook of mixed methods research in business and management* (pp. 41–54). Edward Elgar Publishing. https://doi.org/10.4337/9781800887954.00011

Tzagkarakis, S. I., & Kritas, D. (2023). Mixed research methods in political science and governance: Approaches and applications. *Quality & Quantity, 57*(Suppl 1), 39–53. https://doi.org/10.1007/s11135-022-01384-y

Vogt, W. P., Gardner, D. C., & Haeffele, L. M. (2012). *When to use what research design*. Guilford Press.

Wang, P., Li, K., Du, Q., & Wang, J. (2024a). Customer experience in AI-enabled products: Scale development and validation. *Journal of Retailing and Consumer Services, 76*. https://doi.org/10.1016/j.jretconser.2023.103578

Weyant, E. (2022). Research design: Qualitative, quantitative, and mixed methods approaches (5th ed.). *Journal of Electronic Resources in Medical Libraries, 19*(1–2), 54–55. https://doi.org/10.1080/15424065.2022.2046231

Williams, R. C., & Nafukho, F. M. (2015). Technical training evaluation revisited: An exploratory, mixed-methods study. *Performance Improvement Quarterly, 28*(1), 69–93. https://doi.org/10.1002/piq.21187

Zumitzavan, V. (2011). *The impact of managers' learning styles and leadership styles on the effectiveness of their organisations: A case study from small retail tyre companies in Thailand* (Doctoral dissertation, University of Birmingham).

Zumitzavan, V. (2020). Learning preferences and brand management in the Thai housing estate industry. *International Journal of Management and Enterprise Development, 19*(1), 42–57.

Chapter 11
Discussions of Research Findings

11.1 Introduction

This chapter outlines how to discuss research findings, incorporating relevant examples from the management discipline. It provides strategies for interpreting data, drawing meaningful conclusions, and linking results to theoretical frameworks. Additionally, it highlights best practices for presenting findings in a clear and impactful manner, ensuring they contribute effectively to the discipline of management research.

11.2 The Discussion as an Artful Science: Interpretation, Creativity, and AI

Whilst the preceding chapters have detailed the systematic 'science' of data collection and analysis, the discussion chapter is where the researcher's 'art' truly comes to the fore. This section is not a mere summary of results; it is an act of intellectual craftsmanship, where data are synthesised, meaning is constructed, and a compelling narrative is woven. This creative process, fundamental to all research, is now being both confronted and amplified by the rise of AI.

Furthermore, the transition from 'results' to 'discussion' represents an interpretive leap. It is the art of seeing the greater picture, linking different findings, and contextualising them within a wider theoretical and practical landscape. The researcher serves as a storyteller, transforming statistical correlations or qualitative themes into a coherent and persuasive argument that answers the fundamental "so what?" question (Ankeny & Leonelli, 2024). This requires creativity to formulate novel explanations for unanticipated findings, intellectual courage to challenge existing theories,

© The Author(s), under exclusive license to Springer Nature Singapore Pte Ltd. 2025

V. Zumitzavan, *Social Science Methodologies for Management Research*,
https://doi.org/10.1007/978-981-95-4318-2_11

and reflexivity to acknowledge how individual's own perspective forms the interpretation. This artful synthesis is what raises a study from a simple report to a genuine contribution to knowledge.

Besides, the 'science' of crafting a discussion is evolving with the integration of AI tools, particularly Large Language Models (LLMs). Beyond data analysis, AI can function as a powerful catalyst during the interpretation phase. It can rapidly synthesise massive bodies of existing literature, serving researchers to more effectively position their findings within the academic discourse and identify novel contributions (Alqahtani et al., 2023). In addition, AI can operate as a 'critical friend' by proposing alternative interpretations of the data, highlighting potential logical fallacies in an argument, or identifying gaps calling for further explanation. This improves the scientific rigour of the discussion by compelling the researcher to fortify their interpretive claims.

However, the role of AI must be approached with critical awareness. AI models do not hold true understanding; they cannot grasp the sophisticated socio-cultural context of management phenomena or make the ethical judgements inherent in articulating practical implications (Ankeny & Leonelli, 2024). The 'art' of the discussion—the deep insight, the contextual wisdom, and the ultimate responsibility for the narrative—remains an exclusively human endeavour. The skilled researcher, therefore, uses AI not to write the discussion, but to polish their own thinking, ensuring the final product is a robust and insightful fusion of artful interpretation and scientific evidence.

11.3 Discussions of Quantitative Research Findings

To initiate a discussion of research findings, it is pivotal for the researcher to unambiguously define the research question. In this instance, the question is framed as: "To what extent does a relationship exist between managerial leadership styles and organisational performance?" This query is accurately articulated, as it probes a specific and pertinent relationship, namely leadership styles and organisational performance, thereby making it applicable across a wide range of sectors within management subdisciplines, including both profit-driven and not-for-profit organisations such as retail establishments, hotels, healthcare institutions, and public governance institutes (Zumitzavan, 2011; Zumitzavan et al., 2025; Michie & Zumitzavan, 2016). The aim is to provide well-founded recommendations for harnessing effective leadership styles to enhance organisational performance, hence establishing a robust foundation for the subsequent analysis.

In addition to this question, several other research questions can be formulated, considering the urgent needs observed across different industries. For example, one might ask: "What strategies can retail firms implement to increase sales volumes during seasonal promotions?" This question stems from the phenomenon of fluctuating sales during specific periods, such as holidays or major sales events. Retailers often struggle to maintain consistent sales growth, making it essential to explore effective promotional strategies (Richards, 2006).

Another pertinent research question might be: "How can hotels enhance levels of customer satisfaction through improvements in service quality?" The hospitality sector is notably competitive, with customer satisfaction playing a pivotal role in fostering repeat business and brand loyalty. This question arises from observed trends highlighting the significant impact of service quality on customers' experiences (Zaibaf et al., 2013; Zumitzavan, 2022). By exploring factors such as staff training, customers' feedback mechanisms, and personalised services, the research could provide valuable insights for optimising hotel operations.

A further example is: "How can the implementations of different types of innovation increase productivity in manufacturing organisations?" In a rapidly evolving manufacturing landscape, organisations are under pressure to enhance productivity whilst remaining competitive. This question arises from the increasing adoption of technologies such as automation and lean manufacturing processes (Jung et al., 2021). Researching how various innovation types, be they process, product, or organisational innovations, contribute to efficiency improvements can help manufacturers identify best practices.

Following the summarisation of research questions, it is essential to summarise the key findings succinctly, providing a clear reference point for subsequent analysis. For instance, one might state that a research study found a significant positive correlation between Transformational Leadership and level of organisational members' engagement ($r = 0.76$, $p < 0.001$), suggesting that leadership style plays a pivotal role in influencing organisational motivation and performance.

The findings should also be related back to the original research questions and objectives in order to reinforce the relevance of the study. For example, these findings substantiate the research objective of analysing the relationship between leadership styles and organisational performance, particularly highlighting the varying degrees of levels of effectiveness of Transformational Leadership in enhancing levels of organisational members' engagement across diverse sectors, such as healthcare and retail (Zumitzavan, 2011; Michie & Zumitzavan, 2016).

Engaging with existing literature is critical in order to position the findings within the broader academic discourse. This comparative analysis demonstrates how the research contributes to, or challenges, current knowledge. For instance, one might note that these results corroborate the conclusions of Verma, Verma & Abhishek (2024), who ascertain that Transformational Leadership is a driver of organisational performance. However, one might also note that unlike their findings, which primarily focused on corporate settings, the study incorporates data from public governance offices, thereby extending the applicability of Transformational Leadership across numerous contexts (Zumitzavan & Udchacone, 2014).

If the study was guided by specific hypotheses, it is important to discuss whether the findings support or refute them. For example, Hypothesis 1 posited a positive relationship between Transformational Leadership and levels of organisational members' engagement, which is strongly supported by the research findings, suggesting that organisations prioritising this leadership style can significantly enhance motivation and performance.

In addition, it is vital to articulate the practical implications of research findings for managers and practitioners within numerous industries. Recommendations founded on these outcomes are essential for effective organisational development. For example, the strong correlation between Transformational Leadership and levels of organisational members' engagement suggests that organisations, particularly in sectors such as healthcare, should prioritise leadership programmes aimed at improving Transformational Leadership skills among managers. This is especially pertinent in healthcare, where organisational members' motivation directly influences patient care outcomes (Avolio & Drummey, 2023). Beyond healthcare, the dynamics of leadership styles across different sectors further enrich the discussion. In the airline industry, the adoption of Transactional Leadership strategies has been associated with improved operational efficiency and levels of customer satisfaction (Nguyen et al., 2022), whilst in retail, Transformational Leadership has been revealed to nurture a culture of innovation and higher levels of organisational members' morale, thus boosting sales performance and significantly enhancing overall organisational performance (Jung et al. 2021).

Concluding the discussion section by identifying potential areas for future research is crucial, as it underscores the limitations of the current research whilst paving the way for subsequent inquiries. A suitable conclusion might be that future research should then explore the longitudinal effects of leadership styles on organisational members' performance across different organisational contexts, including the public sector and non-profit organisations, to further elucidate the dynamics of effective leadership in diverse organisational surroundings.

In summary, crafting a comprehensive discussion of quantitative research findings involves summarising key outcomes, contextualising them within research questions and objectives, comparing them with existing literature, addressing hypotheses, discussing practical implications, and suggesting future research avenues. By following these steps, researchers can create a coherent narrative significantly improving the academic discourse in the management discipline.

11.4 Discussion of Qualitative Research Findings

In qualitative research, the formulation of research questions is essential, as it profoundly influences the depth and richness of the inquiry. Well-crafted research questions not only steer the direction of the investigation but also shape the data collection process (Olazo, 2023). They reflect the complexity of the phenomena under study, aligning with the qualitative approach's purpose of discovering the complex experiences of individuals.

To enhance the quality of research inquiries, researchers should emphasise several key principles. Firstly, questions should centre on the experiences and perspectives of participants, inviting them to articulate their insights and feelings. For instance, asking "How do top executives perceive the impact of transformational leadership on organisational culture and levels of organisational members' engagement?" fosters an in-depth exploration of personal insights (Shao et al. 2024). Such questions encourage participants to share detailed narratives, capturing the intricacies of their subjective experiences at the highest levels of management.

Furthermore, ensuring contextual relevance is vital; research questions should be situated within specific environments in order to discover phenomena as they occur in real-world settings. An illustrative example might be, "How do team members in project-based industries perceive the effectiveness of different leadership styles in achieving project goals?" (Shuck et al., 2011). Grounding questions in particular contexts enable researchers to obtain insights into how situational factors influence perceptions and experiences, thereby enriching the findings.

Openness to exploration is another crucial principle that permits the discovery of unexpected themes during data collection. A question like "What are the subjective experiences of employees navigating changes in organisational culture due to digital transformation?" exemplifies this openness (Zhang & Chen, 2024). Such flexibility simplifies the emergence of new insights and broadens the overall analysis, revealing dimensions that might otherwise remain hidden.

Additionally, research questions should aim for complexity and depth, inviting detailed exploration rather than simplistic answers. For example, "How do the challenges managers faced influence their leadership styles and overall organisational performance?" encourages a comprehensive examination of the intricate dynamics at play (Wei et al., 2024). By posing such multifaceted questions, researchers drive deeper inquiry into the interrelated factors influencing experiences and outcomes.

As qualitative research progresses, themes emerge as fundamental concepts derived from the detailed exploration of data collected through methods such as interviews, focus groups, or observations. These themes encapsulate the diverse perspectives, experiences, and insights of participants within specific research contexts, thereby providing depth to our understanding of complex phenomena. The process of categorising themes involves meticulous analysis to discover underlying meanings and implications that quantitative measures alone may not fully reflect. For example, qualitative research builds upon quantitative findings related to leadership styles (Transformational, Transactional, and Laissez-faire) and organisational performance, exploring deeper into how these styles are perceived and experienced. Whilst quantitative analysis establishes statistical relationships, qualitative inquiry effectively investigates the more sophisticated through the voices and narratives of managers and organisational members, thus elucidating how leadership practices manifest in day-to-day organisational contexts (Canavesi & Minelli, 2022).

Moreover, themes may also emerge from the aggregation of sub-themes into broader categories, illuminating each research objective and addressing the overarching research question. Researchers typically begin with open coding, identifying significant concepts from interviews, and then engage in axial coding to examine relationships between these codes, ultimately developing cohesive themes that embody participants' experiences as related to different leadership styles.

To effectively discuss qualitative research findings, researchers should present the identified themes alongside illustrative quotes or examples from participants in order to support each theme. This discussion not only contextualises the themes within the broader literature on leadership effectiveness but also compares them with theoretical frameworks and empirical studies. Qualitative insights enrich quantitative findings by offering a deeper understanding of the mechanisms and interpersonal dynamics underlying leadership effectiveness.

In conclusion, qualitative research enhances quantitative findings by revealing the diverse perceptions and experiences of leadership styles within organisations, shedding light on how Transformational, Transactional, and Laissez-faire Leadership Styles resonate with both managers and organisational members. This integrated approach considerably deepens the understanding of effective leadership practices, informing strategies to enhance organisational performance and guiding future research directions.

11.5 Discussions of Mixed Methods Research Findings

In writing a discussion of mixed methods research findings, it is crucial to begin with a well-formulated research question capitalising on the strengths of both qualitative and quantitative methodologies. A well-crafted mixed methods research question typically seeks to explore complex phenomena by combining numerical data with rich, descriptive insights, thus enabling a comprehensive understanding of the research topic (Matović & Ovesni, 2023).

To formulate an effective mixed methods research question, researchers should consider key principles. Firstly, the question should address a specific phenomenon that requires both quantitative measurement and qualitative understanding. For instance, a pertinent study from Vietnam investigated the research question: "How do customers perceive the effectiveness of personalised service strategies, such as birthday vouchers, in enhancing their overall satisfaction with retail stores?" This question facilitates both the numerical assessment of customer satisfaction levels and the narrative exploration of their experiences with personalised service (Thai et al., 2024).

Secondly, researchers should ensure that the question promotes the integration of findings from both methods. A useful formulation could be, "In what ways do levels of customers' satisfaction scores correlate with qualitative insights on the impact of special treatment strategies across various retail environments?" This framing highlights the relationship between quantitative data and qualitative insights, allowing for a more in-depth interpretation of the findings (Schoonenboom & Johnson, 2017).

Once the research question is established, the discussion section can be structured to underline the integration of findings from both quantitative and qualitative components. Researchers should begin by summarising the quantitative results, presenting the key statistics and trends that emerge from the data. For instance, if the quantitative analysis reveals that customers who receive birthday vouchers report significantly higher levels of satisfaction, this should be clearly articulated, with supporting data.

Next, researchers should transition into the qualitative findings by connecting them to the quantitative results. This integration is vital, as it demonstrates how qualitative insights enrich the understanding of the numerical data. For example, if interviews with customers reveal that receiving a birthday voucher made them feel valued and appreciated, this context enhances the statistical correlation observed in the quantitative findings. It is essential to incorporate participant narratives and illustrative quotes throughout this section to support and expand upon the numerical data (Molina-Azorin & Guetterman, 2023).

Additionally, the discussion should address any discrepancies or unexpected findings that may arise from integrating both methods. For example, if quantitative data suggests high levels of satisfaction among customers who received special treatments, but qualitative feedback indicates some customers feel the vouchers are merely a marketing gimmick, this divergence should be analysed to understand the underlying factors contributing to these mixed perceptions. Such analysis not only strengthens the research but also provides valuable insights for practitioners (Denscombe, 2023).

Another relevant example could involve a study investigating how organisational members perceive the impact of different leadership strategies on the growth of electric vehicle (EV) manufacturers. A suitable research question might be, "How do organisational members in EV companies perceive the effectiveness of leadership strategies in driving innovation and organisational growth?" This question allows for an exploration of both numerical data on company growth rates and qualitative insights into organisational members' perceptions of levels of leadership effectiveness (Löfsten, 2017; Zumitzavan et al., 2025).

To sum up, the discussion of mixed methods research findings should thoughtfully integrate quantitative and qualitative data, providing a comprehensive narrative that articulates the complexity of the research phenomenon. By effectively bridging the two types of findings, researchers can offer a richer understanding of the topic and contribute to both academic discourse and practical applications within the management field.

Integrating quantitative and qualitative findings in the discussion section of a mixed methods research approach facilitates a comprehensive understanding of complex research questions. The discussion section synthesises the results from both approaches, emphasising their complementary nature and offering a more refined perspective on the phenomenon under investigation.

For example, quantitative analysis revealed a significant correlation between leadership styles and organisational performance measures. Transformational Leadership indicates a strong positive correlation ($r = 0.75, p < 0.001$), underscoring its substantial influence on improving levels of organisational members' motivation and organisational commitment. Similarly, Transactional Leadership demonstrated a positive correlation ($r = 0.45$, $p < 0.01$) with operational efficiency and goal attainment. Conversely, Laissez-faire Leadership was associated with a negative correlation ($r = -0.53, p < 0.001$), highlighting its detrimental effects on organisational outcomes when leadership is characterised by passivity or absence (Zumitzavan, 2011).

In contrast, qualitative findings provided profound insights into how these leadership styles are perceived and experienced within the organisation. Themes emerged from interviews and focus groups, demonstrating the transformative impact of Transformational Leadership in inspiring innovation, nurturing collaboration, and cultivating a shared vision among organisational members. For instance, the participants articulated how leaders who embody this style encourage them to transcend expectations and embrace change. One organisational member noted, "Our leader encourages us to think outside the box and provides the support we need to implement our ideas" (Genç & Karadirek, 2018).

Additionally, in an example in the retail sector, organisational members highlighted how leadership styles affected customer service experiences. For instance, a quantitative survey indicated that stores with transformational leaders scored higher in levels of customer satisfaction measures. Qualitative feedback revealed that organisational members felt more empowered to make decisions that positively influenced customers' interactions. One participant stated, "When my manager trusts us to resolve customer issues, it not only helps the customer but also boosts our confidence" (Ghaderi et al., 2024).

For an example in the healthcare sector, a mixed methods study investigated how leadership approaches influenced team dynamics and patient care quality. The quantitative results indicated that transformational leadership was correlated with improved team cohesion ($r = 0.68$, $p < 0.01$) and better patient outcomes. The qualitative data revealed that staff felt more supported and motivated when leaders actively engaged with their teams, leading to innovative practices in patient care. A nurse commented, "Our leader not only listens to our concerns but also inspires us to develop new methods for patient care, which has made a tangible difference" (Zumitzavan & Udchachone, 2014).

Furthermore, in an example from the context of change management within technology firms, research found that leadership styles significantly influenced the adoption of new processes. Quantitatively, the data indicated a strong correlation ($r = 0.62$, $p < 0.01$) between transformational leadership and employee acceptance of change initiatives. The qualitative insights underscored the importance of communication and support from leaders during transitions. Organisational members reported that clear communication about changes made them feel more secure and engaged. One software engineer noted, "When our leader clearly explains the reasons behind changes and involves us in discussions, we are more likely to embrace those changes" (Genç & Karadirek, 2018).

By intertwining these quantitative and qualitative insights, we can appreciate not only the statistical relationships but also the lived experiences that shape these dynamics. This integrative approach significantly enriches our understanding of effective leadership practices and their implications for organisational performance (Pieterse-Landman, 2012).

In summary, discussing mixed methods research findings requires a question that combines qualitative and quantitative insights, such as customers' perceptions of personalised service strategies like birthday vouchers. Quantitative analysis identifies correlations, such as transformational leadership's impact on performance whilst qualitative insights reveal employee perspectives. The end result might be the discussion noting that research shows that effective leadership enhances innovation, team cohesion, and customer satisfaction, enriching our understanding of complex phenomena in management.

11.6 Triangulation of Results

The corroboration of findings from both quantitative and qualitative approaches significantly bolsters the validity and reliability of research conclusions through triangulation. Triangulation occurs when data collected from various sources or methods converge to corroborate key findings, enhancing the overall robustness of the research. For instance, in leadership studies, quantitative research might reveal positive correlations between transformational and transactional leadership styles and organisational performance measures. A recent study indicated that organisations employing transformational leadership experienced a notable increase in organisational members' productivity, whilst transactional leadership positively influenced operational goal achievement (Kingsley-Smith et al., 2024; Zumitzavan & Kantavong, 2018). These quantitative findings can be enriched by qualitative insights that illuminate how employing these leadership styles enhance organisational culture and vary the levels of organisational members' engagement.

This integration serves a variety of purposes. Firstly, it alleviates the limitations inherent in any singular methodological approach, as qualitative insights provide context and depth to numerical data. For instance, whilst quantitative analysis may represent that organisations led by transformational leaders acquire higher performance scores, qualitative interviews with organisational members can reveal the underlying factors driving increased motivation and engagement. An organisational member might observe that transformational leaders foster an inclusive environment encouraging innovation, thus enhancing levels of morale and productivity (Garengo & Betto, 2024).

Moreover, triangulation enhances the credibility of the research by demonstrating that findings are not merely artefacts of a single method but rather reflections of a more complex reality. Aligning quantitative data, such as organisational members' performance measures, with qualitative narratives exploring organisational members' feelings and perceptions allows researchers to construct a more comprehensive picture of leadership effectiveness. For instance, a quantitative survey might reveal a significant correlation between leadership style and team performance, whilst qualitative feedback could highlight specific instances where organisational members felt empowered to contribute ideas, validating the quantitative results and providing actionable insights for managers seeking to cultivate a positive organisational culture (Ramadhana et al., 2022).

Furthermore, triangulation allows for the identification of discrepancies or unexpected findings. For example, whilst quantitative data may suggest high levels of organisational members' satisfaction in a retail sector organisation, qualitative feedback from exit interviews might reveal that organisational members feel undervalued despite their satisfaction scores. Mitigating such discrepancies can lead to deeper insights into the dynamics of organisational culture and the impact of leadership styles. In this scenario, managers can utilise this information to implement strategies that enhance organisational members' recognition and retention (Moore & Hanson, 2022).

In conclusion, the integration of quantitative and qualitative findings through triangulation strengthens research outcomes by offering a multidimensional understanding of the phenomena under investigation. This methodological approach enriches both theoretical and practical implications, providing organisations with valuable insights into how leadership styles shape organisational members' engagement and organisational success.

11.7 Generalisability and Contributions

In the sphere of mixed methods research in management discipline, the concepts of generalisability and contributions are pivotal in enhancing the overall rigour and applicability of findings. This methodological approach synergistically combines quantitative and qualitative data, thereby allowing researchers to interrogate complex phenomena with a multifaceted lens. Quantitative data typically yield broader generalisable insights by delineating statistical relationships between variables, whilst qualitative data furnish in-depth contextual perspectives elucidating the mechanisms and human dynamics underpinning these relationships.

For instance, consider a research study investigating the impact of leadership styles on organisational performance within the retail sector. A quantitative analysis may suggest a significant correlation between transformational leadership and heightened levels of organisational members' satisfaction across diverse locations (Arnett, 2020). Such findings suggest that transformational leadership practices can be extrapolated to other retail environments, offering invaluable insights for managers seeking to enhance levels of organisational members' engagement and in turn improved overall organisational performance.

Conversely, qualitative findings derived from in-depth interviews with organisational members may elucidate specific ways in which transformational leaders inspire their team members. One participant might articulate, "My manager consistently encourages us to share our ideas, fostering a sense of value and motivation" (Jordan, 2016). These qualitative insights contextualise the quantitative results, providing a deeper understanding of how and why transformational leadership impacts levels of organisational members satisfaction and organisational performance.

Furthermore, the integration of both quantitative and qualitative data can uncover unexpected patterns, significantly improving a deeper understanding of the subject matter. For instance, whilst quantitative findings may reveal a robust association between transactional leadership and operational efficiency, qualitative insights might expose that members of the organisation perceive such leadership styles as overly controlling, potentially weakening morale and stifling creativity (Sokolic et al., 2024). By tackling these intricacies, the research not only enriches the existing body of literature but also provides valuable, actionable recommendations for practitioners, enabling them to tailor leadership strategies to the unique context of their organisations.

Moreover, the contributions of mixed methods research extend to theoretical development and practical applications. By elucidating how particular leadership behaviours influence levels of organisational members' performance, researchers can inform leadership development programmes, thereby improving levels of organisational performance. For example, mixed methods research could advocate for training initiatives focused on cultivating transformational leadership skills, thereby equipping managers with the competencies required to foster and develop a high-performance organisational culture (Halliwell et al., 2022).

In conclusion, the mixed methods approach provides a robust framework for strengthening both the generalisability and impact of research. By synthesising quantitative and qualitative data, researchers can provide in-depth insights into the complex dynamics of organisations, thereby advancing theoretical discourse and informing practical implications within the field of management.

11.8 Implications for Practices

The integration of findings from mixed methods research presents several significant implications for organisational leaders and managers. Firstly, emphasising transformational and transactional leadership qualities through specialised training and development programmes can substantially improve leadership effectiveness. By equipping leaders with the skills necessary to inspire and motivate employees, organisations can foster a more engaged workforce, contributing to improved levels of job satisfaction and organisational performance. For example, training initiatives that focus on the principles of transformational leadership, such as effective communication, vision articulation, and empowerment, can nurture a positive work environment where organisational members feel supported and inspired to contribute their best efforts (Leso et al., 2023).

Additionally, organisations can benefit from implementing mentoring programmes that reinforce these leadership styles. Research indicates that leaders or managers who mentor their organisational members can create stronger bonds and foster a culture of collaboration, which ultimately leads to greater levels of team performance (Megheirkouni & Mejheirkouni, 2020). In a technology organisation, for instance, mentoring programmes that incorporate transformational leadership principles have been shown to bolster innovation by encouraging organisational members to pursue creative solutions and take initiative (Schein, 2016).

Moreover, addressing the pitfalls associated with laissez-faire leadership is crucial for mitigating its potentially adverse effects on organisational performance. Leaders or managers must recognise the importance of proactive involvement and support, particularly in environments where ambiguity can lead to confusion and disengagement among organisational members. Implementing strategies that encourage leaders to take a more active role in steering their teams, such as regular feedback sessions and performance appraisals, can significantly enhance clarity and direction within the organisation. For example, a retail manager adopting a more hands-on approach may foster stronger team dynamics, thereby improving overall customer service and operational efficiency (Natarajan, 2022).

For instance, in the healthcare sector, a study found that effective leadership significantly influenced staff morale and patient outcomes. Leaders or managers who engaged directly with their teams had a greater capacity to implement changes enhancing levels of care quality and organisational members' satisfaction (Nugroho & Wahjoedi, 2024). This demonstrates the necessity for leaders to actively participate in organisational processes to foster a culture of engagement and support.

Another relevant example comes from the hospitality industry, where research has shown that transformational leadership significantly correlates with organisational members' turnover rates. Leaders or managers who inspire, motivate, and empower their teams foster higher job satisfaction and lower turnover, which is crucial in an industry characterised by high attrition rates (Natarajan, 2022). By implementing training programmes focused on enhancing transformational leadership qualities, hotel managers can create a more engaged and stable workforce, ultimately leading to improved customer experiences and levels of organisational success.

Lastly, in the manufacturing sector, a mixed-methods study found that leadership styles directly influence organisational members' safety compliance. Transformational leaders who actively promote safety initiatives and engage organisational members in safety discussions cultivate a culture of safety, which contributes to lower accident rates (Brimhall & Palinkas, 2020). This emphasises the crucial role of leaders in not only driving operational efficiency but also ensuring a safe working environment.

In conclusion, a discussion of the implications of a mixed methods approach in this context effectively synthesises both quantitative and qualitative research findings, yielding a comprehensive understanding of leadership dynamics within organisations. By triangulating results, the research enhances the credibility and applicability of its findings, providing a strong foundation for evidence-based strategies aimed at improving organisational performance and cultivating a supportive organisational culture. Such insights are invaluable for practitioners seeking to navigate the complexities of leadership in contemporary organisational settings, ultimately contributing to sustained organisational success.

11.9 Chapter Summary

This chapter examined the process of engaging with research findings, emphasising pertinent examples from the discipline of management. It presented robust strategies for interpreting data, inferring insightful conclusions, and contextualising results within established theoretical frameworks. Furthermore, best practices for presenting findings in a coherent and impactful manner have been highlighted. By adhering to these principles, researchers can ensure that their work makes a meaningful contribution to the field of management, thereby deepening its academic and practical significance.

11.10 Questions for Future Reflection

1. Beyond simply summarising what was found, what rhetorical and analytical strategies can a researcher utilise in the discussion section to construct a compelling argument for the significance of their study's contribution to the management field?
2. A quantitative study, guided by established theory, hypothesised a strong positive relationship between a specific employee training programme and job satisfaction. However, the results show no statistically significant association (e.g., $p = 0.35$). How should the researcher discuss this null finding? Is it merely a failure to support the hypothesis, or can it be framed as a meaningful contribution to the literature?
3. In discussing qualitative findings, the chapter advises utilising illustrative quotes. How does a researcher move beyond simply using quotes as evidence (i.e., "decorating" the text) to employing them analytically to shape a sophisticated interpretation and develop a theoretical argument?
4. A mixed-methods study on a new flexible working policy finds that quantitative survey data demonstrates a significant improves in self-reported productivity. However, qualitative interviews reveal widespread feelings of isolation and burnout. In the discussion section, how can a researcher synthesise these divergent findings into a coherent and sophisticated conclusion without privileging one dataset over the other?
5. Critically distinguish between "implications for practice" and "recommendations for managers." Implementing the chapter's example of leadership styles in healthcare, provide one example of an implication and one specific, actionable recommendation that follows from it.
6. The chapter emphasises that findings should be engaged with existing literature. Imagine your research on organisational culture produces findings that partially support one major theory but also contradict a key tenet of another. How would you structure this part of your discussion to establish a sophisticated engagement with the theoretical landscape?

7. A researcher conducts a single, in-depth qualitative case study of a highly innovative tech start-up in Silicon Valley. In the discussion section, how should they address the concepts of generalisability (from a quantitative perspective) and transferability (from a qualitative perspective) to frame the applicability of their findings appropriately?
8. The chapter implicitly suggests a specific structure for the discussion (e.g., summary of findings, link to literature, implications). Explain the logical rationale for beginning the discussion with a concise summary of the key findings before launching into a comparison with other studies. What purpose does this serve for the reader?
9. How can a researcher ensure that their "suggestions for future research" are specific, insightful, and logically sourced from the limitations of their own study, rather than being generic or overly broad statements (e.g., "more research is needed")?
10. How might the focus, tone, and depth of the discussion section differ for a PhD thesis versus a practitioner-focused article in a publication such as Harvard Business Review? Discuss how the researcher would adapt their presentation of the findings and implications for each audience.

References

Alqahtani, T., Badreldin, H. A., Alrashed, M., Alshaya, A. I., Alghamdi, S. S., Bin Saleh, K., et al. (2023). The emergent role of artificial intelligence, natural learning processing, and large language models in higher education and research. *Research in social and administrative pharmacy, 19*(8), 1236–1242.

Ankeny, R. A., & Leonelli, S. (2024). Investigating research practices: How qualitative methods enhance philosophical understandings of science. *Qualitative Psychology, 11*(2), 247.

Arnett, J. (2020). *The Relationship between transformational leadership styles and employee satisfaction for manufacturing management in Northeast Ohio: A quantitative correlational study*. University of Phoenix.

Avolio, B. J., & Drummey, K. C. (2023). Building leadership service academies to institutionalize a strategic leadership development focus. *Journal of Leadership & Organizational Studies, 30*(2), 137–154.

Brimhall, K. C., & Palinkas, L. (2020). Using mixed methods to uncover inclusive leader behaviors: A promising approach for improving employee and organizational outcomes. *Journal of Leadership & Organizational Studies, 27*(4), 357–375. https://doi.org/10.1177/1548051820936286

Canavesi, A., & Minelli, E. (2022). Servant leadership and employee engagement: A qualitative study. *Employee Responsibilities and Rights Journal, 34*(4), 413–435. https://doi.org/10.1007/s10672-021-09389-9

Denscombe, M. (2023). *The good research guide: For small-scale social research projects* (7th ed.). Open University Press.

Garengo, P., & Betto, F. (2024). The role of organisational culture and leadership style in performance measurement and management: A longitudinal case study. *Production Planning & Control, 35*(2), 151–169. https://doi.org/10.1080/09537287.2022.2058431

Genç, K. Y., & Karadirek, G. (2018). The impact of leadership on customers satisfaction. *Vadyba Journal of Management, 32*(1), 39–47.

Ghaderi, Z., Omidvar, M. S., Hosseini, S., & Hall, C. M. (2024). Corporate social responsibility, customer satisfaction, and trust in the restaurant industry. *Journal of Foodservice Business Research*, 1–32. https://doi.org/10.1080/15378020.2024.2318523

Halliwell, P. R., Mitchell, R. J., & Boyle, B. (2022). Leadership coaching's efficacy and effect mechanisms–a mixed-methods study. *Coaching: An International Journal of Theory, Research and Practice, 15*(1), 43–59. https://doi.org/10.1080/17521882.2021.1884110

Jordan, D. E. (2016). *Examining the relationship between perceived leadership behaviors and employee engagement among part-time retail employees.* ProQuest One Academic. https://www.proquest.com/dissertations-theses/examining-relationship-between-perceived/docview/1810727801/se-2

Jung, J. H., Yoo, J. J., & Arnold, T. J. (2021). The influence of a retail store manager in developing frontline employee brand relationship, service performance and customer loyalty. *Journal of Business Research, 122*, 362–372. https://doi.org/10.1016/j.jbusres.2020.09.010

Kingsley-Smith, H., Farrier, C. E., Foran, D., Kotze, K., Mahtani, K., Short, S., et al. (2024). Leadership development programmes in healthcare research: A systematic review, meta-analysis and meta-aggregation. *BMJ Leader, 8*(4), 283–292. https://doi.org/10.1136/leader-2024-000976

Leso, B. H., Cortimiglia, M. N., & Ghezzi, A. (2023). The contribution of organizational culture, structure, and leadership factors in the digital transformation of SMEs: A mixed-methods approach. *Cognition, Technology & Work, 25*(1), 151–179. https://doi.org/10.1007/s10111-022-00714-2

Löfsten, H. (2017). Innovation performance and organisational capabilities in the Swedish hybrid electric vehicle technology: A study of 40 SMEs. *International Journal of Technology Management & Sustainable Development, 16*(1), 49–69. https://doi.org/10.1386/tmsd.16.1.49_1

Matović, N., & Ovesni, K. (2023). Interaction of quantitative and qualitative methodology in mixed methods research: Integration and/or combination. *International Journal of Social Research Methodology, 26*(1), 51–65. https://doi.org/10.1080/13645579.2021.1964857

Megheirkouni, M., & Mejheirkouni, A. (2020). Leadership development trends and challenges in the twenty-first century: Rethinking the priorities. *Journal of Management Development, 39*(1), 97–124. https://doi.org/10.1108/JMD-04-2019-0114

Michie, J., & Zumitzavan, V. (2016). The impact of 'learning'and 'leadership'management styles on organizational outcomes: a study of tyre firms in Thailand. In Leadership in the Asia Pacific (pp. 165-188). Routledge.

Molina-Azorin, J. F., & Guetterman, T. C. (2023). Special issues on mixed methods research: Expanding the use of mixed methods in disciplines. *Journal of Mixed Methods Research, 17*(3), 234–242. https://doi.org/10.1177/15586898231183257

Moore, J. R., & Hanson, W. (2022). Improving leader effectiveness: Impact on employee engagement and retention. *Journal of Management Development, 41*(7/8), 450–468. https://doi.org/10.1108/JMD-02-2021-0041

Natarajan, D. (2022). *A study of the relationship between transformational leadership, transactional leadership, and employee job satisfaction in the manufacturing sector* (Master's thesis, Department of Sociology and Social Work, Christ (Deemed to be University)). https://doi.org/10.2139/ssrn.4436757

Nguyen, M. A. T., Yu, M. M., & Lirn, T. C. (2022). Revenue efficiency across airline business models: A bootstrap non-convex meta-frontier approach. *Transport Policy, 117*, 108–117. https://doi.org/10.1016/j.tranpol.2022.01.007

Nugroho, A. D., & Wahjoedi, T. (2024). The influence of the work environment and communication on work morale and its impact on employee performance. *World Journal of Advanced Research and Reviews, 21*(3), 2534–2546. https://doi.org/10.30574/wjarr.2024.21.3.0922

Olazo, D. B. (2023). Marketing competency, marketing innovation and sustainable competitive advantage of small and medium enterprises (SMEs): A mixed-method analysis. *Asia Pacific*

Journal of Marketing and Logistics, 35(4), 890–907. https://doi.org/10.1108/APJML-01-2022-0050

Pieterse-Landman, E. (2012). *The relationship between transformational leadership, employee engagement, job characteristics and intention to quit* (Doctoral dissertation, Stellenbosch: Stellenbosch University).

Ramadhana, M. O., Adioetomo, S. M., Irbansyah, B. M., & Hartijasti, Y. M. (2022). Building acquisition management capability to improve firm performance in acquisitions: An ASEAN context. *International Journal of Asian Business and Information Management (IJABIM), 13*(2), 1–20. https://doi.org/10.4018/IJABIM.289650

Richards, T. J. (2006). Sales by multi-product retailers. *Managerial and decision economics, 27*(4), 261–277. https://doi.org/10.1002/mde.1251

Schein, E. H. (2016). *Organizational culture and leadership* (5th ed.). Jossey-Bass.

Schoonenboom, J., & Johnson, R. B. (2017). How to construct a mixed methods research design. *Kölner Zeitschrift für Soziologie und Sozialpsychologie, 69*(Suppl 2), 107–131. https://doi.org/10.1007/s11577-017-0454-1

Shao, Z., Li, X., Luo, Y., & Benitez, J. (2024). The differential impacts of top management support and transformational supervisory leadership on employees' digital performance. *European Journal of Information Systems, 33*(3), 334–360. https://doi.org/10.1080/0960085X.2022.2147456

Shuck, M. B., Rocco, T. S., & Albornoz, C. A. (2011). Exploring employee engagement from the employee perspective: Implications for HRD. *Journal of European Industrial Training, 35*(4), 300–325. https://doi.org/10.1108/03090591111128306

Sokolic, D., Croitoru, G., Florea, N. V., Robescu, V. O., & Cosac, A. (2024). The Effect of leadership styles on employee motivation and organizational performance in public sector organizations. *Valahian Journal of Economic Studies, 15*(1), 53–72. https://doi.org/10.2478/vjes-2024-0005

Thai, N. V., Trang, B. T. Q., Quy, N. L. D., Huong, N. T. Q., & Huyen, V. T. T. (2024). Factors affecting the successful implementation of customer relationship management in 3-to-5-star hotels in Viet Nam. *Cogent Social Sciences, 10*(1), 2316062.

Verma, R., Verma, S., & Abhishek, K. (2024). *Research methodology*. Publishing.

Wei, X., Liao, H., Zhang, Z. X., Dong, Y., & Li, N. (2024). Does passion matter for team innovation? The conditional indirect effects of team harmonious versus obsessive passion via team reflexivity. *Personnel Psychology, 77*(2), 891–916. https://doi.org/10.1111/peps.12584

Zaibaf, M., Taherikia, F., & Fakharian, M. (2013). Effect of perceived service quality on customer satisfaction in hospitality industry: Gronroos' service quality model development. *Journal of Hospitality Marketing & Management, 22*(5), 490–504. https://doi.org/10.1080/19368623.2012.670893

Zhang, J., & Chen, Z. (2024). Exploring human resource management digital transformation in the digital age. *Journal of the Knowledge Economy, 15*(1), 1482–1498. https://doi.org/10.1007/s13132-023-01214-y

Zumitzavan, V. (2011). *The impact of managers' learning styles and leadership styles on the effectiveness of their organisations: A case study from small retail tyre companies in Thailand* (Doctoral dissertation, University of Birmingham).

Zumitzavan, V., & Udchachone, S. (2014, February). The influence of leadership styles on organisational performance mediated by organisational innovation: A case study of the hospitality industry in Thailand. In International Conference on Economics, Management and Development (pp. 45-52).

Zumitzavan, V. (2022). Practical strategy for maintaining organisational performance in the hospitality industry of Thailand. *International Journal of Management Practice, 15*(1), 108–130. https://doi.org/10.1504/IJMP.2022.119923

Zumitzavan, V., & Kantavong, P. (2018). Increasing organisational success through management styles of managers in housing development industry. *Panyapiwat Journal, 10*, 110–123.

Zumitzavan, V., & Udchachone, S. (2014). The impact of different styles of leadership and levels of organisational innovation on organisational performance: A case of hospitality industry in Thailand. *WSEAS Transactions on Business and Economics, 11*(1), 272–282.

Zumitzavan, V., Prachumrasee, K., & Pathak, S. (2025). Transformational leadership cultivating innovation and transparency in local government organisations, Thailand. *Journal of Open Innovation: Technology, Market, and Complexity*, 100626.

Chapter 12
Recommendations and Implications

12.1 Introduction

This section illustrates best practices in the final part of management research, the recommendations and implications section, emphasising theoretical, practical, and actionable implications. It proposes to offer guidance on recommendations for practitioners and researchers, highlighting the broader impact on the discipline of management. The section must start with a clear introduction that articulates its purpose in relation to the research question and objectives, before addressing the contributions of the research, both theoretical and practical, and its actionable insights.

12.2 The Artful Science of Crafting Recommendations and Implications

Whilst the dynamic relationship between the 'science' of systematic process and the 'art' of human interpretation exists throughout the research journey, it is in the final formulation of recommendations and implications that this artful science reaches its pinnacle. This final stage necessitates more than logical deduction; it demands an imaginative leap to change empirical findings into a compelling vision for the future of theory and practice. The 'art' of this process is embodied in the researcher's role as the primary interpretive instrument. It is the creative act of synthesising disparate data into a coherent narrative that definitively answers the fundamental "so what?" question. This calls for a capacity for holistic thinking and a capability to see beyond the data, interpreting complex findings into meaningful contributions that can inspire action and advance knowledge (Leavy, 2014).

At the same time, the 'science' supporting this artful process is undertaking a significant evolution with the integration of AI. Generative AI tools can serve as powerful strategic partners in this final stage. By rapidly synthesising massive

© The Author(s), under exclusive license to Springer Nature Singapore Pte Ltd. 2025

V. Zumitzavan, *Social Science Methodologies for Management Research*,
https://doi.org/10.1007/978-981-95-4318-2_12

academic and industry literature, these systems can help researchers recognise the most important theoretical gaps their work addresses or contextualise their practical recommendations against emerging global trends (Mabaso & Manuel, 2024). By suggesting alternative interpretations or challenging a researcher's inherent biases, AI can act as a 'critical friend' to improve the rigour and creativity of the final argument (Christou, 2024).

However, these technological advancements require critical engagement. AI lacks the deep contextual, cultural, and ethical understanding required to formulate truly wise and actionable recommendations for intricate human phenomena in management (Danry, 2023). The ultimate responsibility for critical evaluation, contextualisation, and the crafting of the final narrative remains a uniquely human effort. Thus, the most impactful recommendations arise from a sophisticated synergy: the researcher's creative interpretation and deep contextual understanding—the 'art'—is augmented and confronted by the systematic power and novel capabilities of AI—the 'evolving science', promising not just findings, but genuine foresight and wisdom.

12.3 Recommendations and Implications

In constructing the recommendations and implications section of a management research study, it is crucial to commence by distinguishing between academic and practical recommendations. Academic recommendations endeavour to advance the body of knowledge within the field, bridging the gaps establishing based on the existing literature, filling gaps identified in the existing literature, and offering insights that either refine existing theoretical frameworks or propose new avenues for scholarly inquiry.

By distinguishing between academic, practical, and actionable implications, the research provides valuable insights for both scholars and practitioners. Academic implications intend to expand theoretical knowledge, providing new perspectives that may refine existing frameworks or open avenues for future research. Conversely, practical implications concentrate on contributing to actionable strategies and recommendations for organisations to enhance their management practices and improve organisational performance. Whilst academic implications contribute to the development of knowledge and theory, practical implications translate the research findings into real-world solutions, and actionable implications establish how the insights from research can be implemented in practice. The following discussion highlights both the academic and practical contributions of the example studies, emphasising how they complement and inform each other.

12.3.1 Academic Implications

The academic implications of research are primarily concerned with advancing theoretical understanding and offering new avenues for scholarly exploration. For example, research into the impact of ethical leadership on organisational morale offers an opportunity for scholars to investigate deeper into the underlying mechanisms by which ethical leadership shapes workplace behaviour. This would not only improve the theoretical discourse surrounding organisational ethics but also potentially polish existing conceptual frameworks (Lai et al., 2020).

As examined by Zumitzavan (2011), a research study of a tyre firm in Thailand affirmed that the Pragmatist and Reflector learning styles, along with Transformational and Transactional Leadership styles, are the most crucial influences on organisational success. This research addressed existing gaps in the literature, emphasising the strengthening roles of learning and leadership styles in organisational performance (Bass et al., 1996; Honey & Mumford, 2006).

Similarly, Zumitzavan (2020) established the interplay between learning styles, brand management, and organisational performance in the Thai housing estate industry. The research findings proved that brand management mediates the positive association between learning styles and performance, validating gaps highlighted by Chris and Donald (2006) and Tosti and Herbst (2009). The research findings indicated that the Pragmatist and Reflector learning styles benefit managers, encouraging enhanced decision-making, organisational members' engagement, and problem-solving through data analysis before action.

In the same context, research examining remote working practices could pave the way for further inquiry into the long-term effects of hybrid work models on levels of organisational productivity and corporate culture, thus adding nuance to the ongoing conversation around work-life balance, flexibility, and the evolving nature of the workplace (Adesegha, 2024).

In addition, research on transformational leadership's role in enhancing team performance provides a valuable opportunity to enhance leadership theories by emphasising the necessity for leaders to adopt their styles to the dynamic and evolving nature of modern organisations (van der Westhuizen et al., 2012; Zumitzavan et al., 2025). Recent research has also distinguished gaps in our understanding of the impact of digital transformation on leadership effectiveness, urging scholars to reconsider current leadership paradigms in the light of the technological revolution and the unique challenges it presents to organisational leadership (Choudhury et al., 2021).

Lastly, the theoretical implications extend to the realm of learning organisations, with research highlighting the essential role of continuous training and development in bolstering a culture of learning. These insights encourage further scholarly investigation into how organisations can build and sustain such cultures in increasingly competitive environments (Bilderback, 2024).

12.3.2 Practical Implications

From a practical standpoint, the research findings in the examples offer concrete recommendations for organisations seeking to improve management practices, organisational members' engagement, and organisational performance. Organisations could greatly gain from implementing a balanced approach, integrating both transformational and transactional leadership styles. This would comprise cultivating a shared vision, offering targeted mentorship, and empowering organisational members to take ownership of their roles and responsibilities.

For example, organisations could implement mentorship programmes that pair less experienced organisational members with experienced leaders or managers, thereby enabling the transfer of knowledge and bolstering a deeper sense of engagement (Pattali et al., 2024).

For instance, Zumitzavan (2011) scrutinised the connection between learning styles, leadership styles, and organisational performance, finding a positive connection between these variables, with transformational and transactional leadership acting as mediators. The research findings suggested that managers adopt these leadership styles to bolster learning and skill development, including boosting levels of organisational members' confidence, offering feedback, encouraging critical thinking, and distinguishing achievements with suitable rewards. The research underscored the importance of these strategies in cultivating motivation and performance. These concrete insights provide valuable implications for future academic research, guiding further exploration into how leadership styles can be utilised to optimise organisational performance.

In addition, as analysed by Zumitzavan (2020), a relationship exists between learning styles, brand management, and organisational performance. Based on the research findings, he noted that in order to fully obtain the benefits of the research findings, managers should participate in regular communication with organisational members, remain well-informed about market trends, delegate authority effectively, and allocate tasks properly to increase levels of productivity and minimise errors. Moreover, managers must prioritise cost-effective training programmes to strengthen their leadership capability and their ability to facilitate knowledge sharing within the organisation.

Additionally, investing in comprehensive training programmes addressing both technical and soft skills customised to organisational members' specific roles is vital. The research suggests that organisational members engaging in such training initiatives establish heightened task proficiency and improved interpersonal skills, which in turn positively affect levels of organisational performance (Lai et al., 2020).

Furthermore, organisations should focus on cultivating a culture of continuous learning. By nurturing environments that reassure ongoing professional development, organisations can not only improve individual performance but also promote collective productivity. Research indicates that organisational members perceiving a supportive learning environment tend to engage in training, which subsequently leads to greater levels of performance across the organisation (Vito & Sethi, 2020). Regular assessment and feedback mechanisms are also pivotal to guaranteeing the efficacy of training programmes. By continuously refining training content and delivery based on organisational members' feedback, organisations can maintain alignment with organisational needs whilst promoting organisational members' ownership over their professional development (van Assen, 2021).

However, challenges may arise, particularly resistance from senior organisational members with extensive experience. To address this, organisations should implement clear communication strategies and effective change management processes. Involving organisational members in the design and implementation of training initiatives, whilst demonstrating the direct benefits to their job performance, can mitigate resistance and foster greater commitment to the training procedure (Evans & Martin, 2024).

Another challenge organisations may encounter is the allocation of resources, particularly in terms of time and budget for training programmes. However, the long-term benefits of enhanced productivity, as indicated by the research, typically outweigh the initial investment. Therefore, management should emphasise the return on investment (ROI) of such training initiatives, demonstrating how they contribute to overall organisational performance (Srimannarayana, 2017).

Finally, the research underlines the significance of integrating both transformational and transactional leadership to improve management practices, levels of organisational members' engagement, and organisational performance. It establishes the basis for new mentorship programmes and tailored training to nurture skills and bolster a supportive learning environment. In addition, it notes that continuous feedback and communications are indispensable for accomplishing challenges like resistance and resource restrictions.

12.3.3 From Insight to Action

Apart from academic and practical implications, the research findings must be interpreted into actionable phases. Impactful and meaningful recommendations must be offered to empower audiences or readers so that they can fully maximise the insights from the research (Saunders et al., 2024).

For example, as proposed by Zumitzavan (2011) and Zumitzavan et al. (2025), whilst transformational leadership is generally renowned for its positive impact on organisational performance, its practical implementation in profit-driven enterprises is fraught with complexities. A fundamental impediment is institutional resistance to change, particularly within hierarchical and bureaucratic organisational structures. Several traditional organisations, such as housing estate development companies and local administrative organisations, operate within rigid frameworks highlighting centralised authority and procedural adherence. Senior management may exhibit a reluctance to delegating authority or endorsing participatory leadership models because of apprehensions regarding efficiency, accountability, and structural coherence. For instance, in large-scale real estate companies, project managers prone to autocratic decision-making may struggle to embrace collaborative leadership, thereby stalling transformative initiatives. To avoid such resistance, organisations must institutionalise comprehensive leadership development programmes that progressively recalibrate managerial mindsets towards empowerment and inclusivity. Establishing change champions within key departments can further encourage leadership transformation by representing the tangible advantages of a decentralised leadership style.

A further constraint pertains to increased rates of organisational members' turnover, predominantly noticeable in high-demand sectors such as healthcare and high-technology industries. Transformational leadership establishes its efficacy on long-term engagement and workforce stability, yet high attrition rates can hinder leadership continuity and diminish the overall levels of effectiveness of leadership initiatives. For example, as studied by Chong and Zainal (2024) in high-technology companies, software engineers and data scientists frequently migrate across organisations in pursuit of superior compensation and career progression, hence disrupting leadership pipelines. To lessen this challenge, organisations may need to design high-intensity, short-duration leadership development modules offering substantial leadership exposure within condensed timeframes, ensuring that organisational members derive leadership insights irrespective of their occupation. Simultaneously, nurturing an environment encouraging to internal career progression and mentorship can improve rates of organisational members' retention, strengthening the organisation's leadership framework over the long term.

In addition, financial and resource constraints present significant challenges to the widespread adoption of transformational leadership, particularly in industries where cost reduction is imperative. Healthcare sector and local administrative organisations, for example, often operate under strict fiscal restrictions, rendering substantial investment in leadership development infeasible. A public hospital, for example, may prioritise spending on clinical competency and operational productivity over leadership training, regardless of the long-term organisational benefits of fostering transformational leadership. In such cases, assimilating leadership training within existing professional development frameworks can provide a practical alternative. Facilitating digital learning platforms, AI-assisted leadership assessments, and virtual mentoring programmes can further lessen financial burdens whilst guaranteeing comprehensive leadership development (Choi et al., 2016; Zumitzavan et al., 2025).

Next, a critical consideration is the dichotomy between short-term operational imperatives and long-term leadership development objectives. Industries characterised by high-intensity work environments, such as the real estate development and healthcare industries, often prioritise immediate performance measures over leadership mentorship. A property development conglomerate, for example, may focus essentially on rigorous project milestones and revenue benchmarks, therefore sidelining leadership development initiatives (Zumitzavan, 2020).

In a similar context, a healthcare institution may encounter operational exigencies that impede extensive leadership training for administrators and department heads. To address this challenge, organisations should incorporate leadership development into day-to-day business activities, hence assuring seamless integration. Strategies such as incorporating leadership interview sessions into post-project reviews, embedding reflective leadership discussions within executive conferences, and integrating leadership coaching into structured performance assessments can facilitate leadership growth without undermining operational priorities (Zumitzavan & Udchachone, 2014).

As contemporary organisations cope with an era of rapid technological evolution, changing workforce dynamics, and growing global competition, the imperative for transformational leadership has never been more noticeable. Across industries such as high-technology, real estate development, healthcare, and local administrative governance, leaders who champion strategic foresight, organisational agility, and workforce empowerment are best positioned to drive sustainable success. Whilst this section underlines the empirical benefits of transformational leadership, its true impact can only be realised through concerted organisational commitment and proactive strategic implementation.

Looking towards the future, transformational leadership must adapt in alignment with three critical dimensions: technological integration, sustainability imperatives, and workforce resilience. Organisations within the high-technology sector must ensure that leadership frameworks are skilful at steering AI-driven decision-making landscapes whilst simultaneously bolstering creativity and ethical responsibility. In the housing estate development sector, leadership must incorporate sustainability-driven governance, ensuring that urban expansion aligns with both ecological and societal well-being imperatives (Zumitzavan, 2020; Zumitzavan & Kantavong, 2018). In healthcare, transformational leadership must prioritise workforce sustainability, minimising occupational burnout in healthcare professionals whilst upholding exemplary patient care standards (Zumitzavan, 2014; Zumitzavan & Michie, 2015). In the same way, local administrative entities must embed leadership excellence within public governance, ensuring transparent decision-making, enhanced civic engagement, and long-term institutional credibility.

To accelerate the widespread implementation of transformational leadership, senior management, policymakers, and academic researchers must participate in a synergistic endeavour to institutionalise leadership superiority. Top management must recalibrate their organisational philosophies to prioritise leadership development not as a supplementary pursuit but as a strategic organisational cornerstone. For example, leading technology organisations could compete with the leadership academies established by global multinationals such as Google and Microsoft, thereby nurturing a robust internal leadership pipeline. Regulatory organisations and industry associations must likewise champion the founding of sector-wide leadership accreditation standards, guaranteeing standardisation and excellence in leadership practices. For example, national healthcare regulatory agencies could present mandatory leadership accreditation programmes for hospital administrators, bolstering leadership proficiency alongside clinical and operational expertise. In addition, scholars must continue to interrogate the evolving intersections between transformational leadership and emergent industry dynamics, such as the impact of

AI-driven leadership augmentation and the role of transformational leadership in lessening workforce mental health deterioration in high-pressure industries (Zumitzavan, 2014).

In conclusion, transformational leadership establishes a fundamental pillar upon which organisations can foster continuing competitiveness and institutional resilience. Whilst engaging challenges persist, organisations currently prioritising leadership transformation will reap substantial strategic advantages in the future. The demand for action is unequivocal—top management, corporate leaders, policymakers, and academic institutions must converge to embed leadership excellence as the bedrock principle of organisational strategies, thereby assuring that transformational leadership remains a driver for innovation, resilience, and sustainable organisational improvement

12.4 Limitations and Recommendations for Future Research

A crucial aspect of any research study is the section on limitations and suggestions for future research. In this section, it is important to acknowledge the key limitations encountered as part of the research process, concerning factors such as sample size, research methodology, or data collection methods. Transparency regarding these limitations can strengthen the validity of the findings.

A common limitation relates to time and budget constraints. If such challenges were encountered throughout the study, it is advisable to discuss alternative approaches that could mitigate these restrictions. For instance, one limitation of the exemplar research is the relatively small sample size of respondents. Future studies with broader and more diverse samples would offer a more comprehensive understanding of the relationship between leadership styles and organisational members' motivation (Fang & Yu, 2023).

Moreover, a limitation could arise from a reliance on self-reported data, which may not accurately reflect actual behaviours or outcomes. As emphasised by Singh and Ramdeo (2020), "Self-reported measures are susceptible to bias, necessitating a triangulation of data sources for more robust findings". In instances where respondents are asked to evaluate the financial performance of their organisation, it is advisable for researchers to incorporate additional data sources, such as return on investment (ROI), return on assets (ROA), return on equity (ROE), or net profit margins, in order to corroborate self-reported measures. This multi-source approach not only enhances the validity of the findings but also provides a more comprehensive view of organisational performance, allowing for a clearer understanding of the relationships under investigation (Fang et al., 2023). By triangulating qualitative assessments with quantitative financial metrics, researchers can mitigate potential biases and offer a more insightful analysis of the impacts of leadership styles on organisational performance. In a similar way, in management research, self-reported data is frequently favoured for its practical compensations, primarily its cost-effectiveness and the effortlessness with which it can be collected.

Nevertheless, the inherent biases related to this technique warrant careful consideration. Two of the most significant biases that may distort the validity of the findings are social desirability bias and recall bias. Social desirability bias arises when participants provide responses they believe may be viewed positively by others, rather than providing a truthful account of their actions or attitudes. This bias is particularly pervasive in management studies where respondents, such as leaders or organisational members, may exaggerate their competencies or positive behaviours in order to appear more competent or successful. For instance, a study scrutinising levels of leadership effectiveness might motivate managers to positively appraise their own leadership styles. In such cases, managers may be inclined to present themselves as representing ideal leadership traits, such as transformational leadership, even if their actual behaviours fall short. This can result in an inflated opinion of the prevalence and effectiveness of transformational leadership within the organisation; thus, this may skew the research findings (Sarwar et al., 2020).

Moreover, recall bias offers a further challenge, predominantly in studies dependent upon participants' recollections of past events or behaviours. The passage of time and the inherent selectivity of memory suggest that participants may imprecisely remembrance or emphasise certain experiences over others. In the contexts of organisational studies, this is often observed when organisational members are asked to reflect on past leadership decisions or organisational changes. For example, organisational members' opinions of a leadership transition may be affected by their current attitudes or experiences, contributing to a retrospective evaluation that favours either positive or negative aspects suspiciously. This selective recall can distort the overall assessment of a leadership change, as individuals may highlight either the beneficial or detrimental effects, dependent upon their present levels of satisfaction.

To mitigate these biases, researchers are recommended to utilise a multi-method approach comprising self-reported data with objective indicators, such as performance measures or third-party assessments or peer-reviews. In addition, integrating anonymous surveys can help alleviate social desirability bias, as respondents may feel less compelled to answer in socially satisfactory manners. By triangulating data from multiple sources, researchers can cross-verify the information and attain a more balanced, precise understanding of the phenomena under examination (Sarwar et al., 2020). Such endeavours not only enhance the robustness of the findings but also contribute to the credibility and validity of the research, meaning that the conclusions drawn are reflective of genuine phenomena rather than impacted by cognitive biases.

Moreover, researcher bias is a significant consideration in any research, principally in qualitative research, where the researcher's perspectives and assumptions can directly influence the research process. This bias may influence how data is interpreted, how conclusions are drawn, and even which aspects of the data are highlighted. For instance, in a management research project on levels of leadership effectiveness, a researcher with a robust belief in the values of transformational leadership might be more persuaded to interpret data in a manner aligning with this view, theoretically overlooking research findings challenging it.

To minimise this influence, researchers ought to take part in reflexivity, continually reflecting on how their own beliefs, experiences, and backgrounds may shape their interpretations of the data. In addition, utilising researcher triangulation, where multiple researchers independently analyse the same data, can help to lessen the influence of individual bias. Also, peer review processes can provide invaluable external perspectives, guaranteeing that research findings are more robust and not excessively dominated by a single researcher's personal perspectives. Hence, these measures could help improve the reliability and objectivity of the research, enabling a more complex and credible analysis.

Suggesting directions for future research is equally important. This may involve highlighting areas for further investigation that emerge from the gaps and questions identified in the research. For example, with regard to research methodology, one could recommend the incorporation of additional methods, such as qualitative approaches, mixed methods, or longitudinal studies. These methodologies can deepen the understanding of complex relationships within the data (Hitt et al., 2024).

More elaborately, researchers should consider longitudinal studies. The value of longitudinal research in the field of leadership cannot be exaggerated, particularly when taking into account the dynamic and frequently unpredictable nature of modern organisational surroundings. Leadership effectiveness is not a stationary phenomenon; it changes over time, influenced by both internal and external drivers. Longitudinal studies, which track changes over prolonged periods, offer critical insights into how leadership styles and effectiveness vary in response to organisational changes, such as restructuring, mergers, or external surprises such as global crises, like the COVID-19 pandemic. In such turbulent contexts, leadership effectiveness is often confirmed, as leaders or managers must develop to new challenges, recalibrate strategies, and manage shifting organisational priorities. For instance, during a merger, the leadership approach may need to shift to a more transactional style to ensure operational stability or to a more transformational leadership to unite and motivate a different workforce. Longitudinal research can track how these shifts in leadership impact the overall organisational performance and morale of the organisation over time, offering valuable data on the longer-term outcomes of leadership decisions.

Moreover, one of the most fruitful areas for longitudinal studies comprises leadership transitions, predominantly at the level of top management. Leadership changes, such as a new CEO or department head, can have profound implications for levels of organisational performance and organisational members' engagement. A change in leadership can cause changes in organisational culture, organisational strategy, and levels of organisational members' morale, all of which evolve over time. For example, a new CEO might present a more innovative, risk-taking approach, which could initially disrupt procedures but may finally lead to improved organisational performance. On the other hand, leadership transitions can also bring about periods of uncertainty or disengagement if not accomplished effectively. Longitudinal studies examining these transitions can offer critical insights into how different leadership changes impact levels of organisational members' commitment, satisfaction, and productivity, as well as the broader strategic direction of the organisation. Recommended research could explore whether these transitions distribute a temporary dip in performance or a longer-term transformation in organisational culture, offering invaluable lessons on managing leadership changes for optimal outcomes.

By uniting these two areas—tracking leadership effectiveness over time and analysing the influence of leadership transitions—longitudinal studies can offer a more complicated understanding of how leadership impacts levels of organisational success. Such studies would offer evidence on the long-term effects of leadership decisions, serving organisations to better prepare for leadership changes and to accomplish leadership transitions more strategically. The insights obtain from such research could inform leadership development programmes, succession planning, and crisis management strategies, ultimately contributing to more effective leadership and enhanced organisational resilience in the face of ongoing change.

Furthermore, it may be beneficial to identify influential variables that could be integrated into the conceptual framework for future studies. For example, future studies could probe the long-term effects of various leadership styles on organisational performance and consider additional contextual variables that might influence these relationships. Comparative research across different industries and cultures could also result in a more sophisticated understanding (Tahir, 2015).

Another consideration for future research could comprise examining influential variables such as the role of emotional intelligence in leadership effectiveness. As noted by Kim and Kim (2017), exploring how emotional intelligence interacts with different leadership styles could provide insights into enhancing team dynamics and performance.

Additionally, future research could investigate the influence of remote work on leadership styles. As highlighted by Neufeld, Wan, and Fang (2010), given the increasing prevalence of hybrid work models, analysing how leadership styles adapt in remote environments could be insightful.

Moreover, upcoming studies may wish to explore the ramifications of diversity and inclusion initiatives on leadership efficacy. As Gomez and Bernet (2019) contend, assessing the performance of diverse leadership teams in comparison to their homogeneous counterparts could generate significant insights into organisational performance.

As an example, Zumitzavan (2011) scrutinised the relationship between learning, leadership styles, and organisational performance in the Thai tyre industry, highlighting that research findings may be context-specific. Given that the study was concentrated exclusively on Thailand, future research should exercise caution when implementing these research findings in different areas, with different cultures or beliefs. To enhance the generalisability of the results, it would be advantageous for future studies to replicate this research method, compare regional differences, and identify the unique drivers leading to improvements in organisational performance across various industries. This approach could yield valuable insights into how contextual variations influence the effectiveness of leadership and learning strategies in enhancing organisational performance.

More specifically, the size and structure of an organisation can profoundly affect leadership dynamics. Small startups and large corporations frequently organise under massively different organisational structures, influencing the application of leadership styles in practice. In small start-ups, leaders or managers typically embrace participative, transformational, or even laissez-faire leadership styles because of the limited organisational resources, informal organisational structures, and fast-paced nature of these organisations. Startup environments necessitate flexibility, adaptability, and hands-on leadership, with leaders frequently engaging with organisational members at all levels in order to drive the organisational vision forward. Consequently, a transformational leadership is frequently most effective, as it is one where leaders or managers encourage and motivate organisational members to share in the vision, innovate, and take risks.

For instance, in a small tech startup, the CEO may implement a transformational leadership style by engaging the team in brainstorming sessions, encouraging creative solutions, and giving employees the autonomy to contribute to strategic decisions. This hands-on, inclusive leadership style is well-suited to startup surroundings, where organisational members are expected to take initiative and where flexibility and creativity are paramount.

However, in large corporations, leadership dynamics are generally more formalised, hierarchical, and structured because of the size of the organisation and the complexity of its operations. In these cases, leadership is more likely to employ more transactional or bureaucratic models, with a strong concentration on achieving operational efficiency, reaching key performance indicators (KPIs), and guaranteeing that organisational members adhere to organisations' policies and procedures.

For example, the leader or manager of a multinational corporation, such as a global financial institution, may adopt a transactional leadership style, where organisational members are encouraged by rewards and performance-based incentives, and where performance is consistently monitored through formal evaluation systems. The leaders' or managers' roles are often concentrated on upholding operational stability and achieving organisational goals, with decision-making being more centralised and well-defined because of the large scale of operations.

The differences between leadership in small startups and large corporations underline the significance of context when considering leadership models. The agile, innovative environment of a small startup, where leaders are closely involved in all aspects of the business, is very different from the structured, formal environment of a large corporation, where a more hierarchical leadership structure and established procedures are required to organise the intricacy of operations.

Therefore, research recommendations should be cautious in generalising findings across organisations of varying sizes. Leadership theories and practices that work effectively in startups may not be as applicable to large, bureaucratic organisations. Researchers should ensure that they consider the size, structure, and operational context of organisations when nurturing leadership models and avoid one-size-fits-all assumptions.

The limitations section could also highlight that it would also be prudent for future researchers to consider further variables encountered during the research process, whether through the literature review or data collection. For instance, as highlighted by Bel (2010) and Zumitzavan and Udchachone (2014), it can be suggested that different types of organisations may implement varying extents of organisational innovation. Therefore, future research could gain from including the varying degrees and types of organisational innovation as independent variables, thereby facilitating a deeper understanding of how these factors can improve levels of organisational performance.

More specifically, leadership styles can differ significantly between the public and private sectors, determined by variations in organisational objectives, stakeholder expectations, and organisational performance measures. Public sector organisations, such as government departments or public health institutions, are frequently led by the demand for accountability, equity, and transparency (Zumitzavan et al., 2025). Consequently, leadership in these sectors frequently adapts more transactional styles, allocating a significant prominence to adherence to rules, regulations, and established procedures. Leaders or managers within the public sector may focus on maintaining stability, ensuring alignment with public service goals, and prioritising compliance over innovation or flexibility. For example, a transactional leadership in the context of a public sector, such as within a local government organisation, generally involves rigid hierarchies and a focus on procedural conventionality. The role of the leader or manager is typically centred around guaranteeing that policies are followed accurately and that performance is appraised against well-defined criteria. This is especially vital in public institutions, where there is often heightened scrutiny and where risk-taking may be viewed as less desirable because of the requirement for compliance with regulatory frameworks.

In contrast, the private sector is likely to place greater importance on profitability, innovation, and market competitiveness, which generally encourages a transformational leadership style. Leaders or managers in the private sector may be more inclined to take risks, motivate their teams towards creative resolutions, and concentrate on long-term strategic goals. For example, the CEO of a technology startup organisation may implement a transformational leadership style, bolstering creativity, autonomy, and a collective vision for growth and innovation. The focus is regularly on flexibility, speedy decision-making, and an energetic response to ever-changing market conditions.

Sector-specific limitations in generalising leadership research across these two environments derive from these variation priorities and operational constraints. Leadership theories effective in one sector may not translate well to the other. For instance, a transactional leadership style, which relies on structure and rule-following, might be more effective in a public sector organisation, but it would likely be counterproductive in a private-sector setting that values creativity and flexibility. Consequently, recommendations for future research should account for the specific organisational goals, contextual factors, and external pressures present in both public and private sectors in order to avoid over-generalising findings.

Moreover, causal inference presents a significant limitation in the discipline of management research, as several studies dependent upon correlational designs may only identify the relationships between variables without verifying causality. For example, whilst research may indicate that transformational leadership correlates with higher levels of organisational members' satisfaction, it cannot definitively state that transformational leadership causes this increase in levels of satisfaction. Other factors, such as organisational culture or external conditions, may contribute to both variables, confounding causal assertions (Fang & Yu, 2023).

To address this limitation, recommendations might stress that future research could utilise experimental or quasi-experimental designs, enabling greater levels of causal interpretations. For example, an experimental research study could involve training one group of leaders or managers in transformational leadership and another in transactional leadership, gauging the impact on levels of organisational members' satisfaction and organisational performance. A quasi-experimental approach, such as comparing similar organisations exposed to different leadership styles, could also help verify any causal relationships. By implementing these methodologies, management research can offer more definitive insights into how specific leadership styles influence organisational performance, contributing to actionable guidance for management practices.

In terms of the limitations related to cross-disciplinary approaches and interdisciplinary research in leadership researches, leadership research in management frequently allocates importance to how psychology, sociology, and organisational theory can contribute valuable insights into how leaders affect their organisations. However, by restraining itself to these disciplines, leadership research may overlook new perspectives from other areas, such as behavioural economics, neuroscience, and political science. Incorporating these fields could deepen our understanding of leadership and deliver practical insights for enhancing levels of leadership effectiveness.

For instance, behavioural economics concentrates on how people make decisions, often influenced by biases or limited information. Research in this discipline could help clarify why leaders or managers sometimes make decisions that appear irrational or suboptimal, particularly in high-pressure circumstances. By integrating leadership theories with behavioural economics, scholars could generate more precise models of decision-making (Kahneman, 2011).

Neuroscience offers another promising contribution. Brain research has shown that emotional intelligence and empathy can influence decision-making and collaboration. By analysing the brain's response to leadership behaviours, researchers can understand how emotions such as trust or stress affect leaders and subordinates (Goleman et al., 2013).

Political science also offers a useful lens for examining leadership, especially in terms of power dynamics and governance. Leadership styles might be more effective in varying organisational contexts. For instance, transformational leadership could work well in innovative environments, whilst transactional leadership may be more appropriate for bureaucratic organisations (Bass, 1990). By combining political science, leadership theories could be implemented to suit different organisational surroundings. Hence, expanding leadership research to incorporate cross-disciplinary insights from disciplines like behavioural economics, neuroscience, and political science can enrich our understanding of leadership. This integrated approach can lead to more effective leadership strategies customised to real-world organisational challenges.

Last but not least, ethical considerations in the discipline of management research are vital to maintaining the integrity of the research and safeguarding participants. One significant challenge arises in research regarding organisations' surveillance and monitoring practices. As organisations gradually apply digital tools to track organisational members' activity, ethical issues regarding privacy and informed consent become more demanding (Zuboff, 2023).

For instance, research analysing the influence of continuous surveillance on levels of organisational members' productivity may comprise monitoring computer usage or even physical movements. Whilst such research aims to understand how monitoring affects work outcomes, it raises concerns related to organisational members' loss of privacy and the potential psychological toll of being constantly detected (Palmer, 2009). Organisational members may feel uncomfortable or stressed, particularly regarding whether or not they are uninformed that they are part of the research, or whether or not they feel pressured into contributing as a result of their position within the organisation.

In such situations, it is pivotal for researchers to acquire clear informed consent, guaranteeing that participants are fully aware of the surveillance techniques and the purposes of the research (Bazeley, 2015). Furthermore, researchers must ensure anonymity in data analysis and reporting, protecting organisational members from any potential negative outcomes (Martínez et al., 2021). One way to address these concerns could be to investigate organisations that already utilise surveillance tools, thereby lessening direct ethical risks for organisational members.

In conclusion, this section should recognise key limitations, including small sample sizes, time, and budget restrictions, together with potential biases in self-reported data, such as social desirability and recollection bias. To address these, future research ought to apply a multi-method approach and triangulate data for greater levels of validity. Longitudinal studies, leadership transition research, and the exploration of emotional intelligence, remote work, and diversity initiatives can be recommended for further studies. Methodologically, experimental designs should be utilised to establish causal relationships, whilst interdisciplinary insights from disciplines such as behavioural economics and neuroscience could enhance greater levels of understanding. Ethical considerations, predominantly vis-à-vis surveillance, must be thoroughly adhered to, guaranteeing transparency and participant consent.

12.5 Conclusion of the Research

The conclusion of a research study in the management discipline serves as a critical synthesis of the key findings and insights stemming from the investigation. It typically comprises several essential components, beginning with a restatement of the research question and objectives and so providing a clear context for the ensuing discussion. By reaffirming these foundational elements, the conclusion enables readers to fully appreciate the significance of the findings in relation to the original aims of the research (Welch et al., 2020).

The conclusion encapsulates the core concepts and findings emanating from the study. Initially, it addresses the research question and objectives, providing a summary of the principal theories and principles studied. For instance, an investigation into leadership styles, specifically the transformational, transactional, and laissez-faire approaches, highlights their varying effects on organisational performance, as noted by Michie and Zumitzavan (2016) and Meng, Xu, Liu, Zhang, Tong, and Lin (2022).

Subsequently, the key insights drawn from the data analysis are emphasised. The findings can indicate that effective leadership is multifaceted, with the ability to adapt leadership styles to suit diverse contexts being crucial. Additionally, it should be stressed that the research underscores the profound influence of leadership on organisational culture and organisational members' engagement, which are intricately interrelated with psychological contracts (Waddell et al., 2019).

Revisiting the learning objectives outlined at the outset, the conclusion provides a succinct summary of how the content has fulfilled these aims. By the conclusion of reading this research, readers should have a thorough understanding of the diverse leadership styles, recognise their influence on organisational dynamics, and be prepared to apply optimally impactful leadership strategies within their specific organisational contexts (Faraz et al., 2019).

Furthermore, the implications of the research must be delineated. Readers should be sufficiently informed such that they can critically scrutinise leadership scenarios and discern the most suitable leadership style for varied circumstances. In addition, the research should endorse the implementation of pragmatic and efficacious training programmes designed to foster leadership development, thereby equipping practitioners with the requisite skills to strengthen their leadership capabilities (Anyigba & Lartey, 2024).

To facilitate practical implications, the researcher should provide guidance on how readers can utilise the knowledge and skills attained. For example, readers can be encouraged to evaluate their existing leadership styles and assess their alignment with organisational objectives, before formulating strategies to further develop their leadership capabilities (Doran & Jordan, 2016).

Transitioning to future studies, potential paths for inquiry must be proposed. Subsequent studies could scrutinise the influence of team dynamics on organisational success as an independent variable, considering its significant impact on organisational performance (Choi et al., 2016). Building upon the leadership concepts discussed, future investigations might examine how effective teamwork fosters innovation and enhances levels of productivity.

Future research suggestions should also comprise methodological considerations. Researchers are encouraged to explore various approaches, including quantitative, qualitative, or mixed-method strategies, as well as longitudinal studies or case studies, depending on data availability and research design. It is vital to specify whether the focus is on individual or organisational levels, as this distinction may influence the accuracy of the findings (Anyigba & Lartey, 2024; Zumitzavan & Michie, 2015). Hence, careful attention to the selection of the unit of analysis is crucial, as it impacts the classification and selection processes underpinning the study.

12.6 Chapter Summary

This chapter on recommendations and implications explained the distinction between academic and practical insights within management research. Academic recommendations, such as investigating the influence of ethical leadership, serves to deepen theoretical comprehension, whilst practical strategies, such as the implementation of leadership development programmes, offer tangible guidance for organisational leaders. The significance of nurturing continuous learning and training should be emphasised as a means of enhancing productivity levels, alongside an acknowledgment of inherent limitations, such as self-report bias. The chapter's main example stated how researchers could emphasise that future research may scrutinise the role of emotional intelligence in leadership and the necessary adaptations for remote working, ultimately shedding light on leadership's crucial contributions to organisational performance.

12.7 Questions for Future Reflection

1. The chapter distinguishes between findings, implications, and recommendations. Take the hypothetical finding: "A quantitative study found a moderate, positive correlation ($r = 0.45$) between the use of a specific project management software and on-time project completion." Elucidate one academic implication of this finding for theory and one specific, practical recommendation for a project manager.
2. When discussing implications, a researcher must often speculate on the potential effects of their findings. How can a researcher strike the right balance between making insightful, forward-looking statements and engaging in unjustified speculation that goes too far beyond their empirical data?
3. Imagine your research finds that a particular leadership style improves levels of organisational members' creativity (a qualitative finding from interviews) but also associates with a higher rate of missed deadlines (a quantitative

finding). How would you formulate the "Practical Implications" section to suggest sophisticated advice that acknowledges this tension, rather than simply recommending the leadership style?

4. A research study on work-life balance relies merely on self-report data from organisational members at a single, large tech firm. Instead of merely stating this as a limitation, how could the researcher frame it as a "boundary condition" that defines the specific contribution of the study, and how does this framing lead to a more insightful suggestion for future research?
5. You recommend that a manufacturing company employ a new efficiency-monitoring system to enhance productivity. What are the potential unintended negative consequences of this practical recommendation (e.g., on organisational members' morale, trust, or autonomy), and what is the researcher's ethical responsibility to acknowledge these possibilities in their report?
6. The chapter astutely notes that institutional resistance can be a major barrier to change. A researcher's findings recommend a shift towards a more decentralised, empowering leadership model. What specific, actionable advice could they offer to a senior leader in a traditionally hierarchical and bureaucratic organisation to help overcome this resistance?
7. A study finds a strong association between regular employee feedback sessions and lower employee turnover. Why must the researcher be cautious with their use of causal language (e.g., avoiding the phrase "to reduce turnover, managers must utilise feedback sessions") when writing their recommendations? Suggest a more appropriate and carefully worded alternative.
8. The chapter advises suggesting directions for future research. Critically estimate the following suggestion: "Future research should explore this topic with a larger sample size." How could this be enhanced into a specific, theoretically-grounded research question that logically extends from the limitations of the current study?
9. How does the purpose of the formal "Conclusion" section differ from the "Implications" and "Recommendations" sections? What should a conclusion accomplish that these other sections do not?
10. How would the "Practical Implications" section for a study on financial risk management differ in tone, language, and focus if it were written for a top-tier academic finance journal versus a professional magazine for Certified Financial Analysts?

References

Adesegha, J. D. (2024). Organisational change and transformational strategies for enhancing a bank's change and transformation during periods of turbulence. *Journal of Management and Science, 14*(2), 16–23. https://doi.org/10.26524/jms.14.15

Anyigba, H., & Lartey, R. K. (2024). Examining the effect of leadership styles on organizational effectiveness in the oil and gas sector: Does knowledge acquisition capacity matter? *Journal of Management Development, 43*(4), 533–555. https://doi.org/10.1108/JMD-06-2023-0197

Bass, B. M. (1990). From transactional to transformational leadership: Learning to share the vision. *Organisational dynamics, 18*(3), 19–31. https://doi.org/10.1016/0090-2616(90)90061-S

Bass, B. M., Avolio, B. J., & Atwater, L. (1996). The transformational and transactional leadership of men and women. *Applied psychology, 45*(1), 5–34.

Bazeley, P. (2015). Mixed methods in management research: Implications for the field. *Electronic Journal of Business research Methods, 13*(1), 27–35.

Bel, R. (2010). Leadership and innovation: Learning from the best. *Global Business and Organizational Excellence, 29*(2), 47–60. https://doi.org/10.1002/joe.20308

Bilderback, S. (2024). Integrating training for organizational sustainability: The application of sustainable development goals globally. *European Journal of Training and Development, 48*(7/8), 730–748. https://doi.org/10.1108/EJTD-01-2023-0005

Choi, S. L., Goh, C. F., Adam, M. B. H., & Tan, O. K. (2016). Transformational leadership, empowerment, and job satisfaction: the mediating role of employee empowerment. *Human Resources for Health, 14*, 1–14. https://doi.org/10.1186/s12960-016-0171-2

Chong, Y. K., & Zainal, S. R. M. (2024). Employee agility's moderating role on the link between employee vitality, digital literacy and transformational leadership with job performance: an empirical study. *Cogent Business & Management, 11*(1), 2337447. https://doi.org/10.1080/23311975.2024.2337447

Choudhury, P., Foroughi, C., & Larson, B. (2021). Work-from-anywhere: The productivity effects of geographic flexibility. *Strategic Management Journal, 42*(4), 655–683. https://doi.org/10.1002/smj.3251

Chris, M., & Donald, E. (2006). Do real estate faculty teach the skills and competencies needed by corporate real estate executives? *Journal of Real Estate Practice and Education, 9*(1), 37–59. https://doi.org/10.1080/10835547.2006.12091620

Christou, P. A. (2024). Thematic analysis through artificial intelligence (AI). *Qualitative Report*, 29(2).

Danry, V. M. (2023). *AI enhanced reasoning: Augmenting human critical thinking with AI systems.* Massachusetts Institute of Technology.

Doran, J., & Jordan, D. (2016). Cross-sectoral differences in the drivers of innovation: Evidence from the Irish community innovation survey. *Journal of Economic Studies, 43*(5), 719–748. https://doi.org/10.1108/JES-10-2014-0171

Evans, K., & Martin, P. (2024). Navigating resistance to change: Strategies for successful training implementation. *International Journal of Management Reviews, 22*(3), 175–190.

Fang, Z., & Yu, S.-C. (2023). Cross-Level influence of group-focused transformational leadership on organisational citizenship behaviour among Chinese secondary school teachers. *Behavioural Sciences, 13*(10), 848. https://doi.org/10.3390/bs13100848

Fang, Y., Li, L., & Zhang, J. (2023). Examining the impact of leadership styles on employee motivation: Evidence from the service industry. *Journal of Business Research, 142*, 134–143.

Faraz, N. A., Mughal, M. F., Ahmed, F., Raza, A., & Iqbal, M. K. (2019). The impact of servant leadership on employees innovative work behaviour-mediating role of psychological empowerment. *International Journal of Management Science and Business Administration, 5*(3), 10–21.

Michie, J., & Zumitzavan, V. (2016). The impact of 'learning' and 'leadership' management styles on organizational outcomes: a study of tyre firms in Thailand. In Leadership in the Asia Pacific (pp. 165-188). Routledge.

Goleman, D., Boyatzis, R., & McKee, A. (2013). *Primal leadership, with a new preface by the authors: Unleashing the power of emotional intelligence.* Harvard Business Review Press.

Gomez, L. E., & Bernet, P. (2019). Diversity improves performance and outcomes. *Journal of the National Medical Association, 111*(4), 383–392. https://doi.org/10.1016/j.jnma.2019.01.006

Hitt, M. A., Ireland, R. D., & Hoskisson, R. E. (2024). Strategic management: Concepts and cases. *Academy of Management Perspectives, 38*(2), 172–183.

Honey, P., & Mumford, A. (2006). *The manual of learning styles* (3rd ed.). Peter Honey Publications.

Kahneman, D. (2011). *Thinking, fast and slow*. Farrar, Straus and Giroux.

Kim, H., & Kim, T. (2017). Emotional intelligence and transformational leadership: A review of empirical studies. *Human Resource Development Review, 16*(4), 377–393. https://doi.org/10.1177/1534484317729262

Lai, F. Y., Tang, H. C., Lu, S. C., Lee, Y. C., & Lin, C. C. (2020). Transformational leadership and job performance: The mediating role of work engagement. *Sage Open, 10*(1). https://doi.org/10.1177/2158244019899085

Leavy, P. (Ed.). (2014). *The Oxford handbook of qualitative research.* Oxford University Press.

Mabaso, C. M., & Manuel, N. (2024). Performance management practices in remote and hybrid work environments: An exploratory study. *SA Journal of Industrial Psychology, 50*(1), 1–13.

Martínez, C., Skeet, A. G., & Sasia, P. M. (2021). Managing organisational ethics: How ethics becomes pervasive within organisations. *Business Horizons, 64*(1), 83–92. https://doi.org/10.1016/j.bushor.2020.09.008

Meng, F., Xu, Y., Liu, Y., Zhang, G., Tong, Y., & Lin, R. (2022). Linkages between transformational leadership, work meaningfulness and work engagement: A multilevel cross-sectional study. *Psychology Research and Behavior Management, 15*, 367–380. https://doi.org/10.2147/PRBM.S344624

Neufeld, D. J., Wan, Z., & Fang, Y. (2010). Remote leadership, communication effectiveness and leader performance. *Group Decision and Negotiation, 19*, 227–246. https://doi.org/10.1007/s10726-008-9142-x

Palmer, D. E. (2009). Business leadership: Three levels of ethical analysis. *Journal of Business Ethics, 88*(3), 525–536. https://doi.org/10.1007/s10551-009-0117-x

Pattali, S., Sankar, J. P., Al Qahtani, H., Menon, N., & Faizal, S. (2024). Effect of leadership styles on turnover intention among staff nurses in private hospitals: The moderating effect of perceived organizational support. *BMC Health Services Research, 24*(1), 199. https://doi.org/10.1186/s12913-024-10674-0

Sarwar, H., Ishaq, M. I., Amin, A., & Ahmed, R. (2020). Ethical leadership, work engagement, employees' well-being, and performance: A cross-cultural comparison. *Journal of Sustainable Tourism, 28*(12), 2008–2026. https://doi.org/10.1080/09669582.2020.1788039

Saunders, M., Lewis, P., & Thornhill, A. (2024). *Research methods for business students* (9th ed.). Pearson.

Singh, R., & Ramdeo, S. (2020). Introduction to organizational development and change. In R. Singh & S. Ramdeo (Eds.), *Leading organizational development and change: Principles and contextual perspectives* (pp. 3–31). Palgrave Macmillan.

Srimannarayana, M. (2017). From reactions to return on investment: A study on training evaluation practices. *Indian Journal of Industrial Relations, 53*(1), 1–20.

Tahir, H. (2015). Leadership style and organizational performance: A comparative study between transformational and transactional leadership styles. *IBT Journal of Business Studies (JBS), 11*(2), 257–274. https://doi.org/10.46745/ilma.jbs.2015.11.02.19

Tosti, D., & Herbst, S. A. (2009). Organisational performance and customer value. *Journal of Organisational Behavior Management, 29*(3–4), 294–314. https://doi.org/10.1080/01608060903092151

van Assen, M. F. (2021). Training, employee involvement and continuous improvement–the moderating effect of a common improvement method. *Production Planning & Control, 32*(2), 132–144. https://doi.org/10.1080/09537287.2020.1716405

van der Westhuizen, D. W., Pacheco, G., & Webber, D. J. (2012). Culture, participative decision making and job satisfaction. *The International Journal of Human Resource Management, 23*(13), 2661–2679. https://doi.org/10.1080/09585192.2011.625967

Vito, R., & Sethi, B. (2020). Managing change: Role of leadership and diversity management. *Journal of Organizational Change Management, 33*(7), 1471–1483. https://doi.org/10.1108/JOCM-04-2019-0116

Waddell, D., Creed, A., Cummings, T. G., & Worley, C. G. (2019). *Organizational change: Development and transformation.* Cengage Au.

Welch, C., Piekkari, R., Plakoyiannaki, E., & Paavilainen-Mäntymäki, E. (2020). Theorising from case studies: Towards a pluralist future for international business research. In L. Eden, B. B. Nielsen, & A. Verbeke (Eds.), *Research methods in international business* (JIBS Special Collections) (pp. 147–164). Palgrave Macmillan. https://doi.org/10.1007/978-3-030-22113-3_9

Zuboff, S. (2023). The age of surveillance capitalism. In W. Longhofer & D. Winchester (Eds.), *Social theory re-wired* (3rd ed., pp. 203–213). Routledge.

Zumitzavan, V. (2011). *The impact of managers' learning styles and leadership styles on the effectiveness of their organisations: A case study from small retail tyre companies in Thailand* (Doctoral dissertation, University of Birmingham).

Zumitzavan, V. (2014). The impact of different styles of 'Personal Knowledge Management' and 'Leadership' on 'Organisational Performance': A case of healthcare industry in Thailand. *WSEAS Transactions on Business and Economics, 11*(1), 430–441.

Zumitzavan, V. (2020). Learning preferences and brand management in the Thai housing estate industry. *International Journal of Management and Enterprise Development, 19*(1), 42–57.

Zumitzavan, V., & Kantavong, P. (2018). Increasing organisational success through management styles of managers in housing development industry. *Panyapiwat Journal, 10*, 110–123.

Zumitzavan, V., & Michie, J. (2015). *Personal knowledge management, leadership styles, and organisational performance: A case study of the healthcare industry in Thailand*. Springer.

Zumitzavan, V., & Udchachone, S. (2014). The impact of different styles of leadership and levels of organisational innovation on organisational performance: A case of hospitality industry in Thailand. *WSEAS Transactions on Business and Economics, 11*(1), 272–282.

Zumitzavan, V., Prachumrasee, K., & Pathak, S. (2025). Transformational leadership cultivating innovation and transparency in local government organisations, Thailand. *Journal of Open Innovation: Technology, Market, and Complexity*, 100626.

MIX
Papier aus verantwortungsvollen Quellen
Paper from responsible sources
FSC® C105338

If you have any concerns about our products,
you can contact us on
ProductSafety@springernature.com

In case Publisher is established outside the EU,
the EU authorized representative is:
Springer Nature Customer Service Center GmbH
Europaplatz 3, 69115 Heidelberg, Germany

Printed by Libri Plureos GmbH
in Hamburg, Germany